For God & Country

For God & Country

The American Legion, 1919-1941

William Pencak

Northeastern University Press
BOSTON

Northeastern University Press

Library of Congress Cataloging-in-Publication Data
Pencak, William, 1951–
For God and country : the American Legion, 1919–1941 /
William Pencak, completing the work of John Lax.
p.   cm.
Bibliography: p.
Includes index.
ISBN 1-55553-050-8
1. American Legion—History. I. Lax, John, d. 1978. II. Title.
D570.A1P45 1989
369'.1861'09—dc19
88-30300
CIP

Designed by Mike Fender

This book was composed in Bembo by DEKR Corp.,
Woburn, Mass. It was printed and bound by Edwards
Brothers, Inc., in Ann Arbor, Michigan. The paper is
Glatfelter Offset, an acid-free sheet.

Manufactured in the United States of America
93   92   91   90   89   5   4   3   2   1

For
Anneli, Peter, and Jimmy Lax
Marnie Greenwood Kiwak
Harriett, Charles, Richard, Pat, and Patrick Pencak

Contents

Illustrations

Preface

This book is both less and more than a history of the American Legion. Less, because to write the definitive story of an organization with over ten thousand local units and more than fifty state and international departments would be impossible. The Legion promoted education, engaged in veterans' benefits and welfare work, investigated, exposed, and combated radicals, fostered national defense, and sponsored a host of community-service activities. Every congressman and state legislator since World War I, local, state, and national government agencies, and civic groups throughout the nation possess Legion material in their files. The Legion itself maintains an impressive archives of its correspondence and library of its publications. Organized by Verna Grimm, widow of a Legionnaire killed in a skirmish with the Industrial Workers of the World in Centralia, Washington, on Armistice Day, 1919, and managed in superlative order by Thomas V. Hull and his wonderfully cooperative staff, the library contains millions of items and occupies half a floor of the Legion's block-long headquarters at 700 North Pennsylvania Street in Indianapolis. Even limiting the story primarily to the interwar years, when the Legion established its influence and stirred up the most controversy, at best reduces an Everest of paper to a Kilimanjaro.

But this book is also more than a history of the American Legion. I hope to show how the Legion carried on an ideal of nationalism—"one-hundred-percent Americanism"—into the twentieth century in various ways. The importance of this theme first struck me on August 8, 1980, when Ronald Reagan accepted the Republican presidential nomination by quoting John Winthrop's "City upon a Hill" speech. He maintained that if we adhered to the familial, civic, religious, and moral values embodied in traditional American institutions, we could again shine forth as a model for the world. If a nationalism based on the individual's obligation to the community has represented the dominant strain of "Americanism" for some three hundred and fifty years, the American Legion takes on major significance. Although Americanism probably would have survived had an American Legion never existed, the Legion exemplifies the manner in which public and private power have interacted throughout American history to instill a culture of patriotism in successive generations. The Legion's methods, successes, and failures thus possess more than historiographical importance. To the extent that its vision of Americanism has survived the turmoil of the Red Scare, the Great Depression, and the sixties, the Legion must be given substantial credit for the survival and triumph of traditional Americanism in the twentieth century.

Few Americans are aware of the American Legion's historical importance. Formed on February 15, 1919, by 20 officers of the World War I expeditionary force, it numbered 840,000 men and was a national power within a year. Immediately following World War II, over 3,500,000 veterans belonged; there were 2,700,000 Legionnaires in 1987. Over six decades, the Legion's boosters have praised it as "the greatest organization the world has ever known," whereas its detractors have warned that a "Fascist" "King Legion" seriously threatened American democracy.[1]

Measured by laws enacted and dollars obtained, the Legion ranks as one of the greatest lobbies in history. Without the Legion, the Veterans' Bureau (founded in 1921, and as of 1930 the Veterans' Administration) would never have come into existence so quickly or accounted for up to a fifth of annual federal expenditures before the New Deal. The GI Bill of 1944, written by former Legion Commander Harry W. Colmery, distributed $120 billion to World War II veterans in its first quarter century. In the 1980s, the Veterans' Administration ranked fourth in federal spending behind the cabinet departments of Defense, Health and Human Services, and Agriculture.[2]

The Legion's record on national security has almost equaled its success in obtaining veterans' benefits. Throughout much of the 1920s and 1930s, the Legion's was almost the only respectable voice crying that internal radical subversion seriously menaced the nation. Its persistence ultimately bore fruit in the Dies (later the House Un-American Activities) committee and a greatly strengthened FBI, which, beginning in 1940, Legionnaires in eleven thousand posts officially assisted. During the interwar period of isolationism, the Legion clamored for strong military preparedness to deter foreign aggression. In 1941 it proved instrumental in persuading Congress to retain the nation's first peacetime draft for a second year and then organized much of World War II's local civilian defense.[3]

The Legion has strongly influenced local community behavior. It has sponsored Boy Scout troops, Boys' State camps, high-school essay and citizenship contests, and Junior Baseball to convey its gospel of "Americanism" to younger generations. To the same end, the Legion has censored textbooks, kept Communists off the ballot, imposed loyalty oaths on teachers, and prevented certain speakers and activists from making their views known. In a less controversial vein, Legion participation in disaster relief, child welfare, and employment drives has also reached millions of Americans.[4]

The Legion cannot be dismissed even in the 1980s as a group of aging reactionaries notable primarily for swapping war stories and holding raucous conventions. Since World War II, half the members of Congress have joined the Legion, whether they agreed with its policies or not. True, the Legion is no longer regular front-page news, as it was during the twenties and thirties. There are at least two reasons for this. First, much of the Legion's program has been accomplished. A strong national defense, generous veterans' benefits, and the almost total elimination of domestic radicalism have ensured that post–World War II America—aside from the civil rights and antiwar movements of the 1950s and 1960s—has been an America the Legion helped to shape and finds quite comfortable. Second, the Legion has learned from its mistakes. Posts no longer run radicals out of town as the Legion works quietly as a national lobby and community-service association to mobilize support for its programs.[5]

The circumstances under which this book was written show that a historian, like a soldier, can be a hero. In January 1978, John Lax was killed at the age of twenty-seven in an automobile accident while embarked on the herculean research plan he had devised for writing his Columbia University dissertation, "The American Legion between the World Wars." He had spent two years organizing his material at Legion Headquarters, working in manuscript collections in Ohio, Iowa, and Indiana, writing a fifty-page prospectus bursting with ideas and research in history, sociology, and political science, and drafting the chapter "The Legion and Labor." I am grateful that John's already well-developed historical talents are preserved in an article, "Chicago's Black Jazz Musicians in the Twenties," in the *Journal of Jazz Studies* (June 1974)—based on his undergraduate thesis at Brown University—and in a piece we coauthored, "The Knowles Riot and the Crisis of the 1740s in Massachusetts," which appeared in the Bicentennial issue of *Perspectives in American History*.

I regret that aside from his contribution to this book there will be nothing more.

John became my closest friend in graduate school. We were the two students who never shut up in class, and a two-hour seminar was not much time to explore the mysteries of covenant theology, slave rebellions, or twenties' speakeasies. Conversations with an exceptionally close circle of graduate students continued for hours at the Graduate Lounge, Hungarian Pastry Shop (seductive graveyard of dissertations), and in a study group whose notes still form the core of my undergraduate lectures.

John and I complemented each other. We both had a tremendous passion for music—in his case jazz, in mine classical. I still remember how he relaxed a group of nervous first-year students, invited to Bill Leuchtenburg's house for the first time, by playing some ancient jazz records and telling us about his interviews with the performers. (These interviews are available at the Columbia Oral History Collection.) Soon we were hanging out at the West End Bar near Columbia, listening to some of the same musicians live, and sharing recordings at John's parents' apartment on Central Park West.

When you became friends with John, you also became friends with his family, his friends—and their friends. John made friends with everybody. He seemed to know every janitor, coat-check lady, and elevator operator at Columbia. I sometimes think he chose to write his dissertation on the American Legion because its members are one of the few groups of people not much in evidence on Manhattan's Upper West Side, and he wanted to know them, too. Tom Hull, the Legion's genial librarian (now retired), and I used to tell each other stories about John. Most centered on our amazement that John would work harder than anyone we had ever seen and yet keep up a social life that seemed like a full-time job in itself.

John's capacity for work was legendary among those who knew him. Tom would tell me how he gave John the key to the Legion library, allowing him to work well into the night. He spent nearly two years there, photocopying the documents and taking the notes that form the core of the present study. His formidable research agenda for the book, which the bibliography describes, took me several summers of cross-country travels to fulfill.

My most memorable time with John was the week I stayed at his house in Cambridge, Massachusetts, in the summer of 1976. We had seven days to cut our 120-page article on the Boston Impressment Riot to a manageable 50 or 60. Fortunately, Bernard Bailyn gave us good advice, and twenty-five-year-old graduate students not only think they can do anything, but sometimes do it. John and I spent the week arguing over and rewriting virtually every sentence, sometimes typing away until three or four in the morning, which drove the neighbors crazy. People who knew us both at the time would not have believed it was John, not I, who insisted we leave a party—the one break we took that week— about ten o'clock to get back to work. "But I was just getting acquainted with the ladies," I protested in vain.

I did not see John much the last year and a half. We were off working on our respective dissertations; I was teaching at Columbia and the Stevens Institute, John was lecturing to tremendous acclaim at Mt. Holyoke (where an annual lecture commemorates his achievement). I know he was a great teacher, for he taught me to appreciate jazz and twentieth-century history. Perhaps most of all he taught me a good scholar could have it all: there was no need to hole up in the office and library all the time; the more stimulating one's friendships and the more varied one's outside interests, the better a scholar one could be.

This book was not supposed to be the end of our partnership. John and I planned to write a series of articles on American crowds, the first of which was the "Knowles Riot." We hoped to examine change and continuity in violence, crowd motivation, and government responses by looking at several major riots over the course of American history. We had decided rather early in graduate school that to specialize exclusively in one era or subject would make our careers less interesting. John used to say you could learn 90 percent of what you needed to know about anything in a few months, but to learn the rest would take a lifetime. For the practical purpose of having major fields and obtaining jobs, we went forth to write our "books"—we never doubted our dissertations would be anything else. We then looked forward to many years of collaborating on topics the future would suggest. If John's death ended this possibility, by finishing his book I have tried, however imperfectly, to keep the faith of our agreement and to offer a glimpse of what John might have accomplished.

Having nearly completed my own dissertation and most of the work for a subsequent book on Thomas Hutchinson at the time of John's death, I resolved to finish his work on the Legion. John and I had talked enough about his work for me to realize he had chosen an exciting topic. I did not want his efforts to be lost or to turn up as footnotes in someone else's book.

I realized at the outset, however, that merely to write up John's notes, or to adhere strictly to his tentative outline in the prospectus, would do neither his memory nor the cause of scholarship much good. Many of the ideas in the book are his. But considerable research remained to be done in the primary sources, and books change as they are written. Since John had drafted only one chapter, which he had planned to revise, it made the most sense to incorporate his notes and ideas into the best book I could write. I am therefore in the pleasant position of being able to take responsibility for all of this work's faults while allowing John to receive credit for much of what is valuable.

The remaining credit for any of the volume's virtues must also be shared with many institutions and people. The American Legion's friendly and knowledgeable archivist, Thomas Hull, allowed John and me access to the manuscripts, provided photocopies and microfilms of thousands of documents, and was always willing to answer questions. During our lengthy trips to Indianapolis, he and his staff were true friends who made the months away from home tolerable. At the Archives of the American Civil Liberties Union in the Mudd Library, located at Princeton University, Nancy Bressler and Jean Holliday directed me to the voluminous material the ACLU had gathered on the Legion with the same assiduousness that the Legion had investigated radicals. Mrs. Holliday was not only glad to see me each morning for over two months, but she told me about the fascinating "Fight for Freedom" records that provide indispensable information on the Legion's mentality. Robert Byrd, Manuscript Librarian at the Perkins Library, Duke University, and Connie Cormier of the Suzzalo Library, University of Washington, also stand out as models of helpfulness among the unfailingly courteous librarians I met throughout the nation. I thank the archives and the institutions mentioned in the bibliographical essay for permission to examine their material. Congressman Hamilton Fish (who began his talk with me by recounting his exploits as an all-American for Harvard's football team of 1910) and Harry Foster of San Diego kindly allowed me to interview them about the Legion.

Many colleagues and friends at various universities were generous with friendly criticism and encouragement. Jeffery Stewart (George Mason), James Sandos (Redlands), James Smith Allen (Phillips), John Chambers and Tony Troncone (Rutgers), Harry Scheiber (Berkeley), William Breen (LaTrobe), Kevin Byrne (Gustavus Adolphus), Calvin Davis and I. B. Holley (Duke), Steven Rosswurm (Lake Forest), Joanna Cowden and Charles

Harvey (California State University, Chico), Lawrence Stone, John Murrin, Sean Wilentz, James Oakes, Tom Knock, Richard Challener, Michael Bernstein, and Daniel Rodgers (Princeton), Roberta Kevelson (Penn State), Bill Olejniczak (Allegheny), Michael Fellman (Simon Fraser), J. R. Hale (University of London), Patrick O'Brien (Oxford), and Daniel Baugh (Cornell) provided key insights and read all or part of the manuscript, thereby saving me from those errors I did not persist in committing. Michael McGerr (MIT) gave the manuscript an especially thorough critique. I will always owe a special debt to R. Jackson Wilson (Smith), Jack P. Greene (Johns Hopkins), Alden Vaughan (Columbia), and, most especially, Chilton Williamson (Barnard) for teaching me how to be a historian. I know John felt the same way about Tom Gleason (Brown) and Kenneth Jackson (Columbia). Our greatest thanks go to William Leuchtenburg, formerly of Columbia and now at the University of North Carolina, Chapel Hill, John's dissertation adviser, who reads a manuscript with a unique care for language, logic, and research. His legendary ability to inspire students will undoubtedly be familiar to many readers of this book. I am sure John would also like to join me in thanking our fellow graduate students at Columbia, who provided the special atmosphere in which our love for history developed in the mid 1970s.

I thank Duke University for awarding me an Andrew Mellon Fellowship in the Humanities for 1979–80, and the National Endowment for the Humanities for providing me with the Fellowship for College Teachers that allowed me to spend 1982–83 as a Fellow at the Shelby Cullom Davis Center for Historical Studies at Princeton University. The Pennsylvania State University, Berks Campus, provided both research funds and a semester of released time to enable me to finish the manuscript. My mother typed the entire manuscript several times and let me know when it had stopped making sense. My father provided encouragement and financial support when I roamed the country, doing research over the summers, as I carted around my earthly possessions in a Toyota Corolla on the way to a series of five one-year jobs and fellowships. Northeastern University Press has been a model of courtesy and helpfulness. If I only mention William Frohlich, Deborah Kops, Emily McKeigue, and the superb copyeditor Frank Austin, it is because they have represented to me an organization dedicated to easing an author's path to publishing as much as possible.

I dedicate the book to those we love the most; their support and faith have made possible many wonderful days and sustained us in the darkest nights. Anything I could write would fail to do them justice.

Reading, Pennsylvania
1988

For God & Country

CHAPTER ONE

The Legion's Americanism

Friends, do you wonder that the American Legionnaire hates a wobbly after having served under that glorious old flag of red, white, and blue, after many of us facing that living hell of gas and burning fire and every torture invented by the enemy, leaving many a comrade in a grave or foreign soil, we came home joyously anticipating a deserved peace, to be met by a "wobbly" who stayed at home safe from the agony of war, and hear him boast about pulling down the Stars and Stripes and hoisting up a red flag.

Raymond *(Washington)* Herald, *April 1, 1921**

Persecution can never kill an idea. As long as conditions exist whereby people go hungry in a land that a few short months ago was boasting that it could feed the combined allied armies and yet have enough for its own people, there certainly must be something fundamentally wrong and no amount of flag waving or calling people names is going to remedy the evil. Why not be broadminded enough to investigate the remedy suggested by the Industrial Workers of the World whereby they suggest trying industrial democracy as a cure for the existing common disorder?

Pfc. W. I. Fruit to Theodore Roosevelt Jr.*

Your leadership is unattuned to modern social ideas; your membership is so moribund and unenlightened, all this because you have opposed dangerous radicalism.

Senator David I. Walsh, 1938 American Legion Convention*

O N NOVEMBER 3, 1936, the National Americanism Commission of the American Legion, a World
War veterans' organization dedicated since 1919 to
promoting "one-hundred-percent Americanism,"
suddenly realized that it lacked "an adequate and
precise definition of the term Americanism." In
fact, "various sincere and honest efforts to arrive at
a suitable definition seem[ed] only to confound the issue." The
Commission decided to think about the problem over the winter,
and entrusted to Chairman Stephen Chadwick the unenviable task
of polling the members and determining exactly what the Legion
stood for. The following May, he presented his synopsis of the
collective wisdom. "The elements that go to make up what we
call Americanism," he announced, comprised:

> Attitude to homeland; belief in the principles that created it and
> have supported it through every crisis in peace and war, storm and
> stress; a sound educational system capable of creating a compre-
> hension of these principles; an undivided and individual allegiance
> to these principles once they are understood and accepted; a firm
> belief in parliamentary tradition which is simply the right of the
> people to choose their own representatives and through them to
> make their own laws; a firm conviction that the law comes before
> and transcends men; cooperation on a grand scale that permits any
> of us to do as he will provided he does not thereby infringe on his
> neighbor's freedom to do likewise.

Chadwick's colleagues had little appreciation for his efforts.
Their comments included: "it doesn't mean a thing" and "over
the heads of college graduates." Commissioners offered their own
definitions: "make it short; it is the right of the people to make
their own laws and the Bill of Rights," and "Americanism is an
ideal which confronts changing conditions with an old and as yet
unfulfilled mandate." One member thought Chadwick failed to
stress adequately "that in order to merit the protection of government and its privileges, one must be willing to fulfill one's
obligations to the government." On the other hand, National
Commander Harry Colmery, who had tried to inspire the Commission by proclaiming that "the big job the Legion has done in
America is to Americanize Americans," considered "the freedom

Long-time Americanism director Homer Chaillaux points out the Constitution to Legion leaders at a 150th anniversary exhibit. Courtesy of American Legion National Headquarters.

of effecting a method of orderly change" a glaring omission. He also warned that "if you slip up on a word or something you give a wrong impression and you are going to be subject to a hell of a lot of criticism." Several members thought the preamble to the Legion's constitution contained all the theoretical Americanism most citizens needed. A lengthy discussion then ensued in which Chadwick protested that he had merely wished to set forth "a guide to the men who write Americanism speeches . . . or something of that kind." Finally, the Commission seconded the judgment of one delegate, who exclaimed "the hell with it."[1]

It may appear startling that an association of almost a million veterans that had provoked nationwide controversy by condemning "un-American" radicals and sponsoring "Americanism" programs in ten thousand communities could not define precisely what it believed in. Upon further reflection, however, the Legion's very difficulty in encapsulating the ideology its members practiced so confidently provides an important insight into what "Americanism" meant.

For most Legionnaires, "Americanism" was so ingrained that to define it would reduce a spirit, a tradition, a way of life to a series of axioms. If the Legion's best minds had trouble *defining* their basic assumptions, Legion boosters never lacked eloquence to *evoke* Americanism and America as subjects of mythical and historical grandeur. Nebraska Legion historian Robert Simmons, for instance, in an unpublished work written in the 1920s, displayed none of the uncertainty exhibited by his more illustrious counterparts. He presented Americanism as something akin to the Hegelian Spirit, moving through the centuries to realize an idea of freedom where nation and citizen perfected each other:

> This association has been dedicated to God and Country. The same God to whom Washington knelt in the snow at Valley Forge and prayed. The same God to whom Lincoln turned to consolation and strength during the trying hours of the Civil War. And the same God in whom the American people have always had an abiding faith. Dedicated, too, to that country conceived from a vision in the minds of God-fearing, free-thinking men; born in the struggles of the Revolutionary War, united by fratricidal strife in the days of the Rebellion, and purged of all unworthiness and selfishness by final action in the war against Germany. [The United States Constitution] for almost a century and a half has been the guiding faith and principle of liberty-loving people which at the present time embodies the hope and is the foundation of the one government to whom the world is looking for political salvation. The American Legion believes that the instrument and the principles and doctrines that are founded upon it are worthy of every sacrifice of blood and treasure. To the preservation of that document and the orderly growth of the government founded upon it, the American Legion is unalterably pledged.[2]

If most rank-and-file Legionnaires would have felt more comfortable with Simmons's evocation than with the Americanism Commission's definitions, one similarity emerges. At the core of the Legion's vision stands the belief that personal freedom requires responsibility to a community defined both morally and historically. Nor can it be used to deny the right of that community to exist. "Undivided allegiance," "willingness to fulfill obligation," "cooperation on a grand scale," "purged of all unworthiness and selfishness," "worthy of sacrifice," and comparable phrases appear in Simmons's history and the Commission's minutes to describe the individual's proper relationship to a society where "law transcends men." Legionnaires asserted the communal foundations of freedom over and over again. At their 1921 meeting, the Americanism Commissioners agreed that too many schoolteachers did not "know what American liberty means" and instilled in the child the "distorted" view that "liberty is something for him, it is a useful thing that he gets under the American flag" instead of "a liberty for service." Replying to an American Civil Liberties Union pamphlet of 1927 denouncing the Legion as "the most active agency in intolerance and repression in the United States today," National Adjutant Lemuel Bolles testily enquired "whether or not the principle of equality of obligation of all citizens as incident to the privilege of living in this country, is one of the principles which the Civil Liberties Union upholds."[3]

As members of an organization forged by the men who had fought the Great War, the Legionnaires' insistence that personal sacrifice for the common good preserved the nation and ennobled the citizen is understandable. Willingness to lay down one's life for one's country, the Legion believed, served as the ideal test of Americanism and established whose voice ought to be heeded on questions of political importance. Denouncing pacifist Sherwood Eddy, and defending the Legionnaires who prevented him from speaking in various cities on a 1927 tour, National Commander Edward Spafford, "with a fiery look in his sharp brown eyes," exclaimed that "a man who would preach such doctrine is unworthy of the protection of the nation for which we gave our very best efforts and for which our brave dead are sleeping under white crosses in France." Insisting that the Legion had no objection to the First Amendment, he nevertheless added that "the only place in which the American Legion has questioned the right of any one to speak has been when that person was trying to tear down the ideals which we zealously guarded back in '17 and '18." A decade later, Commander Daniel Doherty again held up the veterans' war record when an audience hissed him at Columbia University. Doherty urged that the institution rid itself of "baneful influences" to undo its reputation as "the Big Red University." He told the undergraduates that "the reason you have an opportunity to be here tonight is due in large measure to the fact that young men in 1917 and 1918 interposed their bodies between you and shrapnel." For Legionnaires, to be an American required more than lawful behavior and residence within the nation's borders: it demanded positive allegiance demonstrated by appropriate acts of loyalty to a moral and historical community. As Americanism Director Henry Ryan defined the Legion's mission in 1921: "The beginning and end of our work is nationalism, to create a national consciousness. . . . The radical is constantly printing, speaking, working. Why? His soul is a flame. The soul of America must be a flame."[4]

Much of the controversy surrounding the Legion's notion of Americanism concerned who deserved to participate in the body politic—the problem of free speech and expression. Although the Legion's leaders preferred to use legal means to combat subversion, they never admitted that advocacy of subversive doctrines merited the dignity of "free speech." When, after twenty years, a Legion national commander, Milo Warner, finally debated Roger Baldwin of the ACLU, he took the affirmative side on the question: "Should Communist and Nazi organizations be outlawed?" "The individual liberties of those who would destroy the United States do not include any right to endanger the lives of the people of this country," Warner insisted. He informed his fellow citizens that in 1940 they did not face "trifling expressions of opinion, subject to protection under the right of free speech, and assemblage, but acts of murder and treason." Pointing to recent events in Europe, he warned the American people that they faced the same "fifth column enemies" who had undermined France, Belgium, Holland, Norway, and Denmark.[5]

Legionnaires stated repeatedly that they simply followed the Supreme Court and the Constitution by insisting that "free speech" gave no one the right to advocate a doctrine anticipating the violent overthrow of the United States government. Arguing that Eugene V. Debs and other war resisters were "Traitors— Not Political Prisoners" and deserved harsh punishment, Legion lobbyist John Thomas Taylor observed: "There is no such thing as the right of unrestrained free speech in this country, never has been, and never will be." He further remarked that "the fundamental basis of these accepted restrictions [against incitement to crime, obscenity, and libel] is that we must be extremely careful in making statements which will offend, injure, or infringe upon the rights of others." Describing the Legion's official position, Frank Morse in 1938 named several forms of expression the government had always legitimately censured: those which "endanger the foundation of an organized goverment and threaten to overthrow it by violent means," "[are] inimical to public welfare," "corrupt public morals," "incite to crime," or "disturb the public peace."[6]

The Legion's theory of the First Amendment provoked virulent controversy on two practical points. What statements, and which people, threatened to destroy the United States; and what action ought private citizens and public authorities take to combat them? Although Legionnaires disagreed among themselves, the organization developed a consensus that reveals much about the Legion's conceptions of Americanism and the civic community.

The Legion usually adopted a "worst possible case" scenario of the actions of domestic radical groups. It looked at the Industrial Workers of the World and the Communist Party as powerful "unAmerican" and "alien" agents of international conspiracy. The Legion's first National Convention indiscriminately "condemn[ed] all forms of anarchy and Bolshevism" and pledged to "attack the red flag wherever it may be raised as a symbol of disorder, riot, and anarchy." For the Legion, the legitimate sphere of freedom of speech and freedom of expression was the adjudication of questions of policy and power within established American institutions. "We want and need every One Hundred Per Cent American," Commander Frederic Galbraith declared in his 1920 Armistice Day speech. "And to hell with the rest of them." The predominantly middle-class Legion either ignored—or simply could not conceive—that the IWW and the Communist party attracted small numbers, mostly poor unskilled workers who were far more likely to be the victims than the initiators of violence.[7]

The Legion's definition of un-American, however, extended beyond those who overtly advocated a new social order. Socialists, pacifists, and liberals whose doctrines overlapped significantly with those further to the left, who expressed sympathy with their grievances, or who went out of their way to defend freedom of speech for militant radicals also felt the Legion's wrath. The Legion could not imagine how people of goodwill could propose disarming the United States in the face of the Bolshevik menace, or why they would expend so much energy defending the rights of Communists to speak their minds. The *Huddle*, the monthly newsletter of the Americanism Commission, warned posts to beware of "the Communist, in the guise of the professional pacifist," who "spreads his doctrine to palsy the arm of our national defense." The Legion enthusiastically endorsed the "spider-web" chart, a means of identifying Bolshevik sympathizers developed in 1923 by General Amos A. Fries, the head of the United States Chemical Warfare Division and an active Legion leader. Lining up organizations like the National Council for the Prevention of War, the Women's International League for Peace and Freedom, the National League of Women Voters, the General Federation of Women's Clubs, and the Women's Christian Temperance Union (a special bête noire of the Legion for its Prohibitionist activities) on one side of a page, Fries listed known Communists who belonged to them on the other. He thereby proved to his satisfaction that they all formed part of "an international conspiracy directed of course from Moscow." More respectable members of these groups, he could only conclude, were either secret Communists or unwitting dupes.[8]

Legion correspondence is replete with similar deductions about the menace of organizations "sincere in purpose, but of radical thought." Americanism Commission Director Homer Chaillaux used opposition to the Legion's plan to bar the Communist party from the ballot in state and national elections as a means to smoke out closet Reds. "Communist affiliated and sympathetic organizations in the United States, such as the American Civil Liberties Union," he declared, "have rushed in with all their strength to defeat this bill. It has brought out into the open many sympathizers with Communism who were not known before to the Legion in those various states." National Commander Edward Hayes summed it all up when he argued in a speech, "How Red Is America?" that "our premise is that the large percentage of those really doing the work of Communists or real Reds in this country would deny any association with the World Revolutionary Organization."[9]

The Legion's very broad definition of "Communism" provoked considerable criticism of red-baiting from various sides. An ACLU member expressed the opinion of many that "the Legion is attacking every healthy movement of people in the United States" by insisting that "any liberal-minded organization or individual who does not hate Communists are Communists themselves." Within the Legion itself, liberal members found themselves "up against the constitutional problem of the freedom of the press." They argued that the Legion would only appear "foolish and break down" if it tried "to get at somebody else besides the man that throws the bomb." As early as December 1919, in what the Socialist New York *Call* humorously termed a "heavy gesture," portly former President Taft joined "socialists and other defenders of old-fashioned Americanism" in "deprecating one hundred percent lawlessness" masquerading as an equally pure patriotism. Seventeen years later, the Legion's Commander Colmery still worried that "even the most conservative" newspapers denounced Legion efforts to keep Communist speakers from appearing.[10]

Not only the Legion's willingness to lump its opponents together as subversives and Communists, but the methods it used to deprive them of a public forum generated much ill will. On rare occasions, such as a debate at Brooklyn's Erasmus Hall High School in 1938, in which a Legionnaire and a Communist argued the merits of Americanism and Bolshevism, the Legion confronted its adversaries in an open forum. But most Legionnaires would have agreed with the pugnacious Homer Chaillaux, who, when asked if he would debate Communist leader Earl Browder, responded, "I'll meet him in an alley any time, but I'll never dignify Communists by meeting them on a platform." The Americanism Commission confessed that "our first impulse is to take these disciples of sovietism, line them up on the border of the sea, and give them the command, 'Forward March!'" Such feelings were especially strong during the Red Scare of 1919–20 and the period of labor unrest in the mid 1930s. The Legion did not hestitate to act on these feelings. On November 22, 1919, Legionnaires in Los Angeles declared "a war of extermination against members of the IWW and against Bolshevism" and began running them out of town. National Commander Franklin D'Olier, aware that "many posts in some states have acted unlawfully," urged that the National Executive Committee members return home and "diplomatically or as well as we can curb this over-enthusiasm on the part of some of our Legionnaires."[11]

Still, D'Olier's principal concern was not the civil rights of radicals, but rather that "no thoughtless act of ours . . . lose us the support and approbation of the one hundred million American citizens." He publicly praised "the stand of the ex-servicemen . . . for the maintenance of law and order" as "the greatest single factor in curtailing the activities of those radicals who would do injury to our institutions by force." In 1937, after Legion violence during the sit-down strikes, Ray Murphy, the Legion's most liberal commander between the wars, felt the same way: "Perhaps

an individual Legionnaire in one case or another might have gone
too far, but the principles of the Legion were sound." Murphy's
attitude explains why the Legion's critics felt their National Commander's warnings that posts "stay within the bounds of American institutions" was just window dressing.[12]

Some commanders went out of their way to discourage Legion
violence. One was Harry Colmery, commander during the great
strikes of 1936–37 that led to Legion outbursts. He warned Legionnaires not to "deny the right of free speech or peaceful association to any person or group, even the ones we despise."
Colmery argued with Legion posts that had used "mob tactics"
to break up union and Communist rallies that they caused "im-
measurable harm" to the Legion's public image. How could veterans use force and violence to oppose those the Legion
condemned precisely because they "sought to overthrow our government by force or violence?" But like Murphy and D'Olier,
Colmery did not go beyond such missives. Not one Legion post
was ever expelled or formally censured for excessive zeal in combating the radical menace.[13]

Nevertheless, Legionnaires usually realized that mob violence
was counterproductive. It generated sympathy for its victims and
hostility toward the Legion. They therefore followed three alternative strategies. First, between the world wars the Legion at the
state and federal levels supported a host of bills to outlaw the
Communist party, launch investigations of subversion (which
culminated in the creation of the House Committee on Un-American Activities and a greatly strengthened FBI), require teachers'
loyalty oaths, and outlaw "criminal syndicalism" (or most efforts
to organize unskilled workers). Second, the Legion urged that
school boards and public officials deny known radicals the use of
auditoriums and refuse them permits to speak. National Headquarters eagerly provided lists of such characters. "I am perfectly
willing to admit," Americanism Director Garland Powell told his
colleagues on the Commission in 1928, that "the American Legion
had what we called, not a blacklist, but a list of men who were
revolutionaries." Commander Chadwick seconded him a decade
later: with respect to persons "of violent radical thought, I see no
reason why the great majority of the people should furnish the
light and heat for their raving and ranting. Let those who want
to rave and rant hire a hall." Finally, if an "un-American agitator"
did succeed in obtaining access to a meeting place, the Americanism Commission urged posts not to go "off half cocked." The

Legion did not care much about the rights of the "skunk," but feared that an excess of zeal "will belittle the name and dignity of the American Legion":

> When one of the Communist speakers is billed to appear in your town, do not give him any publicity by opposing. Go quietly to the office of your district attorney. Tell him what you know of this character, and the sort of unlawful revolutionary doctrines he is spreading. Ask the district attorney to place his representatives there, quietly and without publicity, to listen in. When the speaker oversteps his rights and abuses the privileges of free speech, as defined by the Supreme Court of the United States, arrest can be made. Prosecute the culprit! When he commits the overt act—and he will do it if he thinks the authorities are not looking—nail him to the mast! Strip him of the robes of martyrdom!

In keeping with these directives, Americanism Director Russell Cook informed the Illinois Department, for instance, not to worry that no federal law forbade "Communist or radical agitation." "Utterances against the public welfare" could easily be prosecuted in accordance with the Supreme Court's guidelines. Illinois Adjutant William Mundt planned to trap W. E. B. Du Bois and Scott Nearing, among others, in this manner. Aware that "ballyhoo stuff" where patriotic groups became carried away only enabled "the Communist speaker to slyly capitalize the incident as an excuse to pose as a martyr to the cause of maintaining the right of free, lawful speech," the Legion found the mantle of law and order a practical expedient as well as an ideological rallying cry.[14]

To civil libertarians, the Legion's efforts to exclude very broadly defined "Communists" from the political arena both smacked of Fascism and offered proof that the Legion represented "a cat's-paw in the interests of big business, of the jingoists, and of the red-hunters." They thought it also marked a new phase in American history. As liberal Texas politician, ACLU member, and lapsed Legionnaire Maury Maverick wrote in 1933: "For the first time in American history citizens have been obliged to organize to maintain civil rights in this period since the World War. Before that time public opinion and the courts were more alert to defend minority rights and unpopular causes. The war legislation changed both the law and public attitudes. The Russian Revolution and the radical movement since have only intensified the struggle."[15]

The Legion, of course, preferred a different interpretation. Far from pioneering a more restrictive definition of free speech and a militaristic version of Americanism, the Legion asserted that it responded to an unprecedented challenge that accompanied World War I. Chaillaux explained the international context Legionnaires used to justify their Americanism campaigns: "We cannot afford to dismiss Communism, Fascism, and Nazism with a contemptuous smile as something foreign and crazy. Such conditions have swept the majority of the larger countries . . . and are at work in almost every corner of the globe." Chaillaux did not hesitate to remind his listeners in 1936 that "there are more Communists in the United States today than there were in Russia when the government was overthrown." Therefore, the Legion insisted, "from a crusading standpoint, the average American citizen must see and feel the real menace of Communism."[16]

Looking back with a half century's hindsight in a United States where domestic radicalism is almost nonexistent, it is easy to dismiss the Legion's "paranoia." Nevertheless, an average middle-class American in 1919 and 1920 could find much evidence that the radical forces which had made a revolution in Russia and were battling demobilized veterans throughout Central Europe constituted at least a potential threat to the United States. Less than a month before the Legion's planning session in February 1919, a general strike with IWW leadership had shut down Seattle. The American Legion's first caucus, held in Paris in March, practically coincided with the creation of the Third Communist International. Throughout Germany, Hungary, Austria, and Italy, leftist and rightist veterans battled each other as public authority collapsed. Scarcely two weeks before the Legion's first domestic caucus in St. Louis in May, someone mailed bombs to eighteen prominent American officials. Between the St. Louis caucus and the Legion's first convention, which met in Minneapolis on the first anniversary of the Armistice, the American Communist party came into being. Over 90 percent of its members did not speak English. Karl Radek, secretary of the International, claimed to be funneling vast sums of money into the United States to promote a Bolshevik revolution. During the summer, the Boston police, the United Mine Workers, and laborers at United States Steel walked out, making 1919 the greatest year of labor unrest in American history, with the possible exception of 1877. In the 1920 presidential election, Socialist war opponent Eugene Debs won a million votes, 6 percent of those cast, from his prison cell in Atlanta, Georgia.[17] Much as President Wilson intended to use his vision of a world made safe for democracy to counteract Lenin's appeal to the workers to overthrow their bourgeois governments, the Legion hoped its program could thwart the red menace on the domestic front. As Theodore Roosevelt Jr. told New Jersey Legionnaires:

> There never was a time in the history of our country when so many un-American forces are at work. When men are hungry and they are tired, when they are down, when they are naked it is a good time for Bolsheviks, for the Communists, for the Soviets, for the IWWs, for the Third Internationals, to come and pat him on the back, shake his hand and say—"Come, we will feed you." And they do feed them. His own country that cheered him on in time of war now forgets him and only the un-American enemy remembers him.[18]

It is possible to explain the Red Scare that swept postwar America by stressing mass hysteria, efforts to find scapegoats for postwar problems, ambitious politicians hoping to pin red tags on undesirables to further their own careers, or conservatives seeking to destroy radical and reformist groups. But to explain why nearly a million former soldiers joined the American Legion, it is necessary to note that a real wave of postwar unrest frightened returning veterans. The newly created Legion capitalized on the Red Scare to emerge as America's leading anti-radical organization.

The Legion's notion of community and free speech thus represented an effort to preserve an "older" America from a "newer" America of immigrants and cosmopolitans, who sought a better life and acceptance for their culture and ideas rather than passive assimilation to a "given" social order. In response to a pluralist vision of the nation, believers in an older, more homogeneous America reacted by refusing their challengers' right to compete on equal terms to define the body politic.[19]

The chief ideological spokesman for those who challenged the Legion's Americanism during the interwar years was the American Civil Liberties Union. Also a product of the Great War—it took its present name in February 1920, after having functioned during the war as the Civil Liberties Bureau—the ACLU represented those who regarded the suppression of dissent before and after the Armistice as manifestations of unprecedented intolerance rather than as signs of renewed patriotic fervor. As the Legion embodied an ideal of American freedom based on service to an established community, the ACLU regarded freedom primarily as the unfettered right of disgruntled elements to offer alternative visions of America's future. The Legion's elite Manhattan Willard Straight Post—its most outspokenly liberal unit and a perpetual thorn in the side of National Headquarters—issued a pamphlet entitled "Americanism: What Is It?" that articulated the ACLU's viewpoint:

> The true American Spirit—"Americanism"—is expressed in a determined and magnificent human struggle to achieve Democracy, Justice, and Liberty. The fundamental aim of this struggle is to maintain for all Americans the opportunity to enjoy the abundance of nature and to acquire such products of their cooperative labor as are essential to their life, liberty, and pursuit of happiness. . . . Liberty means opportunity for self-expression and self-development. It guarantees, among other Freedoms, the Freedom of Religious Worship, and—above all else—Freedom of Speech because without Freedom of Speech there can be no search for the Truth. This search is vital to "Americanism"; for unless great numbers of people constantly seek and discover new Truths, we cannot know how to make our world a better place in which to live.[20]

"Struggle," "development," "constantly seek and discover," "make our world a better place"—the language of the Straight Post contrasts sharply with official Legion pronouncements stressing sacrifice and cooperation. It assumes the United States is imperfect, and that the existing order does not yet fulfill the basic human needs of many citizens. In his debate with Commander Warner, Roger Baldwin added two more reasons to bolster his vision of Americanism. First, he argued that "no government has ever been overthrown by free speech . . . but by the suppression of free speech." Repression of dissent without efforts to solve the social problems that provoked it only augmented unrest and prevented adjudication of disagreements through open debate. Second, censorship required a "political police," which would lead to an authoritarian society founded on fear and conformity. Legionnaires, on the other hand, developed a political Gresham's law, holding that bad ideas drive out good ones. They insisted that even where workers and immigrants had legitimate grievances, they would only become radicals if misled by un-American agitators.[21]

Although the Legion and the ACLU regarded each other as enemies, the two shared important similarities. Each spent a great deal of effort investigating the other's "excesses." The ACLU was as quick to describe the Legion as Fascist as Chaillaux was to brand the ACLU a Communist front. Both organizations engaged in a dialogue, acrimonious to be sure, in which each elevated the aspect of Americanism it cherished the most into Americanism itself. When asked by Peter Odegard, president of the American Political Science Association, to debate Roger Baldwin and others on "the meaning and development of civil liberties" and "equality, social justice, and civil liberties," Chaillaux remarked that the Legion was "not particularly interested" in such matters. Similarly, the ACLU never paid much attention to the arguments of conservative political theorists that free speech can only work in a community with shared moral and cultural values.[22]

The real nature of the "communities" to which the Legionnaires belonged goes a long way toward explaining their Americanism. Most Legionnaires were middle-class—self-employed business-men or clerical, skilled, and professional workers. The Legion exercised its strongest influence in small-town America and the Midwest, areas where "older" Americans were used to living in homogeneous enclaves that accepted the verities of "American-ism" as a matter of course. But to identify the Legion geograph-ically is misleading. Posts in New York City, Detroit, Boston, Chicago, and San Francisco played important roles in civic life and in combating the highly visible left-wing presence in the largest cities. Even here the social world of most citizens revolved around a circumscribed neighborhood. Many Manhattanites shared to a large degree the values and behavior of a small town. As two of Al Smith's speechwriters noted, "They were unques-tioning, like the people in the Middle West. A point of view of life had come to them and they accepted it. . . . Theories about what society owes to the individual were not topics of conver-sation."[23]

The organizing methods used by the ACLU and the leftists were precisely those that would upset locally oriented Legionnaires. "Agitators" unconnected with a community would "invade" it, give a speech, call attention to grievances, attempt to form labor unions, encourage political activity, and depart to do the same elsewhere. When the traveling lecturers were not immigrants or workers themselves, they tended to be people who might be broadly described as intellectuals. The clergy and members of women's organizations who spoke for pacifism, the civil libertar-ians, and the college professors whom the Legion attacked as

"Communists" for questioning the sanctity of American institutions had all liberated themselves from a community based on neighborhood residence. They belonged instead to a nationwide network sharing an ideological commitment to the critical evaluation of existing institutions. Legionnaires unused to examining their Americanism disliked being compelled to do so by those who rejected their values.

But the Legion was forced to think about what Americanism was because it came into being precisely at the moment when the intolerance and suppression that accompanied World War I had borne fruit in a greater concern for protecting dissidents. As Paul Murphy has pointed out, Americans previously "drew the line when the value of freedom of expression seemed outweighed by the danger to more essential values. The fundamental sanctity of the family, of an essentially Christian establishment, and of the Union were shielded from expression which might undermine them." Murphy describes the crusade for civil liberties not as a campaign to restore traditional rights, but as the effort by "aroused, articulate private citizens" to create "a new freedom for the individual." Libertarians cared especially that "depressed" groups could "lessen the gross inequalities of the times" in a more open atmosphere. Legionnaires were correct in viewing the new Americanism as an innovative threat to their way of life. To quote Murphy again, "The good old days, to which civil libertarians of the 1920s pointed," were more "a useful frame of reference for a later repressive day than a functional reality."[24]

The Legion's idea of freedom in fact corresponds with those communitarian visions that have successively dominated American life. The spirit that insisted the self can only attain real freedom through altruistic social service appeared in the Puritans' vision of New England as "a city upon a hill." If people worked, prayed, and strove together—one might almost add the Legion's motto, "For God and Country"—then their land would become a "model" for all the world. A spirit resembling the Legion's surfaces again in the ideology of "republicanism" that Bernard Bailyn, Gordon Wood, Joyce Appleby, and other historians have identified as the principal tenet of the Revolutionary generation: "liberty" can flourish only where a "virtuous" people, willing to take up arms in defense of freedom, remains uncorrupted by the temptations of selfishness and power. For the early nineteenth century, Lawrence Friedman writes of "spread eagle" patriots who "invented" a promised land "that would combine moral perfection with social stability, that would serve as an untainted exemplar to the world, and that would recapture for the United States the predictable order of pre-Revolutionary days." Public schools, penitentiaries, and city police were their crowning achievements.[25]

Still other forerunners of the Legion's brand of patriotism appear in veterans' organizations formed after earlier wars and in such voluntary associations as the Boy Scouts, the YMCA, and the Salvation Army. The direct inspiration for "one-hundred-percent Americanism" came from the Progressivism of President Theodore Roosevelt, whose New Nationalism sought to rally all classes behind a government acting energetically for the public good. The Legion's espousal of veterans' benefits and numerous educational and community programs in fact conforms to a Progressivism defined as the use of state power for the general welfare in cooperation with voluntary efforts of public-spirited citizens. Also present in the Legion was an exceptionally strong dose of the Progressive fear that America needed a classless nationalism to keep "un-American" influences at bay.[26]

Yet if the Legion could successfully claim a long line of ancestors, its style of Americanism by no means enjoyed an unsullied history. Legion willingness to commit illegal acts and stifle dissent legally in the name of "law and order" was consistent with the vigilante tradition whereby respectable Americans have sought to monopolize the political process in their communities. Upper- and middle-class Americans have often regarded "the law" as the guarantor of their customary, local, "legitimate" traditions, rather than as a "legal" reading of constitutions and codes that guarantee free expression and personal rights. Much as the Puritans drove out Anne Hutchinson and Roger Williams, colonial mobs expelled Tories, "gentlemen of property and standing" attacked abolitionists, and southern (and northern) communities lynched blacks and persecuted radicals after the Civil War, the Legion's "one-hundred-percent Americanism" begged two questions put to it by one exasperated critic: "Shall we violate the Constitution in supporting the Constitution? Shall we violate the law in insisting that the law, as we interpret it, shall be obeyed?" Claiming to be a representative American institution, the Legion fulfilled one major condition thereof—it kept alive the practice of identifying "the nation" or "the community" with the status quo and refusing to allow significant dissent.[27]

The Legion's idea of Americanism has therefore received powerful theoretical criticism as being harmful to society and subversive of democracy. In *Freedom and Its Limitations in American Life*, historian David Potter notes that Americans have always identified liberty with "freedom from" aristocracies, monarchies, and established churches, and "freedom to" earn a living as best they could within given social and economic arrangements. Freedom has rarely meant the right of the individual to adopt a life-style or opinions of his own in defiance of communal norms, or the right to criticize the legitimacy of established society. Potter cites Alexis de Tocqueville's *Democracy in America* to show that "American conformity, far from being something extraneous to American freedom, developed integrally along with freedom in a social context of authority rejected and fixed status overthrown."[28]

Tocqueville's own commentaries on the Americans' belligerent patriotism and his famous account of the "tyranny of the majority" could easily be updated a century later as strictures on the Legion's communitarian notion of liberty:

> Nothing is more embarrassing, in the ordinary intercourse of life, than this irritable patriotism of the Americans. . . . America is therefore a free country, in which, lest anybody should be hurt by your remarks, you are not allowed to speak freely of private individuals, or of the state, the citizens, or of the authorities; of public or of private undertakings; or, in short, of anything at all except the climate and the soil.

> In America, the majority raises formidable barriers around the liberty of opinion; within these barriers, an author may write what he pleases; but woe to him if he goes beyond them. Not that he is in danger of an auto-da-fé, but he is exposed to continued obloquy and persecution.[29]

If some thinkers have denounced the Legion's concept of freedom as narrow, it has on the other hand received ample countenance from conservative political theorists. The Legion's defense of an Americanism based on the populace's acceptance of its duty to a historically rooted community finds powerful support in Edmund Burke. Burke insisted that a nation is "a partnership in all art, a partnership in every virtue and in all perfection . . . not only between those who are living, but between those who are dead, and those who are to be born." Legionnaires would find much to applaud in Burke's rejection of "solitary, unconnected, individual, selfish liberty, as if every man was to regulate the whole of his conduct by his own will." Admitting to "love a manly, moral, regulated liberty," Burke defined liberty as "*social freedom* . . . that state of things in which liberty is secured by the equality of restraint."[30]

Theorists of "populist" democracy, as Robert Dahl has termed the Legion's Americanism, stress that for republican government to exist at all, a shared consensus of basic values must prevent selfishness and factionalism from undermining social harmony. John Hallowell, in *The Moral Foundations of Democracy*, has proven an eloquent modern defender of this notion:

> Democracy rests upon consent of the governed. Now real consent is a positive force arising out of inner conviction. It is not synonymous with passive acquiescence. It is found as the basis of government . . . only in nations where there is a community of values and interests, where there is a positive affirmation of certain fundamental values common to the large majority.[31]

Hallowell's statement could easily serve as a theoretical justification for what the Legion has attempted to accomplish.

Opposed to the "populist" democracy advocated by the Legion and conservative theorists, Dahl postulates "Madisonian," "liberal," or "pluralist" democracy of the sort endorsed by the ACLU. Society is not a self-evident community with shared values, but is composed of "autonomous individuals" and groups "with wills and interests peculiar to themselves" who compete to define the body politic. Critics of this notion, including the Legion's Russell Cook, found it not only inconsistent, but dangerous, when "individuals accepting the rights and privileges of American citizenship exceed [them] . . . when they openly advocate the overthrow of our government by force and violence." Hallowell agrees, and believes that liberal democracy slights "the organic nature of community." A free government requires not merely "formal" or "voluntary" consent, but a "natural and essential" agreement "springing from the relations of social life."[32]

Did the American Legion live up to its ideal of Americanism? One way to approach this question is to examine the controversy over whether the Legion was a Fascist organization that recurred during its first two decades. For if the Legion really resembled the novel European militaristic parties and societies that attained great power between the world wars, then it was no traditional, hundred-percent-American organization, but a radical right-wing innovation much like its counterparts.

The Legion sometimes put its foot in its mouth by welcoming identification with Fascism. In 1923, Commander Alvin Owsley remarked that "if ever needed, the American Legion stands ready to protect the country's institutions and ideals as the Fascisti dealt with the obstructionists who imperilled Italy. . . . Do not forget that the Fascisti are to Italy what the American Legion is to the United States!" Owsley went so far as to say that the Legion would take over the government to counter subversive or Communist groups if they managed to gain undue influence. Commander John McQuigg, in turn, called "the Fascisti the Legionnaires of Italy. Their aims and ideals, though not their methods, are identical with those of the American Legionnaires." The Legion even invited Mussolini to speak at its 1930 Convention, and appreciated the great consideration the dictator showed for Italian-American veterans and Legionnaires who had returned to Italy.[33]

Nevertheless, as John Diggins has shown, Legionnaires did not stand alone among Americans in believing that Mussolini provided a reasonable solution for Italy's chronic instability; indeed, *Il Duce* remained fairly popular in the United States during the twenties. Of far more importance than the Legion's opinion of Mussolini is its own behavior. Did it, as Marvin Gellerman charges, "bear a marked similarity with the Fascists in Italy and the Nazis in Germany?"[34]

The Legion's principal resemblances to Fascism stem from its identity as the American version of organizations founded by World War I combatants throughout the world. Between the wars, former servicemen built powerful associations based on the comradeship and nationalism the war had fostered. However, the form such groups took depended on the degree of unrest in each nation and the legitimacy its government retained in the postwar era. In Italy, Germany, and eastern Europe, where nations without long democratic traditions emerged from the war either defeated, weak, or divided, Fascist parties took over the government. In France, veterans' groups supported a variety of Fascist, conservative, leftist, and moderate parties that struggled for supremacy. In England, Australia, and Canada, the veterans became guardians of the established order while lobbying within it for specific benefits and to instill their patriotic fervor in the general population.[35]

The American Legion resembled its Anglo-Saxon counterparts in many ways, but went beyond them in its use of force against opponents and in its intolerance of leftist ideologies. Here Legion behavior flowed out of the American experience of the Great War, as only in the United States did large numbers of Socialists and other radicals provoke repression by refusing to endorse the national cause. But Legion opposition to leftists stopped well short of the persecutions in Fascist lands. Legion violence was sporadic. Legionnaires did not systematically attack radicals, but ran them out of town when they invaded "their" communities. Commitment to free speech always received some support within the organization itself, in part because of outside criticism, but also because many Legion leaders were troubled by the contradiction between professing Americanism and violating the law. If National Headquarters did not do much—such as firing Homer Chaillaux or expelling law-breaking posts—to moderate excesses, the Legion's Americanism Commission minutes reveal divided sentiment on how to combat "un-Americans."

Of course, the Legion might well have been more violent had it not accomplished so much within the limits of American democracy. Besides the Veterans' Administration and its system of benefits, the Legion obtained loyalty oaths, Congressional investigative committees, a strengthened FBI, restrictive immigration policies, control and influence over school systems, and a restricted definition of free speech in many courts and communities. Could one postulate, therefore, that the Legion had no need to subvert the government because much of Americanism was, in fact, virtually synonymous with Fascism?

Such an interpretation is unfair to the Legion. It is useful here to introduce historian Arno Mayer's distinction among counterrevolutionary, reactionary, and conservative right-wing movements.[36] While all three are strongly anti-Communist, nationalistic, appreciative of military virtue, and critical of left dissent, Fascists (whom Mayer classifies as counterrevolutionary) seek radical social change. They reject parliamentary democracy in favor of obedience to a charismatic leader, seek to establish a corporate state where government economic planning directs capital and labor, attract considerable support from workers, farmers, and the lower rungs of society, undertake imperialist expansion where possible, and persecute alien radical or religious groups. Reactionaries seek to turn back the clock by, for instance, restoring monarchies. Conservatives support the traditional order of church and state. In the United States, this order included such values as states' rights, limited government, free enterprise, freedom of speech (within limits), and freedom of religion.

Even at its most unsavory, the Legion behaved in the manner of American conservatives and crowds over the span of the country's history. The strain of vigilantism present in the Legion has periodically characterized respectable society's response to unsavory "intruders," from colonials mobbing British press-gangs to southern lynch mobs. The organization was "one-hundred-percent American" in the strict sense that both its flaws and its virtues mirrored those of conservatives in the greater society over history.

In this book, I do not wish to pontificate on the merits or defects of the competing visions of Americanism put forth by the Legion and its critics. However, during the 1920s and 1930s the perennial debate between the forces of "law and order" and dissidents over the foundations of American democracy did frequently center around the Legion's ideas and activities. This work sets forth the Legion's principal programs, discusses the controversy they engendered, and seeks to provide the reader with the framework and information—not the conclusion—needed to assess the Legion's impact on American life.

CHAPTER TWO

The Legion and Its Predecessors

He cut his own path clean and straight and millions followed him toward the light.
He was frail; he made himself a tower of strength.
He was timid; he made himself a lion of courage.
He broke a nation's slumber with his cry and it rose up.
He touched the eyes of blind men with a flame and gave them vision.
Souls became swords through him; swords became servants of God.

Resolution of the Boy Scouts of America upon the death of
Theodore Roosevelt*

Never again will the men who served in 1917 and 1918 know what it means to be free in that sense.

Former Legion National Commander Frank N. Belgrano, September 9,
1941*

T HE AMERICAN LEGION represented the culmination of two sorts of associations traditional in the
United States. First, veterans of every major American war have organized because, as citizen soldiers,
they held a position both privileged and precarious.
Second, the Legion's campaign for "one-hundred-
percent Americanism" brought to modern times a
crusade waged by a variety of groups between the Civil and First
World wars linking Christianity, conservative reform, cultural
uniformity, and American nationalism.[1]

Beginning with the Order of the Cincinnati in 1783, United
States veterans organized voluntary societies for three reasons. As
the citizen soldiers who won and secured independence, they saw
themselves as heroes with the obligation to preserve their achievements in peacetime. In the words of the American Legion's initial
publicity, they joined together "to keep the spirit of the great war
alive," rid the land of subversive elements, and instill their fervent
patriotism in the nation. But the veterans who returned home
covered with glory lacked programs to care for the wounded,
widows, and orphans, or to help the unemployed adjust to civilian
life. They therefore also joined peacetime associations to devise
assistance plans and to lobby the government to reward their
sacrifices. Finally, they formed veterans' organizations simply because, as Alexis de Tocqueville put it, "Americans of all ages, all
conditions, and all dispositions constantly form associations." In
a country of widely scattered small towns and farms, veterans
have assembled much as the Masons, Elks, and Rotarians to enjoy
each other's company, engage in charitable endeavors, and organize patriotic celebrations, thereby intensifying their own sense
of "comradeship" and instilling a more general community spirit.
The American Legion fits well among the associations described
by Arthur Schlesinger Sr. in his 1944 article "Biography of a
Nation of Joiners": "Reaching out with interlocking memberships
to all parts of the country, embracing all ages, classes, and creeds"
they have served as America's "greatest school of self-government" and "one of the strongest taproots of the nation's well-
being."[2]

To be sure, not all veterans have joined an association, let alone
participated actively. But an unusually large number have: a 1981

poll revealed that throughout the twentieth century, about 30 percent of American adults, disproportionately upper- and middle-class white males in smaller communities, have belonged to at least one association. Given this statistic, veterans' societies have attracted an astonishing percentage of the expectable number of recruits. In 1890, 409,000 of about 900,000 surviving Union veterans belonged to the GAR. Thirteen years later, the United Confederate Veterans numbered 80,000 out of 240,000. The United Spanish War Veterans peaked with 126,000 members in the early 1930s, thirty years after 345,000 volunteers enlisted in the "Splendid Little War." The World War I American Legion attained its greatest strength on the eve of World War II, when it enrolled 1,100,000 people out of a potential pool of about 4,000,000.[3]

Membership in veterans' societies has traditionally peaked twenty or more years after each conflict. War of 1812, Mexican War, and Confederate veterans did not form significant organizations until 1853, 1874, and 1887, respectively. The first of these marked a last-ditch effort by aging nationalists to hold the nation together. The latter two were Southern responses to the Northern Grand Army of the Republic. Middle-aged men, having raised families and attained status in a community through stability of residence and a respectable income, have enjoyed the leisure to revive dormant fraternal ties. The veterans' need for government assistance to deal with psychiatric or chronic disabilities, which increased with age, may also have induced them to turn to those groups fighting for enlarged benefits.[4]

Although veterans of all previous United States wars created the tradition that gave birth to the Legion, the Grand Army of the Republic was its most immediate model. As boys, future Legionnaires "felt something more than a natural excitement" watching "the long lines of blue go by" in GAR parades, and spoke of how deeply they had been moved "when the veterans of the Civil War used to come around on Memorial Day or some other times and told you what they had done during the war." Sometimes such enthusiasm went beyond both discretion and accuracy, as in 1921 when Legion Commander Hanford MacNider exclaimed, "the Grand Army of the Republic dominated the United States for years after the Civil War, although it had but 20,000" men. "What an opportunity for the Legion!" Such statements did not win much goodwill for an organization already accused of possessing too much power and wielding it in undemocratic ways.[5]

Southern Legionnaires found resemblances with the GAR so strong that they feared this would hurt recruitment in the South and nullify the Legion's claim to be nonsectional and nonpartisan. Former Secretary of War Newton D. Baker, a native of Virginia, explained that "having spent my youth under the shadow of Republican domination forced upon the country by the Grand Army of the Republic . . . it is a fortunate thing that the veterans of this war came from all sections of the country." The Legion was careful to invite commanders of the Confederate War Veterans to national conventions and assisted that organization in its ceremonial duties to counter suspicions that it was either a society of Northern or Republican veterans.[6]

Still, similarities between the GAR and the Legion were striking. The GAR was in part a political machine for Union war veterans during the Gilded Age. Confronted with a spoils system that rewarded the faithful and shut the door on others, the demobilized troops joined astute Republican politicians to form the GAR. Much like city bosses and their immigrant clientele, the GAR shepherded the veterans through the rapidly changing post–Civil War world. Living in an era when government responsibility for social welfare consisted primarily of patronage, veterans had to join together, much as their counterparts in the slums and the factories, to compete for a share of America's wealth. They also united to reinforce their sense of identity and community in an increasingly diverse and unstable world.[7]

Like the Legion in the 1920s, the GAR won so many benefits for veterans in the 1880s and 1890s that critics compared it to the Roman praetorians. As a powerful arm of the Republican Party in the late nineteenth century, the GAR obtained preference for appointive government jobs. In 1870, the GAR persuaded Congress to amend the Homestead Act and reduce by the length of their military service the time veterans had to spend on their plots to secure full title. The GAR's greatest accomplishment, a bill to pension every veteran who served more than ninety days, passed in 1890. Over 450,000 Union veterans ultimately received some sort of pension. Grover Cleveland, the only Democratic and non-veteran president from Grant to McKinley (he had purchased a substitute to avoid the draft), earned the soldiers' hatred by vetoing some 322 such laws. Generous payments to Union soldiers prompted historian Wallace E. Davies to entitle a chapter on the GAR in his book *Patriotism on Parade* "The Veterans Discover the Welfare State."[8]

The GAR did not limit its efforts to veterans' welfare. It promoted a host of educational and ceremonial programs, in part to divert attention from charges that its members were "public plunderers," but also because of genuine comradeship and patriotism. The preamble to the GAR's constitution began by explaining that the soldiers, "activated by impulses and convictions of patriotism and eternal right, and combined in the strong bands of fellowship and unity by the toils, the dangers, and the victories of a long and vigorously waged war, feel themselves called upon to declare in definitive form of words and in determined cooperative action, those principles and rules which should guide the earnest patriot, the enlightened freeman, and the Christian citizen." Many men who never sought or received a pension believed every word of it.[9]

Much of the GAR's activity conformed to this declaration. The veterans built rest homes, orphanages, and hospitals for needy comrades and their dependents. By the 1890s, the GAR spent over $200,000 a year to aid fifteen thousand veterans. It lobbied successfully to establish Decoration (later Memorial) Day as a holiday. The GAR took a special interest in the younger generation, organized a "Sons" auxiliary, and launched crusades for public schools to "Teach Patriotism." Veterans presented flags to schoolhouses throughout the nation, instituting on a large scale the custom of displaying the flag at public and private buildings, now taken for granted. It campaigned for a regular procedure to salute the flag, which eventually resulted in a standardized Pledge of Allegiance. To ensure correct instruction in American history, the GAR created a National Committee on School Histories, which exercised sufficient influence that scholars of the caliber of John Bach McMaster and John Fiske sought its approval before publishing their manuscripts. Arguing that "no man is worthy to be a citizen of a free country who is not willing to bear arms in its defense," the GAR unsuccessfully urged Congress to pass a law requiring every male citizen "to defend his country in time of need in person and not by substitute." Failing to achieve this end, the veterans lobbied for military instruction in the public schools. As one GAR commander phrased it, "Our country, right or wrong . . . is the kind of loyalty that we have to instill into the minds of our children."[10]

The GAR embodied the spirit that led to the formation of at least six hundred fraternal orders in the United States between 1865 and 1900. Annual camp reunions anticipated American Legion conventions by attracting hundreds of thousands of participants and visitors, who drank so boisterously that the GAR's leaders joined with the temperance movement, without success, to tone down the veterans' exuberance. On the local level, the GAR built clubhouses and organized so many balls, minstrel shows, plays, and pageants that it drew criticism for emphasizing theatrical performances at the expense of more constructive work.[11]

Much as the Legion would, the GAR vehemently denounced unpatriotic elements in American society. Although it numbered some laboring men in its ranks, it staunchly supported law and order whenever strikes threatened to disrupt the civic peace. The organization officially condemned the great Pullman strike of 1894 as a "rebellion, varying only in degree from that which came to nearly effect the total destruction of our government." It generally blamed popular discontent on "violent, anarchical, and revolutionary movements." Like the Legion, it favored restricting immigration: the grounds were that "the poverty and crime of foreign lands" would join forces with "copperheads and ex-rebels, for verminous warfare against the soldiers in the direct interest of Free Beer, Free Whiskey, Free Tobacco, and Free Trade."[12]

The GAR regarded each of its crusades as an effort to keep the spirit of the Civil War alive. It strongly opposed the restoration of rights to former Confederates, damned Cleveland for returning captured battle flags in 1887, and saw to it rebel soldiers never received any pensions from the nation. A United Confederate Veterans organization, formed in 1887 primarily for memorial rather than political purposes, won only its wrath. Even pensions for disabled Mexican-American War veterans—who did not organize until 1874—required thirteen years before Congressional approval was received because most of these men were southerners. Like any good trust, the GAR did its best to restrict competition.[13]

But recitation of the GAR's formal activities cannot do justice to its influence. It led the nation in glorifying the Civil War and the heroes who fought it. Gigantic Roman arches and obelisks extolled the Union's triumphs—the Grand Army Plaza in Brooklyn and the Civil War Memorial in Indianapolis are spectacular examples. Civil War soldiers who became presidents (Grant, Garfield, and McKinley) found eternal rest in colossal tombs. In the half century after Appomattox, Americans transformed their national tragedy into a triumph—with tremendous effect on the generation that carried the same spirit to the western front.[14]

The Legion would subsequently borrow much from the GAR. Legion conventions, parades, rituals, lobbying, and educational and antiradical programs all resembled the GAR's. During the Legion's early days, organizers consulted with Civil War veterans as to which GAR policies should be copied and which avoided. Henry Ryan of Massachusetts suggested that the Legion send speakers to appear at schools and patriotic celebrations to counter radical lecturers, arguing that "if you think back to your childhood, a talk from one of the men who had the least part in the war will be a lot more good than reams of bull piled on by professional orators."[15]

The Legion would also seize every opportunity to associate in public with its illustrious predecessor. In 1919, at the Legion's first Convention, and again in 1924 and 1928, commanders of the GAR and the United Confederate Veterans sang the nation's and the Legion's praises. This reconciliation symbolically called attention to the Legion's sectional diversity and political neutrality during presidential elections, when both Republican and Democratic servicemen's organizations courted veterans' support. As the Civil War veterans grew too few and too feeble to manage Memorial Day celebrations, Legionnaires took their places. The Legion acquired considerable goodwill by caring for aged veterans in hospitals and by lobbying for increased benefits for them during the inflation following World War I. In return, the Civil and Spanish-American war veterans lent their prestige, voices, and letters to Legion drives.[16]

Like any younger generation with a mission, the Legionnaires not only tried to equal their ancestors, but to surpass them. A hint of rivalry can be detected in statements that measured the Legion's success by claiming that it excelled the GAR and its other predecessors. Legionnaires congratulated each other for obtaining a better system of veterans' benefits after one or two years than the soldiers of the Civil and the Spanish-American wars had after twenty. They pointed to the Legion's initial membership of eight hundred thousand as the greatest ever achieved by a society of former servicemen. They also took pride in the contrast between their nonsectional and nonpartisan organization and the Northern, Republican GAR.[17]

The GAR was only one of a host of mutually reinforcing associations and movements that shaped the late nineteenth- and early twentieth-century world in which the American Legionnaires grew to manhood. To be sure, not all of the thousands of associations formed during this era supported the GAR's brand of nationalism: peace, temperance, immigrant, farmer, labor, and radical groups also competed to define America's destiny. But the patriotic societies that countered them dominated the world in which the Legionnaires grew to maturity. Complementing the GAR's militant patriotism, they linked moral reform, Christianity, survival of the physically and mentally fittest, and nationalism. Several—the Spanish-American War veterans, the YMCA and the physical-fitness movement, the Salvation Army, and the Boy Scouts—directly influenced the Legion's formation.[18]

The GAR's impact ensured that the Spanish-American conflict— fought entirely by volunteers—spawned a number of veterans' societies. These quickly coalesced into two main bodies—the United Spanish War Veterans, formed in 1904, and the still-powerful Veterans of Foreign Wars, which was organized in 1913 and admitted only men with overseas service. Both adopted programs that duplicated the GAR's: enhancing patriotism—ranging from keeping out "un-American" immigrants to lobbying for "Hail Columbia!" as the national anthem—memorializing their deeds, and securing aid for the disabled, widows, and unemployed. However, the United Spanish War Veterans stressed national unity to distinguish itself from the sectional GAR. Its officials included not only General Nelson Miles and Theodore Roosevelt, but the black Colonel Hamilton Blount and Southern Generals Fitzhugh Lee and James H. Tillman. The VFW also recruited men nationwide. It took as its emblem the cross of Malta and ostensibly modeled itself on the Knights of St. John, "the world's first great brotherhood of men who fought to free the oppressed and administer to the sick and needy." Both organizations sought to use their military experience as an agent in the "Road to Reunion," as Paul Buck has described the gradual reintegration of the South into the body politic, and as a bulwark against class, sectional, and rural/urban tensions. On this count, the Legion owed more to the Spanish-American than to the Civil war veterans.[19]

The Legion also appointed itself guardian of a physical-fitness movement that hoped to achieve equally lofty goals. America first heard of this crusade in the 1850s through the Young Men's Christian Association. Founded in London in 1844 "for the improvement of the spiritual and mental condition of commercial young men," YMCAs soon appeared in the United States. Henry

Ward Beecher, between preaching abolition from his pulpit in Brooklyn Heights and sending "Bibles" (guns) to "Bleeding Kansas," became the nation's first prominent advocate, recommending the "Y" as a place "where every young man might find various wholesome exercises and withal good society, without the temptations which surround all the alleys and rooms of our city kept for bowling and billiards."[20]

The ripple of support for physical activity became a torrent during and after the Civil War. Soldiers in both armies learned to play baseball and football. Within a few years of the peace, in addition to numerous "Y"s, private athletic clubs, sports leagues for business employees, parks, and playgrounds appeared. Colleges organized team sports and the NCAA. Professors and statesmen urged physical activity to ensure the Anglo-Saxon race would survive as the fittest. The *Army and Navy Journal* enthusiastically applauded the nation's newly acquired sports consciousness: "One good, at least, from the great evil of the late war, came from its accustoming two millions of our people, most of them young or in the prime of life, to military training." Since "no great war . . . is likely to occur for many years, for the physical training of the people, we must rely on the popular national sports."[21]

The argument that physical fitness led to other forms of excellence culminated in the idealization of Theodore Roosevelt. The future president developed his body through pugilism, ranching, hunting rustlers in the Dakota Badlands, and leading a memorable if mythical charge up San Juan Hill. Roosevelt linked sports, virility, morality, patriotism, and the military ethos in both thought and deed for the men who fought the Great War and capped their achievement with the American Legion:

> In a perfectly peaceful and commercial civilization such as ours, there is always a danger of laying too little stress upon the more virile virtues—upon the virtues which go to make a race of soldiers and statesmen, of pioneers and explorers by land and sea, of bridge-builders and road-makers, of commonwealth builders—in short upon those virtues for the lack of which, whether in an individual or in a nation, no amount of refinement and learning, of gentleness and culture, can possibly atone. These are the qualities which are fostered by vigorous manly outdoor sports.

At the conclusion of its first caucus in St. Louis in 1919, the American Legion delegates rose for a tribute of silence in memory of their beloved former president. They had earlier tried to draft Theodore Roosevelt Jr. as their national chairman.[22]

Following in the footsteps of Roosevelt and his predecessors, the American Legion has sought to convey the benefits of sports to younger Americans. During the 1920s and 1930s, the National Americanism Commission spent as much time debating the rules and praising the merits of Junior Baseball as worrying about the radical menace. The Legion also lobbied with considerable success for required physical-education courses in schools and colleges. Moreover, as James W. Webb has observed, Legionnaires frequently defined their entire Americanism program by using the words "teamwork" and "fair play": "The American Legion, it seems, saw life as a game and the nation as a team."[23]

In 1878, the Salvation Army arrived from England to join the YMCA and fitness enthusiasts. General William Booth founded the Army to combat the lower classes' hostility to the elitist, non-evangelical Christianity of many traditional churches. Uniformed "soldiers" commanded by "generals" "attacked and captured towns" with fervent "kneedrills" (prayer meetings) and martial hymns. Although the "respectable" denominations at first feared competition from the Army, they soon welcomed it as a bulwark against radicalism and atheism. In turn, the Army backed the Spanish-American and world wars.[24]

The Salvation Army and the YMCA were present everywhere in the camps of the doughboys who formed the American Legion. Both organizations opened canteens, which brought comfort to the soldiers while trying with limited success to keep them free from the impurities (alcohol and sex) offered by their grateful allies. If the YMCA ran 90 percent of the canteens, the Salvation Army won tremendous respect for its willingness to serve closest to the front. In 1919, Theodore Roosevelt Jr. wrote to General Evangeline Booth that the change in attitude of one doughboy epitomized the Salvation Army's growing prestige: "Before the War I thought them Salvation Army people were only good to make fun of. If I see a man making fun of them now I'll bounce a brick off his head." Booth reciprocated by sending the Legion $100 and, more important, endorsed this "virile and wholesome organization." The YMCA did its part, too: it turned over its entire $500,000 profit from the war canteens to meet the Legion's initial expenses.[25]

Just before World War I, future Legionnaires received a further opportunity to demonstrate their nationalism: Lord Baden-Powell brought the Boy Scouts to America in 1910, and many future Legionnaires were thus likely recruits. Baden-Powell hoped to turn "the rising generation, of whatever class or creed, into good citizens." He prepared boys to be soldiers, and modeled "Scout Law" on "the romance of the Knights of the Middle Ages [which] has its attraction for all boys." In the United States, the scouting idea spread rapidly: sixty thousand boys joined by 1911, six hundred thousand belonged by 1920.[26]

Many parallels demonstrate the Scouts' influence on the Legion. Theodore Roosevelt, the Scouts' hero, served on the National Council. The Scouts' motto—"Be Prepared!"—was echoed in the "preparedness" campaign on the eve of World War I, and the Legion perennially used the same term to describe its defense programs. The Scout oath began, "On my honor I will do my best to do my duty to God and my country"; the Legion's motto became "For God and Country." Like the Legion later, the Scouts in 1916 acquired a federal charter, an honor shared by no previous association except the Red Cross in American history. Scouts performed notable services during World War I as messengers, signalers, farmers, and fund-raisers for Liberty Loans—three hundred thousand Scouts brought in an average of $880 each. The Scout handbook insisted on "absolute loyalty" and commanded Scoutmasters never to "make an utterance or give instruction which the Scouts interpret as unpatriotic"—under penalty of expulsion. The Scouts' contention "that at no time in our history as a nation has there been a greater need for one-hundred-percent Americanism than today" could well have come out of the Legion's constitution. But the men imitated the boys. The Legion reciprocated by sponsoring more Scout troops during the interwar period than any other organization except the Methodist church.[27]

The young men (average age, twenty-five) who founded the American Legion in 1919 had thus spent their youth watching the GAR parade, listening to the speeches of Theodore Roosevelt, and attending the YMCA, Boy Scouts, and schools that encouraged sports and patriotism. They shared a nationalistic idealism fueled in part by insecurity about the position of America's traditional elite in an era of immigration, large-scale capitalism, and political bossim. (Southerners especially felt a need to demonstrate their loyalty following the Civil War.) Faced with the closing of the frontier, where successive generations of their ancestors had forged the United States, it was only logical they find their frontier and place in history overseas. After World War I broke out in Europe, future Legionnaires joined their elders in the various preparedness and civilian defense societies whose personnel and policies carried over into the postwar American Legion.[28]

Finding Woodrow Wilson's foreign policy insufficiently pro-Allied, Theodore Roosevelt and the East Coast, Ivy League elite that idolized him decided to do the president's job. In January 1915, they formed the first "American Legion" to "remedy by unofficial means the official shortcomings of Congress" and catalogue volunteers who possessed military experience or technical skills useful in wartime. The Legion advertised itself as a "new organization for the defense of the United States," while attempting to disarm critics (who charged that it was a front for interventionists) by claiming to be "not much more warlike than the card index in a public library." Despite its best efforts, however, the Legion attracted only some fifty thousand prospective volunteers, whose names it turned over to the War Department in April 1917.[29]

Far more successful was the Training Camps Movement, founded on May 10, 1915, three days after the sinking of the *Lusitania*. Over the next three summers, twenty thousand young men, including members of the nation's most prestigious families, paid $100 for the privilege of attending officers' training camps, the most prominent of which was located in Plattsburgh, New York. Three of the American Legion's principal founders—Theodore Roosevelt Jr., Hamilton Fish, and Eric Fisher Wood—were among the movement's organizers. The Plattsburghers—nearly all of whom enlisted immediately once war broke out—in turn trained the two hundred thousand reserve officers who commanded most of the American Expeditionary Force.[30]

The Plattsburgh Movement left other legacies to the Legion besides its spirit and organizers. Its headquarters, the Harvard Club at 19 West 44 Street in New York City, served as the American Legion's temporary headquarters in 1919. The Legion also tried to extend the Plattsburgh experience to the nation's military-age population by supporting large allotments to train citizen soldiers through the Citizens' Military Training Camps after the war. In 1940, the Legion would join forces with the Training Camps Movement to lobby for peacetime Selective Service, obliging young men to undergo the training they themselves found so exhilarating.[31]

Preparedness was not enough for some six thousand Americans who crossed the border into Canada and joined a second American

Legion, composed of five Canadian battalions that recruited their neighbors with slogans urging them to participate in "The Biggest Adventure in the World." With former Presidents Taft and Roosevelt and Supreme Court Justice Oliver Wendell Holmes enthusiastically backing the venture, American courts did not enforce the law requiring loss of citizenship for enlistees in foreign armies. And sixteen thousand more Americans, including Legion founder Eric Fisher Wood and the writer Ernest Hemingway, either belonged to the Lafayette Escadrille, fought in foreign armies, or provided medical service for Allied troops on the western front.[32]

The Roosevelt-inspired preparedness movement never enlisted the support of most Americans. When President Wilson (who won reelection in 1916 with the slogan "He kept us out of war") endorsed preparedness, it was because he believed a strong defense would forestall the military involvement the movement's Republican organizers desired. But preparedness anticipating belligerency attracted a significant minority of Americans of English stock from the upper and middle classes, the group that enlisted most eagerly once war broke out.

A host of wartime civilian associations succeeded the preparedness movement. The American Defense Society, the National Security League, the American Protective League, the Liberty League, and the picturesquely named Terrible Threateners, Sedition Slammers, and Boy Spies marked the culmination of a half century's efforts by patriotic groups to purge the nation of suspected traitors. War provided these superpatriots with government cooperation and coercive power to stifle dissent as they tracked down real and alleged Huns, slackers, and Bolsheviks.[33]

Americans volunteered with equal zeal to fight the enemy overseas. Many future Legion leaders took great pains to go to war. Congressmen Thomas W. Miller of Delaware, Luke Lea of Tennessee, and Bennett Champ Clark of Missouri, all of whom played key roles in the Legion's history, gave up their seats. Several future National Commanders of the Legion enthusiastically entered the fray. Louis A. Johnson of West Virginia, later secretary of defense as well, left his state's legislature. Paul V. McNutt and Harry Colmery resigned professorships at Indiana University and the Carnegie Institute of Technology. Ray Murphy, another eager recruit, had previously joined the Iowa National Guard by lying about his age (sixteen). Before that he had volunteered for the Mexican campaign against Pancho Villa. Future Assistant Secretary of War Hanford MacNider (Harvard,

1911) enlisted for both the Mexican campaign and the European war over the strenuous objections of his father: he received more decorations than any man in the AEF save Pershing. (In his fifties, he volunteered for combat duty and served as a brigadier general in World War II.) Of other Legionnaires-to-be, National Adjutant Frank Samuel, having tried unsuccessfully to enlist in the Canadian army, put on weight to persuade the American doctors to accept him; National Americanism Chairman Homer Chaillaux dropped out of Indiana University; and future National Adjutant James Fisk left Berkeley to join the ranks. They were not alone. The historian John Chambers has estimated the army could have raised up to a million volunteers without the threat of a draft.[34]

The man who symbolized American participation in World War I more than any other was Theodore Roosevelt Jr., whose career was a continuous attempt to duplicate his father's. A Harvard graduate, he left his business to volunteer the day after Wilson's war message. He then turned down a desk job and joined the small advance combat force sent over in June 1917 to boost Allied morale. This specially selected volunteer group not only included Ted and his brother Archie, but Americans born in Germany, France, Italy, Poland, Russia, England, and Greece. In the field, he went AWOL from the hospital to rejoin his unit. At the conclusion of the war, Roosevelt set in motion the plans for an American Legion and served as assistant secretary of the navy just as his father had. However, his principal bid for political office failed— he lost the 1922 New York gubernatorial election to Al Smith. In World War II he signed up again and insisted on combat duty, winning command of the advance battalion during the D-Day invasion. Observers reported he leaped from his boat into waist-deep water, determined to be the first man on the beach at Normandy. Six days later, he died at the age of 58 of a heart attack induced by exhaustion; he was posthumously awarded the Medal of Honor. If he could not be president, he at least created a viable American Legion and fought in a European war as his father could not.[35]

Young Ted's career suggests that something more than the idealization of American wars, veterans, and virtue led so many men from respectable families to seek glory on the battlefield. Here was their one chance to escape the routine of business and social life and emulate, rather than honor, their ancestors. Examples of this attitude abound. David Kennedy notes that servicemen measured their deeds by the standards of Walter Scott and the Crusades, indicating a profound need to escape a present "truly artificial and bare," without "romance or color," as one marine put it. War brought release from the drudgery and confinements of civilian society. George B. Forgie has described this mentality in Northerners and Southerners before the Civil War. Having listened to praise of the Founding Fathers from their cradles, mid-nineteenth-century Americans, like future Legionnaires, had to assume an equally heroic mission to be worthy heirs of the American nation.[36]

But the eagerness of World War I soldiers to fight may even go beyond a collective desire to escape the routine of early twentieth-century existence. If the Victorian family functioned as the contemporary and scholarly literature indicates it did, parents demanded children exercise great self-control and accomplish much at school, at work, and even at play. For the young men who comprised most of the troops, enlistment and then combat could be regarded as a declaration of independence, of manhood, from the restraints of authoritarian domesticity and standardized work. Hanford MacNider's enlistment in blatant defiance of his father's wishes is suggestive here, but once again Theodore Roosevelt Jr. epitomized his contemporaries' experiences. Much as Theodore I had made an asthmatic future president smoke cigars and take twenty-mile hikes in the Alps, Theodore II taught Theodore III to swim by dunking him in water. The boy's mother, after he came home bleeding from a fight, would tell him to get into the bathroom and keep the carpets clean. Young Ted suffered from emotional problems that tended to disappear when his father was away from home. Significantly, Theodore Jr. began his war reminiscences, *Average Americans*, with the chapter "Boyhood Recollections." His outstanding childhood memory was that

> from the time we were very little boys we were always interested in military preparedness. My father believed very strongly in the necessity of each boy being able and willing not only to look out for himself, but to look out for those near and dear to him. This gospel was preached to us all from the time we were very, very small.

Chapter 2, "Sins of the Fathers," an attack on the United States lack of preparedness in the early twentieth century, ended with a quotation from a letter his father wrote in June 1918: "When the trumpet sounds for Armageddon, only those win undying honor and glory who stand where the danger is sorest." Participation in

Theodore Roosevelt Jr. (1888–1944), principal founder of the American Legion.
Courtesy of American Legion National Headquarters.

the war freed young men from the "Sins of the Fathers." Their spirit could then compensate for their fathers' follies, and equal their forefathers' achievements.[37]

Some of the most striking characteristics of the AEF confirm the soldiers' need to escape the constraints of their upbringing: the profusion of swearing, gambling, smoking, and sexual intercourse that observers, especially YMCA chaplains, regarded with dismay. Bishop George Brent noted in his diary: "How do these boys cuss and swear! G-- d--- is as common as 'and' . . . and yet I do not believe they intend to be blasphemous. War is a violent trade and its temper colors even the language of the soldier." By March 1919, 9 percent of the AEF had contracted venereal disease, a figure Brent considered "low." The army could not keep President Wilson's pledge to return the boys to their mothers as pure as when they left home, despite the prohibition of prostitution near the camps. Brent complained that the French refused to cooperate. They "harp on the value of the *maison tolérante*. I saw a letter the other day written by the Mayor of Cannes advocating the system. You would have supposed he was singing the praises of a school for morals." But the soldiers' eagerness to circumvent the strictures of their moral guardians indicates they preferred the mayor's "school" to the chaplains'.[38]

In a speech to the Nebraska Legion, Frank Edgerton justified the soldiers' rambunctiousness and condemned the unreasonableness of those who expected the doughboys to superimpose civilian niceties on army life:

> You were given a privilege that had never been yours before. You were told to give the Kaiser hell and if giving the Kaiser hell meant . . . raising a little hell of your own it was all right. Stories came back of all kinds—poker games, crap games, and the ladies. Parents who had believed that their Willie would never smoke or swear visited his training camp, found him doing both—and returning to brag of it! . . . Too much was expected of us. Our army experience clung to us. . . . If we grumbled it was the unpardonable sin. If we had become attached to cigarettes we had gone to the dogs. If we swore, we were roughnecks. . . . Men do not go through hell unsinged. That is why they swear like devils, play poker, tell tall stories, and drink to excess. War is not only a matter of heroes. It is men gone brutes. It is a civilization gone mad.[39]

In "keeping the spirit of the Great War alive," the Legion not only preserved the war's patriotic fervor. Its meetings, raucous conventions, and flamboyant parades gave the veterans, for a few hours and days here and there, the same freedom from the workaday world they had enjoyed during the war.

Fortunately for many soldiers, army life conformed fairly closely to the glorious adventure they had expected. Few Legionnaires regretted their days in uniform. In training camps modeled on colleges, the leniency and camaraderie of reserve or national guard officers and noncoms with the troops exasperated the handful of available regulars. The willingness of uncoerced, demobilized enlisted men to join an American Legion organized by their officers speaks volumes for relations among the two groups. Other positive features of army life included teaching illiterates to read and write, providing basic instruction in hygiene, and giving to thousands technical and vocational skills useful in civilian life. For many of the rural and urban poor, even the austere barracks represented the finest living accommodations they had ever enjoyed. War hero Sergeant Alvin C. York of Tennessee symbolized the poor, rural American for whom the war gave life a grander meaning. Army maneuvers did not seem that onerous to men used to working ten hours a day. As Mark Sullivan wrote in *Our Times*: "If the drilling, the sentry duty, the regularity of reveilles and K.P. grew monotonous for the soldier, this was . . . completely balanced by baseball, football, boxing bouts, and track meets, William Farnum and Mary Miles Minter on the screen, Elsie Janis and Harry Lauder in the flesh, pooltables, songfests, phonograph records, *Life* and *Judge*, ice-cream sodas and cigarettes."[40]

Once they reached the western front, the doughboys were spared the horrors of extended trench warfare endured by their French and British allies. Only 2 million Americans went overseas, and of these only 1.2 million saw action, out of a total of 4.7 million who were mustered. Although the United States sent token reinforcements to the French and British in 1917 to boost morale, General Pershing did not mount an American offensive until August 1918. Few soldiers saw more than four months of combat. In contrast to the tremendous casualty rates of the other powers—90 percent for the Austrians, 75 percent for the French and the Russians, 65 percent for the Germans, and 35 percent for the British Empire—only 49,000 men in the AEF were killed and 230,000 were wounded. Influenza claimed more lives than battle.[41]

Nonetheless, those American soldiers who did see action suffered casualties, proportional to their time in combat, at least equal to the Europeans. Of 1.2 million combatants, 279,000 were killed or wounded in a period of only a few months. Thousands more came down with tuberculosis and mental disorders after the war. The Legion was thus created by two groups of men—those for whom war had been hell, and those for whom it had been a great adventure. Fierce fighting and high casualties led the Legion to insist that justice be done for the disabled; a short, successful, and painless war kept the crusading spirit alive for many.

Morale in the American army remained high until the fighting ceased and the men clamored to go home. Observers noted how the troops loved to sing, especially such cheerful tunes as "Over There" and "Mademoiselle from Armentières"—"the folk song of the AEF." Sullivan wrote that "literally every soldier sang it, and years after the war, veterans moved to song found expression for every mood, solitary or gregarious, in one or another of the countless incarnations of the charms and adornments of the maid—if she was a maid." In addition to upbeat music, the ditty sported lyrics that cockily proclaimed America's superiority to the aging European "mademoiselle" who "hadn't been kissed in forty years" and would trade a French Croix de Guerre to "wash a Yankee's underwear." Legionnaires were particularly fond of two lines: "'Twas a hell of a war, as I recall / But a damned sight better than no war at all."[42]

For young men, many of whom had never held a steady job or traveled more than a few miles from home, army life was a chance to escape and see the world. One soldier spoke for many others: "I want to thank the local [draft] board for sending me: this is the first time in my life I have been treated as a man." Men assigned to stateside or support tasks regretted their misfortune. One West Virginia Legionnaire complained: "Here I am in Boston when I expected to be in France. It is some disappointment, and I get quite peeved at times when I pick up the *Exponent* and see that some draftee with only a few weeks' training is over there." Soldiers kept scrapbooks in which they pasted photographs of their comrades and postcards of the historical sites and resorts to which the government sent them when on leave. In 1927, Legionnaires returning to France looked back nostalgically on the days "When a Buck Private Was a Billionaire" who could "Sleep in Queen Victoria's bed at Aix and Watch the Wheel Spin in Monte Carlo." The *Stars and Stripes*, the soldiers' newspaper, printed reports of the Central Powers' catastrophic losses and the terrible influenza epidemic in North America. Such articles assured the men that the American front lines were the safest place on the globe. Commenting in 1927 on the exuberant mood of an American Legion that held its convention in Paris, Britain's *New Statesman* remarked:

> The fact of an American army's fighting in Europe was so incredible that it could only be made real by . . . clothing it in romance. Peace was attained when the greater portion of the vast new American army was still outside the fighting zone, and two results, among many others, followed. First, the manhood of America came out of the war without the profound disgust and satiety which was the universal feeling of war-stricken Europe; and second, the American doughboy went home by the hundred thousand with his war-time illusions intact.[43]

The soldiers' principal "illusion" was to consider themselves crusaders, disinterested idealists helping the beleaguered Allies. "We were really crusaders," commented Alpha Kenna, Chaplain of the Kansas Legion. "It was to end all war, and it was to make the world safe for democracy. There was crusading spirit in it, manifest in the songs that we sang." "Mother" Kate Barrett, president of the Legion Auxiliary, viewed the medieval crusaders as the doughboys' only true historical predecessors. On another occasion, she asserted that "young men of today, up to the age of thirty and even beyond, are nearer perfection in conduct, morals, and ideals than any similar generation of young men in the history of the world." The Legion's organizers even considered naming it "The American Crusaders." Addressing the Legion's Paris Convention, General of the Army Pershing praised the men's disinterested idealism: "No orders from any government could ever create the spirit, the nobility of purpose which marked the individual American soldier in this war. A continuation of this spirit and the desire to preserve and consecrate our military experience led to the formation of the society of veterans known as the American Legion." By "Keeping the Spirit of the Great War Alive," especially for the majority who served briefly and away from the front, the Legion made it possible for a largely unbloodied army to participate vicariously in one of the most successful wars ever fought by any nation. Speaking to the Legion at its New York Convention in 1937, General Hugh S. Johnson joked that "half the Legion was not in service six months but somehow these lads invaded New York and captured it in three days." He then went on to talk as though the Legion was an AEF that had never disbanded: "You could put those men into olive drab tomorrow and they would still be an army."[44]

Most Legionnaires shared these feelings. A poll conducted in 1939 by Fight for Freedom, an organization devoted to enlisting aid to the Allies during World War II, asked a sample of 553 Legionnaires at the Boston Convention to describe their impressions of World War I: 38% considered it a "great experience"; 25% were less euphoric, but were still "glad to serve their country and to do their duty"; 10% learned a trade; 11% attained self-discipline; 8% called their time in service the "best time of their lives." Only 8% regretted having served. Typical comments ran: "This is a great country and worth sacrifices on the part of every man in order to preserve it." "My boy says he wants to be like me. I told him that it helped me to be strong and obedient. I wish he were old enough to be drafted." David Kennedy's analysis of war diaries and narratives indicates the Legionnaires did not stand alone on this count: soldiers' journals and letters rarely mentioned fighting, and resembled the journals of tourists or college students.[45]

The Legionnaires' positive attitude toward their time in service is intriguing, since 44 percent regarded the war as a mistake. Disillusioned respondents sarcastically observed that "all we got out of the last war were debts," and "talk to the boys in the hospitals if you think war is a good thing." However, the survey attributed this disillusionment "more to a feeling of futility now in view of the blunders after the last war and the tremendous destruction underway, rather than an opinion that our own part in the World War was an error." General Johnson, speaking at the behest of the Legion's isolationist leadership in 1939, captured the ambivalence perfectly: "With smiles and smirks our associates accepted our childish enthusiasm. Then they took our money and our lives. We were the world's prize fat boy with the bag of candy among a horde of hungry urchins. And with Texas Guinan's greeting I salute us all—Hello, suckers." The Legionnaires regretted the outcome of the war, while glorying in the role they themselves had played.[46]

The comradeship and sense of community acquired during the war worked to accomplish the other great social end desired by the war's supporters. "The biggest thing we got out of this war was a spirit of nationalism," Theodore Roosevelt Jr. later wrote. "All classes, all grades in society" mingled to give everyone "new ideas, a broader outlook on life, and a more complete understanding of our country." Such rhetoric should not be dismissed out of hand. Physical and mental tests caused many lower-class people to be rejected as unfit for service, whereas enthusiastic volunteers from the wealthy ensured that not only did a broad cross section of American society in fact serve in the AEF, but the upper class actually contributed more than its numerical proportion. Two major exceptions stand out. The army placed blacks in segregated units and rarely assigned them to combat, despite requests by black leaders to "let the race prove itself." Alien immigrants could not be forcibly inducted at all, and few volunteered. The nature of military participation, therefore, tended to give native-born white Americans of different classes and regions a common, positive experience. Save for the advance unit of 1917, which by design mingled people of various nationalities and statuses, men served in units organized by region and community. This policy minimized personal contact among potentially hostile groups, while maintaining the sense that everyone was working toward one goal. Military service brought young men together at a crucial time in their lives and gave them a common experience they could then define as "Americanism." Groups that did not join their crusade—aliens, radicals, and profiteers—could be lumped together as "un-American" for having failed the ultimate test of loyalty.[47]

As the years passed, American Legionnaires tried to keep the war alive in ways other than excluding un-American groups from the body politic. Each major drive the Legion launched, whether for veterans' benefits or military preparedness, became a crusade where the values of comradeship and nationalism could be resurrected. In 1932, Commander Harry Stevens urged the American people to "unite their efforts as they all did in 1917 to the end that the war against the depression be very quickly concluded." On the eve of World War II, "Old Soldiers" looked forward to "the opportunity to complete our service record." "It's only the beginning, fellows, it's only the beginning. We've got a lot of fight in us yet and we're willing to fight like we did in 1918 to show the new veterans we can do it in 1941." The American Legion not only used the "analogue of war," as William E.

Leuchtenburg has described the national attitude toward fighting
the depression, against economic hardship. It sought to revive
wartime enthusiasm in dealing with labor relations, education,
antiradicalism, and national defense.[48]

Besides death and disease, one thing spoiled the AEF's experience: the regular army. "A rancorous dislike of the regular establishment" prevailed "through all ranks," according to Theodore
Roosevelt Jr. When the Legion was organized, Roosevelt had to
use all his influence "to prevent a membership clause in the Legion's Constitution excluding the regular army." Staunch Legionnaire Congressman John MacSwain echoed America's
citizen-soldier heritage by attacking "the un-American and unnecessary as well as the unconscionable methods of handling the
enlisted men," and the "Prussian methods that the regular establishment forced upon them." The Legion's first convention in
Minneapolis showed that the American distrust of a regular army
as an "engine of despotism" had received a powerful reinforce-
ment during the war. The Legionnaires resolved that "a large
standing army is uneconomical and un-American. National safety
with freedom from militarism is best assured by a national citizen
army based upon democratic principles of equality of obligation
and opportunity for all."[49]

General dislike of the small core of regular officers and General
Headquarters grew following the Armistice. Legion lobbyist John
Thomas Taylor recounted how once the war ended, instead of
sending the heroes home, "the army put into existence immediately the same thing they had done back here in the training
camps. Started to making soldiers of us all over again after the
war was over and they rebelled against it. And every day, every
week, AWOLs by the dozen, the scores, the hundreds." The situation became so bad that General Pershing commissioned twenty
popular civilian officers "to figure out a way to stop this mass
uprising and the terrible conditions in the army overseas." At
their meeting on February 15, 1919, the twenty recommended
that General Headquarters "send the fellows home," give them
some recreation, [and] "let them see the country they fought for."
At the same conference, they created the American Legion.[50]

Founded three months after the Armistice by troops who believed their exertions had quickly ended the bloodiest war in
human history, the American Legion viewed itself as the apogee
of a triumphant patriotism that during the war had vanquished
un-Americanism at home and authoritarianism abroad. The Le-

gion was formed to preserve the victory for which the GAR, the Boy Scouts, Theodore Roosevelt, the preparedness movement, and the wartime patriotic societies had so valiantly fought. Having made the world safe for the virile Christian nationalism they equated with democracy, a large percentage of the demobilized AEF was eager to continue its crusade at home.

CHAPTER THREE

The Legion's First Year

For God and Country, we associate together for the following purposes: To uphold and defend the Constitution of the United States of America; to maintain law and order; to foster and perpetuate a one-hundred percent Americanism; to preserve the memories and incidents of our association in the Great War; to inculcate a sense of individual obligation to the community, State, and Nation; to combat the autocracy of both the classes and the masses; to make right the master of might; to promote peace and good will on earth; to safeguard and transmit to posterity the principles of justice, freedom, and democracy; to consecrate and sanctify our comradeship by our devotion to mutual helpfulness.

Preamble to the Constitution of the American Legion, adopted at the St. Louis Caucus, May 1919

Four million young men united! Four million men who fought, or sought to fight, for American ideals—men of the North and South and East and West—fused with the common purpose of perpetuating those ideals. Truly an inspiring conception!

George Putnam in Outlook *122 (May 21, 1919): 104*

B Y 1920, an American Legion formed only the year before counted 843,013 dues-paying members, some one-fifth of those eligible. If this figure fell short of the organizers' dream that nearly all AEF veterans would enlist, it still represents a remarkable accomplishment. The first Legionnaires had no easy task. They had to weld together former servicemen of different regions, political affiliations, religions, classes, and ethnic groups into a united force based upon a mutually acceptable definition of "one-hundred-percent Americanism." The Legion owes its rapid success to such visionaries as Theodore Roosevelt Jr., Eric Fisher Wood, Bennett Champ Clark, Franklin D'Olier, and Rev. John Inzer, who conveyed their fervor to the veterans. Had they not moved to unite the host of veterans' societies forming rapidly after the war, an organization of the Legion's power and durability would not have arisen.

The Legion's creation falls into two stages. From February to May 1919, the founders established its supremacy among its rivals. They set up the machinery to recruit members in France at a caucus in Paris, and then launched the organization stateside at one in St. Louis. Beginning in May, they undertook a tremendous publicity blitz, culminating in the Legion's first national convention in Minneapolis in November.

The idea for the American Legion seems to have originated with Theodore Roosevelt Jr. As early as October 1917, with only his advance First Division in combat, Roosevelt wondered "how were the disabled to be taken care of with no hospitals, no organization." He especially worried about the shell-shock victims. When asked "what will we do when the Germans are licked," his usual reply was "go home and start a veterans' organization for the good of the country." But Roosevelt held no monopoly on the idea. Former servicemen spontaneously began to organize somewhere between the 8 or 10 societies casually mentioned by Roosevelt and the 762 John Thomas Taylor either counted or made up.[1]

One major threat to the Legion came from Comrades in Service. Founded in January 1919 by Iowa's Ora D. Foster and Episcopal Bishop Charles Brent of New York under YMCA auspices, Comrades shared the Legion's aims of "carrying forward the all-American struggle against a common foe" and preserving the "genuine comradeship and fellowship between the great historical religious groups." Working through the AEF's Chaplain's Service, which Brent headed, Comrades recruited two hundred thousand members by April with the aid of endorsements by President Wilson and General Pershing. Recruiting teams that judiciously combined Protestants with Catholics and officers with enlisted men scoured the camps for members.[2]

However, on April 7, in what he later termed "the thing I have to repent most the rest of my days," Brent "sold out" the Comrades to what he eventually lambasted as "a designing, boozing organization." But at the time, Brent's move seemed sensible. Comrades was coming under attack as a potential tool for a presidential bid by either Wilson or Pershing. Further, the doughboys found the Legion provided the same camaraderie and ideology as the Comrades without the obnoxious moralizing of the chaplains. The *Stars and Stripes*, under the thumb of Roosevelt's group, helped by giving the Legion favorable front-page publicity while interspersing small stories about the Comrades among attacks on Prohibition and draft evaders who became chaplains.[3]

Veterans had many other choices besides the Legion and the Comrades. The most prominent was the Veterans of Foreign Wars. However, this group, while possessing a similar ideology, admitted only those who actually went overseas. Although they still had a potential membership of 2 million men, they never exceeded 300,000 before World War II. Lacking the Legion's prestigious leadership and nationally promoted "Americanism" campaigns, the VFW offered a more down-to-earth alternative with a similar attitude toward patriotism and veterans' benefits. The Legion and the VFW disputed credit for much of the veterans' legislation adopted during the interwar years, but the latter only became an important rival following World War II. Probably for social reasons, a fair number of veterans joined both organizations. Disabled veterans could join the Disabled American Veterans, which suggested programs the Legion frequently made its own. As some 350,000 veterans ultimately received some disability payments, the DAV's average membership of about 25,000 was disappointing. More specialized societies also existed: Catholic and Jewish War Veterans, the Military Order of the World War (officers only), and such ad hoc groups as the Bonus Marchers and competing anti-Bonus groups. Republican and Democratic servicemen's organizations supported their respective candidates and included many Legionnaires. Clearly, veterans anxious "to keep the spirit of the great war alive" had many choices if the Legion repelled them.[4]

Perhaps the most meaningful rival the Legion faced was a loosely federated radical group known most frequently as the Private Soldiers and Sailors Legion of the United States of America or, more simply, as the World War Veterans. Under the presidency of Marvin Gates Sperry, this group drafted a "Declaration of Principles and Constitution" that circulated throughout the nation as early as March 1919. Whereas the Legion proclaimed an identity of interest between officers and men, capital and labor, and government and people, the Soldiers and Sailors rejected such unities and adopted a radical program. It demanded that the government punish "incompetent and unfit officers" who had subjected "thousands of soldiers . . . to needless hardships and privations . . . in courts-martial for insignificant, petty infringements of military discipline." Not "intending to starve or beg," it insisted that the government provide a job for all veterans and a $500 (as opposed to a $60) discharge bonus to tide them over until they got one. It urged the government to distribute "hundreds of millions of idle acres of good agricultural, mining, and timber lands and vacant city lots" to "the soldiers who are conceded to have saved civilization at $30 per month," and wanted to expropriate surplus, underutilized private property as well. The radical veterans hoped many of their comrades would agree with one Ted Booth: "Who am I that I should join a gang of officers and dog robbers when the World War Veterans exist." Consciously Marxist, the Soldiers and Sailors denounced the Legion as a tool of "monopoly and privilege."[5]

But despite its claim of having attracted up to 700,000 men by standing up for the average soldier, the World War Veterans had as little mass appeal as its fellow radicals in the IWW or the Communist party. If it initially attracted large numbers because of promised benefits and disgust with officers, profiteers, and the government, it faded quickly. By 1921, following harassment during the Red Scare and the increasing reemployment of veterans, it was moribund.[6]

The large number of veterans' groups founded after the Armistice supports Eric Wood's contention that "the Legion was not initiated by any single individual, nor was it organized by any clique. It sprang into being as the result of a universal demand among the soldiers and sailors for an effective nation-wide organization which would enable us to carry to the problems of peacetime the teamwork we had so well learned in time of war." Yet Wood and Roosevelt could also brag about how they created the Legion "out of our hip pockets" through an "imaginary committee." Nevertheless, they did not "circumvent," as critics charged, a "spontaneous expression of purpose by the millions of American veterans." Rather, the Legion's originators channeled a mood common throughout the AEF. They manipulated the rank and file in the sense any competent leadership suggests and implements policy, issues self-serving publicity, and tries to paper over internal conflicts. The Legion's leaders made no secret of their aims: they detested "Reds" and "slackers," cooperated with local, state, and national government officials, established friendly ties with the business community, and lobbied for veterans' benefits. This was the "Americanism" they accepted uncritically. Individuals and smaller groups joining the Legion knew where they stood. Some may have joined simply to meet with old comrades or to gain greater access to veterans' benefits and to those local notables whose favor they sought. But the Legion also provoked enough negative publicity for veterans to hear both sides. It speaks volumes for World War I military experience that even had every officer in the AEF joined the Legion in its first year, three-quarters of its members would have been enlisted personnel.[7]

Planning for the Legion itself began in January 1919. According to Eric Fisher Wood, it was "first thought up and initiated by four men, all four starting World War I from scratch, [who] fought their way to become lieutenant colonels of infantry, each of them wounded in action more than once, all four active in World War II." Wood might have added that all four attended the Plattsburgh Training Camp. They were Roosevelt, Wood, George A. White of Oregon, and New York's "Wild Bill" Donovan, who was to become head of the Office of Strategic Services in World War II.[8]

After talking about the organization among their acquaintances, the four next had to find an occasion to recruit members. As army officers, they confronted a rival, Comrades in Service, officially endorsed by both their commanding general and President Wilson. Their opportunity came early in February when Roosevelt was visiting General Headquarters in Paris. He was at the time "plotting to go home" and launch the new association there. General Pershing, suddenly aware of his army's rapidly deteriorating morale, asked the immensely popular Roosevelt for advice. Then, as Wood related: "Ted didn't care particularly about morale problems. But, always mentally quick on the trigger, he saw a chance to correct the impasse. . . . Suggested a morale conference—to be made up exclusively of civilian soldiers—and the four of us to pick the list. SMART!!!"

Pershing approved Roosevelt's suggestion, little suspecting its true purpose. Roosevelt handpicked twenty officers he could depend upon to contribute the ideas and the energy needed to attract grass-roots support. Most important, they would keep the prospective association a secret until they presented General Headquarters with a fait accompli. The group included Bennett Champ Clark, son of the former Speaker of the House of Representatives and himself formerly a Democratic member from Missouri; Captain Ogden Mills (who later replaced Andrew Mellon as President Hoover's secretary of the treasury); Major Franklin D'Olier, a millionaire textile manufacturer from Philadelphia who organized the AEF's supply system and became the Legion's first elected national commander; and another member of the Roosevelt clan, a cousin, George. Eight of the twenty hailed from New York City, the rest residing in such large cities as Philadelphia, Boston, Seattle, and Chicago, where they could initiate regional organization.

The morale conference lasted three days, February 15 to 17, from 10 A.M. to 4 P.M., "with plenty of time out for lunch," Wood noted. "Lunch" and evenings until midnight "were spent rigging up the Paris Caucus," scheduled to meet on March 15. Although morale problems took a back seat, the soon-to-be-born Legion was helped when its leaders persuaded Pershing that his army no longer needed an exhausting drill regimen. Most important, Pershing released and adhered to a demobilization schedule whereby men waiting to return home could look forward to a definite date of departure.

If Pershing accepted the officers' morale recommendations with good grace, he was "furious" that they had surreptitiously started an unauthorized veterans' organization to undermine the one he and President Wilson supported. Pershing summoned the four original conspirators to Paris with orders marked "urgent" to confront them. But he realized he had no choice but to approve their plans. If he forbade the Caucus, he would open himself to accusations of using Comrades in Service to further his presidential ambitions. But the Caucus's organizers could use the fact that he permitted delegates to attend to spread the word that he tacitly sanctioned its aims. But there is no truth in the charge of some Legion critics and scholars that the army set up the Legion to control the veterans' society that was emerging from the war. Rather, as Wood wrote, the reverse occurred: "General Headquarters opposed the Legion until it picked up so much steam that it ran over General Headquarters."[9]

The Caucus Wood and his colleagues "so boldly called together" met quietly on March 15 at the Cirque de Paris. Wood called the meeting to order in the absence of Chairman Roosevelt, already busy organizing the Legion in the States. As executive secretary ("a high falutin' word for stenographer," he claimed), Wood was nearly "worked to death" sending out wires and letters to persuade enough doughboys to show up. Despite his best efforts to corral a large number of enlisted men, to refute the predictable criticism that the rank and file were being manipulated by their officers, the latter greatly outnumbered the former. Of 450 registrants, only 47 held ranks below lieutenant. No one from the navy appeared at all until the final day, when two sailors were "kidnaped off the sidewalk" and another wandered in hoping to see a show. Many enlisted men who were summoned decided to enjoy a vacation in Paris instead of attending to business. Even the officers were sorely tempted: only 230 delegates "stuck it out and stayed off Paris." Yet ignoring the numerical disparity between officers and enlisted men, the *Stars and Stripes* obligingly stressed the initial call for a broadly representative group rather than emphasizing the top-heavy one that materialized. It also played up speeches and anecdotes involving enlisted men to demonstrate the Caucus's "true democacy."[10]

The small attendance and the officer majority actually worked to the organizers' advantage. Guided by an inner circle of Clark, Wood, D'Olier, and Mills, the Caucus accomplished much in two sessions lasting a total of seven hours. It put out the call for a stateside caucus to be held in St. Louis in May for the soldiers who had "returned to America and many other troops [who] were denied the great privilege of coming to France to fight the Germans." It set a precedent for future Legion conventions by adopting the parliamentary procedure of the House of Representatives. Debate was strictly limited to a five minutes' speech per delegate on each topic. The Caucus refrained from committing the Legion on such potentially divisive questions as how black posts should be organized and whether to take a stand on the

League of Nations. (Wood commented that most delegates were hostile to the League, but deferred a resolution against it because President Wilson was then in Paris. Wilson, associated with Comrades in Service, was "too busy" to speak to the Caucus.) From its very inception, then, the Legion established its neutrality on issues that might significantly divide veterans.[11]

Although only five paragraphs long, the temporary constitution the Caucus adopted helped the Legion considerably. It extended membership to all veterans of 1917 and 1918, whether they served in France or not. This provision gave the Legion twice the potential size of the Veterans of Foreign Wars, which limited participation to men who actually went overseas. The Caucus also stipulated that the state would be the Legion's basic unit, with the right to handle its internal organization, "except that the requirements and purposes of the national constitution as adopted shall be complied with." By endorsing strong state sovereignty, the Legion conveniently buried the racial problem and allowed each state to adopt the programs it thought best. Finally, to confirm a broad "Americanism" and to avoid taking almost any other stand, the Caucus adopted a provisional preamble heavily based on the Grand Army of the Republic's:

> We, the members of the Military and Naval Services of the United States of America in the Great War, desiring to perpetuate the principles of Justice, Freedom, and Democracy for which we have fought, to inculcate the duty and obligation of the citizen to the State, to preserve the history and incidents of our participation in the War, and to cement the ties of our comradeship formed in service, do propose to found and establish an association for the furtherance of the foregoing purposes.[12]

In addition to giving the Legion a constitution, the Caucus also gave it a name. Participants suggested several: Comrades of the Great War, American Legion of the Great War (whose initials, A.L.G.W., were those of Abraham Lincoln and George Washington), Liberty League, Army of the Great War, The Legion, American Comrades of the Great War, Society of the Great War, Great Legion, and American Comrades. Other possibilities considered at both the Caucus and back home included American Crusaders, The Grand Army of Civilization, and Grand Army of the World. The committee on a name preferred "Legion of the Great War" but the Caucus overruled it. Memories of the earlier American Legions created by Theodore Roosevelt Sr. and by those who

First Caucus of the American Legion, Paris, February 1919. Note the large
number of empty seats. Courtesy of American Legion National Headquarters.

served in the Canadian army determined the final choice. The
name "American Legion" permitted even men who had not left
boot camp to identify with those on the front lines and to acquire
some of Roosevelt's prestige.[13]

When the Caucus broke up, most prominent Legionnaires left
for home to join Theodore Roosevelt Jr., who was already recruiting with great vigor. First, he sent telegrams to every state,
asking prominent officials, acquaintances, or those who had already started veterans' societies for "the names of men you feel
are representative," and stressing the need for enlisted men to
counter propaganda that officers were running the Legion. He
also asked their permission to use their names to publicize the
Legion. On April 10, Wood mailed a letter to the governor of
every state, emphasizing the Legion's nonpartisan and patriotic
nature and requesting that they "take an active interest in the
formation of the American Legion." Roosevelt and Wood then
sent follow-up telegrams asking all who accepted the invitations
to arrange state caucuses and local publicity.[14]

Yet with only a month before the St. Louis Caucus, states
lacked the time to enroll members and formally elect delegates.
Basically, everyone showed up who wanted to. Illinois, which
topped the list with 112 delegates, sent "a number of free-lancers
with selfish ambitions." The mayor of Tampa picked Florida's
delegation. Bronson Cutting, a newspaper publisher and future
United States senator, coughed up $598 to accompany his friends
from New Mexico. To forestall confusion about the number of
legitimate delegates present, the Legion's Executive Committee
and Caucus Chairman Henry Lindsley allowed each delegation
twice as many votes as its strength in the House of Representatives
and then left it alone to figure out how to cast its ballots.[15]

Despite such makeshift organization, the St. Louis Caucus
proved far more "representative" than the one in Paris in terms
of participation by enlisted men. Generals, colonels, and majors
numbered about 17 percent of those present; but overall, officers
still accounted for 55 percent. Further, a glance at their occupations, which the Caucus delegates recorded, reveals the enlisted
men were mostly upper-class. They included wealthy enthusiasts
who had enlisted as privates but had failed to rise in the ranks.
(One J. P. Morgan of Hawaii, who listed his occupation as "fin-
ancier," began as a private and worked his way up to lieutenant.)
The large number of upper- and middle-class enlisted men at the
Caucus thus enabled the Legion to publicize a group able to take

a week off from work and subsidize their convention expenses as one where "rank counted for nothing."[16]

The Caucus's organizers had a clear idea of what they expected it to accomplish. First, they hoped to secure a good deal of favorable publicity—sixty-six of the delegates were newspaper reporters, editors, or publishers, including New York's George Putnam and Chicago's Robert McCormick, publisher of the *Tribune*. Second, they prepared very broad resolutions against slackers and Bolsheviks and in favor of veterans' benefits to which it was expected no patriotic citizen could reasonably object. Third, the Legion's prime movers hoped the Caucus would permit the Executive Committee to continue its work, leaving all substantive and potentially divisive matters to be smoothed over before the November Convention.[17]

The Caucus did not fail its organizers. On the surface, Roosevelt, Wood, and Clark appeared to have a hard time keeping "the enthusiasm and spirit" of over eleven hundred young men within bounds. Dorothy R. Harper, historian of Hawaii's Legion, has written, "The St. Louis Caucus was one of rip, roar, and tear, as every man pawed the earth to make himself heard and get his ideas over. The melee was inconceivable, disorder reigned supreme, and it looked like the outcome would be a failure." But this confusion worked to the leaders' advantage. It permitted the delegates to let off steam debating and voting on matters with little substance but much publicity value for two out of three days. They spent the two days choosing a chairman, five "representative" vice-chairmen from various branches of the services and sections of the nation, and the site of the Legion's first convention in November. Wasting time electing ceremonial officials and choosing a meeting site ensured that the exhausted men passed the proposed agenda rapidly on the final day.[18]

While the Caucus established its Americanism and nonpartisanship through speeches and ceremonial elections, Legion committees, including those on the constitution, publications, and resolutions, met at night. It was here that the rank and file threatened to undo the nonpartisanship the organizers had planned. Delegates discussed the possibility of taking stands on the League of Nations, admitting regular-army men to the Legion, a peacetime draft, whether Secretary of War Newton D. Baker should be impeached for being "soft" on slackers and conscientious objectors—he freed some after the war ended—Prohibition, the desirability of universal military service in peacetime, and the organization of black posts. An unequivocal stand on any of these matters might have torn the Legion apart. While the Caucus spent its time on symbolic issues, the committees tried to avoid burdening the Legion with the great issues polarizing American society.[19]

To control the situation, Rev. John Inzer of Alabama stepped in with what may have been a prearranged speech. On May 9 before the Executive Committee, and on the 10th before the whole body, as historian Dorothy R. Harper relates, Inzer "put the right dope on the ball. He whanged the gong of cooperation . . . he threw out all the partisan resolutions and behold, the differences fell from us in a half hour." Inzer's oration must have been something to hear; it is still something to read. He harangued the delegates "to take up matters of importance and leave off matters that should not be taken up, and to solidify this body in a great spirit of Americanism that shall last for fifty years as the greatest organization that the world has ever known." "Dreaming dreams and seeing visions of the years to come," Inzer predicted the Legion would become "the jewel of the ages," possessing an opportunity that "the great seers of the past ages have dreamed and longed for." The practical condition of this heavenly prospect was unanimity at the Caucus: "If there is anything that everybody in this convention won't immediately agree upon here today, and which would hinder us from sending out to the nation a message that we are going to pull together, that we have caught a mighty vision, and that we have a great spirit, then brethren, let us postpone that thing until next November." The Caucus then settled down to business, and on its final day rapidly approved the measures the leaders had proposed and that Inzer had urged in concluding his oration. The veterans resolved to ask "the United States Congress to pass a bill for immediately deporting every one of those Bolsheviks or IWWS." Other resolutions were vague but firm requests that Congress help veterans obtain jobs and adequate medical care and provide pensions for widows and orphans.[20]

The Caucus also refused to act on issues that divided the veterans. The Bonus was the sorest point. Many delegates believed that they deserved a bonus of $15 to $30 per month of service, as "many left lucrative employment upon joining the colors . . . at a time when many of the aliens [who] remained in safety at home were enjoying the advantage of an exceptionally high war wage." When the resolutions committee recommended that the

Caucus endorse the payment, Chairman Lindsley, who had moved things along quite rapidly, slowed the pace and questioned whether a bonus was consistent with the Legion's "most splendidly high patriotic attitude." Then Theodore Roosevelt Jr., who had not spoken officially in three days except to refuse the chairmanship, brought his enormous prestige to bear. Insisting that the Legion "put something into the government instead of subtracting something from it," he urged the men to refute the railroad conductor he had encountered on his trip to St. Louis, who thought that "Young Teddy is . . . going out to St. Louis to get the men together and sandbag something for them out of the government." Roosevelt's rhetoric, like Inzer's, carried the day.[21]

The Caucus presented one final problem. In his speech, Inzer warned the men to "cut out every last bit of hoodlum." As the hall was filled with sympathetic newsmen, accounts of the Caucus did not mention the sort of foolery associated with later Legion conventions. But a fair amount occurred. New Mexico's Bronson Cutting, in a letter warning State Chairman Manuel Otero "not to drink up all the booze till I get back," described the event as "some party." He noted that Vice-Chairman Humphreys, "next to Ted Roosevelt, was easily the best known man in St. Louis, and anything he overlooked in the way of chorines and millionaire jewesses was not worth getting." Largely because both press and public forgave the rambunctious young heroes, the Legion avoided another potentially damaging criticism at this formative stage.[22]

Besides taking a strong stand on veterans' benefits and anti-radicalism, the Caucus set up the machinery that enabled the organization to flourish in the next few months. The Legion confined its declarations of principle to high-sounding paragraphs written by a committee chaired by New York's Hamilton Fish, which ultimately became its constitution's preamble. The temporary constitution provided for an Executive Committee of one hundred (two members from each state and the District of Columbia, plus a chairman and a secretary, Lindsley and Wood) to grant charters to state organizations, which in turn chartered local "posts." (The Caucus decided that the Legion would be a society of posts rather than "billets" after Yeoman Edward McGrath of New Jersey argued that a "billet is some place where you lie down and sleep, and the American Legion is not going to lie down and sleep." Posts could not be named after living people, whose political connections might compromise the Legion's effort to be nonpolitical.) A publicity committee also geared up for work. It offered a prize for the best design for an emblem Legionnaires would wear on their buttons and use as their official insignia. After a minute of silence in honor of the late Theodore Roosevelt, "the greatest statesman that this nation has ever produced, the President who defied Wall Street and every other combination," the Caucus pledged its "fidelity to the mothers of America" and adjourned.[23]

Eric Fisher Wood considered the St. Louis Caucus a "tremendous success"[24] in forging a group of dedicated veterans pledged to go forth and create the Legion, but even more difficult tasks lay ahead. The Legion was still an idea in search of a concrete form. Roosevelt, Wood, and their colleagues had no trouble persuading American soldiers that "one-hundred-percent Americanism," freedom, justice, and democracy ought to be protected in peace as in war. But could the patriotic fervor that maintained a broad consensus in war be continued in a peacetime nation bitterly rent by disputes between labor and capital, wets and drys, isolationists and League of Nations advocates, radicals and conservatives, blacks and whites, Catholics and Protestants? Even the carefully selected delegates at the Caucus only agreed to bury a number of hatchets with difficulty. Now the Legion had to take its case to four million veterans, not a thousand.

Between May and November 1919, the Legion's "kingmakers," as Legionnaires half-affectionately dubbed their principal leaders, needed every ounce of tact and energy that they possessed. They made numerous speaking tours to line up American businessmen, newspapers, and political figures behind the Legion. They blanketed the United States with propaganda to convince the country that the Legion not only constituted "the" society of AEF veterans, but that, as Wood wrote, in a nation surrounded by "world-wide social and economic displacements, the American Legion will be the greatest bulwark against Bolshevism and anarchy." In a land gripped by the Red Scare, the Legion successfully appointed itself America's leading anti-Bolshevik organization.[25]

With the Legion officially launched at the St. Louis Caucus, the prime movers lost no time reestablishing control. The Executive Committee of One Hundred could not function: most of its members had to leave St. Louis and get back to their jobs. At its only formal meeting, on the evening of May 10, Roosevelt reassumed the prominence he had eschewed during the public proceedings. He suggested the unwieldy group delegate its authority to Chairman Lindsley, Secretary Wood, and fifteen others (ten chosen by Lindsley, five elected by the other twelve). The seventeen included many familiar names: Clark, D'Olier, Bishop Brent, Mills, Inzer, and Richard Derby, Roosevelt's brother-in-law. Wood reported that "Roosevelt himself sincerely resisted his appointment but the rest of them felt that the Legion was not yet strong enough to survive without him." The Committee of Seventeen then reduced its number further at a full meeting on June 9 in New York City. It empowered five men—Lindsley, Wood, Clark, D'Olier, and Derby—to "devote their entire time to Legion work," although the committee continued to meet. Between June and November, the Legion's "National Headquarters" and organization consisted of this New York directorate.[26]

The Legion's organizers prepared a strict timetable to ensure that a powerful association emerged from the November Convention in Minneapolis. June was devoted to raising money through loans until membership dues started coming in. July witnessed the creation of state departments. By August, they hoped to establish a post in every county in the United States: Wood considered this drive 80 to 90 percent successful. Posts were established at meetings called by Legion organizers sent out by National Headquarters, which organized a Speakers' Bureau headed by J. F. J. Herbert of Massachusetts. Theodore Roosevelt Jr., for example, spoke in thirty states, and John Inzer canvassed the South. In other cases, existing local veterans' groups simply applied for and received Legion charters. In September, the Legion acquired the sort of national charter only the Boy Scouts and the Red Cross had previously obtained, giving it a legitimacy never enjoyed even by the GAR. The same month, posts elected delegates to state conventions scheduled to meet in October, which chose representatives for the forthcoming National Convention in Minneapolis. The state conventions in turn adopted for the most part the measures suggested by National Headquarters in memoranda and by regional organizers in speeches. The plans worked splendidly. As Wood put it: "To have done the work outside of the above schedule would in the long run have caused a loss of valuable time, and in addition would probably have given the Legion such a reputation for inefficiency and have caused so many needless confusions, that it might completely have ruined any prospect of success."[27]

The nation's press also deserves to share credit for organizing the Legion: the young group received reams of free publicity from newspaper and magazine editors terrified that Bolshevism menaced the United States. The *Los Angeles Express, New York Herald, Ladies' Home Journal,* and *Collier's,* among others, opened their columns to the Legion and gave it wholehearted support. Newspaper publishers Robert McCormick in Chicago, Bronson Cutting in New Mexico, and George Putnam in New York were the chief organizers in their states. Future Secretary of the Navy Frank Knox, who published the *Manchester* (New Hampshire) *Union,* raised $10,000 in his state. At its Minneapolis Convention in November, the Legion would make a special point to extend its "most deep appreciation and loyal thanks to the press and all papers, magazines, and publicity committees who have so generously assisted the American Legion."[28]

The Legion soon added its own voice to that of American journalism. On July 4, 1919, under the direction of George White, National Headquarters in New York began publishing the *American Legion Weekly.* Early issues featured articles by Seattle's Mayor Ole Hanson on how international Communism and "un-American" aliens, rather than legitimate grievances, triggered the Seattle general strike and nearly all domestic unrest. The magazine presented the Legion as a panacea for the troubles of the veterans and the nation. As White captioned a comic strip in the first issue: "After reading on one page of your newspaper all about the spread of Bolshevism—and on another of the terrors of Russian Sovietism—and your desponding and gloom increases as you read of riots on another page—and coming to another page, more high cost of living news—bad news—and just as you are reading about starving Europe and sinking into the last stages of melancholia— you read about The American Legion—Oh-h-Boy!! Ain't it a Gr-r-rand and Glor-r-rious Feeling?"[29]

To complement the *Weekly,* the Executive Committee hired one of the nation's leading corporate publicists, Ivy Lee of New York—who had convinced much of the world to consider the Red Cross the leading emergency association in times of disaster— to mount an advertising campaign. On June 9, the Committee gave Lee a discretionary fund of between $5,000 and $10,000 per month for five months, out of which he would pay the necessary salaries and take his profits. Lee ultimately charged $7,500 a month for a nationwide blitz that included advertisements in every newspaper in the land with a circulation of 150,000 or more. He also printed 300,000 posters of upper- and middle-class men walking arm-in-arm with a laborer urging former soldiers "Back into cits [civilian clothes] and the American Legion."[30]

Government officials did their part, too. The governors of Colorado, Kansas, Ohio, and Maine headed their states' preliminary organizations. New Jersey's William Runyon and other governors appeared at Legion state conventions, exhorting Legionnaires to "cast Bolshevism into outer darkness," and praising the former soldiers: "You don't know how grateful the state is to the Legion." General Pershing buried the hatchet with the Legion and supported it both in a public letter and as the chief speaker at a June rally of fifteen thousand people at Madison Square Garden. At the rally, in a dramatic gesture, he resisted a plea by New York's Mayor John Hylan to leave the stage in a dramatic gesture as Hylan assured him that the Legion's founders wished to embroil him in their political schemes. By remaining to give his speech, Chairman Lindsley commented, "You saved it [the Legion], by your ringing words and then, throughout the country, on your triumphal tour on its behalf."[31]

The federal government also supported the Legion. President Wilson endorsed it and predicted that the soldiers' spirit of "service, and the continuation of that service in the American Legion, will make it always an inspiration to the full performance of high and difficult duties." As early as August 1919, the War Department gave the Legion "official recognition and assistance." It permitted the Legion to recruit men still in service, agreed to furnish Legionnaires with advice and assistance in obtaining federal benefits for veterans, and soon issued guns to Legion posts "for ceremonial purposes." But Legionnaires and their radical opponents realized that in the event of an insurrection these guns would have more than "ceremonial" uses.[32]

The Legion's greatest coup, however, was persuading Congress to put its seal of approval on the organization with a federal charter. The charter passed without debate in the Senate and with only mild questioning in the House. Some Congressmen wondered about the Legion's representativeness, its openness to all honorably discharged veterans, and the possibility its thirty-four incorporators (the Committees of Seventeen from St. Louis and Paris) might dominate the Legion for ulterior purposes. However, Legionnaire Fiorello La Guardia—who like Grenville Clark soon became an opponent of the Legion's version of "Americanism"— assured his colleagues that it was "an absolute democracy." The father of a Legion founder, Missouri's Champ Clark, led the floor fight, insisting that the incorporators could not hold onto the organization "to save their lives. The other fellows would take it away from them the first minute they endeavored to." The House passed the charter legislation without a division on August 27, the Senate on September 6, and President Wilson signed it on September 15.[33]

During the Red Scare of 1919, state and national politicians hastened to give the Legion everything it wanted. In Missouri, for example, "no office holder dares to decline to do any service required of him by the state chairman, this through fear." In New Mexico and elsewhere, states offered the Legion free headquarters in their capitols. As "Buck" Private Mendenhall noted in his tract, "A Spasm Relating to the American Legion Headquarters and the Use of Unnecessary Red Tape," this had advantages besides free rent:

> When the Legion officials needed anything, they called on the Governor, the Adjutant General, the Attorney General, and they got what they wanted RIGHT ON THE SPOT. There was no unnecessary red tape or correspondence, there were no letters to get into the hands of a secretary or a stenographer, because the Legion secretary would go direct to whoever he wished to see, AND GET RESULTS PRONTO.[34]

In such states as Illinois, Michigan, and Massachusetts, where the Legion enjoyed enthusiastic organizers and cooperation from both public and private sectors, it took off like a rocket.

In Illinois, Legion founders included General Milton Foreman and the department-store magnate Marshall Field, who systematically enlisted support from "the conservative labor leaders, the conservative foreign element of the large cities, the prominent negroes, and all the prominent business and professional people of the state." Rather than appealing directly to veterans to join up, Legionnaires canvassed their neighborhoods to discover which soldiers were not taking advantage of their War Risk Insurance policies or vocational-training benefits. The Legion then set up a Service Section to deal with these matters and employment problems. Observers found it "an inspiration [to] . . . see the effective and courteous manner in which the cases are being handled." The service offices provided impoverished veterans with meal tickets usable at local restaurants, kept lists of the services and vacancies of every hospital in the state, and followed up on the care given to the men. By 1920 some fifteen thousand former servicemen had availed themselves of such programs. Organizers in Illinois were especially attuned to the problems of recruiting in Chicago, where neighborhood ties were sometimes less important than occupational associations. There, the Legion organized businessmen's, advertising, labor, and newspapermen's posts in addition to chartering one post per community, a model followed in such other cities as New York and Los Angeles. Throughout the interwar years, Illinois remained one of the most imaginative and productive Legion departments: it originated the Boys' State program and put the Legion squarely behind the army's own defense program.[35]

The Michigan Legion enjoyed equal initial success. In the four years after the war, Michigan voted some $11 million to former servicemen, capping its efforts with a state tubercular hospital in 1921 that required $685,000 in cash and $1.5 million in bonds. The state raised another $30 million in bonds to give its veterans a bonus. In the private sphere, Henry Ford employed some fifty thousand veterans recommended by the Michigan Legion. If anything, the department was too successful. By 1922, Wayne County posts were complaining to National Headquarters that "they would rather be rid of the American Legion than give in to the money-grabbing schemes of the state department." That year, the Michigan Legion controlled $240,000 in welfare funds.[36]

But the Legion's greatest early success came in Massachusetts. As in Illinois and Michigan, Massachusetts Legionnaires seemed to be spurred to great heights by an awareness that their urbanized, heavily immigrant, and significantly Catholic population needed special attention. The state's membership of sixty thousand, which exceeded that of the Solid South, New York, or Pennsylvania the first year, led the United States. The Bay State Legion benefited especially from cooperation with the administration of Governor Calvin Coolidge and alarm created by the Boston Police strike. The Legion set up headquarters in the State House, took over the state employment bureau for veterans, and received $700 per week as a subsidy for expenses. Within a year, the legislature had the Proceedings of the St. Louis Caucus printed at state expense; authorized Legion parades and entertainments, even on Sunday; restored to government employees the difference between their service pay and their peacetime salaries; granted the Legion tax-exempt status; and gave every state veteran a $100 bonus.[37]

Not all departments pressed ahead with equal vigor. Though

most did well, the Legion fared badly in several Deep South states for a number of years. As late as 1925, Alabama Adjutant S. C. Crockett described his state's Legion as "a one man affair, by which I mean an adjutant has been paid a salary and it was supposed and presumed by every Legionnaire in the state that he is to do all the work." In 1920, an Alabama adjutant went insane from shell shock and lost the state constitution, while the finance officer absconded with both the records and most of the funds. In Georgia, National Adjutant Lemuel Bolles reported that "the Department Adjutant is working in a bank and only gives part of his time," while "all over Georgia, the boy in the country is owned body and soul and heart by that most disgraceful, unpatriotic, and during the war pro-German [Senator] Tom Watson. They swear by him." Mississippi was plagued by a struggle between two rival Legions (one of them financially corrupt) and by stiff competition from the Ku Klux Klan. In 1925, the department was "still struggling," in debt, and without either a historian or an annual report. However, following the great flood of 1927, in which local Legionnaires manned the front lines and received material assistance from the entire nation, Mississippians joined the Legion in such numbers that the state frequently led the Legion parade at its annual conventions, an honor reserved for the state with the highest membership percentage of surviving veterans.[38]

But the principal obstacle to the growth of the Legion in the South was race. From the beginning, the Legion did not know what to do with black veterans. On the one hand, they constituted over half the veterans of these states. On the other, they had been largely excluded from combat and thus segregated from both the rest of the army and "the spirit of the Great War." The Legion's principal organizers, including Roosevelt and D'Olier, hoped to put "a few" black and women veterans on the Legion's Executive Committee to encourage recruits. In Louisiana, which briefly chartered black posts, a "rich negro" even paid for a black alternate delegation to attend the St. Louis Caucus to protest the refusal of white Louisianans to accept them. (They were turned away.) Some Southern organizers hoped for "separate but equal" posts, including Louisiana's John Parker, who told Roosevelt that "if it came time for a question of excluding the colored soldiers entirely I would resign."[39]

But the Southern delegates in favor of all-white departments carried the day. Were blacks admitted to the organizations, they would have to be allowed to vote in the Legion, even though they could not vote in general elections. Moreover, they would dominate their states by sheer numbers. Rev. Inzer insisted that "Alabama would burst wild on that and so would Mississippi and Georgia and various and sundry other states." The South, he noted, feared the effects that military training and exposure to less racist societies overseas had had on its black population. Inzer appealed to the rest of the nation, where black veterans could join either segregated or integrated posts, not to interfere in the South's internal problems. While admitting that "we must give them their rights, because those that had the opportunity were good soldiers," Inzer depicted Southern blacks as potential revolutionaries if they were granted membership in the Legion. Rather than lose Southern whites, Northern supporters of black equality allowed each state to reach its own racial solution. Despite sporadic protests from blacks during the interwar years, the Legion persisted in this states' rights policy on the race issue.[40]

Some blacks did join the segregated posts adopted throughout much of the nation. Northern black veterans usually formed their own posts without incident in communities with substantial black populations. The largest black post in Louisville, Kentucky, had 110 members and sponsored a jazz orchestra and a Boy Scout troop. But most blacks had little enthusiasm for an organization that had no greater commitment to equality than American society as a whole. North Carolina, for instance, could only attract 500 black veterans out of 20,000 in 1926 when it launched a drive to organize them. Even a black veteran who moved to Georgia from New York, where blacks both joined integrated posts and formed their own, lost his membership under the rules of his new home state. Wright Patman responded to complaints about Texas's exclusion policy with "What's the alternative?" But the quickly extinguished idealism of Roosevelt, D'Olier, and even some white southerners suggested that for a brief moment after World War I—far briefer, even, than a similar moment after the Civil War—some Legionnaires believed that rhetoric about the democratization achieved under arms applied even to blacks.[41]

Outside the South, however, most states responded enthusiastically to the initial Legion appeals that resulted in the formation of local posts. Veterans clamored for personal appearances by "Teddy," or, in his absence, by men "whose names and whose records have a real meaning to these boys and who can put the Legion up to them in a way to bring them to their feet, *with their faces toward the platform.*" Roosevelt spoke with "extraordinary success." Such local enthusiasts as future National Commander Harry Colmery of Kansas saddled up their horses and scoured the backcountry. In California, Harry Foster traveled throughout the state, speaking to rallies in Fresno, Modesto, Bakersfield, and San Diego. Inzer covered fifteen states and claimed he could "fill up a dozen ordinary sheets, and that typewritten, telling you how gratified I am with the program of our great organization."[42]

Besides sending out powerful speakers, the Legion's National Headquarters provided the organization with a sound financial base. By early June 1919 "not one single contribution had been received," and a panicky Eric Wood even believed that "the situation has reached a point where serious consideration should be given to the advisability of curtailing or even completely closing the national office." To meet initial expenses, Colonel John W. Prentiss lent the Legion $20,000; D'Olier and Roosevelt lent $5,000 each. But to cover expenses from June through October, the Legion still needed to obtain a loan of $250,000 from sixty-six banks and wealthy individuals. New York's Morgan Guaranty Trust put up $100,000; affluent Legionnaires personally guaranteed the loan. Critics charged that the loan constituted proof the Legion was started by "Wall Street" and capitalists, but this argument puts the cart before the horse. The Legion came to the bankers, not the other way around, and it had to pay back the money at 6 percent interest.[43]

But if the Legion and American business shared an interest in opposing radicalism, the Legion's new crusades in the 1920s against profiteers and economy-minded businessmen who opposed the Bonus soon demonstrated that the Legion functioned independently of its supposed manipulators. In fact, while the Legion accepted gifts of buildings and office space from states and localities, rented advertisements in bulletins and magazines, and gladly took such special bequests as surplus local war-chest funds and $500,000 from the YMCA's canteen profits, most departments and the national office refused gifts from individuals to avoid accusations that the Legion was anybody's tool. Nevertheless, criticisms of the $250,000 loan put the Legion on the defensive. It never again sought such financial support.[44]

In addition to skirting the racial issue and solving financial problems, the Legion had to decide whether and to what extent it was "political." Nearly all Legionnaires realized partisan support of electoral candidates would destroy the organization. Democrats' fears that Theodore Roosevelt Jr. was using the Legion to launch a presidential bid had to be dealt with quickly. Roosevelt himself was aware of the problem, and aside from retaining his post membership played no role in Legion affairs after 1919. By 1920, Legion founders with political ambitions had established the precedent that candidates for public office could not be officers of the Legion. This rule transformed the leadership completely. Wood, Roosevelt, and Ogden Mills all went into Republican politics; Bennett Clark and J. F. J. Herbert entered the Democratic lists. As Wood put it, once the organization was launched, it was time "to let the rank and file who had not been G-- d--- colonels run the Legion as was their right." Curiously, for all the complaints of the Legion's great influence, its founders had a mixed record in politics. Roosevelt won election to the New York Assembly in 1920, but lost the 1922 gubernatorial race to Al Smith. Eric Fisher Wood's efforts on behalf of Leonard Wood did not bear fruit. Herbert lost his race for lieutenant governor of Massachusetts. On the other hand, Clark, who was elected to Congress from Missouri, Mills, who represented New York's "Silk-Stocking" district before becoming secretary of the treasury, and Hamilton Fish, Franklin D. Roosevelt's home-district congressman and nemesis, all won election.[45]

Other questions of politics besides partisanship in elections threatened to undermine the Legion even when it attempted to avoid them. Despite Inzer's pleadings, in Tennessee the state convention endorsed a soldiers' bonus and the League of Nations. Legionnaire Noel Gaines "vigorously" protested to National Headquarters that "one of your committee [is] going from state to state trying to influence legislation." Gaines won the fight to have Tennessee endorse a specific bonus (one dollar per day in service per man) and complained that Inzer's position was "a boyish straddle." As for the League, Gaines insisted that "President Wilson has said there is no politics in it" and regarded the League as a real, as opposed to a "farcical," form of "one-hundred-percent Americanism." (The Tampa Post's and Georgia Department's resolutions endorsing the League appear in the *Congressional Record*.) Gaines concluded his protests with a quotation from Acts (6:14) against preachers who preached anything but religion. Chairman Lindsley patiently explained that because the leaders at National Headquarters were personally divided on these questions, the Legion should not jeopardize its unity by taking a stand.[46]

For all the leaders' caution in keeping the Legion committed

The first Legion National Convention parade, Minneapolis, 1919. Future parades would be less somber. Courtesy of American Legion National Headquarters.

only to policies on which its members shared a consensus, such as anti-Bolshevism, agreement broke down at the Minneapolis Convention in November. The Legion's membership raucously debated six major issues: whether national dues should remain at twenty-five cents a year or be increased to a dollar to fund the *Weekly*; what sort of stance against "Bolshevism" should be taken; what ought to be done about a Bonus for veterans; whether the War Risk Insurance Board ought to be condemned; who should be the national commander; and what should be the site of National Headquarters. Response to these issues coalesced around "leadership" and "opposition" positions. The Legion's leaders favored high dues, a firm but moderate condemnation of lawlessness, not supporting a soldiers' Bonus, working to improve the War Risk program without resorting to scathing denunciations, the election of "insider" Franklin D'Olier as commander, and Washington, D.C., as permanent headquarters. On the other hand, many delegates favored lower dues, wholehearted manifestos against both radicals and civil-service incompetence, a ringing endorsement of a specific Bonus plan, a commander who had not been associated with the New York leaders, and Indianapolis as the Legion's home. In Minneapolis, the delegates had to decide what sort of Legion they were going to have.

By far the most hotly and lengthily debated issue at the Convention was that of dues. Legion leaders insisted that without a well-funded *Weekly*, members would have no way of knowing "what the Legion stands for" and it would "lapse into disconnected, disjointed, uncoordinated groups of posts." But such a journal would require dues of at least four times the current level of twenty-five cents. Delegates from states with low dues and high memberships, such as Massachusetts, charged the increase would reduce membership and limit it to upper- and middle-class veterans. But after two raucous roll calls and some parliamentary skullduggery by Ogden Mills and Eric Fisher Wood, national dues of a dollar won, 384–300.[47]

The question of what stand the Legion should take against radicalism also prompted debate. A Resolutions Committee consisting of members from every state went far beyond the law-and-order position of the New York–based leaders. It came dangerously close to confirming some members' fears that the Legion was a paramilitary organization, "the tool of the capitalists and being financed by capital to put down the laboring men." The resolution urged "every post of the Legion . . . to tender and volunteer its services and the services of its individual members to the constituted government authorities for use in any time of public crisis to preserve law and order." It went on to suggest that states and localities draw up formal plans of cooperation so that "the full force and power of the Legion can be swiftly mobilized and used on the side of the constitutional government and American Liberty, so that our slogan shall be blazoned to the world: All for one, one for all, all for America." This resolution establishing the Legion as an American *Freikorps* received an unexpected boost by being read immediately after Washington's John Sullivan gave a biased account of how four veterans had been "murdered" by the IWW while marching in an Armistice Day parade in Centralia, Washington.[48]

Several delegates rebutted Sullivan. One questioned "whether you consider this a civilian organization," and insisted that were the resolution to be adopted the Legion would lose many of the "one-eighth" (his estimate) of eligible veterans who currently belonged. Another termed the resolution "amateurish": "We can be called upon in any crisis to put down any kind of disturbance whatever, whether the disturbance is a disturbance which ought to be put down or not, whether it is a legitimate protest against any condition, or whether it may be a threat to law and order and the established authority of a community." Sullivan retorted that such remarks embodied "the spirit of compromise, and the American Legion will not compromise with wrong." But "Wild Bill" Donovan had the last word. Belying his nickname, he exhorted the delegates to maintain their "sanity and clearheadedness," and said, simply, that "such a resolution goes too far." Heeding such prestigious advice, the Convention directed the Resolutions Committee to draw up a statement more consistent with civil liberty and article two of the Legion's constitution, by which Congress chartered it as a civilian organization.

The final resolution, which the Convention's leadership dared only to introduce during its final minutes, when many delegates were running off to catch their specially priced trains, asked posts to cooperate with the authorities in "the suppression of riots and mob violence" where "anarchistic and un-American groups" were involved. No mention was made of preemptive plans of attack against "nests of reds." The Legion at least officially therefore limited its role in combating radicalism to acting in consort with community consensus as voiced by elected officials and police. The Legion thereby mitigated some criticism that it was a strikebreaking, lawless force for "law and order." But while the Legion's resolution may have been moderate, many posts were not. Within a month, Commander D'Olier pleaded that Legionnaires refrain from mob violence against radicals. By taking a middle-of-the-road position at the Convention, the behavior of the Legion's more extreme members in various localities invited libertarian critics to charge it with hypocrisy as well as hooliganism.

The question of whether AEF veterans deserved a bonus and its possible nature caused an even bigger stir. Eric Wood noted that "every political demagogue in the country was yelling 'Bonus' for his own selfish ends beginning about November 12, 1918." Congressmen had already introduced some fifty-five bonus plans, involving in different combinations cash, farm- and home-purchase assistance, land reclamation and settlement programs, and vocational training. Many congressmen hoped the Legion would sort matters out for them.[49]

Three attitudes emerged within the Legion. Some members,

usually the wealthy to whom a few hundred dollars made no difference and who feared they would bear the tax burden, agreed with Oklahoma's General Roy Hoffman. The delegates at Minneapolis hissed him loudly for saying: "You are trying to place a cash value upon the services rendered when you say 'give us this back money.'" The Legion's prime movers—Roosevelt, D'Olier, and Wood—hoped that by avoiding any stand on the issue, they could keep both the Legion's pro- and anti-bonus members. Many delegates argued that such a vague position "pass[ed] the thing right back to Congress, when Congress passed the buck to us and said fix it." But "avoiding a stand" could easily be interpreted as opposing the Bonus. At Minneapolis, the Legion approved adjusted compensation in principle without endorsing a specific plan, thereby reversing its St. Louis position. On the Bonus, the Legion could not win: the following May, the National Executive Committee had to come up with a specific Bonus plan in response to overwhelming grass-roots discontent and Congress's failure to act. If the Legion lost fewer members by favoring a Bonus, it was nevertheless bound to lose some regardless of where it stood on the issue.[50]

In yet a fourth significant controversy, the Legion had to decide what form to give its dissatisfaction with the much-criticized War Risk Insurance Board, temporarily in charge of most veterans' benefits. Many delegates objected when the Resolutions Committee, this time siding with the New York organizers, only asked the Board to "employ more ex-servicemen, give prompter attention to inquiries directed to the Bureau, and Get Busy!" Voices on the floor demanded a more vigorous denunciation, as "only within the last two months have they done any work, and they have done that because of the criticisms of members of the Legion and members of the press." But committee chairman Inzer, worried that any specific condemnation would bring the Legion into politics against the Wilson administration, successfully persuaded the majority "not to condemn the past but to build for the future."[51]

The election of the national commander revealed the same conflict apparent on other issues. The Legion's Executive Committee arranged for California to yield to New York to nominate Franklin D'Olier, who had served stateside in the supply corps, to attract noncombatants who served at home. However, Hamilton Fish took the floor and put forward Iowa's Hanford MacNider instead, stressing his nine combat decorations and his residence in Iowa, "west of the Mississippi," far from the New Yorkers who had run the show until then. Kentucky then introduced a third candidate, Emmett O'Neal, who "drove the Red forces out and helped to drive from the pulpit in Kentucky a man who under the cover of religious teachings was preaching the doctrine of Bolshevism." D'Olier won overwhelmingly, but the significant opposition that emerged on the grounds he was neither a combatant nor an enlisted man indicated restlessness among rank and file Legionnaires. However, since over 75 percent of the delegates had not been to either Caucus and had no real chance to organize a campaign for an alternative candidate, the Legion's founders retained control for at least one more year.[52]

On the issue of a permanent headquarters, however, the leadership met its match in Walter Myers of the Indiana delegation, who proposed Indianapolis as the Legion's permanent headquarters. Theodore Roosevelt Jr. believed any sensible person would want the main Legion office in Washington, where it would make its primary impact as a legislative force. But Myers and his Indianapolis supporters pulled out all the stops. They accused Washington of being a den of "corruption and rottenness." Setting up Indiana state headquarters in the hotel housing the Legion's national officers, the delegation bought all the elevator girls a five-pound box of candy "to let off anyone asking for headquarters at our floor" to meet the maximum number of delegates. (One of those so misdirected was Roosevelt himself.) The Indianans also purchased and distributed scores of straw hats with bands urging the delegates to vote for Indianapolis. These tactics did the trick. On the seven-way first ballot, Indianapolis came in second, with 226 votes to 282 for Washington, beating out such enticing offers as a gift of $2.6 million from Kansas City for a Legion building, the promise of never-ending sunshine in Tucson, and the best cigars and tobacco in the nation in Wheeling. On the second ballot, Indianapolis won, 361 to 323. Just as the Founding Fathers of the nation, 130 years earlier, had removed the nation's capital from Philadelphia to the Potomac to escape the influence of mobs and merchants, the American Legion preferred to convey the voice of the veteran to the government uninfluenced by the wiles of the politicians themselves. One can only speculate whether and to what extent the Legion's decision has shaped its subsequent development into a body representative of conservative middle Americans.[53]

The Legion accomplished much in its first hectic months. To

be sure, it never attained original expectations that "very shortly no man who wants to have it known and who is proud of having been in the service will go on the streets without a Legion button on."[54] But given the obstacles it faced, the wonder is not that the Legion failed to reach its full potential or even to hold all its members. By waffling on the Bonus, taking a firm stand against radicalism, denouncing corruption in veterans' welfare agencies, and ignoring the race problem and the League of Nations, the Legion probably attracted more members than it could have with any other course of action. On the other hand, setting dues at a dollar a year enabled a middle-class organization to support intensive lobbying and publicity. Judged not by the Legion's own overly optimistic expectations of recruiting all veterans, but by its creation of a viable association with both national and local clout, the Legion must be accounted a success. That it attained great power within a year is a tribute to the prudence of its founders in cajoling, persuading, and at times manipulating so many veterans to subordinate and compromise their differences behind a commonly held vision of "one-hundred-percent Americanism."

CHAPTER FOUR

Membership and Organization

The resolutions which the Legion adopts, even though they do roll through the convention on a wave of *viva voce* votes, must be regarded as representing the views, not only of the average Legionnaire, but of the average American whom he so typically portrays. Peace through preparedness; no dealings with Red Russia; chase the subversives out of the country. . . . The American Legion . . . is really the problem of American democracy gathered in one organization. In the good-natured but uninformed man in the Legion cap, who sought to express his patriotism by marching in the parade and to satisfy his need for comradeship by mingling in the horseplay in the streets, is to be seen the citizen from whom votes must be gained in every drive for a majority. . . . In the careful calculations of the office-holders and office-seekers, intent on pushing their own fortunes by serving the special privileges of the group, is to be seen the reason why larger national interests are often at the mercy of local programs. Rather than dismiss such an organization with indignation at its mistakes and shortcomings, it is part of wisdom to take it as posing the problem, in dramatic and concrete form, as to how American democracy can be made to serve the highest interests of America and of the world.

Christian Century, 50 (October 19, 1933):1295

I do imagine that those of us who are unfortunate enough to be called Legion politicians view ourselves somewhat seriously and that to the casual observer we present a rather pathetic appearance, mayhaps comical. Anyhow after the battle is over and sanity has replaced rumor, crimination, and recrimination, we all ought to laugh and join with the French in the expression of "c'est la guerre" and then remember the old bard of Avon and say "all is well that ends well."

*Bryan Purfelt, congratulating Jesse W. Barrett on his election as Missouri State Commander, September 6, 1932**

PEAKING TO THE NATION on NBC Radio on March 23, 1931, National Commander Ralph T. O'Neil maintained that "to condemn the American Legion is to condemn the American people, for we are a representative cross section of the nation." The Legion not only crusaded for "one-hundred-percent Americanism" in its programs, but spokesmen insisted that the organization's membership and internal structure marked "the truest expression of democracy" in three ways. First, as the *Milwaukee Sentinel* described the 1941 National Convention, the Legion contained within its ranks "a slice of America cut right across." Second, it therefore spoke for "the" world war veteran with the "voice of five million," as Marquis James wrote in the Legion's first published history. Finally, the Legion's legislative procedure, Commander Henry L. Stevens explained, made it "the most democratic institution in America." He described how local posts passed resolutions that worked their way up to the popularly elected state and national conventions. The latter then issued "army orders, definitely binding" to the national commander, whom Stevens compared to a mere "sergeant in charge of the detail."[1]

Critics found little truth in the Legion's claim to represent democratically both the veteran and the nation. Writing to his former commanding officer, Theodore Roosevelt Jr., a San Francisco private questioned "an organization that assumes the right to speak for the returned soldier, although it does not represent a majority of the returned soldiers." At that point, 843,000 veterans, fewer than a fifth of those eligible, had paid their Legion dues. And who in that minority ran the organization? "Well-to-do conservative gentlemen who have little or nothing in common with the rank-and-file veterans, small farmers, industrial and white collar workers, shopkeepers, and professional people," charged William Gellerman in 1938 in *The American Legion as Educator*. They permitted "no opposition from the rank-and-file" and prostituted the Legion as "a cat's-paw in the interest of big business, of the jingoists, and of the red hunters," as "the instrument of the privileged classes in American society which have frequently used the state as an instrument of class control." Roger Burlingame termed the Legion "the most perfectly disciplined organi-

zation of its kind in the world . . . a dictatorship." The Legion
was thus undemocratic on two levels. Its wealthy members represented neither the average veteran nor the average American,
and within the national body, the "kingmakers"—as insiders
dubbed prominent Legionnaires—ran the Legion as an oligarchy.[2]

Should we believe the Legion or its critics? Their quarrel re-
sembles the debate between the champions of pluralist and elitist
theories of American government and society. Pluralists argue
that public officials genuinely represent popular sentiment, albeit
imperfectly and filtered through the interest groups necessary for
reaching decisions in large modern societies. Elitists, on the other
hand, maintain that a small wealthy group monopolizes access to
power and effectively stifles challenges through control of the
media, education, party apparatuses, and—in the last resort—
force.[3]

To assess the Legion's role in American life, several important
facts about both World War I and voluntary associations in the
United States need to be kept in mind. Otherwise, an analysis
cannot proceed beyond simplistic assertions that the Legion was
in fact "democratic" ("proven" by its constitutional structure) or
"elitist" ("proven" by showing that active Legionnaires included
a disproportionate number of wealthy people). For instance, Legion promotional rhetoric notwithstanding, World War I veterans
did not in fact proportionately represent all groups within the
nation. Immigrants who had not yet taken up citizenship and
industrial and agricultural workers who received occupational
deferments did not serve in the AEF to the same degree as middle-
and upper-class Americans who supported the war and enlisted
in large numbers. Furthermore, it would be foolish to look for
more "democracy" or "representativeness" among Legion leaders
than in, say, the United States Congress or the major political
parties. People with the wealth, leisure, and wide connections to
devote time to Legion affairs would hold most high offices. It
would make as little sense to expect most veterans to become
active Legionnaires as it would to expect most citizens to participate in local politics. Finally, as a voluntary association dependent
for its existence upon dues-paying members, the Legion could
not have been expected to move beyond a broad consensus of its
members on key issues. Over and over again, Legion leaders
adopted policies designed to retain and attract as many members
as possible. If the Legion was to be aggressive and innovative in

promoting veterans' benefits and anti-Communism, it would have to avoid or straddle such problems as Prohibition, race, and the Ku Klux Klan, which could have split the Legion as surely as they divided American society. For the Legion to have gone against contemporary attitudes on race relations or social welfare would have set its members at odds and sacrificed its effectiveness in obtaining benefits for former servicemen.

Therefore, this chapter poses three questions, and attempts to avoid predetermining their answers. Did the Legion attract a reasonable cross section and proportion of veterans? Were the rank and file able to make their voices heard in Legion affairs and to enjoy the sort of organization they wanted? Finally, and most important of all, who exercised power in the Legion and to what end?

In 1938, to increase its advertising revenue, the *American Legion Monthly* commissioned the Ross Federal Research Corporation to conduct a survey of Legion members' economic status and consumption activities. At a time when the average family income in the United States was $1,244 per year, 92% of all Legionnaires earned over $1,000, 64% over $2,000, 27% over $3,000, 11% over $4,000, and 6% over $5,000. Sixty-three percent owned refrigerators, 65% vacuum cleaners, and 52% washing machines, compared with national averages of 42, 37, and 37%.[4]

The Legion was clearly a middle- and upper-class group, but of a special sort. Fewer than 5% of Legionnaires were retired or unemployed. Less than 10% received the veterans' benefits for which they lobbied so hard. By 1938, the average Legionnaire was forty-seven years old, an age at which middle- and upper-class men tend to be well-established in their business and professional lives and at the peak of their earning power. Having achieved stable residence in a community, they would be more likely to participate in civic activity. An occupational profile of Legionnaires points to solid middle-class respectability rather than great wealth: 12% were in government service, 13% were skilled workers, and 8% each were self-employed professionals, sales or office clerks, and supervisors. The largest number (24%) owned retail businesses, with automobile-related shops (14% of that group), clothing stores (9%), restaurants (8.5%), and food stores (8%) heading the list. In contrast, only 2% of Legionnaires were farmers and 4% unskilled workers, occupations that between them counted half the nation's population. A total of 10% held jobs that in many cases would indicate significant wealth rather than middle-class respectability: executives, wholesale merchants, manufacturers, and hired professionals.

Geographically, although the Legion has a reputation, as its historian Richard Jones notes, for thriving "in the smaller cities and the towns and rural sections of the United States," the Legion was also an important force in urban America. A 1931 Legion survey showed that 34 percent of the members lived in towns of over 25,000 people, as did 36 percent of the nation's population. In 1937, 39,000 Legionnaires lived in the five boroughs of New York City, 12,500 in Philadelphia, 28,000 in Chicago, 10,000 in Los Angeles, and 15,000 in greater Boston. If the Legion did not become in the cities "the largest and most impressive civic group," as it did in small-town America, even there it played a prominent role in antiradicalism and lobbying. The Legion was weakest in the South, because of initial Democratic suspicions of the predominantly Republican founders and because black veterans could not join in several states. The South also was the nation's poorest section, and the Legion did not thrive in impoverished communities. As the Ludovici Post of Georgia remarked in a questionnaire in 1930: "Ours is a small country post and no moneyed men among the number, the members are not very energetic." Seven years earlier, a post in Sedalia, Colorado, elaborated on the same theme: "We are all working men and farmers, and have not the time or money" to put into civic activities. "It is hard enough to earn a living these days, without giving it away afterward."[5]

The Legion's strength varied temporally as well as geographically. It reached a high of 1,107,075 dues-paying members during 1941; in 1925 it numbered only 609,407. Of a total 4.5 million AEF veterans (of whom about 600,000 had died by 1941), roughly 15 to 25 percent were Legionnaires at any one time, although many more belonged at different times. (Since there were only 200,000 officers in World War I, the vast majority of Legionnaires at all times must have been enlisted men.) Though critics have used these percentages to brand the Legion an unrepresentative minority, the proportion of joiners is impressive, considering that only 30 percent of Americans were likely to belong to any voluntary association in the twentieth century. If, therefore, we accept 30 percent of AEF veterans as the maximum membership pool, the Legion enrolled half that number at its lowest point. From 1939 to 1941, when it topped the million mark, 80 percent or more of veterans likely to join any organization belonged to the Legion.[6]

The number of Legionnaires rose and fell through four phases. Between 1920 and 1925, membership declined from 843,000 to 609,000. From 1925 to 1929, the Legion grew to 794,000. At the onset of the Great Depression, when the initial impact of hard times might have been expected to thin the ranks, the Legion had soared to 1,053,000 by 1931; then a catastrophic two-year loss reduced it to 770,000 veterans by 1933. But the Legion regrouped and increased in membership every year until the end of World War II.

Disputes over the Bonus account for early fluctuations in Legion strength. Between 1920 and 1924, one of the most hotly debated issues in America was "adjusted compensation" to make up the money veterans had lost in forsaking civilian employment for low army pay. Although the Legion's St. Louis Caucus had avoided taking a stand, by the time the National Executive Committee met on February 10, 1920, both congressmen and rank-and-file Legionnaires were clamoring for the nation's leading veterans' organization to provide some direction. As a Michigan Committeeman put it: "Are we going to live or die this afternoon? The Bonus proposal is straight up to us. . . . We took a noncommittal wishy-washy course at Minneapolis because it was the ladylike thing to do. Now, let's take a regular honest hope-to-die course and hit the thing bang on the nose."[7]

Forced to take a stand, the Legion chose the Bonus. But if anything was hit "bang on the nose," it was the Legion itself. Legionnaires protesting that patriotism had no price, and that service in war had been a privilege, not a burden, left the organization in droves. William Percy, a wealthy Mississippian who served on the National Americanism Commission, explained that "the American Legion stands very poorly in my part of the country." One post shrank from 190 members to 40 because the men erroneously believed publicity that "the whole work of the Legion was for the Bonus for the able-bodied men and that sat very heavily on the chests of patriotic Americans." Anti-Bonus posts passed resolutions in defiance of the national body and of Legion rules forbidding dissension from convention mandates. Many of the protests came from "upper-crust" Legionnaires, those individuals to whom a few hundred dollars would make little difference ordinarily, but who were members of the small minority of

Americans who paid federal income taxes at the time. The Legion
thus put itself in opposition to Secretary of the Treasury Andrew
Mellon and the "war profiteers," a rather difficult fact for those
who accused the Legion of supporting upper-class hegemony. If
anything, the Bonus struggle suggests division within the upper
reaches of American society between great and moderate wealth.[8]
     After Congress approved the Bonus in 1924, the Legion grew
in strength, for it could concentrate on less controversial matters.
As the national commander for 1923–24, John Quinn, later re-
membered:

> I was the commander who presided over the American Legion
> when its membership was at its lowest ebb. When we received the
> message that the Bonus had been passed over the President's veto,
> did we rejoice? No, my friends. The most dramatic incident that
> it has ever been my privilege to be connected with occurred. No.
> There was a silence, a hush, that fell over the body. Then what
> did we do? We offered up thanks to the Deity that the American
> Legion could now go forward separated from controversial polit-
> ical issues.

Quinn made this observation in a speech to the 1930 National
Convention, when the Bonus again reared its divisive head. In
the intervening years, the Legion realized, as had Grenville Clark
as early as 1919, that it "can't live forever on the social benefits
to its members or on perpetuating the incidents of the Great War.
It will have to stand for some great national movement, and have
settled policies in which the entire country is interested." Beginning in 1924, the Legion emphasized community and youth work,
such programs as Junior Baseball, educational activities, disaster
relief, and cooperation with other local groups to build playgrounds, hospitals, and airports. It also raised a $5 million en-
dowment to care for disabled veterans and the orphaned children
of former servicemen. When the Great Depression struck, far
from losing strength, the Legion's much-publicized campaign to
find jobs for a million veterans brought it to its highest level of
membership ever. The Legion stressed that the unemployment
problem was largely a *veterans'* problem: "It is reasonable to assume that a majority of the unemployed are world war veterans,"
Commander Ralph O'Neil stated with more enthusiasm than
accuracy. Many veterans joined a Legion that "provided that
contact necessary between the veteran without a job and the man
who has a job."[9]

The Legion's patriotic support of Presidents Hoover and Roosevelt, despite their hostility to the Bonus and opposition to key veterans' benefits, undid the effects of the employment drives. Veterans insisted on early payment of the Bonus (due to be paid in 1945) both to ameliorate their own financial woes and to inject over a billion dollars into a collapsing economy. After tabling the question of immediate payment in 1929, and rejecting it in response to personal appeals from President Hoover at its 1930 and 1931 conventions, the Legion finally endorsed the measure in 1932. Such vacillation did not help: the Legion lost 130,000 members in 1931 and another 160,000 the following year. The Legion's fortunes hit bottom in 1933, when the New Deal's Economy Act slashed veterans' benefits by about 25 percent. But as the Legion resourcefully fought to undo the cuts, continued its community work, and took active roles in military preparedness and antiradicalism, it again raised its numbers to above one million as World War II approached.

Although economic distress encouraged some veterans to join the Legion to receive help, it also kept others away, and both Bonus controversies coincided with hard times. Of thirty-three questionnaires surviving from 1923 (of the thousands the Legion national office mailed to find ideas for rebuilding the ailing organization), twenty-one posts had lost at least a quarter of their membership since 1920. Nine listed economic difficulties, sometimes in the form of young veterans migrating in search of jobs, as the primary cause. Similarly, in the early 1930s, Missouri posts responding to State Commander Jesse W. Barrett's membership drive reported that many members were out of work and too poor to pay their dues. Fred Holloway, adjutant of a formerly energetic black post in St. Louis, complained that "many of the most active members can't carry on and are unemployed." Post dues of $3 per year and a combined state and national levy of $2.25, both average figures, proved a real burden. The number of Legionnaires might well have sunk even lower had not many posts served as both employment and relief agencies during the 1921–22 recession and the Great Depression. Fourteen of the thirty-three posts surveyed in 1923, for instance, including all those with over 200 members, performed this function. Omaha's, the "largest post in the world," with 2,580 veterans, claimed to have found jobs for 5,000 veterans during the recession. The Legion took care of more than its own.[10]

The Legion attempted to increase its ranks in a variety of ways.

National Headquarters encouraged states to compete in membership drives. The state with the highest proportional enrollment
headed the parade at the National Convention, with others following in order. The *Washington Veteran* in 1920 outlined an ideal
recruitment campaign: solicit endorsements and advertisements
in local publications from prominent citizens; give veterans who
had not joined economic assistance to win their goodwill; and
"make note of the names and addresses of men who refuse to join
the Legion for some fancied reason," then have a "corps of special
salesmen who will call on these hard prospects and sell the American Legion to them." Legion leaders were acutely aware that "we
must use every medium of advertising" to market the Legion, as
"a manufacturer would sell a new product to the public." As early
as 1926, twenty-nine Legion departments sponsored radio broadcasts. The Legion's National Publicity Division, established in
1937, thanked NBC and CBS for "splendid cooperation," which
included twelve coast-to-coast broadcasts that year. Earlier, an
American Legion Film Service offered posts the use of "Flashes
of Action," "Man without a Country," and "The Last Battalion"
to attract audiences and members. Over five million Americans
saw them in 1924 alone. And the American Legion News Service
made available 48 weekly stories to 2,100 papers, a six-column
article every three weeks to 1,000 journals, and a 2,000-word
column every week to the dailies of twenty large cities. By 1927
it was distributing 250,000 stories each year. Such hard-sell techniques as Hanford MacNider's branding of non-Legionnaire veterans as "slackers" tended to backfire.[11]

Despite such favorable coverage, the Legion sometimes complained that newspapers ignored its finer accomplishments in favor of exposés of rowdy conventions and "red-baiting." National
Commander Harry Colmery objected that the activities of the
local posts meant "nothing to the wire services, only in the particular area in which the incident happens, unless it is something
very sensational. The newspapers today are just looking for that
which is sensational." Colmery privately assailed the reporters
assigned to him as "a bunch of G-- d--- kids who don't know
anything about the Legion," paid no attention to his serious pronouncements, and were "only seeking something that will drive
a wedge in [public] opinion and that starts a controversy." Another problem he located was that the Legion's National Headquarters in Indianapolis was not on the wire services' trunk lines.
Material put out by the Washington office had a much better

chance of wider publicity.[12] Nevertheless, the plethora of articles and radio transcripts does not suggest an organization ignored by the media.

A more serious problem confronting the Legion was the passivity of Legionnaires who paid their dues and did nothing more. As early as July 14, 1920, Commander Franklin D'Olier complained that there were "not enough real Legionnaires." Questionnaires from Legion posts, such as one returned by Rocky Ford, Colorado, in 1923, confirm that far too many members were "willing to let the other fellow do the work." A membership drive by the Rose City Post of Portland, Oregon, similarly foundered in 1933. The minute-taker recorded: "An attempt to enlist all present in the drive to secure the renewals of last year's members was met with a hearty response: 'Let George do it.' " Future Chief Justice Earl Warren, in 1931 district attorney for Oakland, California, believed "nine out of ten of the members take no part in the administration of the Legion." Harry Hough, commander of Omaha's enormous post, even advanced the heretical notion that "if all the dead timber were out of the post, the post would accomplish just as much, and be held in just as high esteem." He recommended the Legion only accept voluntary "enlistments" and eschew membership drives. Hough thought five hundred, rather than twenty-five hundred, the optimal size for his own post. Legion questionnaires suggest, in fact, that members' attendance at post meetings averaged between one-fourth and one-third.[13]

Do tales of Legion apathy indicate widespread malaise? Or do they merely reflect the usual grousing of extremely active workers in any group who fail to realize that most members have higher priorities? Most Legion posts contained enough active members to support significant community activities. By 1931, 10,300 Legion posts sponsored 1,500 Boy Scout troops, 3,000 auto-safety programs, 1,600 park and playground programs, 3,000 emergency-relief units, and 4,835 miscellaneous community services. The hundreds of thousands of Legionnaires who attended conventions and wrote letters to congressmen also suggest that if some members only paid their dues to meet with old friends, many did not.[14]

If Legion leaders complained of local apathy, posts and state departments sometimes felt out of touch with National Headquarters. Earl Warren believed "the veins of the great silent majority are very often in conflict with the leaders." Legionnaire William Gellerman was inspired to write his highly critical study when he contrasted the helpful community-service and educational programs sponsored by local posts with what he considered the hysterical antiradicalism of the National Americanism Commission. Commander Franklin D'Olier commented that the typical Legionnaire felt "the less we hear from Indianapolis the better," and Hanford MacNider thought most Iowa Legionnaires could not even name the national commander. Writing to a friend in Pittsburgh, he maintained that "Iowa could wheel right along without any National Headquarters and never know the difference."[15]

One issue symbolic of the differences between National Headquarters and the local posts was the question of American Legion ritual. National Adjutant James Fisk expressed the official view that the Legion's founders exhibited both "artistry and vision in their writings, for in our manual of ceremonies we have ritual beyond compare, capped as it is by a preamble so beautiful in thought and expression that it will undoubtedly survive among the imperishable documents of this century." They considered the ceremonies for meetings, initiation of new candidates, installation of officers, dedication of halls, funeral services, and Memorial Day and Armistice Day essential "to stimulate membership" and assist "the average Legionnaire to become enthusiastic about the Legion." Regular rituals would persuade the men to regard the Legion post as a "temple of justice, freedom, and democracy" instead of a site for "sociability and frivolity."[16]

Local posts, however, thought otherwise. The 1923 questionnaires reveal that only fifteen out of thirty-three posts used the ritual: the rest did not because the members had voted it down or because too few attended to make it worthwhile. At the very time the Legion was campaigning to make "The Star-Spangled Banner" the national anthem, Legionnaires found it "too difficult to sing." (The revised 1934 ritual manual substituted the first stanza of "America.") Other criticisms came from ministers and religious Legionnaires objecting to the prayers as a violation of the "separation of church and state." The national Legion solved this problem by substituting thirty seconds of silence for prayer if any member objected. By the mid 1930s, some Legionnaires even thought that the word *comrade*, so noble and "American" in World War I, smacked of Bolshevism and suggested it be replaced by a "good American form of salutation." Summarizing much grass-roots sentiment on the ritual, Florida Adjutant Howard Rowton wrote to his national counterpart Frank Samuel that he should "prohibit National Headquarters fellows from coming around," since "they are a whole hell of a long ways from knowing what the boy out at the crossroads thinks." The American Civil Liberties Union was not alone in believing that "the rank and file of the Legion often have no sympathy with what the national officials do in their name."[17]

The mutual recriminations of Legionnaires at the local, state, and national levels resemble complaints about the federal system, much as the debate over the Legion's popular and elitist features mirrors the scholarly controversy over American democracy. In political structures where power and responsibility are widely dispersed, zealous participants are apt to feel overworked and underappreciated. Grass-roots members lament powerlessness and remote, unconcerned leaders, who in turn object to popular apathy. Such criticisms need not indicate an ailing organization. They could also show that the Legion attained the precarious balance between the unity necessary for national prominence and the openness necessary to accommodate veterans of different ethnicities, religions, economic interests, and political views. Local posts had the option of devoting themselves to a wide variety of activities—the 1930 questionnaires suggested over 150—with whatever degree of enthusiasm they chose to muster. The diversity of Legion activities and the latitude available to the departments and posts argues powerfully that a voluntary dues-paying association of a million men could not be run as a machine. As the Bonus debates showed, the disgruntled could—and did— simply quit: "The storm followed because the leadership got out of step with the rank and file."[18]

The manner in which departments chartered posts and posts accepted members, the process by which the Legion selected its officers and passed legislation, and the presence of a professional bureaucracy to complement short-term elected officials enabled the Legion to speak effectively with one voice on such critical issues as Americanism and veterans' benefits.

The fundamental Legion unit was the post, with between ten thousand and twelve thousand existing during the interwar years. Posts varied in size from Omaha's twenty-five hundred or more Legionnaires, who met in one gigantic hall, to some units that fell below the 1919 constitution's minimum of fifteen members. Once established, state departments could grant or deny charters to groups of veterans; each post could similarly enroll prospective members at its discretion. In practice, the Legion sought to max-

imize its strength and only rejected applications when there was
a powerful reason. Sometimes existing posts successfully objected
to the chartering of potential rivals. For instance, in 1932 Portland,
Oregon's, Rose City Post opposed the city's Italian Americans
banding together on the ground that "the American Legion rec-
ognizes neither class, race, nor creed among its members." Posts
in a region would privately circulate names of "undesirables" who
had disrupted meetings or otherwise affronted local standards of
acceptable deportment, such as by wearing their old uniforms
while peddling. Posts and departments could expel members or
local units for violating the Legion's constitution. They rarely did
so, however, except in the most extreme instances. Even Manhattan's Willard Straight Post, which consistently opposed the
national position on radicalism and veterans' benefits, was not
expelled by the New York Department until 1933, following
years of complaints and a three-month "warning suspension."
Posts that objected to the Bonus were expelled (Pennsylvania) or
merely ignored (Ohio), depending on the state department's attitude. At the national level, the Legion's Executive Committee
suspended the New Mexico department in 1933 because the state
Legion had become a blatant political tool of Senator Bronson
Cutting. Such an admission and expulsion policy, generally characteristic of large broad-based political and social organizations,
minimized dissension within posts and departments while allowing different posts and departments to function autonomously.[19]

In addition to official state departments and local posts, Legionnaires formed numerous internal associations. States had district and county organizations where post leaders could exchange
information and decide who they would support for Legion state
and national office. (New York, for instance, had nine districts.)
Legion delegates from neighboring states also participated in regional conventions, where they worked out deals to present a
united front at the National Convention. In 1937, for instance,
the Far Western states worked out the "batting order" for their
national vice-commander for the next eleven years. Every state
from Montana, Wyoming, Colorado, and New Mexico westward
could pick its man in turn.[20]

Legion regional groupings encouraged as wide a distribution
of positions and perquisites as possible, thereby roughly satisfying
veterans throughout the nation. By 1923, the Legion routinely
chose one vice-commander each from the East, South, Midwest,
and Far West, with one slot rotating (Puerto Rico, Hawaii, and

Panama all had one vice-commander between the wars). The Legion's first twenty-two national chaplains included eleven Protestants, ten Roman Catholics, and one Jew.[21]

The Legion also rotated convention sites and the national commandership to satisfy as many members as possible. From 1919 to 1941, Chicago, Cleveland, Boston, and Minneapolis–St. Paul each hosted two conventions, with Detroit, New York, St. Louis, Philadelphia, San Francisco, and Paris, among others, taking their turns. Fourteen of the twenty-two conventions occurred in the center of the nation, however, both because it was a Legion stronghold and because it was easier and less expensive to reach. Similarly, political, religious, and regional considerations figured in the choice of the national commander primarily in an effort to represent different elements within the Legion. By 1935, the Legion had chosen nine Democrats and seven Republicans for the post; of those commanders for whom religious affiliation is known, four were Episcopalian, three Presbyterian, one Methodist, one Baptist, one Congregationalist, and one Roman Catholic. (The first two churches disproportionately represented the higher socioeconomic groups, as did the Legion.) The Legion used such diversity to publicize its sectional and denominational impartiality. In 1922, Ferre Watkins of Illinois praised the election of Texan Alvin Owsley as "one of the finest things that has occurred since the Civil War. . . . Before this war, no man regardless of his abilities or attainments from a Southern state could have been elected the head of an organization such as this." On the other hand, Owsley's election produced criticism that he had only triumphed over his closest rival, New York's Major William Deegan, because the latter was a Roman Catholic. But in 1934 and 1938, Edward Hayes of Illinois and Daniel Doherty of Massachusetts attained the Legion's highest office, a quarter century before the United States elected its first Catholic president.[22]

Though formally the Legion's annual convention elected its national commander, in practice candidates were chosen by leading Legionnaires whom both critics and members sometimes dubbed "kingmakers." Service within the Legion was the primary criterion for election: only to publicize the Legion's "pilgrimage" to Paris in 1927 did General of the Army Pershing consent to serve as honorary commander, but he turned down all suggestions that he actively take part in the Legion's affairs. (Sometimes he did not even pay his dues, which offended his hometown post in Lincoln, Nebraska.) Usually, effective state commanders or men who served actively on Indianapolis committees received consideration. To win, they had to undertake elaborate campaigns, sometimes for several years in a row. Prospects would first obtain endorsements from powerful Legionnaires and politicians. They then sent out thousands of flyers and letters and lobbied at conventions. Iowa's Ray Murphy, who finally won the commandership in 1935, began seeking support in 1931. Texas's Wright Patman among others backed him because he wanted a commander "who was at one time a private in the American army." In 1935, Murphy defeated his closest rival, Harry Colmery, by 560 votes to 414. Colmery in turn won the next year. Only one interwar commander, Alvin Owsley, whose work as director of the National Americanism Commission inspired Legionnaires throughout the land, earned his post through the Legion's bureaucracy.[23]

Legion leaders preferred a unanimous one-ballot election. They went to great pains to work out preconvention deals that allowed candidates from different regions and factions to support each other in turn. For example, in 1926 New York's Edward Spafford threw his support to Howard Savage of Illinois in return for Savage's backing the following year. Washington's Stephen Chadwick, who served as one of the most important members of the National Americanism Committee in the 1930s, yielded to Daniel Doherty of Massachusetts in 1938. Five of the ten unsuccessful serious candidates in 1940—Milo Warner, Roane Waring, Edward Scheiberling, Warren Atherton, and Lynn Stambaugh—were to serve as commander by 1945. The "kingmakers" sought to avoid donnybrooks, which consumed two conventions in the 1920s. In 1923, California's John Quinn bested Washington's James Drain after eleven ballots; in 1926, Howard Savage of Illinois triumphed over South Carolina's Monroe Johnson after twenty-one. Such scenes were usually preempted by such actions as former Commander John Emery's telephone calls in July 1930 to two "important friends." He asked them to "subdue their natural instincts," as "a considerable number of key states are already pledged to certain candidates whose names were thoroughly discussed during the last executive committee meeting in Indianapolis."[24]

Informal politicking does not appear in Legion records, but Legionnaires used scheduled business meetings as opportunities to forge alliances and forestall potential dissension. When Missouri's Jesse W. Barrett responded to a request for information about the "kingmakers," he noted that "the term kingmakers is used only by the groups who are unsuccessfully trying to name a commander of their own." He thought the term "Legion leaders" more appropriate. "That is what distinguishes our organization from a mob and shows the beginning of wisdom in our ranks." Barrett argued that "even a pure democracy needs leadership. There is no use bothering about the destruction of an existing leadership unless for some reason it deserves to be overthrown and can be supplanted with something better." But other Legion leaders, like New York's Hamilton Fish, maintained that the elaborate behind-the-scenes maneuvers that determined the national commander "consumed far too much time and importance." Even worse, they lessened the Legion's national influence by diverting veterans from "intelligent consideration and discussion of the important problems of the nation." Iowa's Daniel Steck also felt "sick and tired" of "the peanut politics" played at state conventions, which involved "wholesale trading" of support "for various positions among parts of the state." Legion complaints that personalities sometimes overshadowed issues again mirror those about the nation's political system.[25]

Besides meritorious service in the Legion itself, major qualifications for a Legion commander included being a tireless traveler and a dynamic speaker who could favorably impress the nation with the Legion and its program. Upset with the lackluster Commander John Quinn, Hanford MacNider complained, "there has got to be a roar in the air all the time to make Congress remember us." Other commanders did better. Alvin Owsley covered sixty-five thousand miles and lost twenty-five pounds during his year in office. Michael Cohen of Montpelier, Vermont, described how Owsley's "clear, forceful words that ring with truthfulness and unselfishness" gave the local posts "a new lease on life." By the 1930s, commanders were averaging ninety thousand miles per year. Ray Murphy managed to give 285 speeches, broadcast fifty-two radio addresses, and film twenty-two newsreels during 1935–36. His successor, Harry Colmery, spent only sixty-five days administering in Indianapolis and eighteen days lobbying in Washington. The commander symbolized the Legion, much as the president did the nation.[26]

Even more than the national commander, the annual convention held in late September or early October—in time for the Legion to convey its wishes to politicians seeking election—brought the Legion to the nation's attention. Legion conventions

More characteristic Legion parades at Louisville (1929) and, next page, Chicago (1933). Courtesy of American Legion National Headquarters.

had two sides, which gave both Legionnaires in search of a good time and those seriously concerned with national issues what they wanted. They featured much-publicized brouhaha, while leaders worked to hammer out a program acceptable to the major factions.

Legion conventions are perhaps the organization's best-known feature. National Adjutant Frank Samuel exaggerated only slightly when he described them as events that "in size, wholesome hilarity, and elaborateness . . . overtop all other nationally known conventions . . . a combination of Mardi Gras, the Fourth of July, and New Year's Eve." But the Legion's critics had serious doubts about the "wholesome" aspect of the conventions. New York's Socialist *Call* termed the 1921 Kansas City gathering an affair of "rum, rowdyism, and riot," where Legionnaires "openly patronized bootleggers and under the influence of liquor terrorized people in the streets."[27] Rowdyism and hijinks of various sorts marked Legion conventions. "Cities prepared for the coming of the Legion much as the inhabitants of Georgia prepared for the coming of Sherman," the *Nation* reported in 1921. That year in Kansas City, Legionnaires made drums for impromptu late-night parades from the town's new metal trash cans; a policeman who complained about the racket found himself rolled down a hill inside one. One Legionnaire brought a steer into the lobby of the Baltimore Hotel; another attempted to drive his car in. Still oth-

ers, to honor the Boston Tea Party, disguised themselves as Indians, raided a pawn shop, and threw the entire contents into the street. Philadelphia's 1926 meeting featured Colorado's Legion turning loose a menagerie of mules, coyotes, and other Western beasts as "Broad Street Turned into a Dance Hall." Harry Gardiner climbed to the top of William Penn's statue on city hall to observe the festivities. In 1938 in New York City, Legionnaires capped an eighteen-hour parade by pouring into Times Square and stopping traffic for the first time ever except on New Year's Eve. Sometimes, though, others had the last laugh: in 1940, Boston hotels frustrated Legionnaires accustomed to dropping laundry bags filled with water on pedestrians by cutting off the corners of the bags.[28]

One persistent feature of Legion reunions was the abuse of alcohol. This especially shocked respectable folks during the Prohibition Era. A reporter for the *Christian Century* wrote of the Louisville Convention in 1929 that "never have I seen such a flood of alcohol in one spot. . . . Men and women had lost every vestige of orderliness and self-respect. [There were] tipsy men and women hanging out of hotel windows, swearing and shouting. . . . The visitor to cities in which these conventions have met in the past will still hear their inhabitants talking, as of a scourge, of the debauchery they witnessed." Historically tolerant New Orleans sought to repeal Prohibition for the Legion convention in 1922, only to be overruled by a federal court. Legionnaires

A "Forty-and-Eight" wreck. The boxcars are miniatures of those used to trans-
port troops in France. A secret society, the Forty and Eight consisted of many
of the most active Legionnaires. The Legion divested itself of the all-white, all-
male group in 1960. Courtesy of American Legion National Headquarters.

responded by denouncing this act of "uncalled-for bureaucracy"
and self-righteously terming the court injunction "superfluous so
far as it concerns a convention of those by whose pledge the laws
are held sacred." Journalists found it a suspicious "coincidence"
that "most of the cities chosen to entertain the Legion have either
been on [an international] border or notably wet."[29]

In official pronouncements, Legion leaders denied any blame
for violations of legal and moral norms. "If there is trouble, the
Legion will stop it, not start it," Adjutant Samuel insisted. Prominent Virginia Legionnaire John J. Wicker observed with "regret
and disgust" the "disgraceful conduct of some rowdies and hoodlums who have no connection with the American Legion." But
at the 1941 Convention in Milwaukee, Ben Hilliard, chief of the
Forty and Eight, a secret society within the Legion open only to
white males and noted for organizing "wrecks" at conventions
(the Legion divested itself of the Forty and Eight in 1960), contradicted him. Claiming that his group was "as usual, sacrificing

itself for the Legion," he explained: "We are glad to do the drinking for the Legion; we are glad to go to jail for the Legion; we
will do anything for the Legion."[30]

Privately and sometimes publicly, Legion leaders agreed with
their severest critics on the matter of unruly conventions. The
Minnesota Department, in 1925, informed post adjutants that
"fun is the finest thing in the world when it is fun. But fun as
portrayed by open drunkenness, open gambling, even lewdness,
fighting, etc. only places a stigma on the Legion." At the 1925
Omaha Convention, the chairman of the Resolutions Committee
criticized the delegates for "too much tomfoolery in the streets of
the convention city. Unless the Legion, faithful to the public of
this country of ours, attempts with power and force to kill the
bad order and misbehavior and disgraceful conduct of Legionnaires in the convention city, then that disgraceful conduct will
kill the Legion." He received warm applause for these remarks.[31]

Public officials subordinated their desire to keep conventions
orderly to their willingness to put up with considerable nonsense
to stimulate the local economy. Hundreds of thousands flocked
to Legion conventions. Chicago's 1933 convention brought in an
average of $20 for each of 400,000 persons, apart from hotel bills.
Cities bid openly, the amounts announced on the convention
floor, to host the following year's affair. In 1936, New York's bid
of $62,500 topped St. Louis, Denver, and Los Angeles, which
had each offered $25,000 to host a 1937 convention attracting
250,000. Chicago came up with $100,000 in 1938. Contributions
went to cover official Legion convention expenses. City governments also promised Legionnaires a good time, which in practice
meant loose enforcement of disorderly conduct laws. As the police
chief of Kansas City put it in 1921: "The town is yours. Take it
apart. Scruff it up to your heart's content." Sixteen years later,
New York's Mayor La Guardia promised Legionnaires a bash that
would make "California's superlatives look like anemic diminu-
tives." At the Paris Convention of 1927, Legion leaders arranged
for the equivalent of extraterritoriality: rowdy conventioneers had
their own American judge. The attitude of law-enforcement officials toward Legion hijinks is perhaps best symbolized by the
chief of police in Emporia, Kansas, who threw away the key to
the jail when the Kansas Department held a convention in his
town.[32]

Of all the Legion conventions, the most ambitious was the 1927
"Second AEF," the "Pilgrimage" to Paris touted by its principal

sponsor, Henry D. Lindsley, as "the greatest peaceful invasion in the history of the world." Lindsley and his supporters had to overcome doubts that "French politicians and financiers endeavoring to have America assume European war debts" would "create ill will towards Americans." Others feared an "egotistical" attitude toward the French would promote resentment, and the Legionnaires would "become involved in broils and riots."[33]

In fact, the "greatest good will pilgrimage in history," as General of the Army Pershing phrased it, drew mixed reviews. Correspondents repeatedly called attention to the twenty-five thousand doughboys' spirit of "holiday gaiety" and "carnival of comradeship." Despite the leaders' usual warnings to behave themselves, twenty-eight Legionnaires were hauled before the special tribunal created for conventioneers, "most of them [for] drunkenness in its wildest forms, because the gendarmes had been instructed not to arrest Yanks who merely wanted to pull their whiskers or pull the birdies out of their hats." One Arkansas veteran hurled a couple of tables and waiters through the window of a café that had cheated him in 1918.[34]

Such shenanigans seemed inappropriate to many. The *Washington News* commented that "France is still a house of mourning," whereas "America has forgotten the war and become the greatest, richest, happy-go-luckiest country on earth." An anonymous Frenchman put it even more bluntly: "The war? You made the war and you made it well, but it never touched you." Leftists found even more to criticize. The *Nation*'s Ida Treat regarded the visit as a "mobilization day for the [French] church, the army, the fascists, the police, Montmartre, and Montparnasse [bourgeois sections of Paris]," a chance for the ruling element "to show that for all their noisy demonstrations, the radicals do not yet rule in France." The American Civil Liberties Union's Roger Baldwin protested the Legion's pilgrimage by undertaking one of his own. He dedicated the Place Sacco-Vanzetti in the radical town of Clichy in honor of the recently executed anarchists, whose martyrdom angered the French more than most Legionnaires suspected.

Nevertheless, to the convention's joie de vivre and its antiradicalism, the Legion added a plea for peace that the world applauded. Once the convention ended, most Legionnaires set out "at the earliest possible moment for the battlefields and cemeteries to visit the graves of their comrades-in-arms." Both the official speeches and ceremonies, and thousands of personally arranged trips to the western front, conveyed the desire of a traumatized civilization to "abolish war [and] make sure that such a calamity as the World War never shall again overwhelm the world." French journals applauded the Legionnaires' "direct diplomacy . . . of the heart" and featured cartoons praising the Americans as "brothers, not foreigners." American papers agreed that "the coming of the American Legion to France has gripped France as few things have gripped her these last ten years" and concluded that "it was a great day for the United States, for France, and for the world."

Once the Legion returned home, the "Pilgrimage" left a bitter aftertaste that symbolized the Legion's racial difficulties. Only two black veterans, who came on their own, marched in the Legion parade. The Legion travel bureau had refused to accept reservations from black veterans, and blacks refused to be satisfied with Travel Director John Wicker's excuse that steamship companies would not accommodate blacks on the same ships as whites. The Legion's failure to search for a line willing to provide equal treatment demonstrated, according to José Sherwood, the leading black Minnesota Legionnaire, that "at no time has the Legion asked for a clear-cut declaration of equality of treatment for all servicemen," but contented itself with "flinch[ing] the issue and send[ing] out some subterfuge" to placate black Legionnaires. Sherwood voiced blacks' general disappointment that "the glorious sentiments expressed in the preamble" to the Legion's constitution had not become "the match which will raise the sleeping consciousness of at least a moderate sized group of fair-minded people" on the subject of racial equality. But in the context of the generalized goodwill and favorable publicity the Paris Convention generated, such protests found few sympathetic ears.[35]

Legion leaders, besides enjoying a good time themselves—there was more than a fair amount of carousing in 1921 when a group visited France—were keenly aware that the opportunity to attend conventions at reduced hotel and railroad rates attracted members. Legionnaires with sufficient time and money could take advantage of both department and national conventions in addition to local or regional gatherings each year. Missouri Commander Jesse Barrett, writing at the height of the Great Depression, nicely summarized the Legion's effort to balance a rousing four-day party and national spectacle with more substantive aims:

I don't want the boys to lose the fun they have in thinking of the Legion as a playground. Especially these days, a fellow's soul gets hungry for a place where he can forget his troubles and enjoy an easy-going and convivial comradeship. I do wish, however, that our boys would understand the strength and the power and the influence of this mighty organization—at least our gravity and seriousness of purpose.

The function of a Legion convention as an escape from the routine of everyday work and the constraints of community life appear as a recurrent theme in Legion poetry collected by the Wisconsin Department in preparation for the 1941 National Convention in Milwaukee. (Several of these poems are reprinted following the notes to this chapter.) Escape took the form of pranks and rowdyism, drinking, and reliving one's youth through telling old war stories. Journalist Margaret Doty captured the convention spirit, where "the shoe clerk from Sandusky, the tailor from Yakima, the iron smelter from Pittsburgh, the grocer from Montpelier forget the humdrum routine of their post-war years and recreate the incredible thrill life once gave them. . . . They cut loose. Rum and rowdyism are taboo the rest of the year at home— but they're in the army now."[36]

For veterans the Legion convention was their college reunion, much as army life had been their higher education. Bordentown, New Jersey,'s Presbyterian minister Robert Williams compared Legion conventions "favorably with Princeton reunions as regards sobriety, consideration for others, and intelligent action on questions of serious moment," adding that "Princeton alumni represent of necessity a far higher average of culture, wealth, breeding, and religious training than is true of war veterans." Observing New York's 1937 National Convention, columnist Heywood Broun found in the Legion's "violent horseplay" comforting proof that far from being a "well-disciplined potentially fascist threat to American democracy," as critics feared, Legion antics "resembled the Yales and Harvards after a football game." "Just imagine," he wrote, "a gathering of Nazi storm troopers putting on a jamboree in Broadway in which they tied up city traffic."[37]

Williams and Broun probably overstated their case. Legion conventions, through sheer size, caused more damage to hotels than any other. Especially during Prohibition, the contrast between conventions many obviously attended to get drunk and raise hell jarred noticeably with the Legion's belligerent "one-hundred-percent Americanism" and law-and-order posture. The Legion developed as the nation's premier "party" organization even as it emerged as its number one antiradical force.

While the "friendly run of the mill Americans" who comprised the rank and file were listening to speeches praising the Legion and enjoying both planned and spontaneous entertainments, the conventions' serious work went on. Committee spokesmen argued for programs and legislation they deemed especially important. Sometimes the president (Hoover on the Bonus in 1930 and 1931, Roosevelt in 1933 and 1941 to urge support, respectively, for the Economy Act and for national defense) or cabinet officers would dramatically urge the Legion to pull together in peace as it had in war. At the end of the convention the Legion adopted the resolutions it would recommend to and lobby for before Congress. Debate only occurred when the Resolutions Committee was severely divided; the outgoing national commander, who presided over the convention, then arranged for principal supporters and opponents of the committee's majority and minority reports to present their cases before the delegates. Usually one to three items received such thorough discussion at each Legion meeting. Some of the most notable debates occurred over the Bonus in 1920, 1930, and 1932; whether to condemn the Veterans' Bureau in 1922; and what stand to take on the Ku Klux Klan in 1923, the World Court in 1924, and Prohibition in 1930 and 1931. Before the United States entered World War II, Legion arguments over the "universal draft" of capital as well as labor (1938 and 1941) and whether to endorse aid to Britain (1940) and Russia (1941) attracted nationwide attention. The Legion, like political parties, strove for consensus and only aired differences that also severely divided the American nation.[38]

Although in theory any delegate could speak to any point, in practice the commander moved things along smoothly by recognizing prominent Legionnaires and limiting discussion time. During the interwar years, the Legion annually adopted one to two hundred resolutions filtered through the various committees and then through the Resolutions Committee. Americanism Director Garland Powell commented that "delegates seldom, if ever, know exactly what they are voting upon." Resolutions had to be forwarded by a state department, but those that became prominent items on the national agenda reflected the interests of influential Legionnaires at National Headquarters. Leaders complained that the departments would forward and the convention approve "a flood of resolutions at the last moment pertaining to everything under the sun." Legion insiders sometimes found it convenient to arrange for symbolic resolutions to pass without extensive debate to placate the membership and then leave matters to the appropriate committee. Committees in turn could make resolutions "part of the Legion's major program" or simply ignore them. For instance, faced in 1931 with a grass-roots demand for registration of aliens, the National Americanism Commission refused to act: "If our hands are tied by every resolution that is passed by a National Convention, then of course it is useless for us to talk about these resolutions at all." In 1935, the commission voted to do nothing about a resolution asking that Congress investigate use of "marajuhana" on the grounds "this does not seem to be germane to the Legion program."[39]

The Legion's committee structure ensured that resolutions that were "the hobby of some individual in some department" did not distract attention from vital national issues. By 1936, the Legion had twenty-four standing committees that decided what resolutions to implement within the Legion and to emphasize in Washington. The most important were Finance, Rehabilitation, Child Welfare, Americanism, Legislation, Defense, World Peace and Foreign Relations, Veterans' Preference, and Resolutions Assignment. At the head was the National Executive Committee, where the National Commander and Vice-Commanders met with one representative of each department to implement Legion programs between conventions. Committee members were appointed by the National Commander: most served for only a year or two and participated irregularly. If the surviving minutes of the National Americanism Commission are any indication, a small number of active Legionnaires vitally concerned with their committee's work dominated the proceedings and to a large extent shaped policy. Hamilton Fish explained the passivity of many committeemen by noting that "very often Legionnaires of limited experience are appointed to important Legion Committees, merely because they were active in the successful campaign of the new commander."[40]

Even more than leading committee members, however, the Legion's paid permanent bureaucracy provided continuity and expertise. The National Adjutant, Judge Advocate, Director of Americanism, Chairman of the Legislative Division, Director of Rehabilitation, and Director of Child Welfare all had small staffs (an assistant and one or two secretaries) and usually served for long periods. During the interwar years the Legion had only four adjutants (who served as the head of Legion administration). The Judge Advocate handled the Legion's legal matters and advised it how to construe some of its charter's vaguer positions; Ralph Gregg (1935–60) held this post the longest. Homer Chaillaux (1935–45), Emma Puschner (1927–50), and Watson B. Miller (1921–41) became virtually synonymous with the Americanism, Child Welfare, and Rehabilitation departments. From the Legion's Washington office at 1608 K Street, Miller directed fourteen regional offices set up in 1921 to parallel the structure of the Veterans' Bureau. From 1920 to 1950, the legendary John Thomas Taylor ran the Legion lobby—the National Legislative Committee. State departments usually employed a full-time adjutant and service officer to help with veterans' benefits. Departments and posts set up committees parallel to National Headquarters to handle Americanism, Education, and whatever other activities suited their needs and abilities.[41]

Although critics circulated rumors of the Legion's great wealth acquired from its hidden backers, the Legion in fact operated on limited funds. It tried to obtain needed support from diverse elements in the nation without antagonizing others. The Americanism Division handled everything from National Education Week to Junior Baseball to the Legion's antiradical and public-safety activities for around $25,000 a year. Frequently, the Legion provided organizational guidance and manpower for programs funded by others. Americanism Director Garland Powell confessed in 1925 that "we stretch a point when we talk about our campaigns. I have swiped, literally stolen, six or seven campaigns from other organizations. You see this 'Get Out the Vote' Campaign which cost the Manufacturing Association hundreds of thousands of dollars. I walked in and took it right away from them." Twelve years later, Stephen Chadwick remarked how the Legion "chiseled" its traffic-safety-program pamphlet from the automobile industry, and "hit the National and American Leagues up for Junior Baseball." The American Education Association took care of National Education Week; several leading newspapers sponsored the oratorical contest. Legionnaires in turn would man tables, give speeches, put up billboards, distribute pamphlets, coach baseball teams, judge contests, and supply publicity. Still, Americanism members remarked bitterly that for all the Legion leaders' rhetoric about Americanism being the core of the organization, the Finance Committee was quite stingy with the budget. Amos Fries, Chairman of the Defense Committee, had even more cause for complaint: he had a grand total of $500 to publicize the nation's military needs in 1934. Such state departments as

Missouri and Minnesota operated on less than $20,000 per year. The Legion's national budget for 1935 was $589,000. Dollar-a-year dues from almost a million members covered most expenses.[42]

If the American Legion was a "substantial business enterprise," as critic William Gellerman suggested, it was a nonprofit one. Scandals tainted a few state departments: they never touched National Headquarters. Scarred by charges concerning the original $257,000 loan, the Legion was careful not to open itself to more criticism than necessary. It only obtained money for specific purposes from organizations not likely to offend members or average Americans. For instance, it was logical for the Legion to team up with the big leagues for Junior Baseball, the auto industry for traffic safety, or with teachers to foster education. In 1921, the Americanism Commission resolved that there "were many wealthy men that might be moved by very laudable impulses to give money," but still they ought to be politely refused, as "the money could be considered tainted money." The principal form in which the Legion accepted support came from advertisements in Legion publications: some of the Legion's faithful supporters in the *Monthly* included American Telephone and Telegraph, various tobacco companies, and the New York, John Hancock, and Prudential life insurance firms. In local post publications and convention bulletins, public officials, businesses, and local notables also tendered their compliments. Most of this money, however, financed the publications and specific related activities.[43]

The Legion's concern not to receive "tainted money," while accepting indirect corporate support through advertisements, provides an important index of the organization's nature. The Legion was not dominated by Wall Street. However, there was considerable coincidence of interest and sentiment between the conservative small businessmen who made up the Legion's rank and file and other right-wing groups in America. The Legion did not need to be manipulated when it came to antiradicalism, on the one hand, or proposing community-service programs, on the other. On the great issue of veterans' benefits, however, the well-to-do Legion leaders ran up against the very rich, and fought them fiercely. This conflict illustrates that there could be major divisions within the nation's upper echelons not explicable through the class analysis frequently employed by the Legion's leftist critics.

Similarly, the Bonus question shows that the Legionnaires in the posts, who generally ran their own show and let National Headquarters do likewise, were quick to dissent and leave the organization when Indianapolis took an unpopular stand. On the Bonus, as on the Ku Klux Klan, Prohibition, and foreign policy on the eve of World War II, factions in the Legion struggled to control policy not only for reasons of principle, but also to retain membership. Division occurred within both the leadership and the rank and file. Debate therefore ensued all the way from the posts to the national conventions, with the majority winning. Fluctuations in membership resulting from the Legion's controversial public positions thus checked the leaders from taking such stands without taking possible defections into serious account. On the other hand, the vast majority of Legionnaires remained in the ranks following these crises, indicating commitment to the Legion and its principles generally overshadowed anger at a particular stance.

But in most cases, consensus was the rule in the Legion's ranks. With few exceptions, veterans who were not virulently anti-Communist or in favor of substantial federal benefits for the disabled quit the organization. Other Legion activities were generally noncontroversial, and the posts, states, and National Headquarters cooperated in educational, athletic, patriotic, and local-betterment projects of which the nation approved. The Legion was not composed of a cross section of all Americans or even of all veterans, as it liked to claim. It was, however, representative of those groups that dominated the civic culture and identified themselves as "the nation" and "the community."

CHAPTER FIVE

The Legion in Politics

Probably the most serious offense an American Legion post, department, or national official can commit against his organization is to use his office in the Legion for partisan political purposes.

> *National Commander O. L. Bodenhamer, July 1930; the* Huddle, AL

The mistake is frequently made of ruling the American Legion out of politics because of its Minneapolis action [the constitutional interdiction against politics]. It should be understood that the American Legion is very much in politics. . . . But they are merely keeping their collective voice free from party entanglements. They are not keeping their organization out of the political life of the country but out of the clutches of practical politicians. . . . The American Legion merely escaped its extinction when, at its charter convention, it refused to divide its strength into rival political camps and cast its hat with a whoop into the political arena.

> *Marcus Duffield, "The American Legion in Politics,"* Forum *85 (May 1931):263*

Congress may rant against the power trust, it may denounce and bludgeon Wall Street, it may suborn powerful foreign governments, and it may choose to deny the President, but inevitably it bows to the will of the Legion.

> *Clipping from the* New York Sun, *January 30, 1932,* ACLU, *vol. 523, 119*

WRITING TO THE POSTS of Massachusetts in September 1921, State Commander James T. Duane urged Legionnaires to concentrate on "beneficial veterans legislation rather than politics." Calling upon the Legion to become "a brotherhood not a party," he observed that "the American Legion is composed of men of many minds on political questions, of Republicans, of Democrats, of Socialists." The Socialists did not remain long, but Duane had pinpointed one of the Legion's main dilemmas: where did "beneficial legislation" end and "politics" begin? Could the Legion accomplish the former without engaging in the latter and thereby plausibly represent all of America's veterans?[1]

The Legion's Constitution tried to gloss over the problem by equating nonpolitical and nonpartisan. Article 2, section 2, declared that "the American Legion shall be absolutely non-political and shall not be used for the dissemination of partisan political principles nor for the promotion of the candidacy of any person seeking public office or preferment." The only remarks explicating this high-minded passage forbade veterans who held "remunerative" office in the Legion from holding "elective" public office. Legion committeemen and the rank and file could enter the lists.[2]

But the constitution did not so much solve the political question as open it. Several founders who held no formal Legion office went into politics almost immediately after the Minneapolis Convention of November 1919. Were they not using the prestige they had gained in creating the Legion to further their own careers? New York's Socialist *Call* was not alone in linking the Legion with the presidential ambitions of Republican hopeful Leonard Wood, for whom Eric Fisher Wood and Theodore Roosevelt Jr. both worked. The Legion's first legislative representative in Washington, Delaware's Thomas Miller, briefly retained that post while serving as Wood's campaign manager. A Michigan Legionnaire complained that "the first thing we will hear back home is 'I see the American Legion is backing Wood for President.'" Those searching for a political Legion could also point to the National Executive Committee's decision on August 7, 1920, to conduct its own investigation of Assistant Secretary of Labor

Louis Post, who did his best to save victims of the Red Scare, for "refusing to enforce the laws relating to the deportation of aliens." Six weeks before a presidential election, the committee accepted the report of two Southern Democrats and a Virginia Republican demanding Post's removal on the grounds that he had tried to "negative an act of Congress," a "most radical tendency inimical to the principles of our Constitution." Although one Western committeeman objected that the Legion was taking a "political" stand, most Democrats on the committee agreed with Joe Morrison of Arkansas: "We are not concerned with the election. We are concerned with rectifying a state of facts. It is a crime if they exist." Legion lobbyists then began to confront Secretary of Labor William Wilson concerning his subordinate's behavior.[3]

Legion partisanship abounded in the 1920 election. The most emotional plea that the Legion be allowed to participate in political campaigns came from Georgia. There, Legionnaires conducted a bitter fight against Tom Watson's bid for the United States Senate, denouncing him as a "Bolshevist" who had consistently opposed the war and tried to organize a nationwide movement against conscription. The Georgia Legion openly supported his opponent financially, and uniformed Legionnaires even heckled and physically disrupted Watson's rallies. Watson, for his part, mobilized the Ku Klux Klan and attacked the Legion as "a Republican organization; . . . a sectional organization; . . . [and] an organization dominated by tyrannical officers." Legion headquarters did not interfere with the Georgia Legion. Watson, however, turned its opposition into one of the key issues that won him an overwhelming victory.[4]

A similar case occurred in Ohio's Fourteenth Congressional District. C. L. Knight managed to win the Republican primary over the opposition of "several prominent Legionnaires" who claimed to be "acting entirely as individuals." Knight then attacked the Legion as political; it replied by branding him "pro-German" and "disloyal." The State Commander responded by urging "every loyal citizen in the district" to unite behind the veterans against Knight, a stand that National Commander Frederic Galbraith, himself an Ohioan, approved. He argued that "even though the American Legion takes no part in political contests between loyal Americans, it stands however for loyal American principles at all times and in all holders of public office." The Knight case raised the interesting questions of whether the Legion as a body could completely disassociate itself from actions taken by members "as individuals" and whether the National Commander and organization could make exceptions to nonpartisanship by opposing especially obnoxious candidates.[5]

The Wisconsin Legion, on the other hand, removed State Adjutant R. M. Gibson from office in part for his stand against Senator Irvine Lenroot. In a statement widely publicized during the 1920 campaign, Gibson accused Lenroot of "aligning himself with Socialists and other elements of unpatriotic citizens." Gibson's stand was idiosyncratic; many Wisconsin Legionnaires supported Lenroot against Robert M. La Follette, whose "pro-German and Socialist" support was more substantial. When State Commander Claudius Pendill and National Adjutant Lemuel Bolles asked him to retract the criticism, Gibson claimed "the issue could not be considered at all in the light of partisan politics." Gibson's indiscretion and stubbornness served as one of the grounds for his removal, but doubtless charges that he misappropriated funds, did not appear at his office, and quarreled constantly with Pendill carried more weight.[6]

A similar conundrum surfaced in New York. A state appellate court judge up for reelection in 1920 had just declared New York's bonus for former servicemen unconstitutional. His son, Legionnaire Paul Shipman Andrews, circulated a petition among state Legion leaders urging that they "understand the necessity for not penalizing a fearless judge and voting against him simply because his conscientious decision ran against the wishes of the American Legion." Theodore Roosevelt Jr. put a stop to the petition, which he termed "exceedingly bad policy" because the Legion had not attacked Judge Andrews openly. Roosevelt explained:

> From letters of this sort no matter how carefully worded, the ex-servicemen and the American Legion will gather the impression that individual Republicans are endeavoring to deliver the American Legion for a Republican candidate. They will gather the impression because it is a fact. I think such a letter will be a boomerang. If there is one thing the average American Legion man does not like it is for people to try to deliver it.[7]

Andrews won reelection, but his case illustrated that by the 1920 Convention in Cleveland, it was all too clear to the National Executive Committee that the Legion's "nonpolitical" clause was too vague. An Oklahoma delegate complained that "it was being interpreted differently in practically every state." Still, the convention turned down 963 to 142 Eric Fisher Wood's suggestion that the Legion be permitted to support candidates openly who agreed with its "policies and principles."[8]

After 1920, the Legion reached a consensus. It did not deal with hostile congressmen by openly supporting their opponents, but restricted itself to publicizing their disagreements with the Legion on specific issues. Occasionally, a legislator would receive an angry letter, as did New York's John Taber from an anonymous source in 1935: "Hundreds of Republican Legionnaires are watching your efforts to deprive them of their Bonus. Hoover is resting peacefully in California and the Auburn [New York] sunshine may work wonders for you." (There is little sunshine in upstate New York.) But prudent Legion leaders realized such belligerence only entrenched hostility, and contented themselves with "barrages" of letters and telegrams making clear their positions on matters of importance to veterans.[9]

Legionnaires therefore found ways to influence aspiring politicians without openly endorsing them. As Marcus Duffield noted: "Politician X is running for Congress against incumbent representative Y. Mr. X, who, as a matter of course nowadays has contact with some Legion post, gets that post to write to the National Legislative Committee in Washington for his opponent's record." Stafford King advised Minnesota Legionnaires to get their congressmen to commit themselves on issues of concern to the Legion. He recommended that Legionnaires personally acquainted with their congressmen persuade them to speak at post meetings, where they would either commit themselves to the Legion or face its wrath.[10]

Thus, while remaining technically "nonpartisan," members of the Legion could be extremely political. Legionnaires used the organization as a springboard for their careers, they closely associated with and displayed public admiration for sympathetic lawmakers, and they tried to influence legislation and appointments. In practice, as Marquis James predicted, the Legion's "nonpolitical" character became a matter of "a sort of Legion common law." What was political became a subject of "considerable delicacy," as Minnesota Adjutant Raymond Scallen put it in 1928 when ruling on whether a Legion post commander could openly support presidential candidate Herbert Hoover "as an individual." (He could.) Legion department and national headquarters tried to allow Legionnaires maximum leeway to exercise their duties as citizens without raising a public outcry that the Legion had become the tool of any political party or pressure group.[11]

To avoid charges of partisanship, most of the Legion's founders quickly severed all connection with the organization except for retaining membership in a local post. Theodore Roosevelt Jr. stopped attending conventions because "I am always afraid of hurting the Legion by giving people an opportunity to say that I was using it for my own personal advantage." For Hamilton Fish, the problem was rather that involvement in Legion politics could jeopardize his position in Congress. Fish easily won election to New York's Putnam-Dutchess congressional seat in 1920 with the bipartisan help of veterans. He retained their support, for his achievements included introducing legislation giving veterans bonus points on civil-service tests, authorizing the Tomb of the Unknown Soldier, suggesting a (never-constructed) monument to black troops such as those he had commanded, and ensuring the erection of a veterans' hospital for his district. But after a few Legion elections in which he backed at different times Republicans and Democrats for New York Commander, he ceased participating in the state Legion, fearing that candidates he opposed in the Legion would reciprocate when he ran for Congress. Franklin D'Olier took a third way out. The Legion's first elected commander, a millionaire textile manufacturer and future president of the Prudential Life Insurance Company, D'Olier refused to run for elective political office or to accept any government appointments "to show that the [Legion] office should not be used as a stepping stone" to state or national positions.[12]

If many prominent Legionnaires retired to private life after their Legion careers, others did not. President Harding appointed Legion founder Theodore Roosevelt Jr. assistant secretary of the navy; unlike his father and cousin Franklin, however, this was the highest position he attained. Thomas W. Miller, Harding's choice for alien property custodian, had previously been a congressman from Delaware. He was convicted in 1927 of transferring property illegally and served thirteen months in jail. The *New York Times* editorialized that "so many good berths have gone to Legion men in the Harding administration that it would be possible to organize a Federal Jobholders Post." Other Legionnaires who used their position in the organization to gain higher office included National Commanders Hanford MacNider (assistant secretary of war under Coolidge); Paul McNutt (governor of Indiana; federal security administrator in World War II); James Drain (McNutt's assistant); and Louis A. Johnson (assistant secretary of war under Franklin Roosevelt; secretary of defense under Truman). McNutt would have made a bid for the White House in 1940 had Roosevelt not chosen to run for a third term. State commanders who rose in public life included Harry Woodring (governor of Kansas; assistant secretary and later secretary of war under FDR); and United States Senators Lewis Schwellenbach of Washington and Daniel Steck of Iowa.[13]

Eligible politicians joined the American Legion much as Legionnaires entered politics. As early as 1924, the Legion claimed 14 of 21 members of the newly created House Veterans' Affairs Committee and 1 of the 5 senators on the Senate's Veterans' Sub-Committee. Proudly surveying the Legion's Milwaukee Convention in 1941, Ohio's Governor John Bricker noted 9 of 21 state governors who were Legionnaires in attendance. The same year, 24 United States senators and 145 congressmen also belonged.[14]

Although not in their capacity as Legionnaires, former National Commanders and other leaders also organized veterans behind the Republican and Democratic standards. The Republicans were first. In July 1924, former Legion commander Hanford MacNider, Theodore Roosevelt Jr., and other prominent Legionnaires formed the Republican Service League to elect President Coolidge and other GOP candidates. They considered it a "marvelous opportunity to get the best of our generation actively into the councils of our party." Chairman MacNider sent out letters to prospective organizers in forty states, bypassing only the "hopelessly Democratic" Solid South and a few other states "infested with Klan troubles" of the sort the Legion carefully avoided. MacNider made a minor gaffe at the outset by contacting Democratic Congressmen Millard Tydings of Maryland and Bronson Cutting of New Mexico (who was supporting Progressive Robert La Follette). Tydings promptly "blew the whistle" to the *Baltimore Sun* and challenged MacNider to debate Coolidge's record. Both he and Cutting called attention to the Bonus vetoes and a Republican-run Veterans' Bureau "responsible for the most colossal graft in American history." Nevertheless, with help from state leaders among Republican veterans who contacted local notables in much the same way the Legion itself had been born five years earlier, the Republican Servicemen's League enjoyed immediate success. It boasted committees in ninety of ninety-nine counties in MacNider's home state of Iowa and no fewer than twenty organizers in Wyoming. A gift of $20,000 from the Republican National Committee paid organizing and printing expenses.[15]

The principal target of the League was Wisconsin Senator Robert La Follette. Even after the Democrats' 103-ballot brouhaha in New York, Republicans feared La Follette might win enough liberal members of the GOP to give the election to the Democratic presidential nominee, John W. Davis, or, less probably, win it himself. MacNider was amazed at "how many Legionnaires were supporting that damned La Follette," "a traitor to his country in time of war" whose obstruction of the mobilization "caused many thousands of deaths." "How any man who wore the uniform could want to see him anywhere outside of the hotter regions is more than I can understand," he declared. The Service League arranged for the *Iowa Legionnaire* to publish an editorial by Frank Miles "La Follette and [Senator Burton] Wheeler [his running mate] Have Putrid War Record," which called them "red-hyphenates." One critical veteran sarcastically predicted that a La Follette cabinet might consist of Eugene V. Debs, boxer Jack Dempsey (who evaded military service), the IWW's Big Bill Haywood, German sympathizer George Sylvester Viereck, and radical Kate Richards O'Hare.[16]

The Service League mailed fifty thousand copies of Miles's editorial to veterans all over the nation. It provoked a storm of protest. Despite the organizers' intention "to be very careful . . . not to give the impression that we are using our associations in the Legion for political purposes," Legionnaires could see "that the Republicans were trying to capitalize on" MacNider's and Roosevelt's reputations. Howard Hess of Madison, South Dakota, member of a post where he reckoned 50 Legionnaires were for Coolidge, 12 for Davis, and 230 for La Follette, claimed that many men had vowed to quit the Legion since MacNider had, in effect, branded them as "unpatriotic" for supporting La Follette. MacNider tried to argue that "the Legion is not being used nor perverted to the issues of the Party and any such allegation is a *lie*." Rather, he maintained that "if there is any one way to keep the Legion out of politics, it is to give the servicemen avenues in every party which they may wish to affiliate with."[17]

Confronted with a president and a party that had offended veterans by stinginess and the residue of the Harding hospitals scandals, and with a challenger who had opposed the war, Democrats might have been expected to seek votes from the former servicemen with a vengeance. Ohio's Robert Black, for one, "heartily welcome[d] MacNider's idea," and wished that the Democrats would imitate it. MacNider himself encouraged Democrats to do so, both so that the Legion would be a power in both parties and to avoid "misunderstandings and battles" resulting from the misconception that it had become a Republican tool. In 1924, however, the badly divided Democrats had trouble even getting together an advisory committee of prominent Legionnaires. Two of the most important who received offers—former New York State Commander William Deegan (an Al Smith booster) and Tennessee labor leader George Berry, who disliked corporate-lawyer nominee John Davis—were especially unhappy and declined to serve. Deegan had joined Democratic labor leaders to support the nomination of former Legion Vice-Commander Berry for vice-president. (The Legion had assigned Berry, past president of the International Printers, Pressmen, and Assistants Union, the task of reconciling the Legion with the American Federation of Labor.) Just as Berry had forged a "splendid relationship" (an overstatement) between the two groups when they "had become a little bit strained because of false propaganda" (an understatement), Deegan predicted a man of Berry's skill could reunite a political party severely torn "between reactionary conservatism and extreme radicalism." The Berry boomlet, however, never got off the ground.[18]

In 1928, a Democratic Veterans' Organization headed by General Henry T. Allen competed with MacNider's group on equal terms. Stressing scandals in the Veterans' Bureau and repeated Republican presidential vetoes of the Bonus in the early twenties, Allen argued that "through the Democrats and in spite of two Republican Presidents' opposition, the Congress has maintained America's traditional policy to generously care for the veterans." Flyers emphasized Governor Al Smith's support for veterans' preference and benefits in New York. Allen also appealed to the Legion's religious openness by attacking the anti-Catholic rhetoric to which some of Smith's opponents stooped: "We are fighting for democracy again now. It's a war against intolerance, bigotry, and religious prejudice." Allen even quoted the opera singer Ernestine Schumann-Heink, "the mother of the American Legion" and a lifelong Democrat, as saying, "I pray for Al Smith every night, just as I used to pray for my boys in the Great War." Allen hoped to make his "organization a vital and living part of the Democratic Party, representing the energy and strength of the young manhood of the party."[19]

For all Allen's efforts, including being "the center of attention" at the 1928 Legion Convention in San Antonio, his group held more problems than promise. Republicans criticized the accuracy of Allen's propaganda—had not Republican votes helped pass the Bonus? did not the Republicans create the veterans' hospital system? MacNider argued that Smith appealed to the former soldiers by arguing insufficient veterans' benefits, but to the nation by attacking excessive Republican expenditures. But Allen's efforts also met with criticism from Democrats still aware of the Grand Army of the Republic. In a confidential letter, former Secretary of War Newton D. Baker claimed to have "not the slightest objection to veterans who are Democrats joining together as a Democratic organization." But he was "fearful that such an organization may after a while become a veterans' organization with a political purpose." Although Allen replied that he was making "a direct appeal to the individual veteran" and was "in no manner attempting to drag any of the standard veterans' organizations . . . into politics," his warm reception by the Legionnaires in San Antonio provoked controversy. The *World Tribune* reported that "the American Legion has a row brewing over some of its most prominent figures," and cited numerous "complaints that Legion leaders were participating in the campaign."[20]

Although men who had held high office in the Legion continued to organize veterans after 1928, such attempts received little publicity and probably had almost no effect. In 1936, former Commander Edward Spafford, a Republican, expressed amazement that Louis A. Johnson had the audacity to chair a Democratic Veterans' Committee that year at all. Citing reductions in benefits under the Economy Act, Roosevelt's Bonus veto, policies that "pit class against class," and a "breakdown in Americanism which . . . caused Russia to be recognized and placed on an equality with God-fearing nations," Spafford charged that "the New Deal candidate for President is giving the veterans a phoney deal." In 1940, twenty-five prominent Legion and VFW leaders, headed by former Legion Commander Harry Colmery, united behind Wendell Willkie.[21]

Legionnaires, if not "the Legion," became involved in state as well as national elections. Missouri Democrat Lloyd Stark's effort to mobilize them behind his successful bid for the governorship in 1936 may serve as an example of the advantages and problems of obtaining the veterans' support. In December 1935, Stark first broached the idea of Stark for Governor Veterans' Clubs to his friend William Kitchin, a prominent Kansas City Legionnaire. He hoped to "work out a systematic plan of contact with the Legionnaires, especially the Republicans." Kitchin set up private meetings between Stark and veterans, but warned him not to emphasize his military record: "I would run as Lloyd C. Stark and not as Major Lloyd C. Stark. A lot of ex-servicemen, corporals and privates, may not like a major. Knowing the veterans as I do, little things like that weigh with them." Stark and Kitchin organized the clubs with the blessings of "Mr. [Tom] Pendergast," the notorious boss of Kansas City, all the while letting "the boys . . . think it is their own original idea." Despite the Legion constitution, at least three posts openly endorsed Stark.[22]

But when Jesse W. Barrett, former commander of the state Legion, won the GOP's nod, Stark had to change his tactics. Another adviser warned him, "Do not at any time stress the Legion too much for your inactivity in the post and in their affairs will produce resentment. . . . They are a sensitive crowd and to alienate even a few leaders means loss of many Republican votes." If Legion contacts enabled Stark to go after Republican votes, it also helped smooth feelings between the two parties. At the state Legion convention, Barrett asked that "Democrat friends of his not get sore at him" for his "plan to make Pendergast a dominating issue in the coming campaign." They understood; they "were used to that issue." The Missouri case shows how Legion and partisan politics could become inextricably intertwined without technically transgressing the rule that the Legion officially endorse no candidate.[23]

Despite the Legion's importance as a lobby, neither its members' campaign drives nor veterans' issues won or lost many elections. Given the strength of party ties, offsetting efforts by Republicans and Democrats, and the large margins that decided every presidential and most other contests between the wars, it is safe to conclude that the partisan campaign drives of Legionnaires mattered little. They only opened the Legion to renewed criticism that its "nonpolitical" stance was a sham. On the other hand, polls conducted by Congressman Wright Patman (who clashed with the Legion over the method of paying the Bonus) in 1935 and by the social scientists Albert Somit and Joseph Tannenhaus in 1957 concluded that congressmen's stands on benefits for former servicemen did not make much difference in elections.[24]

Legion inability to elect candidates, however, paled before the Legion's effectiveness as a lobby for legislation it desired. Historian William Gellerman considered the Legion's "sheer political power" as "singularly effective" among interest groups. The title of Marcus Duffield's diatribe, *King Legion,* speaks for itself. The Legion also encouraged rumors of its own omnipotence, as when John Thomas Taylor asserted, "The American Legion favors it. It is inevitable legislation." While such statements exaggerate the case, they do point to the Legion's influence on Capitol Hill.[25]

Taylor's effective lobbying was responsible for the exaggerated rumors that "opposing a Legion measure is like poking one's political head out of a train window." Head of the National Legislative Committee from 1920 to 1950, he appeared on the cover of *Time* on January 21, 1935, as the man who had "put three presidents in their place." As the Legion's chief Washington lobbyist, "never befuddled by lengthy, well-meaning resolutions passed by Legion members at conventions," wrote Drew Pearson in 1934, "Taylor whittles out a legislative program which he thinks the Legion ought to have; then he proceeds to push it through." After consultation with Legion leaders, Taylor first established such significant matters as adjusted compensation, veterans' benefits, and national defense as his top priority. He would then "deal directly with what he calls the key men in Congress" and draft the bills himself. On minor matters he arranged for friendly congressmen to introduce quickly forgotten bills to mollify special interests within the Legion. "The veterans' lobby? You're looking at it. I'm it," the cocky Philadelphia lawyer, formerly of the Boies Penrose machine, informed interviewers. "An investigation? Sure. I'm for it. I have no secrets to hide from anyone." "A lobbyists' legend," "the great white father of the American Legion," Taylor managed almost single-handedly to make the Legion far more important in passing legislation than, say, the American Federation of Labor, which boasted three to four times its membership.[26]

Historians should be glad to know the secret of Taylor's success was thorough research and its effective presentation. By the mid 1930s, his files included twenty volumes recording how every congressman had voted on every issue in which the Legion had taken an interest since its creation, and sixty volumes of committee hearings. The *New York Sun* called Taylor's files "the most complete statistical information service that can be found in Washington," and attributed to them 50 percent of the Legion's success. Congressmen who forgot their previous votes visited Taylor to find out where they stood.

John Thomas Taylor with Royal Johnson, Congressman from South Dakota, the first chairman of the House Veterans' Committee. Courtesy of American Legion National Headquarters.

After assembling information and arguments to back up Legion-sponsored legislation, Taylor presented it. At committee hearings, he appeared with thoroughly digested quantities of facts and statistics, ready to pounce on any opponent who slipped up or arrived unprepared. Since "his facts are invariably accurate and reliable, the members of Congress have come to look upon them as the most authoritative available," said the *Sun*. After one house approved a major Legion bill, Taylor personally brought it to the clerk's office to be enrolled, and escorted congressional messengers to the other chamber to ensure prompt action.

When Taylor thought the Legion would back him up, he called for a "barrage" of telegrams and letters to let recalcitrant congressmen know Legionnaires considered their stand on a particular issue an important criterion for voting in the forthcoming election. "Freshmen in Congress marvelled when a barrage of 350,000 telegrams descended on Capitol Hill overnight after an unfavorable vote on veterans' legislation," *Time* noted in its "Man of the Year" story. Before Taylor pioneered the "barrage," constituent mail to congressmen had been individual and sporadic; other lobbies soon picked up this technique.

Taylor had a flair for the theatrical. When he fought for pensions for disabled officers, fifty crippled men from Walter Reed Hospital sat in the front row of the House of Representatives' gallery to observe the vote. He presented a petition three feet thick with a million and a half names to urge support for the Bonus. In 1944 he inundated the steps of the Capitol with boxes of petitions in favor of the Legion's GI Bill. In addition to his other activities, Taylor mailed out a news bulletin once a week when Congress was in session to every Legion post in the country, explaining what was going on in Washington and how they could effectively help. He spoke throughout the nation to stir Legionnaires to take as active an interest in the disabled and in national defense as they did in the Bonus. Affecting spats, carrying a gold-headed cane he shook in congressmen's faces, treating freshmen congressmen like "messenger boys," Taylor "bristles with pugnacity," "with the punch-you-in-the-nose spirit," the *North American Review* wrote. He deliberately cultivated the legend of his own invincibility and sought maximum exposure for the Legion's lobby. As the *New York Sun* noted, "There is nothing underhanded or insidious about the Legion's lobbying activities." A Congressional committee looking into lobbying abuses in 1932 considered examining the Legion "a waste of time for the lobby itself deliberately invites the widest publicity." No wonder the more anonymous and less flamboyant lobbyists for disarmament, fiscal retrenchment, and civil liberties regarded the Legion with awe and jealousy.

Taylor, though, frequently got into hot water. In 1927, Commander Howard Savage tried to remove Taylor when Congressman Hamilton Fish charged that he had "bamboozled" the Legion to support the development of poison-gas research because of his personal links with the du Ponts and the chemical industry. When Taylor was mentioned as a possible director of the veterans' bureau, assistant secretary of war, or civil service commissioner in the Hoover administration, he ran afoul of rumors that he held riotous drinking parties at his Washington house and indulged in extramarital affairs. Taylor even managed to offend his stalwart supporter Hanford MacNider by arranging for an appointment for the guard at the Tomb of the Unknown Soldier without consulting the Legion "kingmaker" and assistant secretary of war.[27]

In 1930, Taylor's independent self-assertiveness provoked a recall campaign headed by the Commander of Pennsylvania's Sixth District, compelling National Headquarters to gather opinions from prominent Legionnaires and legislators on Taylor's retention. The Pennsylvania Legionnaire had been severely embarrassed when, after obtaining several congressmen's commitments to a veterans' hospital bill officially endorsed by the Legion, Taylor had thrown his influence behind another bill he claimed was superior. But aside from Fiorello La Guardia, who objected to Taylor's suspect law practice as a conflict of interest and complained that "policy should not be left to any salaried member of the Legion," respondents to the Legion poll all supported Taylor. Florida's Adjutant, who admitted "I do not like John Taylor," still thought that the ouster was motivated by a "small gang of politicians" and any uproar would "break the Legion." Iowa's Ray Murphy, a future National Commander, acknowledged that "Taylor may have incurred much ill-will and resentment," but argued that if he had not, he would not have been an effective Legion advocate: "His equal will not readily be found. He has done a great job." Congressmen Albert Johnson and H. D. Hatfield endorsed Taylor. New Hampshire's Adjutant considered him "the most valuable man on the Legion payroll"; one anonymous senator called him "the greatest lobbyist the world has ever known." Taylor stayed on until 1950. He accomplished his Capitol Hill miracles with an assistant, two secretaries, and a budget of under $25,000 per year.

Through Taylor's leadership the Legion effectively forged what political scientists call an "iron triangle" or "subsystem": a combination of congressional committees, a federal regulatory agency, and an interest group. All three share an interest in maximizing the power and the budget of the agency involved. Because of the highly technical information required for most laws and regulations, and the limited attention detailed points receive from political decision makers, the press, and the public, subsystems usually get their way. The Legion teamed up with a Veterans' Bureau (as of 1930, Veterans' Administration) that it had brought into being and whose staff was largely drawn from its ranks. The House Veterans' Committee and a Veterans' Sub-Committee of the Senate Finance Committee completed the triangle. These were headed through much of the interwar period by Mississippi's sympathetic John Rankin and Legion founder Bennett Champ Clark, respectively. On such matters as what disability payments a soldier should receive for a given injury, what procedures were required to prove its service-connectedness, and how veterans' hospitals ought to be staffed and supplied, the subsystem had its way within budgetary constraints. The Legion also developed close ties with the Dies committee and the FBI on law enforcement and with the Defense Committees of both houses.[28]

Yet the Legion's reasons for effectiveness go beyond Taylor's personal competence and the development of an effective subsystem. Unlike nearly every other lobby, the Legion could plausibly present itself not as a special-interest group but as a broad national movement representing veterans, and thereby Americans, of every class, region, party, and religion that—and this is crucial—restricted itself to those issues on which such a diverse group was more or less united. No congressman could deny that he desired justice for the veteran. As the Legion formulated the most detailed and publicized plans for benefits, Congress had to accept these as at least the basis of discussion. Similarly, national defense and a general, "antiradical" Americanism could be criticized on grounds of fiscal austerity, "militarism," and civil liberties, but only implausibly as special-interest legislation that did not command wide public support. By seeking to increase its membership, the Legion maximized its general representativeness and thereby seemed to set itself apart from "selfish" interests. The almost total absence of any financial corruption or illegality in the Legion's lobbying helped, and by saving its thunder for a few selected areas—benefits, defense, and Americanism—the Legion offended congressmen and the public far less than it antagonized the liberal intellectuals who so futilely fulminated against its influence.

But if the Legion were "king," it was still a limited monarch. It never obtained the compulsory military service it sought until the 1940 emergency. A much-desired Senate Committee on Veterans' Affairs did not emerge until World War II. The Legion could neither obtain Assistant Secretary of Labor Louis Post's removal in 1920 nor prevent President Harding from pardoning Eugene V. Debs in 1921. President Roosevelt recognized the Soviet Union and reduced veterans' aid under the Economy Act of 1933 despite virulent Legion hostility. Even many of the Legion's successes came after controversies lasting years. Only during World War II did the House approve a permanent Committee on Un-American Activities, fifteen years after the Legion had first requested it. Military-preparedness programs only began to make headway in 1940 when the Axis menace obtained nearly universal recognition.

The Legion's wobbling stance on the Bonus also reflected its limited power. In 1920, the Legion reluctantly endorsed the idea, but a bill to pay the money *in 1945* only became law in 1924 over vetoes by Presidents Harding and Coolidge. Similarly, it took four years of lobbying, from 1932 to 1936, before legislators agreed to pay the Bonus ahead of schedule over Hoover's and Roosevelt's vetoes. Defending the Legion against attacks that it "dictated all kinds of policies to the Congress," Hamilton Fish went so far as to argue that "the so-called Legion lobby is a myth and its influence is infinitesimal."[29] But he exaggerated. As the most-interested and best-organized lobby for veterans' issues, national defense, and antiradical legislation, the Legion could set the terms of debate by introducing bills and forcing congressmen to oppose or support them. The Legion would also publicize controversial issues, like the Bonus and defense, year after year until congressional and public opinion finally saw the light.

On the other hand, the Legion sometimes went too far. Legion hostility did not necessarily hurt its enemies. Robert La Follette and Tom Watson had no trouble winning election to the Senate in the face of open Legion opposition. Fiscal conservative Ogden Mills turned the Legion's animosity into votes in Manhattan's "Silk-Stocking" district. And for all his prestige as the Legion's

principal founder, Theodore Roosevelt Jr. lost his 1924 gubernatorial race in New York against Alfred E. Smith.

Nevertheless, because they had been soldiers themselves, felt a
real sympathy for the former servicemen, or perceived veterans'
support as useful in their constituencies, many elected officials
cultivated close Legion ties. On both the national and the state
levels, Commanders set up friendly candidates with the opportunity to make speeches to promote their political fortunes. "A
humorous delegate provided a roar of laughter" at the 1931 Detroit Convention by suggesting that each new speaker announce
"what office he's running for." Greenville, South Carolina's, John
MacSwain symbolized the ideal Legion legislator. As he launched
his bid for a fifth term in the House of Representatives in 1930,
he obtained a note from John Thomas Taylor praising him as
"one of the most active Legionnaires in Congress. He has been
in favor of and voted for every piece of legislation which the
American Legion has proposed to Congress." Two years earlier,
after MacSwain had landed "a wallop between the eyes" in attacking opponents of the Tyson-Fitzgerald Bill, which granted
pensions to disabled AEF officers, the *National Legionnaire*
promptly thanked him in the middle of the campaign. Maine had
a MacSwain in Senator Fred Hale, "a great man" who "never
failed us" according to Legionnaire James Boyle. Boyle's activities
on Hale's behalf after he voted to override President Roosevelt's
Bonus veto illustrate that the lines separating Legion gratitude
from partisan politics, and Legionnaires acting "as individuals"
from official Legion stands, were fine indeed:

> In such a case we do not act politically but I got some fellows
> together and went down to Portland and talked to the head of the
> Gannett Papers and got him to run extracts of a speech in the *Sun
> Telegram* the following Sunday made by our Department Com-
> mander, which I wrote, acknowledging the thanks veterans must
> give to Senator Hale, and these we planned for distribution in the
> several papers.[30]

The Legion also counted many stalwart supporters among state
legislators and governors. For instance, West Virginia's Governor
Conwell, "a Legion man from the top of his head to the bottom
of his feet," spent a week during his 1920 campaign speaking to
Legion gatherings throughout the state. State Adjutant Louis Carr
suggested that a letter from National Headquarters, praising him
even if it did not specifically endorse his candidacy, would be an

appropriate gesture. A Minnesota poll conducted by Stafford King in 1924 revealed fifty-six state legislators (including eight active Legionnaires) favorable to the Legion, three unfavorable, and three with mixed views. Friends of the Legion in Minnesota included Senator J. E. Dieser of Mankato, who regularly attended Legion banquets, spoke at functions, and even paid half the expenses of the local delegate to the state convention. C. H. MacKenzie of Gaylord was a past commander of the local post and was "always doing something for the post," including obtaining captured German cannons for ceremonial uses. Senator L. P. Johnson of Ivanhoe was not only an active Legionnaire who could "not praise the Legion too much," but he "spent his own time and money to help ex-servicemen who were needy and has not charged a penny."[31]

Yet for all its staunch supporters, the Legion did not command automatic allegiance, even from legislators who were prominent Legionnaires. In fact, one of the chief reasons it made little practical sense for the Legion to support or oppose candidates officially was that its greatest champions on some issues would disagree with it on others. In the late 1930s, loyal Legionnaire and United States Senator from Washington Lewis Schwellenbach opposed the Legion's policy to terminate immigration to the United States and to deport radical aliens. Americanism Director Homer Chaillaux explained that even apart from honest differences of opinion, "there was some politics involved with Schwellenbach due to the fact that the Hearst press was supporting solidly the program of the Legion and you know how bitterly they were attacking the Senator." In 1940 Legionnaire Earl Hayley of Burns, Oregon, helped out Oregon Congressman Walter M. Pierce when he won the Legion's ire for opposing the deportation of labor leader Harry Bridges as unconstitutional. Hayley presented Pierce's written justification of his position, won over many members of his post, and believed that this "fine move . . . will make many votes for you in the general election that would have been placed otherwise."

No one exasperated the Legion more than Hamilton Fish, a Legionnaire who introduced much veterans' legislation. In 1927, however, Fish startled the Legion when he denounced a convention resolution that the nation defend itself by stockpiling large quantities of poison gas. In a speech in the House of Representatives, Fish accused the chemical industry of combining with the Legion to block the ratification of a Geneva protocol outlawing chemical warfare. He went on to claim that 90 percent of the

Legionnaires agreed with him in favoring an end to production
of a substance that would cause "countless women and children
in crowded cities [to] be destroyed." Fish's friend Stafford King,
however, expressed the view of most Legion leaders that they
had to put their personal beliefs aside when it came to priority
Legion legislation:

> Whenever a man of your prominence introduces to the general
> public evidence of a break in the ranks of the Legion it takes the
> organization months to rebuild itself in the confidence of the pub-
> lic. Naurally we cannot all agree, but I am of the opinion that for
> the best interests of the organization and especially after a propo-
> sition has been talked out we should show a united front.

Legislative Chairman Taylor could not understand Fish's independence. Although he usually got on well with Fish, he complained that "he likes to be considered as ornery," and "nobody
here understands him and nobody tries to." When the poison-gas
issue blew over, Fish and the Legion again cooperated in exposing
Communists: in 1979, to celebrate the Legion's sixtieth and Fish's
ninetieth birthdays, the National Convention voted him an honorary lifetime National Commander.[32]

   Fish was a thorn in the Legion's side, but the congressman's
lifelong nemesis, Franklin D. Roosevelt, posed even greater problems. Roosevelt and Legion politics first intersected at the Legion's 1932 Portland Convention, when Boston's Mayor James
Curley turned his speech into a violent denunciation of the Hoover administration. He remarked that under Hoover, "the wealth-
iest nation in the whole world" had "lost that which Washington
and his followers gave to them, and since hoped never might be
lost, faith, fortitude, and courage." He went on to compare the
veterans who had been killed when the Bonus Army was driven
from Anacostia Flats to those martyred on the western front:

> How the heart of the great hero [George Washington] would be
> saddened and filled with sorrow with the knowledge that some of
> the victims of our social order, who in the hour of crisis stood
> ready to make the supreme sacrifice that free government might
> not vanish from the earth, because they were victims, because they
> pleaded for that to which they were entitled, that they were shot
> down like dogs in the capital of the nation.

To drive his point home, Curley followed up his convention
appearance with a speaking tour for Roosevelt. Outspoken former
Legion Commander Edward Spafford objected that by allowing

Curley to speak, Commander Harry Stevens, a Democrat, had blatantly engaged in politics. The following year, not only did Roosevelt himself appear to defend his Economy Act, and praise the "patience, the loyalty, and the will to make sacrifices shown by the overwhelming majority of the veterans," but "Mother" Schumann-Heink praised him as "the greatest man" who "loves the Legion" and "trusts that you will help him bring the United States back to where it used to be in the old times."[33]

Officially, the Legion supported Roosevelt, as it did all presidents, as an act of national loyalty, while reserving the right to criticize specific policies. As Watson B. Miller said in an address to the nation on NBC Radio, it was "a matter of profound regret . . . that we find ourselves in disagreement [on veterans' benefits] with a President who has such wide support among us as our great national leader Franklin D. Roosevelt." The Legion realized it had to work with Roosevelt's administration to have any hope of restoring the Economy Act cuts. Nevertheless, conservative Legionnaires attempted at various times, without success, to condemn implicitly key features of the New Deal. In 1934, the National Executive Committee rejected a proposed resolution stating that "any delegation of the legislative power to any central authority endangers the fundamental rights and liberties of the people," and "respectfully" urged Congress to resume its Constitutional powers. Similarly, in 1937, at the height of Roosevelt's efforts to "pack" the Supreme Court, Homer Chaillaux suggested a plan to "pound away for the education of our people . . . [on] the system of checks and balances and complete independence of the three coordinate branches as the bulwark of our form of government," although it came to nothing. The Legion's wisdom in not actively opposing the extremely popular president appeared yet again in 1939, when some Republican congressmen tried to enlist the Legion in their battle against Roosevelt's defense buildup. Beginning in 1940, the Legion realized that "the only way to unite the nation behind a preparedness program," which it had favored all along, "is to back the program of the President."[34]

While the Legion avoided taking open sides in electoral contests, it actively tried to secure appointive posts for veterans in the Veterans' Administration, Post Office, and state and local government. For instance, in 1939 former state commander Fred Boettinger recommended Leon Embry to Missouri Governor Lloyd Stark as an ideal choice for veterans' welfare officer: "He is a stalwart Democrat of the Lloyd Stark type; carriage, appearance, and character of the American Legion type . . . sincere and honest 100% American, the type of man we need." Two years earlier, several prominent Legionnaires endorsed Clarence McGee for Missouri circuit judge. Noting that McGee was the "only ex-serviceman eligible for this appointment," they "would be for him anyways," as "no man has given more of his time and talent to the cause of the ex-soldier than he has." In Minnesota, Stafford King praised the talents of Bill Lyons, a Legion service officer, in seeking to obtain a job for him with the Veterans' Bureau: "I have yet to be in a town where ex-servicemen meriting consideration by the Bureau have not been able to get to him." However, problems arose when more than one former serviceman or Legionnaire sought the same employment. Stephen Chadwick advised a Seattle post commander that "to endeavor to secure a state or federal appointment for an ex-serviceman" was "not considered political provided that there are no other ex-servicemen candidates for office." But sometimes there were. When the Oklahoma Legion was given the right to fill a Veterans' Bureau appointment by Congressman Leroy Gensman, a "scrap" ensued among several prospects. Gensman told them to select their favorite, so "the Legion will be held responsible and not the party organization."[35]

Public officials and those who hoped for public positions used Legion connections to obtain appointments. In 1923, Minnesota's Stafford King won the mayor of St. Paul's nod to be chairman of the state's Veterans' Welfare Bureau. General Frank Parker, seeking to line up Legion and Auxiliary support behind his ambitious preparedness program, appointed the husband of the president of the Legion Auxiliary in Illinois a first lieutenant in the Army Reserve. As assistant secretary of war, Hanford MacNider received numerous requests for federal jobs from members of the Republican Service League in 1925. Indiana State Commander Paul McNutt was similarly called upon to use his connections to obtain state jobs for Legionnaires. Legionnaires could remain "nonpolitical" and yet engage in extensive lobbying, nominate appointees, and run for public office on the strength of past Legion service.[36]

However, the Legion drew a firm line by defining as "partisan" any activity that might split the membership. Specific endorsement of political candidates, either by posts or by members currently holding Legion office, was forbidden. Kansas Republican Harry Colmery obtained an apology from the *Denver Post* for printing a photo of himself and presidential candidate Alfred M. Landon with a caption indicating Colmery supported him. When a post commander urged Legionnaires to "stick with" Minneapolis Mayor Arthur Nelson in the 1928 election, Stafford King found the remark in "exceedingly bad taste." A Comrade Stiles once complained that Minneapolis Legionnaires were not adequately supporting St. Paul's Mayor George Leach for election to the United States Senate despite his good work for veterans; he was "assured by Commander Larsen that properly [the post] could not enter politics without losing ground and would be establishing a precedent." Indiana "Legionnaires active in state or local politics were more or less ostracized," and State Commander C. A. Johnson warned a post adjutant not to endorse a senatorial candidate. On the other hand, in a low-visibility local race, Washington's Stephen Chadwick responded to a request for information by observing that if a post wanted to endorse a comrade who was running, "What is the constitution among friends?" But he was careful to insist "the resolution is to be passed unanimously."[37]

In addition to not taking sides in political contests, Legion posts and officials could not endorse or appear to support policies that might divide the Legion. Oregon's Rose City Post refused to sponsor a speech by the evangelist Aimee Semple McPherson "because Mrs. McPherson is too closely connected in the minds of the public with a religious sect and by our Constitution we are a non-sectarian body." The most notorious such case occurred in 1940, when Missouri Legionnaires complained that O. K. Armstrong, a member of the Legion National Foreign Relations Committee who named his baby after Charles Lindbergh, had been using his position to further the America First cause. One Legionnaire complained to National Commander Kelly that "our Legion members here don't think much of Lindbergh, and I would suggest that Mr. Armstrong be instructed either to keep his political views to himself, or be removed from the speaker's bureau." As a Republican candidate for the Missouri legislature, Armstrong went on to "condemnation of the administration policies and the President of the United States." National Adjutant Frank Samuel warned Armstrong either to cease his political harangues or dissociate himself from the Legion. Samuel's remark that "in twenty-one years of office I have leaned so far backward when it comes to any possible suspicion of political implication that I have undoubtedly missed a lot of thrilling things which are supposed to be available to a private citizen" reveals the Legion's general attitude on avoiding potentially divisive issues. But he still balked at removing Armstrong: realizing that "from the public standpoint it will be virtually impossible to dissociate Armstrong as Legion member and private citizen," he still argued that to censor him "would be dangerous and place him in the category of personal martyr." Samuel advised the National Commander to let the episode wind its course. Privately, Armstrong's Legion friends rebuked him for "the hell of a mess you have started up."[38]

Of all the controversies occasioned by the Legion's entering into partisan politics, none can compete with the New Mexico scandal, which resulted in the suspension of the state department's charter from 1933 to 1935. Despite the Legion's general unwillingness to air its dirty laundry in public, the state Legion had become deeply involved in political and racial issues centering around progressive Republican Senator Bronson Cutting.[39]

A well-to-do Long Islander who had moved to the Southwest for his health in 1910, Cutting used his private wealth and his leadership of New Mexico's Spanish-speaking majority to build up the state's Legion. (He vigorously defended Mexican Americans' right to public instruction in their own language when the national Legion began to lobby for English-only schools; not only were the teachers not available, but "the chance of getting a Spanish-speaking legislature to pass such a bill would be, to say the least, remote.") Using Mexican Americans in the Legion, Cutting turned the state's Republicans in a progressive direction. He took advantage of the Harding scandals to defeat the conservative wing of the party, headed by Albert Fall, and won election to the United States Senate in 1926.[40]

But by 1931, Colonel Harry Hering could argue at the state convention in Artesia that "the time had passed when any one man can control the American Legion in New Mexico," and that "the NATIVES . . . must be eliminated." Learning of this attack, Cutting shot back that "you have been instrumental . . . in injecting into an American Legion convention two things which have no place there: partisan politics and racial discrimination."

Taking their case to National Headquarters, New Mexican Anglos obtained an investigation in 1933. A three-man committee headed by future National Commander Harry Colmery of Kansas found the department guilty of permitting "the American Legion to be used politically and/or to be used for the dissemination of partisan principles and/or for the promotion of the candidacy of persons seeking political office." Most of the indictment listed Legionnaires belonging to more than one post, dummy posts whose members' dues were paid by the Cutting machine, ineligible members, and officials in the state Legion who had, among other things, served as mayors and sheriffs and run for Congress and New Mexico's secretary of state while still holding their posts. As punishment, Headquarters revoked the charters of nearly every Spanish-speaking post in the state, which removed Cutting personally from the organization. New Mexico also became the only state to suffer the suspension of its charter until it could put its house in order to the satisfaction of the National Executive Committee. The *Santa Fe New Mexican* bitterly protested this violation of home rule, asserting that both factions were headed by "capable men and Legionnaires" and that National Headquarters' plan to retain the state's dues "until the members no longer have any politics is fascinating, to say the least." It sounded "suspiciously like the little situation which caused the Boston Tea Party!"[41]

But in its bid to keep New Mexico's Legion nonpartisan, National Headquarters' decision against Cutting could itself be interpreted politically. New York's Edward Spafford charged that the Legion had blundered by attacking a loyal friend of the veterans in Congress:

> The American Legion has kicked out of its membership the man who has done more for the disabled man than any man in Congress. I believe that when Bronson Cutting comes up for election again this fall the Legion has placed him in a defensive position. Perhaps I should not say that the Legion has done this, but the Democrats have done it, using the Legion as their tool. Bronson Cutting has been loyal to the veterans. He has fought our battle in season and out of season. We have made his row tougher to hoe and all of it is due chiefly to the chicanery of the anti-Cutting faction.[42]

The Legion attack on Cutting was probably coordinated secretly with the Roosevelt administration's decision to support Cutting's Democratic challenger Dennis Chavez in the 1934 election. (The man who led the Legion's fight against Cutting was appointed postmaster of Albuquerque.) Cutting not only had opposed the Economy Act in 1933, but he achieved nationwide attention as the leading critic of the Independent Offices Act of 1934. Among other provisions, the bill restricted the criteria under which veterans were presumed disabled during wartime and hence eligible for benefits. Although Roosevelt had originally offered Cutting the secretaryship of the interior, relations between the men cooled quickly. Cutting was the only progressive Senator openly attacked by the White House in 1934. He retained his seat by less than a thousand votes, but was killed in a plane crash shortly thereafter. The whole episode illustrates not just the problems of a Legion department that became politicized, but how the national body could not avoid some kind of partisan involvement once it entered the political fray.[43]

Although the Legion sometimes had trouble deciding what was political and what was not, there were two issues it dodged whenever it could, Prohibition and the Ku Klux Klan. Like the Legion, drys and Klansmen hoped to restore America to a mythical purity. But whereas the Legion sought to encompass a diverse constituency, the drys and the Klan appealed almost exclusively to Protestants and Anglo-Saxons. If the Legion lacked the tremendous impact the Klan and Prohibition enjoyed during the twenties, its prudent maneuvering around these issues and concentration on programs that united its members ensured that it continued to influence national policy long after its rivals had faded into insignificance.

The young men of the AEF had no trouble reconciling their commitment to law and order and Americanism with wholesale violation of the Volstead Act. In their eyes, Prohibition was illegitimate, a war measure prolonged by chance in peacetime as the soldiers waited overseas to be demobilized. The men who made the world safe for democracy could easily rationalize disobedience to a law in whose formation they had no voice.

Legion posts soon became famous as another kind of speakeasy. Indiana Legionnaire Frank McHale estimated that 90 percent of the posts violated the Volstead Act with impunity. Legionnaires near Mexico held meetings south of the border to avoid legal trouble. In 1926, for instance, Nogales, Arizona, veterans treated the state's new commander to "a wonderful blowout, of course in Mexico, where it could be wet." (New Mexican Prohibitionists sarcastically considered starting a "dry post" in 1931, twelve years after all Legion posts were theoretically dry.) With the aid of sympathetic clergymen, Minnesotans imported suspiciously large quantities of "communion wine" from Canada. Concerning a $146 shipment that went astray, Stafford King (who once wrote "I don't think a person can drink too much champagne") jocularly informed the mayor of Winnipeg that "the Legion makes strange bedfellows, and among others it had produced an amazing friendship between Reverend Habermann, a Lutheran, and E. J. Normogle, a Catholic priest," who jointly requested the "wine." District of Columbia Commander Charles Reisner expressed the Legion consensus that given the chance 95 percent of the doughboys would have voted Prohibition down and prevented its adoption. He considered it a measure "railroaded through Congress under false colors. The plea was to turn the ingredients used in the manufacturing of liquors into food for the soldiers in France." The Legionnaires of the "second AEF" demonstrated what they thought of this argument by burying Congressman Andrew Volstead in effigy at sea to the strains of the death march from Handel's *Saul*. And Legion conventions were well known for hosting the rowdiest displays of drunkenness in the nation.[44]

Despite the Legionnaires' general sentiment, they still belonged to an organization pledged to "absolute respect for and enforcement of all laws upon the statute books"—or so the Indiana Legion resolved the year before police had to break up a drunken spree at the Kokomo Convention with tear gas. During the Legion's formative days, posts urged the state and national departments to oppose the newly enacted dry laws. Such statements drew the ire of the Anti-Saloon League, which was quick to discern "desperate attempts on the part of the liquor men to make use of the American Legion to oppose Prohibition and to restore the power of the brewers." National Commander Henry Lindsley and Theodore Roosevelt Jr., worried by the publicity the newspapers gave anti-Prohibition remarks, warned that they "put the Legion in a bad color . . . overshadowing other things which the posts may be doing." Even more important, they unnecessarily offended a dry Congress and the state legislatures, two-thirds of which had adopted Prohibition before 1918.[45]

To keep drys in the Legion and not alienate legislative support, the Legion never officially opposed Prohibition. However, neither did it ever make enforcement a major concern. Practically, it tried to ignore the issue by allowing Legionnaires to work out whatever arrangements they could in their localities. When Mississippians found Legion drinking offensive, the State Adjutant replied that "the Legion does stand for law, order, and Americanism," but that "the organization cannot be responsible for all the law violations by its members." A Ralph Collins of Coral Gables, Florida, expressed his outrage that local Legionnaires were imbibing homemade whiskey. Judge Advocate Scott Lucas, later a United States senator, replied by clothing the Legion in the majesty of the law while belittling Collins: "It is my opinion that any American Legion Post that uses intoxicating liquors within the walls of their clubrooms not only violates the law, but violates the spirit and purpose of the American Legion. You have remedies in your own community to meet a situation of this kind and it is more or less ridiculous to require National Headquarters to interfere."[46]

The Legion's true contempt for Prohibition, as opposed to the "law-and-order" litany its Americanism compelled it to recite, appears in its anger at federal agents who infiltrated and reported on Legion drinking bouts. In 1929, "Con" Hanley fumed to National Commander Paul McNutt that over forty Legionnaires had been convicted after a recent Indiana Convention when a federal agent "used Legion credentials to obtain evidence against fellow Legionnaires." In Bennington, Vermont, enforcement officials used Legion buttons to gain entry to places that sold liquor. (Such buttons apparently were as good as the proverbial password.) These agents, the local post complained, threatened to "stultify the American Legion by using it for selfish purposes" and constituted a "spy system more elaborate than any maintained by Germany during the war." To add insult to injury, the informers first liberally enjoyed the available refreshments. Anger that Prohibition agents would dare to manipulate the Legion to enforce the law, when contrasted with the easygoing toleration of the violations themselves, expressed the Legion's real attitude.[47]

Not all Legion posts were wet. Drys within the organization had to be placated to some extent. The Ketchikan Post in Alaska, for one, helped run bootleggers out of town. In St. Louis, one Legion post complained to Commander Jesse Barrett that another had rented its clubhouse for stag parties and drunken revelry that degraded the Legion: Barrett could only throw up his hands in view of the conflicting evidence and tell them to work it out for themselves. In Palo Alto, California, Legionnaires fought against smuggling bootleg liquor and narcotics into the local hospital, but obtained minimal support. Earl Warren found Legion leaders in California considerably "wetter" than many of the rank and file.[48]

As the twenties roared on, however, Legionnaires clamored for the national organization to take a stand in favor of repeal. In 1924, Judge Advocate Robert Adams informed Paul McGahan, Commander of the District of Columbia Department, that there was "nothing subversive to the Legion" in anti-Prohibition statements by Legionnaires. He humorously added: "There have been a good many resolutions passed by posts demanding 'our beer.' Most of my own experience in the matter leads me to think, though, that . . . what we want is something with a considerably more powerful kick." Still, the drys fought back. In Detroit, for example, the sister of war hero Charles Learned objected that the post named for her brother permitted "itself to be used as a propaganda organization for the liquor interest"—that is, its members drank there. She demanded, unsuccessfully, that its name be changed.[49]

National Commander Edward Spafford began the movement that culminated in the Legion's endorsing repeal. Like "wet" Democratic presidential candidate Al Smith, Spafford hailed from New York, although he was a Republican and an Anglican. Realizing that even within the Legion opinion on Prohibition was divided, Spafford suggested that the Legion sponsor a nationwide referendum to provide Congress and the state legislatures with the sense of the people. He made no effort, however, to hide his own thoughts:

> The American Legion is an all-American organization and cannot but view with grave concern a situation such as this:—Gangsters in Chicago, New York, and Philadelphia; officials profiting by graft; roads covered with illicit liquor; restaurants and clubs closed by padlocks; murder being committed by bootleg and hijack groups. . . . No government can long exist which does not enforce its laws, or which resorts to a breach of liberty in order to enforce some law which has not the sanction of the best thought of the community.

Spafford's pronouncement of December 9, 1927, set the Legion in an uproar. Even such prorepeal Legionnaires as Charles Wardery considered it a divisive political issue, though he added, "If given the opportunity to vote I will vote WET and whenever given the opportunity will drink my conscience." Spafford hoped to give the Legion a boost with his proposal: "Political parties dodge, the Legion dares." But former National Commander or not, the National Executive Committee would not even let him bring up this political hot potato at the next two conventions. He was furious at "not being able even [to] express an opinion," and condemned this "insulting, despicable action." As a parting shot, he expressed the hope that there were some "people who still believe in liberty which extends beyond the narrow bounds of thought."[50]

Repeal finally surfaced at the 1930 Convention, but only because National Commander and Arkansas Prohibitionist O. L. Bodenhamer decided to rule the whole matter out of order. He feared "nothing short of a debacle if we were to permit the American Legion to follow a program outlined and carried on by the Veterans of Foreign Wars, and urged by designing politicians." Bodenhamer firmly refused to allow debate on a resolution that "the Eighteenth Amendment is misplaced in the Federal Constitution in violation of the fundamental American right of self-government in local affairs, and has surrendered to the federal authorities police duties over the habits and conduct of individuals which belong of right to the states." "Bodie" insisted a repeal resolution was "in direct conflict with the political restriction clause of the American Legion Constitution," and diverted attention from "advancing care of the disabled and deserving." Somewhat surprisingly, Legionnaires greeted his bold stroke with approving cheers.[51]

However, as with the Bonus a decade earlier, repeal sentiment was too strong for leaders to contain. The *Chicago Tribune* taunted that "the Legion flinches in the face of a dry foe. Are pensions more important than freedom?" At the 1931 Detroit Convention, where "hell broke loose" in the neighboring Canadian city of Windsor and twenty-five veterans were hospitalized for alcohol-related excesses, the Resolutions Committee recommended that the states reconsider the Eighteenth Amendment. Commander Ralph O'Neil's protest that "there are many much more important matters which should occupy our time" was met with a "boisterous" demonstration and a fortissimo chant of "We want beer!" that went on for half an hour. A reporter for the *Church Advocate* dryly remarked that "many voting for it not only wanted liquor but already had more than the law allows." Delegates gave vent to twelve years of pent-up feelings. One charged that "since the passage of the Eighteenth Amendment, this country . . . has seen the fingers of evil stretched forth into our smaller communities. Across the length and breadth of this land there are minor Capones." Prorepeal forces evoked images of children gunned down in crossfires, flagrant contempt for the law by respectable people, and taxes raised to new heights to fight organized crime. Prohibitionists were booed and their opponents reminded to "be courteous." When the roll was called, the Legion voted 1,008 to

394 for a national referendum on the legal purchase of alcoholic beverages. Former Commander Bodenhamer's home state of Arkansas was joined by Kansas, Mississippi, Nebraska, Oklahoma, Tennessee, Texas, Utah, and Wyoming in unanimously opposing the resolution. Except for two New Hampshire and four Vermont Legionnaires, the entire Northeast unanimously favored it.[52]

Although to balance the score the Legion elected North Carolina's Henry Stevens, "a personal dry from a dry-voting state," as National Commander, no one was fooled by his insistence that the Legion "simply called for the full expression of the opinion of the citizenry." Religious publications predicted that the vote would "arouse resentment on the part of the great mass of Legionnaires who are active members in thousands of our churches." "Fairly boiling with wrath," drys charged that the Legion had been bought by the brewers and "reactionary element" to "throw its influence against moral progress." A more realistic assessment in the *Outlook,* however, noted that the Legion only declared for a referendum after the American Federation of Labor, the American Bar Association, and the American Medical Association had already done so. "So deeply did the Legion feel about the matter" it even "ventured outside its proper province."[53]

Having urged reconsideration of Prohibition, the Legion grew impatient. Judge Advocate Remster A. Bingham warned posts in Pennsylvania and New York that "the Prohibition law is still in effect and in their exuberance they should not transgress under the colors of the Legion." In 1932, one entire Indiana post was hauled off to jail in a Volstead raid; Commander Louis Johnson even threatened posts where drinking could be proven with revocation of their charters. But the cause was lost. August A. Busch published an article castigating the drys in the January 1933 *American Legion Monthly,* four months after a Legion convention finally demanded "immediate" repeal with only 162 dissenting votes.[54]

The Legion's belated stand on Prohibition once again mirrored national ambivalence. While dry sentiment still ran strong, the Legion joined much of the nation in ignoring the Volstead Act. The Legion's 1931 vote probably had little national influence on repeal: everyone knew the veterans had drunk illegally for years. Even so, the Legion prudently refrained from a wholehearted endorsement of repeal until 1932. It instead attacked Prohibition as a violation of states' and personal rights, as a practical failure that did not curtail drinking but led to the rise of gangsterism and violence. Legion leaders did not worry that this belated condemnation of Prohibition seriously reduced membership.

As with its stance on Prohibition, any official position the Legion took on the Ku Klux Klan was likely to engender controversy. Unlike the drys, however, the membership, ideology, and activities of the Klan and the Legion overlapped sufficiently that some identification occurred in the minds of those unfamiliar with the details of either organization. Elizabeth Gurley Flynn, for one, predicted that if Fascism ever came to America, the Klan, the Legion, and the Italian gangsters would institute it. She thereby managed to link a Prohibitionist anti-Catholic association, a nonsectarian, essentially anti-Prohibition group, and bootleggers, many of whom were Catholic.[55]

To be sure, the Klan and the Legion shared some goals and methods. Both claimed to represent "one-hundred-percent Americans." The 1925 *Klansman's Manual* proclaimed the order "dedicated to the principle that America shall be made American through the promulgation of American doctrines, the dissemination of American ideals, the creation of wholesome American sentiment [and] the preservation of American institutions" from foreign perversions. Like the Legion, the Klan promoted "fraternal love" among its members and urged them to develop "a spirit of active good will." The Klan and the Legion both engaged in such community services as sponsoring Boy Scout troops and helping the needy, sick, and infirm.

Here the similarities end. The Legion, although an organization of former servicemen, repeatedly insisted it was not militaristic and structured itself on a democratic, parliamentary model. The Klan, on the other hand, stressed its "military form of government" as essential "for the sake of true, patriotic Americanism, because it is the only form of government that gives any guarantee of success. We must avoid the fate of the other organizations that have split on the rock of democracy." The Klan also identified Americanism with white Protestant Christianity. It openly attacked blacks, Catholics, and Jews as unworthy of citizenship, whereas the Legion admitted all three. Furthermore, the Klan went far beyond the Legion in its devotion to ritual and secrecy. The difference is best symbolized in that the Klan uniform was a sheet and hood that concealed the Klansman's personal identity, whereas Legionnaires simply wore blue suits and the familiar Legion cap. Closely connected with the Klan's secrecy was a prime reason for it: in many states, especially in the South and

West, the Klan engaged in widespread punishment—and sporadic torturing and lynching—of "undesirables." From the Red Scare until the mid-1930s, the Legion was seldom involved in extreme actions in the name of a higher "Americanism"; those that did occur were repudiated by National Headquarters. Finally, the Klan made enforcement of Prohibition statutes (against "Romanist" bootleggers) and sexual morality (it frowned on divorce, miscegenation, and any form of promiscuousness) major aims; the Legion left these matters to the authorities. Ironically, the Klan declined precipitously in the mid 1920s because of personal scandals and pecuniary corruption among its leaders. Except in a few states, the Legion remained free from major accusations, apart from complaints about rowdy conventions.[56]

For all their dissimilarities, the Klan still posed a problem for the Legion. In some parts of the nation, membership overlapped considerably. To add to the Legion's difficulties, the Klan boasted its greatest strength in the Midwest, where the Legion also obtained large enrollments. Kenneth Jackson estimates that of some 2 million Americans who joined the Klan between 1915 and 1944, 240,000 came from Indiana, 195,000 from Ohio, 95,000 each from Illinois and Oklahoma, 70,000 from Michigan, 45,000 from Missouri, 40,000 from Kansas, and between 25,000 and 30,000 each from Kansas and Nebraska. Indiana Legionnaires estimated between 20 and 50 percent of their state's membership also belonged to the Klan. When in 1925 a post in Perry, Iowa, rented its clubhouse to the Klan and National Commander James Drain objected, post commander McDermott could only apologize and explain that they had to approve such an implicit endorsement of the local KKK because "there are so many Legion members that belong to the Klan here."[57]

Further connections between the Klan and the Legion appeared in the 1924 race for United States senator from Iowa. Democrat Daniel Steck, former Commander of the state's Legion, won the Klan's support against incumbent Republican Smith Brookhart, a La Follette booster whose vitriolic attacks angered the Klan more than Steck's mild criticisms. To complicate matters, Senator Brookhart was a bitter personal enemy of Hanford MacNider, head of the Republican Service League, who denounced him as a Communist sympathizer and a friend of neither the farmer nor the veteran. (Brookhart had opposed the Bonus.) When the tightly contested election went to a Senate committee to resolve, MacNider acted as Steck's chief adviser. Steck rejected an offer of Klan funds for legal fees to present his side of the recount, although he employed a noted attorney for the Klan, W. F. Zumbrunn. Depending on whether one believes MacNider or his enemies, his Legion connections persuaded several senators to vote for Steck, whom the committee certified to replace Brookhart by a vote of ten to one. While MacNider and the Republican Service League refused to have anything to do with the Klan—they would not even organize in Colorado, where the Klan "had taken entire control of the Republican party"—in Iowa the two groups clearly worked together or separately to oust a common foe.[58]

Pockets of Legion support for the Klan appeared throughout the nation. In 1925, the state department threatened to revoke the charter of a Factoryville, Pennsylvania, post when it cosponsored the local Fourth of July celebration with the community's Klavern. California was more indulgent. In Santa Monica, post commander James Collins received objections that the Klan and the Legion both marched in the Armistice Day parade of 1923. He responded, "It was fortunate that I was not present that day because I suppose they would have expected me to take each man by the neck and throw him in the ocean in order to keep them from parading." He insisted that if the Klan engaged in "no disorderly conduct or no infringement of the laws," he could see "no angle from which I can attack the matter until some [such] overt act is committed." Whatever the Klan's outrages in other parts of the nation, Collins could see no objection to the organization per se as a community fraternal order. The Klan, like the Legion, functioned in this innocuous manner in many of its local units. But in other cases the two were linked locally with less happy results. When New Jersey elected a Jew, Philip Forman, state commander in 1924 and he proceeded to denounce the Klan, a Lakewood Klansman and Legionnaire responded with a virulent denunciation of the man's war record and the Legion's drinking bouts and stag parties. "I have never heard anything about the policies of the Legion and do not know if they have any, even though I am a member," he said. "The only thing I ever knew them to do was graft on the public, and get out in uniform on a holiday and shout." He concluded, "Take the Klansmen out of the Legion and you have little left to call an organization." In 1923, Ohio Department Commander Gilbert Bettmann was furious to find that Klan and Legion leadership overlapped in the city of Springfield. Three years later, the principal opposition to a Catholic candidate for Illinois State Commander came from the Klan. In Mississippi, the first State Adjutant, Glen Smith, was an active Klansman: his combined recruiting efforts for both groups embarrassed and hindered Legionnaires, and they ousted him. As late as 1930, Legionnaires and Klansmen in Elmira, New York, joined to tear down a red flag at a workers' summer camp, burn a cross, and unsuccessfully attempt to have the two young women who ran it convicted of desecrating the flag.[59]

In general, however, the Legion and the Klan were adversaries and competitors on the local level. Legionnaires in Dallas, New York City, Los Angeles, and Lancaster, Pennsylvania, led their communities' opposition to the Klan. Of eastern Long Island, New York, where the Klan was very powerful, David Chalmers has written: "The only open opposition seemed to come from the American Legion which consistently objected to the Klan taking part in Memorial Day parades." In Smithtown, the Legion post took on the "Klan stronghold" by insisting that Catholic musicians participate in the dedication of the local war memorial on the grounds that "no one asked our buddies their religion when they died for their country."[60]

The Klan provoked vehement and almost unanimous hostility among the Legion's leaders. The main impetus for the Legion to denounce the Klan came from the South, where the Klan was more of a vigilante and less of a fraternal order than in the Midwest and the Northeast. It also represented a "populist," poor-white challenge to the "respectable" Democratic political machines dominated by wealthy, long-established Southern families. Klan support for Tom Watson against the Legion in Georgia exemplified this situation. Legionnaire Percy of Mississippi, whose patrician family stood in the forefront of his state's anti-Klan faction, begged at the 1921 Americanism Commission meeting for "a strong statement from the American Legion that this thing is un-American and against the traditions of our government." His rationale, that an open denunciation "would have large influence on this unthinking portion of the population," illustrated upper-crust southerners' opinion of the sort of members that the Klan attracted and the ease with which they believed the poor whites could be swayed. Texas Legionnaires, however, who also bitterly fought the Klan, "tried to keep the American Legion from being injected into" what they considered a matter of law enforcement and Democratic party politics. If Dallas Commander Royal Watkins slyly accepted the gift of a flag from his city's Klan by

noting that "the only masks the American Legion has any use for
are gas masks," Americanism committeeman Leonard Withington
wondered "whether we can drive it out, and whether [by denouncing them] we are not giving them just the kind of ammu-
nition that they thrive on."[61]

In 1921 the Americanism Commission not only turned down
Percy's request to attack the Klan openly, but even rejected a
milder resolution sponsored by the Kentucky Department:
"whereas certain organizations claiming to be one hundred percent American are using the cover of masks and darkness to usurp
the authority placed by the Constitution in the hands of the peace
officers, be it resolved that the American Legion hereby goes on
record as opposed to any organization which uses the cover of
darkness or masks to achieve its purposes." The substitute not
only begged the question of bigotry but could enable the many
Klansmen whose local activities were primarily fraternal to remain
Legionnaires in good standing. Commander John Emery, though,
saw through the subterfuge. He urged that Legionnaires concentrate on lobbying for the construction of hospitals within the
recently established Veterans' Bureau and not dissipate their
strength. He thought it would make little sense for the Legion to
grapple with a hornet's nest both Congress and the American
Federation of Labor had avoided.

But by 1923, revulsion with the Klan had reached levels where
it could not be ignored. In February, Ohio State Chaplain William
O'Connor "rapped" Commander Owsley when he refused to
support that state department's resolution that "the Ku Klux Klan
is one of the dark clouds on the national horizon and should be
gotten rid of at once." At the May National Executive Committee
meeting, claiming "a feeling as intense as life itself with regard to
the passage of this resolution," Texas Protestant Henry Lindsley
presented a four-count indictment of the Klan. It "perpetuated
religious and racial prejudice"; placed "indefensible restraints . . .
upon freedom of conscience and liberty of judgment on matters
touching the relationship of man to his creator"; subjected "courts
and jurors . . . to improper and unlawful interference"; and—
Lindsley's most forceful criticism—"citizens entitled to due process of law have been and are being unlawfully seized, tried, and
convicted, without hearing, in clandestine courts, of offenses under unknown and invisible laws, and have received, and are receiving, barbarous, cruel, and inhuman punishments." Lindsley
admitted his proposal would provoke a "battle royal" at the fall

convention in San Francisco. But he insisted that this time the Legion ought to stop worrying about alienating a sizable number of members and declare "whether the American Legion stands for the practices of the Ku Klux Klan organization or any organization based as it is on religious intolerance and bigotry." But the Executive Committee substituted a weaker measure by a vote of thirty-six to twenty. It retained part of the 1921 resolution referring to usurpation of the police power and added a more general denunciation of any group or individual that "creates or fosters racial, religious, or class strife among our people." The roll call followed no discernible sectional pattern: Alabama, Pennsylvania, and Kentucky supported Lindsley; New York, Florida, Louisiana, and North Carolina opposed him.[62]

The split that appeared at the Executive Committee degenerated into a near brawl at the National Convention. The Resolutions Committee literally fought over whether to condemn the Klan by name. On the Convention's floor, Charles Kendrick of California demanded that the Legion officially brand the Klan as destructive of American principles and ideals, which nearly started a fight. He argued in vain that "when we stood in the midst of death and when our souls were bare to God, we didn't care whether our buddies standing beside us in that hell were Catholic or Protestant." The debate was frenzied; some Protestant delegates argued for attacking the Klan openly; some Catholics took the opposite side, as a Klan imbroglio would be an obstacle to the Legion's "first duty to the disabled." Other Legionnaires regaled the convention with tales of how posts had lost members because the Legion had not denounced the Klan; others threatened catastrophic losses if it did. Kendrick's proposal lost 815 to 142. Iowa's 45 delegates, 31 of 35 from Massachusetts, 11 from Connecticut, 10 from Kentucky, 9 from South Dakota, and 8 from Indiana formed his principal supporters. None of his California colleagues backed him up.[63]

The Legion's refusal to go on record against the Klan thus appears as a mixture of strategy and sentiment. Many, probably most, Legionnaires in their personal political activities refused to associate with known Klansmen and opposed them for office. In 1923, at the height of Klan influence in Indiana, the state department publicly declared that the "Klan is not regarded by this office as an Americanizing influence." When the outstandingly competent Frank Samuel moved to National Headquarters, the Kansas Department chose Catholic Ernest "Red" Ryan as state adjutant "to demonstrate the American Legion was not connected with the Ku Klux Klan." The National Convention that refused to explicitly condemn the Klan arranged for William J. McKinley, the supervising secretary of the Knights of Columbus, to appear on the program to sing the praises of the Catholic welfare and fraternal society. He emphasized that his organization had spent three million dollars on former servicemen, found jobs for 285,000 of them, and enrolled another 282,000 in evening schools. At the same convention, though, California's John Quinn was elected national commander: he admitted having applied for membership in the Klan, but had never actively participated.[64]

The Legion's effort to avoid a stand on the Klan and Prohibition illustrates both the limits of its influence and the nature of its strength. Although it can never be definitely known, most Legionnaires seem to have been antidry and anti-Klan. Yet for fear of losing a sizable minority of members and creating needless hostility among the general public and legislators, Legion leaders tried to conciliate Klansmen and drys. By realizing that its members shared an overwhelming consensus on two vital issues—"Americanism" and veterans' benefits—and disagreed on much else, the Legion brought its strength to bear precisely where it could accomplish the most.

CHAPTER SIX

The Crusade Against Radicalism:

The Red Scare and the Twenties

I often times like to quote Macaulay—"That America in the twentieth century will be plundered as fearfully as the Roman Empire was in the fifth century"—with this difference: that the Huns and Vandals that plundered Rome came from without its borders, whereas the Huns and Vandals that plunder America will come from within its own borders and be engendered by its own institutions. We have seen that prophecy almost come true in the past few years.

> *Americanism National Director Henry Ryan, National Americanism Commission meeting, March 12, 1921, 181,* AL

Turn deaf ears and blazing eyes towards despisers of our traditions, defilers of the Constitution, violators of the law, boring bigots, pandering politicians, bellowing bolsheviks, howling hyphenates, peace-at-any price pacifists, and insidious internationalists.

> *Frank Miles,* Summary of the Proceedings of the Tenth National Convention *(San Antonio, 1928), 43*

The American Legion is not only the strongest organization in the country, but unless we are careful it is going to be the most intolerant. . . . There is no question that in the early history of the organization we were the most intolerant. We decided who could speak and who couldn't; even in some places, they decided who could play a violin and who couldn't, and the Legion is still suffering from preventing Fritz Kreisler concerts in some communities.

> *Commander Edward Spafford, National Americanism Commission meeting, January 11, 1928, 22,* AL

WHEN I SPOKE to Legion founder Hamilton Fish in January 1986, the final question I asked him was, "What has been the greatest contribution of the American Legion?" He replied without hesitation that the "Legion has been consistent in its exposure of Communism." Fish thereby confirmed the judgment of National Commanders Ray Murphy and Stephen Chadwick. They boasted that if the American Legion had not led the fight against subversion, the United States might well have fallen prey, first to chaos, then to the totalitarianism that overcame much of the world in the twenties and thirties. Murphy stated in 1937 that "at last the American people are completely convinced that the Legion is a great stabilizing force." He warned that "there are encroaching upon us various beliefs and 'isms' which we would not have tolerated or even dreamed of a few years ago." Several years previously, "when the voice of the Legion was raised against various 'isms,' even conservative as well as radical newspapers were inclined to ridicule . . . the so-called 'Red Baiting.' " In 1938, Chadwick compared "twenty years of disorder in the rest of the world" with the peace enjoyed in the United States "under the wisdom and aegis of the American Legion." Referring to the committee established in 1938 (after many years of urging from the Legion) by the House of Representatives to investigate un-American activities, he concluded his speech by mentioning that Chairman Martin Dies "was kind enough to say that the voice of the American Legion was the first voice raised in defense of his ends."[1]

The Legion's self-praise for its leading role in opposing subversion put a friendly face on a campaign against "un-Americanism" that made the veterans' organization one of the most controversial groups in the United States. Keeping alive the spirit of the Great War meant mob violence against radicals and a limited notion of free speech that sought to narrow political discussion to moderate reforms within existing institutions. Although many Legion posts used illegal tactics to defend law and order, National Headquarters, prominent Legionnaires, and other posts rebuked them, even though most equated domestic radicalism with alien subversion. Nevertheless, out of secret sympathy or unwilling-

145

ness to alienate rank-and-file Legionnaires, the national and state bodies did not suspend unruly local units.

Legion posts did vary their tactics against "un-Americans" over the course of two decades. They could hardly beat up Protestant clergymen or Jane Addams as they did Wobblies and Communists. But they never questioned the notion that Moscow directed a vast conspiracy from within against the United States.

Legion antisubversive programs underwent a shift in the decade before the Depression. At first, the Legion continued to battle groups that had opposed American participation in the war. It took stands against pro-Germans and the pardoning of conscientious objectors and war resisters. The Legion fought the Industrial Workers of the World in the Pacific Northwest, the Socialists and Communists in the industrial cities, and the Non-Partisan League in the Great Plains states. Crowds including and led by Legionnaires broke up radical meetings with a frequency that appalled even the Legion's leaders and other conservative public figures.

After the Legion's campaign to keep Eugene V. Debs in jail failed when President Harding released the Socialist war resister in 1921, it modified its tactics for the remainder of the twenties. Especially under the guidance of Americanism Director Daniel Sowers (1927–30), it came to realize that physical persecution of radicals usually gave them publicity and martyrdom that aided their cause and seriously hurt the Legion's image. Instead, the Legion adopted the quieter strategy of persuading local officials to deny "un-Americans" public forums. When this failed, Legionnaires either attempted to refute their arguments or observed their meetings in the hope of overhearing remarks that might lead to prosecution for advocating overthrow of the government. At the same time, with Communism and Socialism almost invisible following the Red Scare, the Legion turned its wrath against "pacifists," who it argued sought to pave the way for a Communist conquest by disarming America. As radicalism became less of a real menace, the Legion found itself attacking moderately left groups that had passed unnoticed during the Red Scare in order to continue its fight against "un-American" elements.

The Legion's campaign against un-American activities began with its birth. The German Americans and radicals who had opposed the Great War received as little sympathy from the returning veterans as they had received from homefront patriots

during the conflict. The armistice of November 11, 1918, did not
mark the end of the mentality that had put thousands of aliens in
internment camps, sent Eugene V. Debs to jail for sedition, turned
sauerkraut into "Liberty Cabbage," and banished the sounds of
Wagner from American operatic stages. The Red Scare of 1919–
20 marked the continuation of the war at home.

During the Legion's formative days, eradication of vestiges of
"Prussianism" constituted one of its major activities. The Legion's
first national convention condemned "the resumption of German
opera, instruction of German in the schools, public performances
of German and Austrian performers, and any other act which
tends to minimize the German guilt." Legion posts especially
focused attention on a concert tour undertaken by the violinist
Fritz Kreisler during October and November of 1919. Kreisler
angered veterans because he had served with the Austrians; then,
after he moved to the United States, but before America entered
the war, he had donated his concert receipts for the relief of
musicians in Germany and Austria. Legionnaires in Louisville,
Kentucky, Ithaca, New York (where they apparently turned off
the lights in a Cornell University auditorium), and elsewhere
followed National Headquarters' suggestion that they take the
lead in "arousing patriotic public sentiment that would unite in
prevention of such performances."[2]

Legionnaires also continued to regard German and Austrian
vocal music, widely banned during the war, as "propaganda"
intended to spread "the most insidious form of Germanophilic
promotion." The Legion successfully stopped German Americans
from presenting programs of "sacred German songs" in Los Angeles and operetta in Astoria (Queens), New York. They abruptly
ended a projected winter season of German opera in Milwaukee
by symbolically training a captured cannon on Pabst Hall. Such
xenophobia was short-lived: as early as December 1919, the New
York County Legion sponsored a Kreisler concert, which won it
considerable praise for "good sense" and "intelligence." The New
York State Executive Committee also urged its compatriots not
to "go to ridiculous extremes" and argued that "good music,
whether it be by Wagner, Strauss, or Sousa, cannot and should
not be killed." While most Legion posts briefly preferred to "hear
our own singers for a while before we throw open our gates to
the horde of fat songbirds from the Rhineland who are eagerly
awaiting the opportunity to garner good American dollars," they

soon turned their attention to the more threatening radical menace. Complaints of Legion opposition to German-American musical performances disappear after January 1920.[3]

By chance, the Legion's final major act to combat pro-German propaganda provided it with the uncharacteristic opportunity to pose as a defender of free speech. In February 1921, one Edmund Von Mach, an impressive, articulate German American, asked Legion Commander Frederic Galbraith to speak at a Madison Square Garden rally sponsored by the "American Committee of Protest Against the Horrors on the Rhine." Falsely claiming that black troops from French African colonies had committed "unspeakable" atrocities while occupying the German Rhineland, Von Mach's organization hoped to sponsor a nationwide series of meetings to show how the Allies had betrayed the ideals for which Americans had fought. He also wished to encourage sympathy for Germany as a misunderstood nation that did not deserve to bear the full moral (and financial) onus of the war. Galbraith responded to Von Mach's request by handing him his hat, showing him the door, and exclaiming that "we fought this war to crush a domineering military autocracy which was a disgrace and danger to the world." He then planted a hundred Legionnaires with forged tickets at Von Mach's rally to ensure that the highly unpopular event occurred without disruption by outraged New York veterans, thousands of whom milled around the meeting and condemned Mayor John Hylan for permitting its occurrence. (New York's Legion expelled a former lieutenant colonel who spoke at the rally.) Von Mach's other meetings never occurred, but the Legion countered their possibility with a dozen well-attended "All-American" rallies in the cities where they were planned.[4]

The Legion's adoption of Austrian-American opera singer Ernestine Schumann-Heink as its collective "mother" symbolized its willingness to reintegrate the nation's long-established, relatively affluent, and basically patriotic German-American community into the body politic. The mother of George Washington Schumann, the great contralto had sung at myriad war-bond rallies and was a naturalized American citizen who had lost sons on both sides during the war. She then acquired a nationwide reputation singing gratis for Legion "buddies." The Legion chose Schumann-Heink to lead the singing of the national anthem at the Kansas City Convention of 1921, attended by the commanders of all the major Allied armies. She continued to appear at Legion affairs until her much-mourned death in 1935. Schumann-Heink stood for the rapid reassimilation of her ethnic group (with the exception of a minuscule number of Bund members who supported Nazism in the 1930s) into the nation's and the Legion's melting pot, much as her compatriot Kreisler had temporarily represented its estrangement.[5]

Even before the Armistice, the Legion had begun to regard the Industrial Workers of the World as a greater menace to the United States than the German Americans. Throughout the nation, Legionnaires, lawmakers, and civic associations made "unalterable opposition to all Bolshevistic, Anarchistic, Nihilistic, i.w.w. or Soviet forms of government" their first priority, and vowed to "stamp out Bolshevik Anarchy and i.w.w.ism," which many veterans viewed as indistinguishable. The hatred directed against these "miserable human vermin," as Washington's Senator Miles Poindexter termed them, can only be understood as a reaction against the symbolic and verbal challenges the "One Big Union" posed to the war effort, capitalism, local community power structures, and the Christian religion—all of which defined the identity of respectable Americans. For by the time America entered the war, the IWW, as its historian Patrick Renshaw writes, had become "increasingly conservative in its methods, acting more like a hard-bargaining industrial union than a revolutionary organization." Furthermore, with over two hundred leaders accused of and jailed for sedition, conspiracy, and violent crimes, the IWW was on the defensive. It had turned into "a full-time legal defense organization," a "grandiose failure" enrolling fewer than a hundred thousand members nationwide. Historian Joseph Conlin observed that it "was neither anarchistic, an advocate of the violent overthrow of the government, nor an organization which approved the assassination of public officials, [nor] a threat to the war effort."[6]

Nevertheless, the very existence of the IWW angered patriotic Americans, especially veterans. During the war, the Wobblies discouraged enlistments by proclaiming "it is better to be a traitor to a country than a traitor to your class." They promised to "resist with all the power at our command, any attempt upon their [the "capitalist masters'"] part to compel us, the disinherited, to participate in a war that can only bring in its wake death and untold misery, privation and suffering to millions of workers." The IWW therefore tended to shoulder the blame for many acts of sabotage. In addition to attacking the war and the "criminally insane," "raving mad" master class that profited from it, the IWW condemned institutional Christianity for its complicity in both the slaughter and the wage system. Once the Soviet government concluded a peace treaty with the Central Powers in March 1918, which released millions of German soldiers to fight on the western front, future veterans joined other Americans in dubbing the IWW "Imperial Wilhelm's Warriors" and refused to distinguish between Communists and syndicalists seeking a classless society and defenders of the traditional German autocracy. Both represented "hyphenated un-Americanism."[7]

The Wobblies shared a hatred of war and capitalism with the Socialists and even some Progressive reformers; what set them apart was their commitment to organizing the "army of transients without residential roots that could be hired cheaply when needed and discharged just as easily when not needed." These "bums" and "hoboes" comprised the migrant agricultural workers and lumberjacks who formed the backbone of what historian Robert Tyler has termed the "frontier economy" of the Pacific Coast, where the IWW was strongest by the late 1910s. Besides frightening conservative citizens by appealing to the impoverished, uneducated men who stood outside any residential community, IWW organizers themselves were transient speakers who could only reach their constituencies by "invading" towns and logging camps and giving form to the workers' grievances. As Tyler eloquently put it: "They entered an American garden as outsiders and outcasts, invited to be the hired gardeners, to be sure, but on the tacit understanding that they would not complain that the garden grew tares and nettles. Their very existence as hoboes and aliens, as well as the rude and heathenish doctrines of class division they shouted so loudly, made them a rebuke to and a denial of the cherished myth." Contemporary newspapers expressed the same theory from the establishment's perspective by commending "the heroic efforts of the American Legion to protect their communities from the contamination of radical ideals."[8]

During the Red Scare after the war, the American Legion replaced the "Red Squads" and vigilantes that cooperated with the Loyal Legion of Loggers and Lumbermen—a company union— as the IWW's principal foe on the Pacific Coast. Throughout the region, "leading merchants and professional men" joined with the Legion in a "war of extermination against members of the IWW." Stockton's Karl Ross Post took the credit "in the ferreting out of certain Bolsheviks and IWWs from our city," and San Diego's

Harry Foster recalled how these "rough characters" were taken to the city limits and told not to return.[9]

The principal clash between the Legion and the IWW, which sparked the regional campaign that practically destroyed the Wobblies, occurred in the small logging town of Centralia, Washington, on Armistice Day, 1919. To this day, the facts of what happened are in dispute. The Legion still maintains that the IWW ambushed unarmed parading Legionnaires, killing four as they passed an IWW hall. The Legionnaires forced open the hall in self-defense after being caught in a cross fire between the building and some men stationed on a hill across the street; the Legion then took the Wobblies in the hall to jail. That night, one of them, veteran Hiram Wesley Everest, was tortured and killed by a lynch mob. The Legion insisted its members played no role in the atrocity. Newspapers and public figures throughout the country seconded the Legion's version that it had acted with restraint and courage following the murder of the "returned heroes," and "unbelievable deed" perpetrated by "radicalism run mad."[10]

The IWW told a different story. *New Solidarity* wrote, "It is entirely beyond reason to suppose that eight or ten men would deliberately agree to station themselves for the sole purpose of firing on paraders from whom they had nothing to fear." The paper charged that "the truth regarding what actually happened at Centralia on Armistice Day is being suppressed. Facts considered favorable to the accused are not allowed to find their way into the news columns, eyewitnesses are not permitted to talk." In the course of a controversy that dragged on until 1936 (when Rayfield Becker, the last of eight Wobblies jailed for second-degree murder, was released), an overwhelming body of evidence emerged to prove that the Legionnaires had planned to attack the union hall, from which the IWW had already been driven twice in the past year. Warren Grimm, one of the four Legion martyrs, had apparently chaired a meeting of the Citizen's Protective League on October 20. At the urging of the Southwest Washington Lumbermen's Association and other business groups, the Legion and the Centralians had resolved that the only way to handle the IWW was to "clean 'em up and burn 'em out."[11]

Moreover, the trial of the IWW members arrested for murdering the Legionnaires was rigged. Presiding Judge John M. Wilson had delivered a eulogy for the slain Legionnaires. Veterans in uniform attended the hearing, threatened the jurors, and spread rumors that thousands of Wobblies were lurking in the woods. Wilson forbade defense attorney Elmer Smith, disbarred for his vigorous denunciation of the proceedings, from introducing evidence of a conspiracy to attack the hall. Smith had to restrict himself to trying to show—which he could not—that Grimm had personally tried to force down the door of the hall. In May 1922, six of the jurors signed affidavits that they only brought in verdicts of second-degree murder because one juror would not vote for acquittal under any circumstances. They feared "that in the event of a hung jury, a new jury would have been called and in the face of the hysteria that then existed, innocent men might have been hung." Wilson responded to their recommendation for leniency by sentencing the defendants to twenty-five to forty years each. One of the eight commented, "He put on every year he could and then some. We didn't look for anything else from a tool of the lumber barons."[12]

Despite the evidence that came to light, an interpretation somewhat more favorable to the Centralia Legion can be advanced. It probably did not intend to murder any of the IWWs, but merely to drive them out of town. No other deaths can be traced to the Legion's anti-Wobbly campaign along the coast. If some of the Legionnaires carried gas pipes and rope (as "a joke," they claimed), the union men, who anticipated an attack, were armed with shotguns. And as Renshaw writes, "It was never proved who fired first, nor whether the firing began before or after the Legion began rushing the IWW hall." If the Legionnaires did not intend to do more than destroy the hall, did the IWW have the right to fire point-blank into a crowd? If so, did the fact they were overwhelmingly outnumbered and obviously terrified excuse them?[13]

Legionnaires throughout the nation had no problems deciding which story to believe. The Centralia post received over a thousand telegrams of sympathy and support within a day; ninety-three Legion posts throughout the nation pledged money to counter a rumored $100,000 IWW defense fund. The promise of the Theodore Peterson Post of Minneapolis to "cooperate to the last man and last cent in running to earth and bringing to justice men guilty of disloyalty" embodied the general spirit. The Centralia incident provided the excuse for a wholesale campaign against the IWW all along the West Coast, described by the Socialist *New York Call* as a "widespread plot to destroy the radicals by unlawful violence." In Oakland, Tacoma, Seattle, Spokane, and elsewhere, Legionnaires cooperated as special deputies with

federal and local officials to put an end almost immediately to the
IWW as an effective organization.[14]

The Legion's attitude toward the Non-Partisan League, which
fell heir to the strong prewar Socialist movement in the "Red
Belt" from the Dakotas and Minnesota to Oklahoma, was more
ambiguous than its passionate hatred of the IWW. The League,
like the Wobblies, had opposed American entry into the war. But
once hostilities commenced, George Creel, Chairman of the National Committee on Public Information, publicly declared that
it "had a better war record than that of many organizations operating in the name of hundred percent patriotism." North Dakota, the only state where the League controlled the government,
instituted what supporter Thorstein Veblen termed a form of
"agrarian syndicalism" and built state grain elevators and mills, a
bank, and low-income housing, while maintaining what historian
Robert Morlan has termed "one of the best" war records. However, other Midwestern states and communities used the antiwar
statements of League founder A. C. Townley and other leaders
as pretexts to bar the NPL from organizing.[15]

The Legion began objecting to Townley and League organizers
as "radical agitators" who "invaded" their towns and "endangered
the peace" after the war. Between June 1920 and March 1921,
Salina, Great Bend, and other places in Kansas forbade League
meetings. In Great Bend, a mob composed mostly of Legionnaires
tarred and feathered two speakers, rolled them around in the dirt,
took them out on the prairie, and left them to find their way back
to civilization. The NPL had its Legion supporters, however, and
Legion leaders reported to National Headquarters that as a result
of this "fight to the finish," the Legion was "being split wide
open." After a meeting in Salina where members of twenty posts
bragged of having participated in the mobbings, one post commander complained to National Headquarters that it resembled
"a meeting of Benedict Arnolds." The Kansas Department tried
to take a neutral stand by permitting members to join "either the
Non-Partisan League itself or any organization which may be
formed to fight it." But many felt too strongly about the League's
radical economic program to maintain such equanimity.[16]

Legionnaires uninvolved in the fracas appealed to National
Headquarters, warning that "unless something is done in Kansas
there will be no American Legion." Adjutant Lemuel Bolles
launched an investigation that revealed that perhaps half of all
Legionnaires in the region supported the League. He tried to

reason with those who did not by arguing that "inasmuch as the Non-Partisan League confines itself to legal political campaigning it should not be interfered with, but should receive the same consideration extended to other political parties." Strongly advocating a "hands-off" stance, Bolles expressed confidence that the "utterly unsound" economic theories of the League "will do the people of the United States no harm so long as they are simply preached." Kansas conservatives, however, found Bolles's orders easy to circumvent and organized "The American Defense League of Kansas," headed by Salina's post commander. With "more eloquence than accuracy," as Richard Loosbrock, the historian of the Kansas Legion, wryly noted, State Adjutant Frank Samuel cheerfully wrote Bolles that the Defense League "does not in any way violate the spirit of our [Legion] Constitution." By enabling Legionnaires and "all interested citizens" to fight the Non-Partisan League, the new organization would "keep the American Legion free of any improper action." Needless to say, the facade of "individual action" fooled nobody, although Legion posts frequently used it to combat undesirables without violating the Legion's "nonpartisan" mandate. Great Plains Legionnaires worried that the controversy cost it members, but the eclipse of the Non-Partisan League during the recession of 1921–22 and the Legion's subsequent strength in the prairie states proved its effect to be short-lived.[17]

The Legion had no doubts whatsoever about the native American Socialist party—founded in 1901—and the new Communist party, which consisted almost entirely of alien immigrants who did not speak English. Before the war, the Socialists, who derived their strength from well-established communities of farmers and workers, were tolerated and even respected by reformers in the major parties. But unlike their European counterparts, the American Socialists vigorously opposed World War I as an excuse for capitalists to reap windfall profits and oppress the working class. This provoked a nationwide crusade against them. The party chairman, Eugene V. Debs, sentenced to ten years in federal prison for sedition, symbolized opposition to the war more than any other American. He won almost a million votes in the 1920 presidential election while incarcerated. Although their stand against the war, and the persecution it engendered, cost them much support, especially in the "Red Belt," postwar Socialists still competed significantly in elections in such cities as New York,

Milwaukee, Cincinnati, Schenectady, and Reading, Pennsylvania.[18]

Eastern and Midwestern Legionnaires had as little difficulty in crushing Socialists and Communists as their West Coast comrades did in attacking the Wobblies. In 1919 and 1920, Legionnaires raided Communist party headquarters in Columbus, Ohio, attacked Socialist halls in Cincinnati and St. Louis, and silenced Socialist speakers in Philadelphia and Springfield, Massachusetts. They rallied to prevent Socialist Congressman Victor Berger from addressing crowds in Milwaukee, the Bronx, and Providence, and broke up a meeting of Young Socialists in Bayonne, New Jersey. In Reading, Pennsylvania, which boasted perhaps the strongest Socialist movement in the United States from the late 1890s until the 1940s, five thousand Legionnaires gathered in a futile effort to prevent James Maurer, the influential president of the State Federation of Labor and Socialist leader, from organizing workers.[19]

Mob incidents against Socialists involving Legionnaires, when added to those against the IWW, Non-Partisan League, and others, were so numerous that the American Civil Liberties Union despaired of counting them. Many attacks went unreported: "Information about the lawless practices of various local posts is quite meager," the ACLU noted. "Newspapers as a rule are unsatisfactory." To call attention to the magnitude of the problem, in July 1921 the ACLU confronted the Legion with a list of fifty selected documented "crimes," charging that "usually it is against the poor, the weak, those whom they know to be hopelessly unpopular minorities, that the presumably gallant defenders of the Constitution have raised their hands." Since National Commander D'Olier and former President Taft had also criticized the veterans for breaking the law in order to preserve it, National Headquarters wrote to every accused post to demonstrate disapproval of such violence.[20]

The posts' responses showed that, as during the war, grassroots vigilantism both preceded and exceeded the desires of leaders who in principle were quite happy to see radicalism routed. The replies ran the gamut from denials Legion men were involved at all (Ithaca, New York, Oakland, San Francisco), to insistence that far from threatening violence, the Legion kept law and order (Centralia, Washington and Jamestown, New York), to maintaining that the Legion acted as deputies for the duly constituted authorities (Oneida, New York). In general, posts denied involvement or refused to take responsibility for members "acting as individuals." The reply of Ohio Legionnaires after the Communist Labor party sued the Ohio Legion and the Bentley Post of Cincinnati for damages resulting from the destruction of their state headquarters is typical: "Some members of the Legion, without any action having been taken by the Bentley·Post or by these headquarters, raided radical headquarters . . . and destroyed literature which was really seditious in its nature. No resistance was offered by any of the radicals or by local authorities. In fact policemen were present and looked on." Acting during the Red Scare as incensed representatives of their communities, few Legionnaires could muster much sympathy for victims of the hysteria on libertarian grounds.[21]

The Red Scare of 1919 and 1920, and the Legion's prominent role in it, raises two significant if unanswerable questions. How important was wartime and postwar repression in thwarting American radicalism? How significant a role did the Legion play? It is possible to argue, as has Aileen Kraditor, that prewar American radicalism never amounted to much, and that as the major political parties began to champion the practical welfare reforms and business regulations favored by the Socialists, the nation's lack of commitment to the latter's collectivist ideology became apparent. The prosperity of the twenties, especially in the cities, can also be credited with the decline of left-wing protest. Yet both Legion and public officials thought otherwise, as does James Weinstein, a historian sympathetic to radicalism who believes it was crushed during the war and the Red Scare. Commander D'Olier agreed that "during these days of unrest and readjustment, the American Legion and the stand of the ex-serviceman for law and order is the greatest insurance policy our nation could possibly have." The Socialists still retained considerable strength in 1920 despite four years of intense persecution. Had not the trials, deportations, and departures of such leaders as Emma Goldman and Big Bill Haywood occurred, the 1921–22 recession (when unemployment temporarily reached 16 percent), the Harding scandals, and a divided Democratic party might have provided a good opportunity for renewed radical activity. A decade later, Communists and Socialists attracted thousands of followers during the Great Depression and elected a fair number of public officials. Economic troubles and political weakness in Germany and Italy in the early twenties reinvigorated left-wing parties there. It can also be postulated that the Legion preempted possible veterans' unrest through employment programs and the launching of the Veterans' Bureau and hospital system. Unlike their European counterparts, American veterans received most of what they wanted through democratic means. In short, it is difficult to deny that the combination of Legion vigilantism and veterans' benefits aided appreciably in almost totally eliminating the American left during the twenties.[22]

By the time the Civil Liberties Union officially proclaimed the Legion's misdeeds in 1921, the Red Scare had ended. Although the ACLU continued to brand the Legion as "the most active agency in intolerance and repression in the United States," incidents in which Legionnaires took the law into their own hands rarely occurred for a decade. Instead, the Legion tried to preempt radical organizing through legislation. With the Legion's sponsorship or blessing, states passed criminal-syndicalism and antisedition laws "to rid our country of this scum who hate our country, our flag, and who prate of their privileges and refuse to perform their duties," as John Thomas Taylor argued in unsuccessfully urging the federal government to enact a peacetime sedition bill. But as radical activity subsided the Legion saw little need to resort to violence. The widespread adoption of legislation outlawing advocacy of overthrowing the government by force, however, indicated Americans in general preferred the Legion's brand of Americanism to the ACLU's.[23]

With radicalism nearly defunct by 1921, the Legion turned to symbolic issues to "keep the spirit of the Great War alive." Perhaps no other issue so aroused "the patriotism that burns in the hearts of men and women in the Legion" as whether the federal government should pardon the 168 war resisters still in jail for violating the federal Sedition and Espionage Acts. The release of these political prisoners generated a lively controversy until President Coolidge pardoned the last of those in federal prisons on December 15, 1923.[24]

For its first five years, keeping the dissidents behind bars became a symbolic crusade for the American Legion. Special attention focused on the case of Eugene V. Debs, serving a ten-year sentence for publicly blaming the war on a "master class" whose destruction he predicted following a Socialist sweep into power.[25]

Legionnaires used several arguments to oppose the release of Debs and his fellow prisoners. First, they insisted that any sign of mercy would betray those who had sacrificed their lives and health in the common cause. Commander Galbraith approvingly forwarded to President Harding the opinion of one Arch C. Clump, who declared Debs's pardon would be "the most un-American act committed since the days of Benedict Arnold," a "rank injustice to not only the boys who were in the army in 1917, but to the parents and friends who suffered the loss of them." In his Thanksgiving telegram (1921) to Harding, Commander Hanford MacNider insisted that "if pardon is granted to Debs or others fairly and justly convicted of treason or sedition during a time when the nation's very life was at stake, the lives of those American boys who lie on the fields of France and those who lie broken in the hospitals and homes of this country have been uselessly sacrificed and our blood has been given in vain."[26]

Aside from a just loyalty owed both living and fallen comrades, the Legion insisted that if Debs and his ilk did not stay behind bars a disastrous precedent would be set. Kentucky Adjutant Emmett O'Neal wrote, "We are fighting now to hold slackers and draft dodgers to strict accountability in order that similar laws in the future may not be considered unworthy of observance. . . . We are making patriotism and loyalty to our country in times of war a pretty compliment rather than a stern necessity." Commander John Quinn cabled the *New York World* concerning Coolidge's 1923 pardons that "I cannot but wonder what the effect will be on the next generation. Suppose another war were imminent. Would the radical, cowardly, unpatriotic, and alien groups within our nation choose service in the armed forces or would they choose spending a limited time in jail?"[27]

Third, the Legion insisted that "reds, pinks, yellows, traitors, IWWs, anarchists, and seditionists," "the full force of destructive radicalism," instigated the whole movement to free the prisoners. Taylor went so far as to claim that "if punishment for traitors can be abolished, recruits for a great revolution would not be so difficult to obtain." When President Wilson's own secretaries of war and labor, his attorney general, and sometime Legion allies Samuel Gompers and the AFL came out in favor of pardons, the Legion termed them "misguided . . . servants of the enemies of the republic."[28]

The Legion did not hesitate to use varying degrees of pressure to silence those who urged pardons. In November 1919, two thousand Legionnaires forced the mayor of Reading to prohibit a protest meeting calling for Debs's release, as "bloodshed" would be the inevitable result. The Legion also saw to it that the principal visiting speakers left town in a hurry—"the radicals recognized the only argument that would appeal to them, that of force." In 1922, when the recently freed Debs planned a nationwide speaking tour to organize support for those still incarcerated, the Legion successfully lobbied the Colorado legislature to forbid him from making a speech in Denver. In Long Beach, California, the Legion persuaded the mayor to deny Debs the use of all city property, including the only sizable auditorium available. The Legion even gagged its own free speech element. At the 1921 National Convention, Commander John Emery, after an enormous shout of "aye" greeted a resolution that Debs remain in prison, found no one accepted his "dare" to stand up and be counted against the "unanimous" vote.[29]

Yet for all the rhetoric, Legion Headquarters realized public sentiment was running against its stand as the Harding administration's benign philosophy of "normalcy" replaced the strident moralism of the Wilson years. While National Commanders wrote strongly worded letters to the chief executive, they sought to minimize illegal actions by posts and negative publicity. Commander Galbraith realized that "there will be a division of opinion on the Debs matter, greater than on any one of the other issues," such as the Bonus, disability benefits, or hospitals, which provided Legionnaires with more tangible proofs of national esteem. Commander MacNider responded to Legionnaires who accused him of soft-pedaling the Debs case by retorting "there was no use hollering when we were defeated" and by advising members "to save our strength for the disabled." With the establishment of the Veterans' Bureau in 1921, the Legion was placed in a situation where the give-and-take required by Capitol Hill politics made it sensible not to take extreme stands on symbolic issues.[30]

Critics of the Legion's attitude on political prisoners did not confine themselves to issues of free speech and the nature of American society. They went after the Legion itself as "un-American" and cowardly. Some, like Emmett Swisshelm of the *Baltimore Sun,* asked the Legion "who were the radicals, the rebels, in 1776," and questioned whether it was more "cowardly to stay home and fight against the brute tide of hysteria, to face the lynchings, the beatings, the castrations and clubs of 100 percent fanatics" than to enlist along with the crowd. Walter Liggett of New York accused the Legion of a "brazen disregard for law and order" by "mobbing musicians" such as Kreisler and "breaking up peaceable political meetings, and displaying a cowardly and contemptuous spirit of 'Hunnishness.' " He suggested that "instead of opposing the pardoning of an old man—a splendid spirit whose boots you are not fit to lace—that you devote your energies to hunting down some of the war profiteers and to curbing the large bully element within the American Legion." In their debate over the fundamental question of who was a good American, the Legion and its opponents hurled back and forth similar charges of disloyalty, endangering class harmony, and being untrue to the spirit of the Founding Fathers.[31]

The debate over the prisoners also involved an interesting semantic question, not unlike the problem of whether jailed Vietnam dissenters should receive amnesty (which implied they had done no wrong) or pardons (meaning they were forgiven for the wrong they had done). Harding and Coolidge solved the problem by not "pardoning" anyone; technically, they "commuted" the sentences of all "political prisoners" so they were eligible for instant paroles. This verbal evasion satisfied neither the Legion, because the "traitors" were back on the streets, nor the former prisoners, the justice of whose cause the government refused to acknowledge. In a remarkable legal brief on the Debs case, Harding's attorney general, Harry Daugherty, admitted that the administration only considered the case because of "the enormous mass of communications received in his behalf." He acknowledged that Debs was indeed a criminal, had materially harmed the war effort, and yet ought to be freed because the eight remaining years of his sentence would consume too much (probably all) of the old man's life! By ignoring the moral and legal questions the Legion stressed, Harding and Coolidge paradoxically helped accomplish the Legion's own end of minimizing the importance of American radicalism. Their peremptory "commutations" ended the last major dispute keeping the Socialist war resisters in the public eye.[32]

For the next decade, the Legion continued to cry that Communism and radicalism, although almost invisible, remained a serious menace. It did so by equating pacifism with Communism. In a 1928 pamphlet, "The Threat of Communism and the Answer," the Americanism Commission explained how the subtle Bolsheviki manipulated well-meaning if soft-headed individuals "under the guise of idealism and liberalism." "At the present time, notorious proponents of radicalism are being financed throughout the country to organize youth under various camouflages into Liberal Clubs, Student Forums, Conferences, etc. for the sole purpose of creating unrest and discontent," the Commission wrote. "Our premise is that the large percentage of those really doing the work of Communists or real Reds in this country would deny any association with the World Revolutionary Organization," Commander Edward Hayes told the United States Chamber of Commerce. But "the immutable, irrefutable truth is that they are giving aid and assistance to an enemy within our gates."[33]

The prestige of those citizens who supported the peace movement required that the Legion abandon the strong-arm tactics it had used with the IWW. "Our problem is much more insidious because the sponsors of it are not unlearned foreigners from across the sea, but those people among the most educated but dissatisfied among our own people," one leader lamented. Pacifist Sherwood Eddy, "a charming, brilliant, cultured gentleman," did not appeal to the "low classes," but to the "finer, cultured people." "Super-intellectuals," sneered Commander Hayes, "supporting forces organized to destroy constituted democracy," who "mistake academic freedom for academic license," used the protection of universities to advance a pacifist position and thereby aid in the triumph of the Soviet Union.[34]

Like the Communist party, newly founded in 1920, the pacifist movement marked another novel threat to the traditional Americanism of Legionnaires. Pacifism "never took hold in the United States until the aftermath of World War I, when a wave of disillusionment with that conflict swept across the country," writes the movement's historian Lawrence Wittner. The National Council for the Prevention of War, founded in 1921 and representing thirty groups, and the Women's International League for Peace and Freedom, begun by Jane Addams in 1915, maintained Washington staffs and headquarters not far from the Legion's own, sent out large numbers of pamphlets and press releases, organized demonstrations, and directed a nationwide network of local units, much as the Legion did.[35]

The pacifists irked the typical Legionnaire. The peace movement seemed to denigrate the man who was "regarded as a hero back in 1917," as the *Christian Century* explained. Legionnaires responded to charges that "war never settled anything" by pointing out that Americans had won the Revolutionary, Civil, and World wars and that "the progress of Christianity has always been at the point of the sword." Moreover, the pacifists were not led by the upper- and middle-class males associated with traditional community and civic structures. Besides "superintellectuals" (that is to say, college faculty and students), "the peace movement appealed perhaps most strongly to women," in Wittner's words. Through the peace groups, both women and young people could assume a greater role in civic life than in the male-dominated political and social organizations with which the Legionnaires were comfortable.[36]

Ideologically, the pacifists' ideals and programs directly confronted the Legion on several counts. In contrast to the Legion's affirmation of nationalism, the pacifists looked forward to a world government more effective than the League of Nations. They also believed that only disarmament could bring long-lasting peace, whereas the Legion favored a strong defense to deter potential aggressors. Finally, the Legion was correct in believing that many pacifists favored a more collectivist economic system. Left-wing pacifists believed that lessening inequalities of wealth would end the incentive of capitalists to provoke wars and would promote peace. The American League Against War and Fascism, founded in 1933, included Communist William Z. Foster among its leaders and remained close to the American Student Union, another group with prominent Communist connections.

Legion opposition to the peace movement represented the more restrained tactics it used to combat its opponents following the Red Scare. In July 1921, a "confidential memorandum" to posts and departments asked that all attacks from radical organizations "be entirely ignored." The Legion followed this strategy in refusing to oppose distribution of the antiwar film *All Quiet on the Western Front* or to counter the arguments in Marcus Duffield's *King Legion,* published in 1931. Rather than "giving them the publicity on which they thrive greatly" and "putting the patriotic organizations in the position of appearing to make a ridiculous ado about nothing," the Legion adopted several courses of action. National Headquarters became a center of information gathering on "subversive" activities and then passed its intelligence on to communities and posts throughout the nation. On a few occasions between 1923 and 1934, Legion posts still opposed their opponents' right to speak publicly. However, they turned more and more to anti-immigration and educational campaigns to strike at those foreigners and educators they perceived to be principal conveyors of "un-American" ideals.[37]

From its very birth, the Legion cooperated with civilian and military authorities in keeping them posted on which groups it thought needed to be investigated and prosecuted. As early as

1921, the American Legion News Service provided publicity to warn unsuspecting communities concerning agitators about to enter their midst. By the mid 1920s, the Legion maintained contacts with the Daughters of the American Revolution, the Department of Justice, and the armed services. The National Americanism Commission became a nationwide clearinghouse for reports on left-wing groups with suspected subversive connections. As the National Civic Federation's president, Ralph M. Easley, realized by 1924, the Legion was invaluable as "the only organization with which all other antiradical organizations can cooperate." The Legion also employed "secret agents" of its own to spy on left-wing groups. Their activities can only be guessed at from Americanism Director Frank Cross's remarks of 1925:

> My informers hold membership in various Communist organizations, but if they were to ask too many questions it would immediately arouse suspicion against them. They have made it a policy to work carefully, act normally, and absorb what information comes their way. . . . I have already asked our agents to investigate several matters.

Cross even claimed to have discovered Communist infiltration of the Boy Scouts, but said he could not deal with the matter openly without jeopardizing his sources.[38]

The Americanism Commission's information network operated in two ways. It published pamphlets and sent bulletins to posts and other interested citizens throughout the nation. These suggested radical speakers be barred from using their communities' facilities if possible or be followed by patriotic Legion or like-minded orators to counter their propaganda. The Legion's most regular publication on Americanism was the monthly *Huddle,* begun in 1928, which in 1935 became the *National Legionnaire.* The Legion also forwarded information on subversion from sources it considered reliable to the Justice Department, the armed forces, and local and state law-enforcement authorities.[39]

The Legion's activities led to charges that it circulated a "blacklist," similar to the DAR's, of undesirable, red-tainted lecturers. While Garland Powell claimed to be "the father of the blacklist" at an Americanism Commission meeting, both he and other Legion leaders greatly resented public use of the term. It was "not a blacklist but a list of men who were revolutionaries, men who advocated the overthrow of the government." However, they could not deny that the Legion would "keep files and send information" in the form of a "Bi-Weekly Report on Radicalism," which National Adjutant Frank Samuel claimed was "just a compilation of material which comes to us from various sources and was passed on without any comment."[40]

The Legion was prone to equate membership in organizations that admitted known Communists with Communism itself. It branded the National League of Women Voters a "radical, pacifist group" and "discovered that Jane Addams, Clarence Darrow, Felix Frankfurter, John Haynes Holmes [a Protestant clergyman and peace leader] are Communists, working hand-in-glove with Joseph Stalin himself." Otherwise, why would these people continue to belong to groups that did not oust Red members? By that logic, the Legion discovered that at least sixteen Congressmen and a hundred university administrators belonged to "interlocking directorates" of yellow (pacifist), pink (progressive), red-radical (Communist), and rose-colored (educational and religious) organizations.[41]

Even though the Legion for the most part stopped roughing up its adversaries after 1921, it still received censure from both without and within the organization for its broad interpretation of subversion and "Communism." As Jane Addams eloquently put it, the Legion had "no right to assume that because we differ we are not patriotic. To assume, in a country that has signed a treaty [the Kellogg-Briand Pact ratified in 1929] declaring war illegal, that a citizen who is against war and wants his country to use non-warlike means of adjudication and settlement of its disputes is unpatriotic, is illogical." Even a significant minority of the Legion's Americanism Commission, including the moderate director Dan Sowers (1927–30) thought many Legionnaires had become carried away with their Spider Webs. "How in the name of Heaven are you going to be able to stick the brand [of Communism] on the individual and do it fairly unless he admits that he is a Communist and subscribes to the political faith. We undertake to name members of various organizations and we are going to get into a hell of a jam." Sowers even discouraged strengthening the FBI, on the grounds that it might build up "a great secret police spying machine," and questioned Legion efforts to have the Communist party outlawed: "My ideas of personal liberty under the Constitution certainly could not be reconciled to anyone sitting in judgment on the legality or illegality of Communists or any political party."[42]

The Legion also rejected identification with some of the more extreme "red-baiters," as Sowers's predecessor as Americanism Director, Frank Cross, called "the chief instigators of the scares which periodically go out over the country." By 1926, Cross had come to realize that information from Harry Jung's Chicago-based American Vigilant Association and Fred Marvin's Key Men of America (located in New York) had to be used with extreme caution. Jung and Marvin discovered "millions" of Communists in America, including leaders of groups close to the Legion, such as the American Federation of Labor and the American Federation of Teachers. Marvin even suggested that Cross himself might be a Communist because he refused to take such accusations seriously. Cross in turn branded Marvin and Jung "utterly devoid of reason and principle" and "unreliable." They failed to realize that people who followed Communist instigators were not necessarily Communists, but "sheep . . . that were merely dissatisfied with their lot and ready to follow any medicine man that whooped up a panacea." Although the Legion continued to file data from these fringe groups, it did not embarrass itself by citing them to bolster antiradical drives.[43]

Although Legion vigilantism declined after 1921, from time to time Legionnaires still tried to silence their opponents. In January 1924, Legion posts in Newark, New Jersey, Springfield, Massachusetts, Hartford, New Haven, Stamford, and Bridgeport, Connecticut, and Wilkes-Barre, Pennsylvania, protested meetings held by radicals to honor the Soviet statesman Lenin upon his death. The mayor of Wilkes-Barre, who claimed to be "in favor of the most enlarged liberties of free speech . . . but not under the red flag of anarchy," even granted the local American Legion the right to veto any future radical meetings, if necessary by breaking them up. Legionnaires in Chicago protested to National Headquarters when former Canadian "Private" Harold Peat—a wounded war veteran—delivered his pacifist message under the auspices of several Legion posts in Illinois. Americanism Director Powell promised to put a stop to any future sponsorships, arguing that he had already made sure the "Pax Special" of antiwar speakers then touring the nation did not stop in "several towns and cities."[44]

Even in the late twenties, some Legion posts still could not control themselves. Chicago veterans protested in January 1927 when Professor Carlton J. H. Hayes of Columbia University delivered a speech containing "ironical" references to the American flag. Several hundred Legionnaires suggested the federal government prosecute Hayes for sedition after he analyzed America's "religion of nationalism with its own churches, images, icons, and relics." The Legion was quick to spot Soviet sympathies when Hayes humorously called attention to old ladies who kissed the crack in the Liberty Bell and the "very curious liturgical forms" attendant upon the "cult for worship of the flag." Also in 1927, the Massachusetts Department went out of its way to take a stand in the Sacco-Vanzetti case. In a "wild uproar" at the State Convention in Fitchburg, the Legion "applauded and expressed its appreciation to the Governor [Alvah Fuller] for his untiring efforts in the interests of justice" when he refused eleventh-hour pleas that he pardon the two "convicted murderers." The Legionnaires "clapped. They yelled in one big chorus. . . . They stood, then they pounded the chairs. Then the band played *America*," the *Boston Globe* reported. When the two anarchists were executed it was the authorities' turn to compliment Legionnaires, "furnishing their own equipment, under adverse weather conditions, and without remuneration," who patrolled the streets of Braintree to forestall an anticipated radical protest.[45]

Curiously, the only other state department to take a recorded stand on Sacco and Vanzetti was Texas, which became the center of a free-speech dispute the following year. State Commander Walton Hood urged National Headquarters to "prevent the parading over the country of the bodies of the two executed anarchists," which he predicted would encourage unrest. But National Commander Howard Savage, who appointed the relatively tolerant Sowers to his post, warned Hood to make no press statements committing the Legion on this still-controversial issue without his approval. Hood found himself frustrated again the following year when he asked the "American Legion and all patriotic citizens" to join him in forcibly preventing a speech that Benjamin Gitlow, a noted Communist leader, had timed to coincide with the Legion's National Convention in San Antonio. Hood falsely claimed that National Commander Paul McNutt had agreed to support this action, a statement that enraged former Texas State Commander and future congressman Maury Maverick. "I stomped and I roared," Maverick wrote in his colorful dispatch to the ACLU. Angry at "about Mr. Hood's sixth unauthorized blabbing on behalf of the Legion," he persuaded McNutt, "a liberal and a Legionnaire," "a lawyer and a gentleman," to rebuke Hood. Claiming to enjoy Gitlow's speech as "the first time I had ever had the pleasure of looking at a real honest-to-

God bolsheviki," Maverick told the ACLU that "if one Legionnaire or one self-respecting citizen stands against such balderdash and claptrap, Mr. Hood or other hooded masters would not get away with it." (Hood had been a "violent Klansman.") Maverick also jocularly urged the ACLU's directors to take a trip:

> You radicals spend all your time agitating in New Jersey and New York, all because you are too lazy to leave a small area. Why don't you come to the dark and dreary South; why don't you come down to the place where a real honest-to-God mob will take you and knock you for a row of telephone posts. (Come to Texas and get murdered.)

The Texas incident was not of major importance for the Legion. But it does show how strongly rank-and-file Legionnaires felt when confronted with symbolic challenges to the nationality they cherished in the name of free speech.[46]

Far more disruptive of the Legion were disputes with Sherwood Eddy in 1928 and the Federal Council of Churches in 1929. A pacifist associated with the YMCA, Eddy undertook a speaking tour of several states in January 1928. Obtaining his itinerary, Legion Commander Edward Spafford sent letters to department and local commanders urging that they try "to prevent his speaking, and failing in that, to see that he is followed up with a good speaker who will instill a little radical nationalism." Although Spafford tried his best "to treat this whole thing rather confidentially" and to avoid any "public propaganda," copies of his circular letters became public—Eddy published them with the names of the addressees deleted in the *Christian Century* on March 1, 1928. Legion pressure had proven instrumental in the cancellation of all Eddy's engagements in Kentucky and three out of six in North Carolina, despite the vehement denials of North Carolina Commander Albert Cox that the Legion had taken a hand.[47]

Prominent Legionnaires joined others in protesting Spafford's heavy-handed tactics. A Baptist minister and Legionnaire from Raleigh, North Carolina, who claimed to "love" the "splendid company of American citizens" in the Legion, objected that "an honest clean American citizen, whose convictions lead him to the pacifist position should have the same right to express his views . . . as a militarist." State Commander John Pipkin of Arkansas expressed "chagrin" over the episode, and feared that the Legion would acquire "the reputation of not standing for the Constitutional rights of freedom of speech," which would "quickly and justly lose it the respect of all intelligent and fearless lovers of human liberty."[48]

Challenged to explain or apologize for his actions, Spafford only became more belligerent. "I did not object to him speaking, but that I didn't like to have Americans listening to him," he replied to one critic. Arguing that wartime standards of free speech ought to apply in peacetime as well, he told Pipkin that "all I tried to do was to discourage people from listening to the words of a man which, if said in time of war, would place that man against a wall before a firing squad." To a psychology professor who accused the Legion of stooping "to the methods of the Ku Klux Klan," Spafford went so far as to argue that those who did not favor strong military preparedness in fact "advocated the murder of our next generation." Spafford remained "proud" of his stand to the end; as late as 1944, the Legion continued to send out information criticizing Eddy as a "radical pacifist" with close links to Communists.[49]

The year after the Eddy imbroglio, Commander O. L. Bodenhamer became the embarrassed opponent of the Federal Council of Churches, an organization founded in 1908 to publicize and lobby for the major Protestant denominations. (Methodist, Presbyterian, Baptist, Friends, Lutheran, and Episcopalian were among the twenty-seven associated churches it represented.) At its 1929 Convention in Louisville, the Legion called upon a United States Senate committee investigating lobbying to look into the Council and nine other groups "engaged in the dissemination of propaganda and the use of other insidious means to hinder and defeat" national defense. While the Council and the Legion clashed on such issues as compulsory ROTC, required military training in high schools, and arms reductions, Legionnaire and Council fundraiser Charles Cole was not alone in calling attention to the "insult" such "an absolutely absurd" allegation offered to the thousands of Legionnaires who belonged to these denominations. The Legion, he said, thereby grouped the Protestant churches with such "crazy" organizations as the Society for the Advancement of Atheism, the League for Industrial Democracy, and the Young Pioneers as possible "Communist fronts" receiving tainted money. Charles MacFarland, general secretary of the Council, had a lot of fun with the Legion's resolution. "Noting with pleasure" that the Legion suggested an investigation, he thought the Senate might be too busy, and in a much-publicized story invited the Legion itself to look into his group. Commander

Bodenhamer could only reply that the Legion convention had authorized the Senate, not the Legion, to do so. His efforts to come up with some hidden left-wing connections among the Council's leaders only revealed the by-no-means-earthshaking news that many of them belonged to the Anti-Saloon League! The Legion soon dropped this resolution, one of many passed without much thought in the midst of its annual convention ballyhoo.[50]

The Legion's run-in with the major Protestant denominations reveals how hard pressed it was in the late twenties to "keep the Spirit of the Great War Alive" by hunting for subversives. Efforts to equate Communism with pacifism stretched the facts too far and were of little national interest during the prosperous Roaring Twenties.

Such extreme charges failed to thin the Legion's ranks. It recouped its declining membership after 1924 thanks to its good work for veterans, community-service programs, and the absence of the Bonus controversy. Also, it is doubtful that many Legionnaires worried much about civil liberties. Time after time, local posts ignored admonitions from higher up to restrain themselves to legal action and plausible targets.

However, when serious unrest finally emerged during the Great Depression, the Legion's crusade against pacifists and its broad definition of fellow travelers assumed a retrospective importance. By preserving the belief that an almost invisible domestic radicalism seriously menaced social stability in an age of "normalcy," the Legion could link renewed labor unrest with a continuous stream of subversion dating back to the world war. Despite moderating its tactics in the late twenties, the Legion never lost its basic consensus on this point. Once it faced union and Communist organizers in the thirties, the Legion did not hesitate to use the same tactics it had used to destroy the IWW.

CHAPTER SEVEN

Veterans' Benefits and Adjusted Compensation

The fight being made on the Adjusted Compensation is simply an incident and an indication of the present condition. It really represents the struggle between the common man and those elements, which for a better term, we refer to as big business or the vested interests. In the last analysis, it is a struggle between human rights and property rights, and that to me is the great issue which America must decide in the next few years if we are to continue our forward progress. At times it does seem that the reactionary elements have the upper hand. To one who loves his country and respects his government as a vehicle for the greater happiness of mankind, it is a saddening thing to note how difficult it is for humanity to make real progress.

National Adjutant Lemuel Bolles to Commander Hanford MacNider, February 17, 1922, History—Iowa—MacNider file, AL

It is a fight between "Main Street" and "Wall Street."

John Thomas Taylor, A History of the Adjusted Compensation Legislation *(Indianapolis, 1921), 25*

B Y THE EARLY 1930s, attacks on the American Legion and the "Billions for Veterans" it had obtained through "The Veteran Racket"—to quote the titles of two representative articles in *Current History* and the *Atlantic Monthly*—commanded nationwide attention. The left, the right, the churches, and the common man all joined in "Scotching the Veterans' Lobby," to cite yet a third essay, this one from the *North American Review*. On the left, Marcus Duffield, the author of *King Legion,* working in tandem with the American Civil Liberties Union, compared the Legion's influence in contemporary America with "the ancient Legions [who] dominated Rome with spears and set up emperors at will." On the right, Roger Burlingame, representing a National Economy League led by Archibald Roosevelt, Calvin Coolidge, Alfred E. Smith, General of the Army Pershing, and Admiral Richard Byrd, argued that slashing veterans' benefits and the resulting swollen federal budgets was the best way to fight the Great Depression. Burlingame wrote of the "Capture of Capitol Hill" by a Legion bent on "tyranny" and "dictatorship." From the pulpit of Grace Episcopal Church in New York City, Rev. R. Russell Bowie mobilized sixty-one religious leaders throughout the nation to support his denunciation of the Legion as a "sinister and deadly cancer upon the body of American life." Privately, his friend President Franklin Roosevelt agreed that "it is time to tell the truth and show a little righteous wrath." And the *Boston Sunday Post* referred to the growing popular consensus in the Bay State that Legionnaires were "plunderers instead of patriots. . . . The crowd who raided the United States Treasury. . . . The birds who browbeat Congress into appropriating millions and millions of dollars for their own fat selves, while the rest of us will have to pay the bills."[1]

A glance at the mounting federal expenditures for veterans as the nation endured its greatest economic collapse lends plausibility to these charges. Veterans' benefits varied little through the twenties, once the Veterans' Bureau was in place, from a low of $612 million in 1925 to a high of $659 million in 1930 for all years between 1922 and 1930. Then they rose to $733 million in 1931, $813 million in 1932, and $805 million in 1933. Given rising government expenditures during the Hoover administration,

171

however, veterans payments continued to fluctuate within a narrow range at around 20 percent of the budget: between 1922 and 1932, the lowest proportion was 17.0 percent in 1932, the highest 21.3 percent in 1927. As the National Economy League was quick to point out, the United States' generosity to its veterans of the Great War far exceeded that of its fellow belligerents. Using one of many inflated figures tossed around, it wondered how America could spend over a billion dollars a year on former servicemen when Germany ($298 million), France ($286 million), and Britain ($174 million) spent far less, although they suffered over ten times as many casualties. Pointing to the higher standard of living in the United States and the nation's greater wealth, the Legion retorted that America expended a mere 1/800 of its national wealth to care for veterans versus 1/170 in France, 1/700 in England, and 1/40 in Germany. Still, despite numerous recriminations over the accuracy of competing statistics, many Americans and even Legionnaires endorsed the *Christian Century*'s position that "the Legion has tasted blood, and its appetite will not be appeased until the nation is saddled with a pension system that will make the prolific source of post–Civil War scandals look like child's play."[2]

The Legion's day of reckoning came on March 20, 1933. Acting on President Roosevelt's pledge to reduce the federal deficit, in one day Congress abolished the entire structure of legislatively guaranteed benefits the Legion had painstakingly erected over the past fourteen years. It permitted the president, acting through Budget Director Lewis Douglas, to draft a new schedule of benefits on his own authority. Even after the Legion succeeded in having many of his original cuts (which amounted to 40 percent) restored, Veterans' Administration expenditures never exceeded $600 million between 1934 and 1940. They then varied between 6 and 9 percent of the far larger New Deal budgets.[3]

However, the Legion responded effectively that it had not sought veterans' legislation for itself, but for the disabled. It brought up the veterans' war sacrifices time and again to contrast with stay-at-home adversaries' lack of civic virtue. By keeping the plight of war-injured veterans foremost in its "constructive and conservative" program, as Commander Bodenhamer termed it, the Legion emerged from its great battles of the mid 1930s bloodied but strong, an organization that had fought sensibly for its constituency while not threatening the public good. Consequently, both former servicemen and the Congress turned to the Legion once again for advice in framing beneficial legislation for

World War II veterans. The resulting GI Bill proved the Legion's greatest triumph.[4]

Unlike their successors of the 1940s, who returned home to a completed, generous assistance package, the returning AEF faced the future without any immediate assistance except a $60 discharge bonus. They confronted an economy plagued with inflation, which almost tripled prices and wages between 1915 and 1920. Workers' salaries and businessmen's profits far exceeded the $30 per month that had been allotted the private soldier, and from which the government further deducted support for dependents and War Risk Insurance premiums. (Soldiers, however, did not have to buy food and clothing, as the Bonus's critics noted.) Even "Southern Negroes getting from eighty cents to a dollar a day working in the fields were suddenly raised to $3.30," Legion Commander Edward Hayes argued in an article designed to shame the nation into appreciating its heroes' financial losses. Eric Fisher Wood justified the doughboys' demand for "Adjusted Compensation" not as mercenary but as an outburst of righteous indignation that their sacrifices had become the means of noncombatants' prosperity:

> The Bonus was probably an unsound proposition from a national point of view. But by God, settling every strike in a war plant during *war* by raising wages of home stayers $2 or $3 a day every time workers stopped sending us ships and arms had been a damned sight unsounder. Maybe two wrongs don't make a right. But that was the way most of us came to feel about it.[5]

However, labor garnered but a small fraction of the Legion's wrath for its wartime good fortune. The veterans saved their choicest epithets for the conflict's greatest beneficiaries, the "powerful selfish interests," that "slacker division of millionaires" "Who Got the Money," as Marquis James entitled a series of articles denouncing profiteers in the *American Legion Weekly*. To compound the injustice and indignity, it was precisely the "magazines and newspapers controlled by big business" who "pounded upon [excessive] veterans costs until the subject became one of general discussion throughout the nation." "Many of those who opposed just benefits for the disabled," the Legion never tired of reiterating, "are those who did not share the burden of war in 1917 and 1918, but instead benefited by the war." John Thomas Taylor captured the Legion's attitude toward war-won wealth when he thundered that the war had made a millionaire for every cross in Flanders![6]

The Legion used resources of research, logic, and rhetoric in attacking Andrew Mellon in the twenties and the National Economy League (NEL) in the thirties equal to those it had used to denounce the Wobblies and Communists threatening "Americanism" from the other extreme. For instance, National Headquarters assembled "twelve classes of facts, figures, and explanations on veterans' costs, authentic records showing the motive behind" the National Economy League, which it branded as the "more or less secret (legitimate or illegitimate) stepdaughter of the Chamber of Commerce of the United States." Legion bulletins, speeches, and publications tried to present "conclusive proof of an apparent scheme to relieve the big-income group of 42,000" who earned over $150,000 a year and paid over 80 percent of the federal income tax that funded veterans' benefits, "by shifting the cost from the big federal income tax-payer to the 'little fellow!'" Arguing that disabled former servicemen would have to be taken care of somewhere by someone, the Legion played up the irony that the nation's wealthiest class would shift much of its financial burden onto the states and localities, with their regressive systems of taxation, at the height of the greatest depression in American history. Pulling out all stops, the Legion insisted that a mere eighth of the income of the nation's wealthiest taxpayers could mark the difference between destitution and comfort, if not life and death, for hundreds of thousands of its wartime defenders. The same amount, $767 million, it also maintained, was far less than the nation spent annually on such frivolities as chewing gum, jewelry, magazines, and travel.[7]

Nor did the Legion scruple to attack its adversaries personally. The veterans showed how many of the NEL's leaders enjoyed some of the nation's largest federal pensions: $21,000 a year for General of the Army Pershing, $10,000 for Admiral Byrd (as a result of a football injury sustained at Annapolis; it did not prevent him from reaching the North Pole), not to mention the $5,000 received annually by the mother of Archibald Roosevelt, the League's principal spokesman, "as the widow of an ex-President who died from no cause even remotely connected with military or civil service." By 1935, Legion Commander Ray Murphy could contemptuously dismiss the sort of detailed accusation from the NEL that between 1932 and 1934 would have filled pages in *Collier's* or the *Forum*: "The National Economy League has so thoroughly demonstrated to the American People that its interest in economy begins and ends with economy at the expense of the veteran that no good purpose will be served by controversial correspondence. . . . Your viewpoint is as twisted as the figures you quote."[8]

Enlisting popular support against rich profiteers who opposed veterans' benefits stood the Legion in good stead. Such tactics played to the same populist mistrust of the very wealthy that elected Franklin D. Roosevelt president. By focusing its attack on a small, unpopular, and clearly identifiable class, much as in its assault on the radicals and outside agitators at the bottom of the economic ladder, the Legion could again appeal to what may be described as middle-class Americans' classless vision of Americanism. "Equal rights for all and special privileges for none was said long ago as a protest of our people against the same influences in our public life that during the war profited on every side," Hanford MacNider reminded a Legion convention. The veterans' crusade for justice could be viewed as yet another of the nation's great struggles to achieve equality and decency for the deserving yet neglected.[9]

Besides capitalizing on the unpopularity of its adversary, the Legion won victories by demonstrating that it worked unselfishly for the disabled. Praising the extraordinary efforts of the late Commander Frederic Galbraith, tragically killed in 1921 in an automobile accident in Indianapolis, his successor John McQuigg pledged to continue the Legion's policy where "our first concern is with the disabled, and it is not until the program for the benefit of the disabled was well under way that the American Legion proceeded to lay emphasis on the Adjusted Compensation measure." Galbraith's speeches and articles in favor of veterans' hospitals and a united Veterans' Bureau served as a standard to which future Legionnaires could repair: at a memorial service, one speaker noted that "I have never yet heard the expression 'we shall give help or advice to help Legionnaires. . . . We think in terms of the disabled and of all the people who served in the World War." Legion apologists never hesitated to point out that most Legionnaires (90 percent) received no benefits. Following the drastic cutbacks of 1933, National Commander Louis Johnson led the Legion in fighting for a four-point program that would restore payments for service-connected disabilities and widows' and orphans' benefits. At the same time, Johnson stood by the president, pledging the Legion's "loyal cooperation" and urging it to "march a million strong into the battle zone of this struggle

for national reconstruction and economic justice." Roosevelt's
first nationwide radio address was in fact on the Legion's show,
where Johnson joined him in a plea for the same "splendid and
generous service" the soldiers had given the nation during the
war.[10]

Half a century after the protracted struggles over the Bonus
and the Economy Act, neither the sums nor the principles involved seem quite so monumental. Following an almost univer-
sally agreed upon GI Bill that spent $120 billion on World War II
veterans in its first quarter century, and a modified welfare state
that spent several times that amount annually on social services
in the 1980s, one can only marvel at statements like Ernest Angell's in the *Nation* that "drunk on power and insolent with success," the Legion's "treasury raids" constituted "a definite menace
to democratic institutions and free government." Yet in the twenties and early thirties the federal government annually spent only
between three and four billion dollars. A balanced budget and
even a substantial surplus to pay off debts were real possibilities,
and mainstream political leaders in both parties regarded federal
welfare programs as threats to the nation's moral fiber and capitalist civilization. As the first major national bureaucracy formed
explicitly to provide health care and financial benefits for citizens
in peacetime, a Veterans' Bureau founded in 1921 had to do more
than overcome the scandals of the Harding years and the preju-
dices of wealthy taxpayers. Both through its internal organization
and through cooperation with Congress and the American Legion, the Veterans' Bureau pioneered in the institutionalization of
an extensive welfare system for at least some Americans. Ironically, because of the large role the Legion played in creating and
molding the Bureau, veterans' benefits could be attacked during
the Great Depression for providing an economic cushion for veterans denied to other equally needy citizens.[11]

Much as with its antiradical crusades, the Legion's struggle for
veterans' benefits went through several stages. Between 1919 and
1924, the new organization fought for the veteran with the same
zeal it fought against the IWW. In five event-filled years, the
Legion obtained substantial disability allowances and hospital care
for the war disabled, helped establish a Veterans' Bureau and
expose its mismanagement, pushed a deferred Bonus (to be paid
in 1945) through Congress over repeated presidential vetoes, and
obtained presumptive wartime disability payments for large numbers of tubercular and shell-shocked veterans who developed these

conditions in the 1920s. The late twenties were relatively unevent-ful, as they were on the antisubversive front. But the onset of the depression and the unpopularity of newly legislated pensions for veterans with non-service-connected disabilities (*not* a Legion measure) in 1930 compelled the Legion to use all its skill to retain its hard-won achievements. It rose to the occasion by obtaining restoration in 1934 of most service-connected disability payments cut by the Economy Act and the immediate payment of the Bonus, again over a presidential veto, in 1936. In the late thirties, New Deal welfare expenditures and foreign-policy problems overshadowed an essentially complete and generally accepted sys-tem of benefits. Only the opportunity to help twelve million GIS readjust to civilian life after World War II again placed the Legion's program for veterans in the national spotlight.

In theory, veterans' benefits for the AEF should not have been a problem. The 1917 War Risk Insurance Act guaranteed all sub-scribers—the vast majority of soldiers—up to $10,000 in life in-surance for a pay deduction of $8 per thousand, plus unspecified but "reasonable" medical care and rehabilitation in the event of disability. Praised by its originator, William Gibbs McAdoo, as "one of the greatest humanitarian measures ever enacted by any government," War Risk Insurance was to have the added benefit of accustoming the average man to the benefits of insurance, as the policies could be carried on in peacetime at the same low rate. A further purpose of the system, congressional sponsor Sam Ray-burn noted, was to "do justice" by avoiding "another saturnalia of pension frauds" such as that which followed the Civil War.[12]

Nevertheless, the quick advent of peace before half the army could even reach Europe proved a mixed blessing for the some 334,000 men then in army hospitals and those who would later come down with tuberculosis or shell shock. "In 1919, when we came back our government didn't know we were going to have any disabled men and there was not a hospital in the country to put our disabled soldiers in"—so John Thomas Taylor would remind Legionnaires of the situation before the Legion sprang into action. At the War Risk Insurance Board (WRIB) in Washing-ton, "employees were crawling all over each other in the hall-ways" in a state of utter confusion, prompting 90 percent of the veterans to let their policies lapse. Without established procedures for determining the extent and nature of disabilities, "men died while officials disputed the question of the rate of compensation to which they were entitled." Hundreds of thousands of claims piled up as Legionnaires complained men received improper advice and ratings from the inexperienced personnel of a Bureau whose "management . . . has been chaotic and surrounded by red tape."[13]

The Legion wasted no time after its 1919 Minneapolis Convention in exploring remedies to a situation where, the *American Legion Weekly* maintained, "thousands of wounded men are abroad, some of them in every community in the land, abandoned by the government they served," thanks to "the crass and inexcusable incompetence of its public servants." Fortunately, the leaders of the WRIB were aware of the problem and more than willing to obtain the Legion's help in solving it. As its supervisor, Assistant Secretary of the Treasury Jouett Shouse, confessed, "the Board has made many mistakes, we realize that it will make many mistakes in the future," and could only plead that "it has had to do a work unparalleled in the history of this or any country, a work so great as to stagger the imagination." Robert Cholmondely-Jones, director of the WRIB, won the admiration of the Legion for his "courageous cooperation" in undoing his own agency and working with the Legion to create the Veterans' Bureau: he literally worked himself to death in his "labors to straighten out the chaotic affairs of the Bureau."[14]

Conferences between the Legion and government officials in Washington in December 1919 and April 1921 began to solve the problem. The first increased disability payments from a maximum of $30 per month, a buck private's pay, to a more realistic $80. The second created the Veterans' Bureau, which combined functions performed by the three government departments previously concerned with former servicemen: WRIB (in Treasury), Board of Vocational Rehabilitation (in Labor), and Public Health Service (in Interior—responsible for hospitalization). The Legion lobbied for both these measures. In 1919 disabled men from Walter Reed Hospital accompanied Legionnaires as surprise guests when they met with congressmen and told them horror stories about red tape and poor care. Within a week, legislation for increased benefits and streamlined claims procedures, previously tied up in committee, passed both the House and the Senate unanimously. During 1920, Commander Galbraith spoke throughout the nation about the shortage of hospitals, his campaign culminating with a dramatic speech in November about 450 stranded tubercular veterans who had migrated to Tucson, Arizona. Although as Marquis James noted "few of the men were actually sleeping on the ground," and most in fact were "being cared for by private charities," the publicity did the trick. Tucson built a temporary hospital, Washington sent doctors and nurses, and the Legion followed up by distributing a lengthy memorial "Directing Attention to the Situation which Surrounds the Rehabilitation of the Ex-Servicemen and Suggesting a Remedy." Criticizing "the suffering, the shameful neglect, and injustice" to which the men who had sacrificed their health making the world safe for democracy were subjected, the Legion painted a graphic picture of veterans as "objects of public and private charity . . . driven to refuge in almshouses and jails. Many have died and if immediate relief is not forthcoming more will die destitute, without proper medical care, without compensation."[15]

Completion of the Legion's program for the disabled required a special hospital system for the large number of wounded. Although the lame-duck Wilson administration failed to act on this point, the Legion obtained incoming President Harding's pledge to begin construction. Upon his inauguration in March 1921, Harding promptly launched an investigation of the former soldiers' situation, headed by Charles Dawes, that confirmed the Legion's diagnosis of the need for hospitals. In August, over the opposition of the Interior and Labor Departments—which argued that the need for rehabilitation and hospitalization of veterans would soon pass—Congress and the president had created a Veterans' Bureau suggested by the Legion as the appropriate way to relieve the disabled. Its first director, Charles Forbes, would supervise an annual budget of some $500 million, larger than that of any other government department.[16]

The Veterans' Bureau eventually lived up to expectations, but for two years its corruption and incompetence forced the Legion to fight for the disabled once more. Problems first surfaced, not with Forbes, but with Brigadier General Charles Sawyer, chairman of the Federal Board of Hospitalization. The Legion had argued effectively before Congress and the public that the rapidly increasing number of tubercular and neuropsychological (mostly shell shock) cases especially required the construction of new hospitals devoted solely to the care of these diseases. Between March and June of 1921, a committee of medical specialists headed by Dr. William Charles White of Pittsburgh had developed plans to spend a congressional appropriation of $18,600,000 to construct these facilities. But Sawyer, "convinced that the peak of hospitalization has been passed," suggested instead placing men in vacant beds in public (usually military) hospitals and continuing to contract with private institutions where possible. Only admitting that new hospitals were needed in New York and Chicago, Sawyer regarded the congressional appropriation, plus an additional $17 million voted in 1922, as best spent in improving existing institutions.[17]

Legionnaires were outraged. The Massachusetts Legion called for Sawyer's ouster: "with the actual war over nearly three years, there is still no definite arrangement for the proper care of our country's wounded heroes," it complained, and termed the hospitalization situation "disgraceful." Wisconsin and Texas, fed up with the delay, built their own veterans' hospitals (Texas's became enmeshed in contracting scandals similar to those of the Veterans' Bureau). Oklahoma's Adjutant protested to his state's convention that "it has gone too far when I see boys dying from tuberculosis in this state and no hospital provided for them. . . . I do not give a damn where they put it if they only give us a location." The *St. Louis Star* declared a "Hospital Emergency" in a situation where "many invalids are unable to gain entry to a government hospital." The paper's investigation found that "several hospitals are virtual firetraps, and that insufficient medical attention is available at others." Legionnaires in North Carolina noted that their buddies were contracted out to hospitals infested with "flies, mosquitoes, and bedbugs," with "many broken panes of glass."[18]

Veterans condemned to mental hospitals suffered especially. In Fargo, North Dakota, the Legion Auxiliary claimed to have "two hobbies: the first to keep our poor boys out of insane asylums," the second to "at least give them a chance to save their minds." The president of the Legion's Women's Auxiliary found "absolutely typical" those "border cases," who might be expected to recover their sanity, locked up with "men in all states of lunacy from chattering idiots to the morbid cases, subject to violent outbursts" or confined to hospitals for six months without outdoor recreation. Such men, "slightly nervous and upset by war experiences," would soon "become a permanent charge on the government." Only the "miniature figure of Brigadier General Sawyer, who donned the khaki in 1920," she charged, was "blocking the path" to hospital construction. She sarcastically urged him to leave his Washington office and find out what was going on, and wondered if his duties as Harding's personal physician consumed all his time.[19]

A. A. Sprague, the Chicago businessman and retired brigadier general who headed the Legion's National Rehabilitation Committee, led the struggle to insist that Sawyer stop impounding funds intended for veterans' hospitals. Sprague backed up his claims that hospitals were needed with the testimony of medical experts selected by Congress that the peak for hospitalization would not occur until 1926. "You have stated that these hospitals will not be long needed. Sir, they are needed now," Sprague exploded in a letter he sent to both Sawyer and President Harding, pointing out that the government "without a whimper" approved three billion dollars to fulfill uncompleted contracts at the end of the war, "scrapping temporary structures right and left." Why were the disabled singled out for "parsimonious treatment?" "It is almost unbelievable," he raged, that "having satisfied Congress that these hospitals were needed and that they should be built to capacity that we now have to reply to your statement that they are unnecessary." Sawyer's gratuitous charge that the Legion as an "outside agency" that had attempted to bully the government met with Sprague's withering reply that the Legion had worked out its plans at the request of Congress along with "the best group of medical consultants in the country."[20]

Anger at Sawyer came to a boil at the New Orleans Convention in October 1922. The Legion did its work well: Sprague prepared a 157-page report detailing serious problems with the Veterans' Bureau in each of its fourteen regional branches. "Strong men with tears in their eyes were cursing at the same time," shedding "tears of sheer sorrow for neglected comrades" while reserving "the bitterest words for those who neglected their sworn duty." Although public criticism, the imminence of the Convention, and pressure from President Harding compelled Sawyer to agree to begin construction just before the Convention began, the delegates demanded Sawyer's removal by a vote of 601 to 375. Sprague argued in vain that having reached an "armistice" with Sawyer, insisting on his removal would undo the Rehabilitation Committee's negotiations. Ohio's Gilbert Bettmann was greeted with "hoots, jeers, and growls" for suggesting that repudiation of the president's physician and friend would only alienate the administration and hurt the disabled. More emotional arguments won out, like Minnesota's Stafford King's description of "men who have died on the doorsteps of contract hospitals waiting to get in" and wondering why "not a cent has been seen" of $36 million allocated throughout the United States.[21]

Sawyer, honest if incompetent and thick-headed, was only part of the problem. The corruption of Veterans' Bureau Director Charles Forbes angered the Legion even more. Forbes began well, authorizing personnel in the fourteen district offices of the Bureau to cooperate with Legionnaires and medical authorities in a "clean-up" campaign to place veterans in hospitals and determine disability payments without having to go through the Washington office. But criticisms began to roll in from Legionnaires about the unqualified and uninterested office-seekers Forbes appointed to the new Bureau. As early as November 1921, Sprague was complaining that the new employees had adopted an "antagonistic attitude toward the applicant for hospitalization and training," while managing offices characterized by "delay, confusion, and extravagance." Forbes refused either to consult with the Legion in making appointments or to take its advice in removing incompetents. Legionnaires charged that the system had become a "dumping ground" for political favorites possessed of "one thought—the holding of their jobs." Competent employees resigned in disgust "on account of conditions being so rotten that I could not tolerate them any longer." They then offered the Legion "all the information they want showing that the Bureau has wasted millions of dollars." Forbes responded by showering the Legion with statistics demonstrating that his agency was spending over a million dollars a day, proving that the United States was "doing more for its disabled veterans than any country in the world," criticizing Legionnaires who inspected hospitals he had contracted "without the formality of first calling upon the directing official," and defending his appointments policy on the incredible grounds that "where a particular individual is necessary . . . and that individual possesses rare abilities and qualifications . . . he should be appointed as a special expert and not be forced to go through the civil service." One of these experts earned his pay by "keeping soused to the gills"; another earned $4,800 for two days' work.[22]

If anything, Forbes's personal irregularities dwarfed his subordinates'. Instead of following the White committee's recommendations for hospital sites, he traveled around the country, ostensibly to ascertain locations, but in fact to be wined and dined "by civic bodies of local boosters who apparently believed that through the display of a gracious hospitality a government institution might be forthcoming." Legionnaire Congressman John MacSwain, for instance, arranged with his friend Heywood Mahon, South Carolina's department commander, for Forbes to be persuaded of the merits of MacSwain's home town of Greenville as a suitable hospital site. Also, instead of completing at least *some* hospitals, Forbes authorized that the $35 million voted by Congress be used to begin work on *all* the recommended sites. "I can see just how far the funds are carrying us," he reasoned, so "I will be able to ask Congress for additional funds if they are then necessary." Presenting Capitol Hill with a number of useless, half-finished hospitals and then demanding additional funds obviously suited Forbes, as his then-undisclosed corruption could continue. But Legionnaire Sprague once again took the lead in denouncing these further delays. In October 1922, he attacked Forbes's "skillfully planned smoke-screens . . . to distract public attention from the real need" and accused him of misinforming the president as to construction progress at actual hospital sites. "Why is it necessary every time we make a slight gain in our purposes to carry out the plan which has been definitely agreed upon, to introduce some reason or excuse for not getting to the point of accomplishment," he asked, as "delays are little less than criminal."[23]

The Legion had already begun to learn that the delays were criminal indeed. While such congressmen as Lewis Frothingham of Massachusetts were demanding (as early as January 1922) explanations of huge rents paid by the Veterans' Bureau for offices, the Legion first learned of a major scandal in California that August. Forbes knew about it. He defended the payment by the Veterans' Bureau of $35,000 to the Mack Copper Company to prevent the bankrupt firm from defaulting on a mortgage it held on the ground where Camp Kearney, a veterans' convalescent home, was located. But not only was the $35,000 annual rental far more than the property was worth, Mack's contention that otherwise the bank that held the mortgage would throw out the veterans at the sanitarium was completely spurious. Even worse, the company had formerly employed Charles Cramer, the general counsel of the Veterans' Bureau, who later committed suicide when he learned the Senate was about to investigate the Bureau. After much soul-searching, the Legion decided not to publicize the California scandal, as the Bonus Bill was soon to come up for congressional and presidential approval.[24]

By 1923, however, the Legion was less reticent. It not only insisted that Congress investigate the mounting charges against Forbes and his associates, but in fact did much of the legwork that convicted them and led to a complete overhauling of the Veterans' Bureau. American Legion district rehabilitation chairmen, such as Augustus Graupner in California, worked closely and confidentially with the Senate Investigating Committee's general counsel, General John O'Ryan. Graupner uncovered such astonishing outlays as $65,000 paid to an architectural consultant to design a hospital at Livermore, $35,000 spent to rebuild a dilapidated structure at Palo Alto (which was torn down instead), and a $62,500 rental for a contract hospital near San Bernardino with an option to buy it for $750,000, which was "beyond all reason." Forbes probably made $300,000 on the Livermore site alone, Graupner contended, and added insult to injury by proving an "unspeakable beast" in his sexual advances to nurses while visiting the state, to the extent of hosting an "orgy" in Stockton. Nevada Senator Tasker Oddie, who along with David Reed of Pennsylvania and David Walsh of Massachusetts constituted the Investigating Committee, commended the California report as "splendid," rendering "my position and that of the Committee so strong that there cannot be any deviation from it." Each of the fourteen Legion rehabilitation districts furnished a comparable report, and worked closely with O'Ryan, the committee, and General Frank Hines, the Veterans' Bureau's new director, in weeding out Forbes's unscrupulous appointees. When the hearings opened, O'Ryan praised the Legion's investigators to the Senate and the nation: "I cannot speak too highly of the generous, efficient, and exceptionally satisfactory manner in which the services of the men were rendered. . . . To me personally, it has been an inspiration."[25]

When O'Ryan had finished, the scandal in the Veterans' Bureau emerged as perhaps the most sensational in American history. The sums involved were huge: in addition to overpaying construction companies and receiving kickbacks, Forbes sold over $3 million (some estimates went as high as $7 million) in bedsheets, medical supplies, and other equipment intended for the hospitals for a paltry $600,000 as government surplus. He planned to obtain much of the difference from the company fencing the goods. But even more shocking than the scale of Forbes's speculation was that the money was taken from former soldiers who waited for hospitals that remained unbuilt. In company with Secretary of the Interior Albert Fall's sale of navy oil reserves for his personal profit and Attorney General Harry Daugherty's illegal disposing—in company with Alien Property Custodian and Legion founder Thomas W. Miller—of German property seized during the war, Forbes's conduct ensured that the Harding administration probed sordid depths reached previously only under Ulysses S. Grant.[26]

In several respects, 1924 was a banner year for the Legion. With the honest and competent General Frank Hines in control, the first new government hospital since the war was finally completed. Over President Coolidge's veto, Congress agreed to pay "Adjusted Compensation" to veterans in 1945. The House created a Veterans' Committee, headed by Republican Legionnaire Royal Johnson of South Dakota until 1933 and then by Mississippi's equally sympathetic John Rankin. It fulfilled Louis Johnson's promise of "a legislative committee which ex-servicemen . . . will have perfect confidence in, to whom we may talk and state facts without fear that our confidence will be violated, and men who understand the detail work that is required." Thirteen of its first twenty-one members had served in the AEF. And Congress, over the opposition of Treasury Secretary Mellon and the American Medical Association, approved the World War Veterans' Act, which not only codified all existing veterans' legislation but granted presumptive service-connected disabilities to veterans who reported a neuropsychological or tubercular condition before January 1, 1925. This was a most important law: 80 percent of disability benefits ultimately went to these veterans.[27]

"All matters of distinctly Legion origins . . . are now definitely disposed of and entered upon the statute books," Commander Edward Spafford bragged at the 1928 San Antonio Convention. Hines backed him up: "There is no legislative problem either administratively or legislatively dealing with the care of veterans which the Veterans' Bureau and the American Legion cannot solve." By the late twenties, occasional grumblings about "red tape" aside, the Legion went "on record as having been impressed with the general effort of the Veterans' Bureau, their desire to afford the veterans every relief offered by law, and their consideration in every way to the American Legion." That over half the Bureau's personnel were veterans as early as 1925, and two-thirds by 1933, thanks to ten added points on civil service exams and the Bureau's hiring policies, also facilitated cooperation. Veterans' preference assured that slightly over one-quarter of all federal employees appointed between the wars were veterans.[28]

For the rest of the twenties and thirties, the Legion and Hines worked out an efficient administrative structure in which the Legion Rehabilitation Service functioned as a quasi-official branch of the federal government. About four hundred Legionnaires could appear before the Bureau and its regional offices in lieu of attorneys, who disliked these cases, as they were forbidden by law from charging more than $10 for prosecuting veterans' claims. The fourteen regional offices of the Legion Rehabilitation Division, each headed by a service officer, paralleled those of the Veterans' Bureau. In Washington, Watson B. Miller, who served as head of the Division from 1923 to 1941, was General Hines's match in longevity, industry, and probity. Total expenses for the Legion's rehabilitation program came to under $100,000 a year, of which the Legion funded less than half through membership dues; $25,000 came from some of the interest on its million-dollar Endowment for the Disabled and Child Welfare, and the sale of poppies made by disabled, hospitalized veterans—which began in 1921—through the Legion Auxiliary raised another $25,000. For this sum, the division handled in a typical year (1928) 38,000 interviews and 23,000 claims, wrote 121,000 letters, and collected $2.7 million for individual veterans, in addition to monitoring, introducing, and lobbying for Congressional legislation. Miller and his subordinates also handled emergency cases, such as saving the life of an impoverished Sioux Falls veteran's child by rushing him $100 worth of serum on thirty minutes' notice. They also fielded questions on such arcane topics as Confederate war pensions, when a certain regiment had sailed for France, tax exemptions for veterans, and whether veterans forfeited their benefits if they violated the Volstead Act (they did not).[29]

Each state and many counties supplemented the National Rehabilitation Division with their own paid service officers. Every post had a rehabilitation officer who was either qualified to assist veterans filing claims or capable of directing them to the next step on the Legion hierarchy. Until 1938, the Legion offered these services to all veterans. That year, however, frustrated that "barnacles hanging onto the organization" had exploited it for years without joining, the Legion gave men using its services the option to join or "handle their own problems." However, the Legion still provided free help to former servicemen who could convince the local post they could not afford to pay dues. Membership, incidentally, increased over two hundred thousand from 1939 to 1941.[30]

Thanks to generous depression-fighting construction programs by the Hoover and Roosevelt administrations that built additional hospitals, by 1941 the Veterans' Administration operated ninety hospitals in every state except Delaware and New Hampshire with a total of more than 75,000 beds, nearly half for psychiatric patients. As the number of service-connected disabilities declined, veterans who could not afford private medical care—of whom there were many during the Great Depression—were admitted: in 1938, only 20 percent of those in veterans' hospitals were treated for ailments incurred during service. Despite some criticisms, the ever-watchful Legion in 1937 rated the care "excellent and comparable to that afforded in community and private hospitals." Several veterans' hospitals pioneered in cancer, X-ray, and allergy research, in addition to psychological problems and tuberculosis. Such prominent physicians as the Mayo brothers volunteered part of their time to help the veterans.[31]

With the Harding scandals out of the way, as the National Rehabilitation Committee reported in 1926 to the Philadelphia Convention, the job of caring for the disabled had become "in the main a day by day grind to keep up with the current load, constant research and study to keep up with the general progress of affairs." Still, before the great struggle to retain established benefits in the thirties, the Legion embarked on two significant and successful projects: to reform guardianship laws for incompetent veterans and for widows and orphans, and to pension disabled emergency officers. A July 1926 amendment to the World War Veterans' Act authorized the federal government for the first time to intervene in state courts if the Veterans' Bureau believed guardianships for veterans and their dependents had been abused. Discovering cases where politically influential attorneys held as many as fifty wards, or instances where unscrupulous relatives had misappropriated funds, the Legion worked with the Bureau to reassign some 25,000 victims and to reduce to five the number of wards under the control of any individual. And in 1929, after a decade-long struggle, the Legion finally obtained passage of the Disabled Emergency Officers' Retirement Act, which permitted any temporarily commissioned officer during the war who was at least 30 percent disabled to retire with three-quarters disability pay for life. The Legion championed this measure on the grounds that it put the heroes of 1918 on a par with regular army officers, who were entitled to such a pension even if they had never seen combat. Opponents within the Legion argued the bill created an invidious distinction between officers and enlisted men. All other benefits applied equally to all former soldiers. Some 6,000 men received an average monthly pension of $140 from 1930 to 1933, when the revised ratings following in the wake of the Economy Act reduced the number to around 1,800.[32]

Legion programs that aroused little animosity were the Employment Drives it undertook whenever large numbers of veterans were out of work. In June 1919, Arthur Woods, chairman of the Federal Employment Service, urged the Legion to take up this task, then handled by a variety of public and private agencies. During the 1921–22 recession, the Legion put half a million veterans to work in three weeks with a nationally sponsored voluntary employment drive. In Kansas, for instance, unemployed veterans were hired to cut timber that unemployed truckers then carted off and sold for firewood, the proceeds going for relief. During the Great Depression, "thousands of forward-looking public-spirited citizens," including executives of the oil, steel, auto, food, and banking industries, put a million veterans to work during the Legion's valiant but futile effort in 1931–32 to combat the depression. Richard Clutter estimated that 80 percent of the posts in Indiana served as depression-era employment agencies. Questionnaires from Georgia and New Mexico for 1930 confirm that except for small, usually rural posts, nearly all posts were as active in finding jobs and providing relief, at least for veterans and their families, as they had been in 1921 and 1922. Even the tubercular veterans at New Mexico's Fort Bayard Hospital found twenty-two jobs for their healthy buddies, while a post with fifteen members in Dalton, Georgia, located two hundred. Commander Ralph O'Neil led the Legion to its first million-year membership during the grim days of 1930 by advertising the organization as "providing that contact necessary between the veteran out of a job and the man who has a job."[33]

In addition to its efforts on the federal level, the Legion obtained similar benefits on a smaller scale in the states. General Henry T. Allen tried to muster Democratic support for Al Smith's 1928 presidential campaign by contrasting his record on veterans' issues as governor of New York with the dismal scandals of the Harding years. New York voted a $45 million bonus for its own veterans, gave them absolute civil-service preference in some jobs, made available $2 million for veterans' relief during the 1922 depression, and foreshadowed the GI Bill of 1944 by providing scholarships to enable veterans to complete their high school and college educations. California Legionnaires fought for bills giving veterans farm and home mortgages at 5 percent interest with twenty years to pay. "It was looked upon largely as socialistic legislation," a bemused Commander John Quinn recalled in the 1960s, "but I shudder now to think how conservative it was compared to other things that have been accepted." By 1931, nineteen states had passed bonus acts providing $351 million. Four years later, twenty-six had veterans' preference laws.[34]

The 1930s ended the relative ease with which the Legion had persuaded lawmakers to enact veterans' legislation. The advent of the Great Depression and the ill-advised 1930 law authorizing non-service-connected disability payments put the Legion on the defensive. It spent the next five years fighting not only for the lives of disabled veterans, but for its own life and the preservation of a system of guaranteed benefits. Its substantial success in the face of the nation's greatest economic emergency and more general New Deal welfare measures testifies to the wisdom of the Legion's moderate course, which avoided the blandishments of such politicians as John Rankin and Texas's Wright Patman, who urged it to favor extravagant programs.

The Legion's first debacle occurred in 1930 through a typical effort to straddle a controversial issue. At its 1929 Convention, the Legion recommended pensions for the widows and orphans of war veterans, estimated to cost $12.5 million a year, as the only significant amendment to the 1924 World War Veterans' Act. However, when the Independent Offices Act, under which the Veterans' Bureau received its annual appropriation, came up for debate the following April, congressmen, responding to pressure from the Veterans of Foreign Wars and the Disabled American Veterans following the onset of the depression, added new benefits and pensioned veterans disabled at least 25 percent for a variety of diseases that surfaced before January 1, 1930. Tubercular and psychological disorders were on the list, but so were gout, hemophilia, rickets, scurvy, leprosy, and obesity, which could not possibly be traced to wartime injuries. John Thomas Taylor found that "the hypocrisy running through the whole proceeding is perfectly disgusting," as congressmen attempting to kill the bill loaded it down with increasingly less plausible diseases. The *American Legion Monthly* denounced these "costly and unreasonable" propositions, which it correctly estimated would cost nearly $100 million a year, as a hindrance to hospitalization and other aid to the legitimately war disabled and their dependents. Iowa Legionnaire Senator Daniel Steck forced Pennsylvania's David Reed to state on the Senate floor that the final product was not a

Legion bill. (In fact, President Hoover and Veterans' Bureau director Hines had secretly sponsored it to forestall passage of a bill introduced by Mississippi's John Rankin, which they estimated would cost four times as much.) Royal Johnson, who had introduced the innocuous initial Legion proposal, turned his back on the "Reed-Johnson" Bill, as it was popularly known, and eventually joined the National Economy League.[35]

Although the Legion lobbied against the 1930 bill before it passed the House in April, it made a serious tactical error by then defending it in the Senate and publicly over the next two years. Representative Chester Bolton of Ohio, a Legion ally, warned Commander Bodenhamer to get on the airwaves and "lose no time protesting." However, the Legion waffled on practical grounds: it could not oppose a bill that ultimately pensioned four hundred thousand veterans over the next two years. Not until mid June did Bodenhamer answer an exasperated Royal Johnson, who wanted to know what the Legion's stand in fact was. Authorizing Thomas to use the "barrage" to ensure the Senate passed the generous bill, Bodenhamer argued that "because the Legion has been fair and conservative in their programs and because of the shortness of time [Congress was anxious to adjourn], we are now willing to support if necessary legislation more extreme than we had originally requested." But while publicly favoring non-service disability pensions, Bodenhamer was furious at the Pennsylvania Legion, which had gone off on its own to lobby for the bloated benefits from the very start. Taylor, although securing guarantees that Congress would not leave for the summer until "our" bill was passed, predicted "the terrible effect the tremendous cost of this legislation will have on the news stories, placing the entire responsibility for it on the American Legion. The average congressman and the public generally look upon the Legion as the spokesman for the servicemen, and they are going to believe, unless we do something to correct it, that this bill was the direct result of our efforts and no one else."[36]

Taylor's foresight soon became apparent as massive attacks on the "veterans' racket" began to materialize in the public press. *Barron's* noted in August 1930 that "the American Legion regarded the new bill with amazement, then it hastened to endorse it. That, briefly, is the story of how pensions came to the American taxpayer." The *Literary Digest* found the Legion's espousal of the new payments the rankest hypocrisy. "The Legion approved, though, incidentally, officials of the Legion have been quoted in the press to the effect that the organization has constantly favored relief for men actually disabled in service, and not until they are fully cared for should veterans who left the service in good health receive aid." Critical articles told of football players and policemen who claimed to have contracted diseases before 1930 receiving pensions. "A veteran who, in 1926, fell off a ladder in his own basement actually received free hospitalization plus a 'disability allowance' for a broken leg," the *Atlantic Monthly* reported. Alarmed by VA Director Hines's reports that the government would be spending billions on pensions by 1945, the House and Senate appointed a joint committee to investigate veterans' benefits, which grew by 25 percent from 1930 to 1932. Also in 1932, Legionnaire Lewis Douglas won election to Congress from Arizona (a state where 20 percent of the adult men were veterans) on a platform stressing the unreasonableness of government budgets unbalanced to care for a select group at a time much of the nation was suffering from hunger and unemployment.[37]

The Legion read the handwriting on the wall. Leaders recognized reduced benefits would be necessary, and scrambled to limit and control the inevitable sacrifice. As early as April 1932, Watson Miller urged that the Legion advise Congress so that "the contraction should be in items of the statutes which all bear the least heavily on the disabled veteran group." When Franklin Roosevelt was elected president after promising to cut government spending by 25 percent, the Legion offered to help the administration work out reductions for veterans limited to that amount. The Legion responded to criticism by insisting that it did not want every veteran's check decreased by a fourth, but was proposing that an overall reduction be worked out, with preference for the war disabled and neediest. In the summer of 1933, Commander Louis Johnson attempted to mollify budget cutters by admitting that the Legion was not "without blame in the overburdening of the World War Veterans Acts with benefits which made it so topheavy that it was certain to destroy itself sooner or later."[38]

Nevertheless, few Legionnaires were prepared for the arbitrary and drastic "Bill to Maintain the Credit of the United States Government," more popularly known as the Economy Act, which passed on March 20, 1933. Proposed by the president and pushed through the New Deal Congress as quickly as possible before the Legion lobby could muster its forces against it—the Legion only learned of the legislation on March 9, the day before it was introduced—the bill scrapped the entire structure of veterans' benefits and left it to the president, or more accurately, to his budget director Lewis Douglas in consultation with General Hines, to work out a new one. Legion founder and Senator Bennett Champ Clark, one of thirteen Senators voting against the bill, wanted his negative inscribed on his tomb. The House was more impressed by the Legion's last-minute cry against "Congress abdicating its constitutional responsibility by granting to the President authority to repeal or amend existing veterans' laws," but the act passed there 266 to 138, with fiscally conservative Democrats joining like-minded Republicans.[39]

The Economy Act presented the Legion with both a fait accompli and the question of what to do next. It would have been folly to oppose a popular new president whom both Congress and the nation felt should be given a fair chance and a free hand in solving the greatest peacetime emergency in American history. On the other hand, the Legion could not abandon its traditional role as the veterans' champion. Commander Louis Johnson was ideally suited to reconcile the Legion and the administration. A Democratic politician from West Virginia who became Roosevelt's assistant secretary of war, Johnson secretly kept the president and his aides informed of Legion politics. Johnson opted for the prudent course of issuing a "battle order" that his men support the president: "The Legion has every faith in the discretion, firmness, and justice with which the "President will deal with this problem." At the same time, Johnson and his chief Washington spokesmen, Taylor and Miller, consulted with the president in March and April in a futile effort to ensure that the cuts for veterans were as mild as possible. On March 15, Miller and Taylor received the president's assurances that Douglas would consult the Legion before making his cuts. Roosevelt joked about his membership in three separate Legion posts and the Legion's and his mutual dislike of the National Economy League, which gave Roosevelt "a pain in the neck." However, Legion efforts to talk to Douglas proved fruitless.[40]

The new regulations promulgated April 1 went far beyond the Legion's worst fears. The Independent Offices Bill proposed for 1934 would have reduced veterans' benefits by $460 million dollars, or 50 percent. Half the veterans currently receiving payments, including nearly all the non-service-connected men, would have been eliminated from the rolls, for a total saving of $361 million on this count. But they were not the only sufferers. Presumption that tuberculosis, mental disorders, and other late-developing diseases were service-connected was eliminated, and disability percentages were reduced across the board. A one-legged veteran, for instance, who had formerly drawn $60 per month would have to make do with $20.[41]

Johnson and his fellow Legionnaires did not lose their patience. Much as the Legion's opponents had presented horror stories of veterans freeloading at the public trough, it was now the Legion's turn to scour the nation for tragedies, such as a Philadelphia veteran who committed suicide so his family could receive a pension, and to bring a legless veteran to visit the president. Taylor spoke to the president on April 12 and convinced him that many of the reductions were "all wrong," the result of misleading figures put out by the Veterans' Administration. On May 10, presidential aide Stephen Early notified the national press that following a conference with Douglas and Johnson, "as a result of the appearance of the veterans' representatives, it now seems that the cut in compensation of service-connection world war veterans with special disabilities has been deeper than was originally intended." The Independent Offices appropriation passed that June restored a hundred million dollars to the veterans, limited cuts for the war-disabled to 25 percent, and permitted veterans whose disabilities were changed to non-service-connected to plead their cases before ninety special review boards set up throughout the nation. Wright Patman, who at first castigated Johnson for not having opposed the Economy Act "tooth and nail," publicly apologized: "With any policy of stubborn opposition to the President, the servicemen would have batted against a stone wall of popular sentiment."[42]

Johnson's wisdom in not antagonizing the president was apparent in other ways. First, Roosevelt had the enormous advantage that the public blamed Hoover for firing on the Legion's "buddies" during the 1932 Bonus March. Second, given the gravity of the depression, many Legionnaires either approved of his policies or were nevertheless willing to make sacrifices in the national interest. New York's Department attracted nationwide attention by refusing to oppose the Economy Act in March. Legionnaires throughout America wrote the president of their support. The Oyster Bay, New York, post condemned "huge sums annually paid to world war veterans for disability allowances not caused or contracted in the line of duty." A post in Portsmouth, Virginia, praised Roosevelt's "courageous and progressive spirit" and offered to "volunteer in that great army of Americans who are ever ready to make any sacrifice to assist the government of the United States." The Versailles, Kentucky, post "re-enlisted for Service in 1933." Furthermore, many New Deal programs specifically aided veterans. Civilian Conservation Corps youth camps were led exclusively by veterans or soldiers, there were special CCC camps for veterans, and veterans' preference applied to federal work programs. The Legion was pleased at the massive public construction programs of the New Deal, as they included both veterans' hospitals and employment opportunities for former servicemen. The support of many New Dealers for a child-labor law won the Legion's wholehearted endorsement, as working children took jobs away from veterans. And the administration's "Buy American" campaign went straight to the heart of the Legion's nationalism. As a result, Louis Johnson confidently promised the president "the greatest reception of your life" when he addressed the Chicago National Convention in October 1933, while predicting, also correctly, that "your presence and example will ensure that we keep the Legion on the right road of conservatism and patriotism." Wearing his Legion cap, the president was greeted by showers of applause and ticker tape as he spoke:

> [I] appreciate the patience and the loyalty and the will to make sacrifices shown by the overwhelming majority of the veterans. . . . The first principle, following inevitably from the obligation of citizens to bear arms, is that the government has a responsibility toward those who suffered injury or contracted disease while serving in its defense. The second principle is that no person, because he wore a uniform, must thereafter be placed in a special class of beneficiaries over and above all other citizens. . . . I personally know that mistakes in individual cases and inequities affecting various groups have occurred during the past six months. But at the same time there stands out the fact which you know—that many of these mistakes have been rectified and that we have the definite purpose of doing justice.

As Roger Daniels has aptly noted: "The bitter pill at the heart of this doctrine—the veteran is, essentially, just another citizen—was sugar-coated with thick layers of presidential charm and blarney."[43]

If Roosevelt himself presented a palatable figure to many Legionnaires, the Veterans' Bureau and its director, Frank Hines, became the scapegoats for the cutbacks, the "evil advisors" who could be attacked when the king himself was untouchable. The Legion especially turned against Hines because it had wholeheartedly supported his efforts to consolidate the Veterans' Bureau, the Bureau of Pensions, and the National Home for Disabled Soldiers into the Veterans' Administration, formed in 1930. The honeymoon between Hines and the Legion had ended that year, when Hines lobbied with both the president and the Congress against nonservice disability claims as "driving toward such a stupendous expenditure by the government, the extent of which cannot be accurately estimated" and "creating a prospective burden for the taxpayer before we have adopted any sound national policy for dealing with the whole problem" of depression and employment. Hines argued at the Legion's 1931 Convention that veterans' benefits had been won when "times were good and money was plentiful," but that "with relief from distress being demanded . . . in many different directions . . . no one group can afford to put forth a policy seeking material advantages at the expense of others." The Legion, in turn, castigated Hines for his much-publicized assertions that veterans' benefits would amount to over $21 billion between 1932 and 1945. Much of this sum, they argued, would go for hospitals and administrative costs: "Do other department heads tell the public voluntarily what their departments have cost since the Revolutionary war, and then make a guess as to what they will cost thirteen years from now?" the Legion queried. Commander Edward Hayes complained of the bureau chief, claiming that "ninety-five percent of the Legion considered him unsympathetic," and John Thomas Taylor obtained some vague, unfulfilled promises from President Roosevelt that he would work for a "New Deal in the Veterans Bureau." Hines kept his job, and National Headquarters quietly buried a resolution from the Illinois and Pennsylvania Departments calling for his removal. Adjutant Frank Samuel realized the folly of further antagonizing the man with whom they were obliged to work.[44]

The Legion also vented its wrath on the review boards that looked at the presumptive war disabled to determine if their ailments were in fact service-connected. Legion field representative Bert Halligan complained that some veterans were completely deprived of their checks on the opinion of one doctor who had no opportunity to examine their files and was insufficiently acquainted with the diseases in question. He also found members of the review boards "caustically critical to representatives of the service organizations . . . their dominant consideration" being "to get the veterans off the rolls, rather than to extend to them the consideration which was the obvious intent of Congress." The Legion prepared statistics to show that, depending on the board in question, only between 23 and 59 percent of presumptive disabilities were allowed, and many of those were reduced. Halligan noted that the "colored boys" in the South fared the worst: only 10 percent retained their benefits.[45]

The Legion still did not give up, and in 1934 it won a substantial victory. At the same Chicago Convention where Roosevelt spoke, it resolved to lobby for a "Four Point Program" that essentially conceded the government's right to eliminate nonservice disabilities but demanded the restoration of the old rates for service-connected ailments, the return of some 29,000 presumptives, and the right of veterans to use government hospitals, if there was room, for diseases and injuries acquired in civilian life. Over Roosevelt's veto, the House passed these measures 310 to 63 and the Senate 52 to 27. Only the Legion's request to pension the widows and orphans of veterans failed to win the lawmakers' approval. John Thomas Taylor hailed the revised legislation as "our most successful yet. Our publicity campaign changed public opinion and that of the press. Legion history has been made in a most dramatic manner." Still, the review boards' closer scrutiny and the almost total elimination of the 1930 act's false presumptives reduced the number of veterans receiving government payments by four hundred thousand, or approximately half, with annual savings of over $200 million.[46]

The irony of whether such savings mattered as the New Deal ran record peacetime budget deficits was not lost on the Legion. "The inference that the budget is being unbalanced by the compensatory veterans' relief legislation is an absurdity when it is considered that the present administration has deliberately unbalanced the budget by some eight billion dollars," the president's nemesis, Congressman Hamilton Fish, complained in 1934. Fish praised the Legion for its "reasonable attitude," and warned the nation that "in these days of radicalism with a tendency toward social revolution" it would be wise to appreciate the Legion, which stood as a "bulwark of law and order and for the maintenance of the Federal Constitution." The Legion's own Rehabilitation Committee also wondered in 1941 why the veteran was made to bear the onus of economy "during an administration advancing other social causes at a rate of expense heretofore unheard of and unthought of in American history."[47]

Nevertheless, by working exclusively for the war disabled and not denouncing the president, the Legion was doing more than playing good politics. It was pragmatically refuting its enemies' charges that it was planning a "racket," or pensions for all veterans. If the Legion lost a quarter-million members between 1931 and 1933, it gained them back by 1939. It also emerged with considerable credit. "The behavior of the veterans in this crisis was admirable," the *Literary Digest* commented. "No rebellious outbursts took place anywhere. A bitter potion had been administered, but it produced no revolt. The veterans were staggered by the shock but they took their punishment like soldiers. One felt an impulse to lift a hand in respectful salute to such men."[48] As more veterans achieved practical relief through regular New Deal programs, the Legion's moderation stood it in extraordinarily good stead when it summoned its prestige to achieve an even better package for World War II veterans, the GI Bill.

The Legion behaved with similar restraint on the most controversial veterans' issue of the interwar years, the question of the "Bonus," or "Adjusted Compensation." It hesitated, changed its mind several times, and ultimately supported a successful measure quite different from the immediate cash payment suggested in the twenties or an inflationary scheme authored by Representative Wright Patman and endorsed by the Veterans of Foreign Wars in the thirties. The Legion's waffling on the Bonus reflected division in both the organization and the nation. Legion leaders and wealthy members frequently spoke out against the payment, as did delegates from such Southern states as South Carolina and Mississippi. They warned that a crusade for a Bonus would demean the Legion in the nation's eyes and interfere with its efforts for the disabled. On the other hand, much as various state legislatures, referenda, and the Congress itself, rank-and-file Legionnaires believed Adjusted Compensation both their just due and, during the Great Depression, an excellent means of stimulating the economy. If public opinion on the Bonus was divided and opposition intense, almost all the criticism came from the wealthy taxpayers who would have to foot the bill and the press they dominated (the Hearst papers being the major exception).[49]

Congressmen were introducing a variety of Bonus bills before the Legion's first Convention, eighteen before the end of August 1919 alone, over fifty by the time of the Minneapolis meeting that November. "There was no idea that I know of among the original men who founded the Legion as to a cash bonus," Theodore Roosevelt Jr. wrote; it was simply "human nature: if I ask if you would rather have $500 or not?" Expecting that something would come of the vast array of bills in the legislature, the Minneapolis Convention "recommended with confidence" that Congress handle the matter, only to find "that confidence had been misplaced." By February 1920, so many "bills kept pouring in upon Congress" that "the Ways and Means Committee . . . sent an s.o.s. to the Legion, asking what kind of legislation the Legion considered best."[50]

For all the surface enthusiasm for some kind of payment, the Legion and Congress were engaged in a classic example of buck-passing. So many positions existed on whether a Bonus was desirable, and if so what sort and how much it should be, that any stand was bound to alienate important segments of public opinion. Legionnaire and University of California president Daniel Barrows called it "a bombshell in the ranks of the Legion." Within the Legion itself, such prominent figures as Ogden Mills, New York State's first commander, argued that "I have never been able to believe that every man who defended his country and thereby performed his duty as a citizen of a free republic is entitled to a gift from the public treasury." Nor was he alone. In various parts of the country, Legion representatives reported that recruitment lagged because among the organizers "there is a bunch of the Legion which is out for the Bonus alone." In the South, especially, Legionnaires feared the effects of unprecedented amounts of cash placed in the hands of black veterans, who for the most part were sharecroppers locked into a system of debt dependency. At the same time it barred black posts, Arkansas protested that in endorsing a Bonus in February 1920 the Executive Committee violated the National Convention's mandate. At the Cleveland Convention that year, which did approve the Bonus, South Carolina's J. Monroe Johnson nearly came to blows with a Pennsylvania congressman who referred to anti-Bonus forces in the Legion as "the enemy within." Johnson loudly refused to allow a "unanimous" endorsement to go through.[51]

In Congress itself, the Republican majority wooed the former servicemen by proposing a host of bills, most of which had no chance of passing. Legion leader Gilbert Bettmann wrote of congressmen that they "fear to come out openly against the Bonus," "so they are trying to kill the thing indirectly" by proposing a variety of taxes to pay for it "until our American Legion has upon its back a tremendous opposition from all over the country." Nor did the nation's press, controlled by the Legion's wealthy opponents, hesitate to publish such statements by congressmen as "the bill is damned bunk, but the Legion demands it," and "the bill is an insult to every war veteran, a shameful disgrace to Congress and the nation, but I will vote for it."[52]

The majority of Legionnaires fought back. First, although they frequently slipped and used the word "Bonus" themselves, from the first they resented the term and insisted on the more dignified "Adjusted Compensation." As early as September 15, 1919, Commander Lindsley was proclaiming "the American soldier is not entitled to a Bonus," but that "there has been a notable failure to discriminate between the 'Bonus' and a service adjustment which would be based on justice." Second, the Legion successfully, and to a large extent accurately, defined the Bonus issue as a class issue. Theodore Roosevelt Jr. took the lead in explaining to his New York associates and former Harvard classmates that "the opposition normally comes from individuals on whom the taxes would most heavily reflect." He dismissed their arguments "that the United States would be financially ruined if this bonus were passed" as "trash." In his *History of the Adjusted Compensation Legislation,* distributed nationwide to aid Legion Bonus speakers in debates they were urged to engage in with representatives of the United States Chamber of Commerce, John Thomas Taylor went even further. Would the nation have been bankrupted if the war went on three more weeks, the approximate cost of the proposed bonus? He dared businessmen "to look an unemployed ex-serviceman in the eye and say to him, not one penny of my war profits goes to pay you a Bonus," or to say to a war widow "you can't expect my wife to give up one of her diamonds simply because your husband happened to get in the way of a bullet." The Legion was aided considerably by Treasury Secretary Andrew Mellon's fiscal miscalculations. He argued that the nation needed tax reductions and budget surpluses to stimulate a lagging economy in the early 1920s. But Mellon's insistence that the nation could not afford a Bonus rang hollow when 1922 produced a $313 million surplus instead of the $24 million deficit he had foreseen. The next year witnessed a $310 million surplus instead of the predicted $650 million deficit, which the Legion promptly dubbed the "Billion Dollar Error." The Legion also gleefully exposed Mellon's and other corporate influence behind supposedly grass-roots opposition to the Bonus.[53]

In the last analysis, both the Legion and the nation overwhelmingly favored some form of compensation. Four successive Legion

Conventions approved a Bonus unanimously or nearly so without a roll call. Bills endorsed by the Legion passed the House 289 to 92 in May 1920, 333 to 70 in May 1922, 258 to 54 in September 1922, and 313 to 78 (over President Coolidge's veto) in 1924. The Senate first approved a Bonus in August 1922, 47 to 22, but failed (44 to 28) to override President Harding's veto in September. In 1924, the Senate did override Coolidge's veto, 59 to 26. If such overwhelming majorities did not reflect Congressional preference, they certainly indicated the legislators' opinion of their constituents' feelings. In those states that held referenda on state bonuses, the margin of victory ranged from a maximum of ten to one (Rhode Island) to a minimum of nine to five (South Dakota), with three to one the ratio in New York, New Jersey, and Wisconsin. Members of the Chamber of Commerce, polled by the national organization to demonstrate business opposition to the Bonus, actually favored some form of compensation 4,116 to 2,657 while readers of the Literary Digest, given the choice of a Bonus or a tax increase, favored the former by a margin of 23,000 votes out of 900,000 cast.[54]

Although the nation accepted the Bonus, the ultimate form agreed upon can hardly be called a total victory for the Legion. Veterans received adjusted compensation certificates, payable either in 1945 or to their beneficiaries if they died before then, to a maximum of $625 based on the number of days they served. With accrued interest, the average payment would be $1,000. Bonus opponents fearing high taxes were placated, as the money would be gradually paid into the treasury over twenty years with no major tax increase necessary. Provisions for home and farm loans, the latter a particular favorite of Senator William Borah, also dropped by the wayside as the recession of 1921–22 ended and few veterans needed further assistance to adjust to civilian life. The Legion's leaders achieved exactly what Theodore Roosevelt Jr. wrote that Commander D'Olier was attempting. He "is doing the best he can and likes the cash bonus no more than the rest of us do. His part as I understand it is to get the overwhelming sentiment into the best channels possible."[55]

The Bonus compromise that the Legion and its Congressional allies worked out in 1924 did not survive the Great Depression, Wright Patman, and the Veterans of Foreign Wars. Although a Legionnaire, the Texas congressman got nowhere in Legion circles with his 1929 drive for immediate payment of the entire amount due in 1945 as a "reflationary" measure to increase pur-

President Herbert Hoover at the 1930 Convention in Boston, urging Legion-naires not to endorse immediate payment of the Bonus and to maintain their confidence during the Great Depression. General of the Army John Pershing is at the center, looking at the camera. Former President Calvin Coolidge sits between two women, on Pershing's left. Courtesy of American Legion National Headquarters.

chasing power and productivity. Herbert Hoover himself ap-peared at the Legion's September 1930 Boston Convention, the first time a president had ever spoken before the annual meeting. Prepared by none other than John Thomas Taylor, who urged an appeal to the Legionnaires' "idealism and this striving of theirs, touching upon the constitution and maintenance of law and or-der," while "tell[ing] them how generous the government has been," Hoover's Legion supporters laid the immediate-payment question on the table 967 to 244. Patman complained "the reso-lution did not receive fair consideration" and made a vigorous speech denouncing war profiteers and the reduction of debts owed by foreign nations that could have paid off the veterans. A firm Prohibitionist, he even argued that the Legion's leaders had traded the immediate-payment question for a congressional vote against Prohibition. However, the following January the Legion Executive Committee, inspired by a four-million-signature petition presented by the VFW and an increasing number of grass-roots Legion resolutions in favor of immediate payment, repudiated the Convention's action. Patman celebrated by leading a fife and drum corps parade down the capital's Pennsylvania Avenue.[56]

The Committee's action infuriated Legion "kingmakers," among them Hoover's Assistant Secretary of War Hanford MacNider and Washington's Stephen Chadwick, who denounced Commander Ralph O'Neil's administration as "the weakest since our organization began" in failing to "hold the Legion against the selfishness of individuals" who wished to "impose the ex-serviceman and his program as a burden upon the country." They successfully plotted to reverse the Executive Committee's about-face at the 1931 Detroit Convention, where a repeat surprise appearance by the president asking the Legion's aid in "this war against world depression" led to a 902 to 507 vote against immediate payment. The debate was so virulent, with Patman again speaking for the minority, that the Legion for the first time published much of it in its summary of the proceedings. In concluding the Convention, the Legion elected as its commander a North Carolina Democrat, Harry Stevens, who for the next year adamantly stood by the Republican Hoover on the issue even if it meant, as he joked, "the spectacle of a National Commander being boiled in oil at the Portland Convention" scheduled for 1932.[57]

Portland, birthplace of the famed Bonus March of 1932, proved an ironic choice for the Legion's meeting. Some twenty thousand veterans from all over the nation had marched on Washington in May, pledging to stay until the Bonus was paid, only to be driven out by General Douglas MacArthur on July 28. (MacArthur acted without authorization from the president, but Hoover did not repudiate his rough tactics, giving the impression he had ordered them.) The Legion took no formal stand on the Bonus March. In many communities, Legionnaires fed and arranged transportation for the traveling veterans, in part out of sympathy, in part to hurry the ragged contingents out of town before they caused trouble. In Johnstown, Pennsylvania, on the other hand, over the formal demand of the local Legion and Chamber of Commerce that the marchers be kept out of town, Mayor Eddie McCloskey responded, "To hell with everybody—Let 'em come." Congressman Royal Johnson tried to persuade Legion Commander Stevens to intercede with the Bonus Marchers to leave Washington and to arrange for their transportation home, "but he seemed to be afraid of it."[58]

If the Legion carefully avoided taking a stand on the controversial march itself, it had no difficulty in condemning the veterans' brutal expulsion from Anacostia Flats. The Massachusetts State Convention invited Bonus March leader Walter Waters to be their keynote speaker. He proceeded to denounce the "most desperate precedent ever established by a President in time of peace." National Economy League leader Admiral Byrd could not even gain the floor. At the National Convention, Hoover's supporters in the Legion arranged for Secretary of War Patrick Hurley to present his case that the Bonus Marchers were criminals, whose disorderly conduct had provoked their expulsion. (Some 22 percent had been arrested at some point in their lives, mostly for trivial offenses; the administration, despite a great deal of effort, could find no evidence that they were dangerous radicals.) Pelham Glassford, Washington's police chief, whom the administration criticized for his sympathy with the veterans, ripped Hurley's charges to shreds in newspaper articles that when read aloud at the Convention were greeted with "whistling and stamping and cheering" by the Legionnaires. Boston's Mayor James Curley, who had previously welcomed the Bonus Marchers with the freedom of the city, delivered the Convention's most famous speech, charging that Hoover had ordered the veterans shot down "like dogs." Hearst reporter Floyd Gibbons also won cheers for praising the "Americanism and patriotism" of starving men who had "retreated without resistance to the bayonets and tanks and tear gas and the fire which was used against them."[59]

As the Convention itself deteriorated into a "mob"—with army units standing by to keep order in case violence broke out—Commander Stevens arranged a debate on the Bonus, even while judging beforehand that "it will pass by an overwhelming majority." Wright Patman promised the Bonus would put five billion dollars in circulation and end the depression. New York's Edward Spafford countered that fiat money would "wreck our whole financial structure" in a manner similar to postwar Germany. Spafford was only one of many prominent Legionnaires who had originally favored the Bonus in the twenties—Hamilton Fish and Royal Johnson were two others—but who opposed prepayment in the thirties. To no avail, however, as only 107 of 1,274 delegates stood by the president. Hoover's lieutenants in the Legion were grateful they were able to escape with a demand for immediate payment in order that "the Legion keep on friendly terms [with] both parties and refuse [to] pass any resolutions condemning [the] President or anyone else." Eight states had insisted the Legion take the unprecedented step of censuring an incumbent president. Frank Hines and Legionnaires in the Veterans' Administration secretly worked to prevent more from doing so.[60]

The Legion shifted course again in 1933, resolving to give President Roosevelt the same chance as his predecessor. Patman's bill for immediate cash payment did not even reach the floor. Instead, former Commander Stevens put forth an intriguing theory that "the inflationary spending program" of the government came from "people yonder in Wall Street who desire to recoup their losses sustained in 1929 by manipulation of the stock market." Opera star Ernestine Schumann-Heink praised Roosevelt as "the greatest man," who "loves and respects the Legion."[61]

By 1934, however, with the New Deal relief programs in full swing and the Economy Act cuts modified, the Legion was ready to take on a fourth president who opposed the Bonus's payment. Once again the Legion took its unique position between two extremes. It continued to oppose Patman's bill, which he insisted be funded by fiat money to increase purchasing power, and substituted a measure sponsored by Kentucky Congressman, Legionnaire, and future Chief Justice Fred Vinson, which left the manner of payment open. Patman's bill had passed the House of Representatives as early as 1932 by a 209 to 176 margin, although the Senate rejected it 62 to 18. It passed again in 1934, 295 to 125, but failed to be recommended by a Senate committee expecting President Roosevelt's veto. In 1935, the Patman bill narrowly edged the Vinson measure 202 to 191 before the whole House approved it 318 to 90. Although the Senate passed the bill 55 to 33, unlike the House it later failed to override Roosevelt's veto. January 1936 witnessed immediate payment's last triumph as Patman and the VFW finally agreed to the Legion bill, although at the 1935 Convention the Legion had booed the Texas congressman for alleging Legion leaders—especially Commander Frank Belgrano, son-in-law of Bank of America president A. P. Giannini—were financially "interested in the Vinson Bill," which would "make millions for the bankers." All in all, as one delegate wrote of the outdoor Miami Convention that approved the Bonus for the last time, "the boys had a hell-roaring time and wound up passing resolutions to make the Bonus safe for democracy."

The following January, Congress overrode the president's perfunctory veto—he merely referred them to his powerful message of the previous year—325 to 61 in the House and 76 to 19 in the Senate. Although immediate payment was Patman's brainchild, the final bill and credit for its passage rested with the Legion.[62]

Writing of the Legion's long and checkered history on the Bonus, historian Dorothy Culp commented that "in this phase of its legislative activity, at least, the Legion belied the accusations of its opponents that the organization is an autocracy, for the impetus for the Bonus came not from the officials of the organization but from the rank and file, whose demands were adopted only after a strenuous opposition." But the Legion's indecision on the Bonus provides four clues to the nature of the organization. First, it showed that the Legion was no tool of its leaders on this key issue. The rank and file repudiated prominent, wealthy Legionnaires who would have preferred no Bonus at all. Second, the Legion proved no tool of big business: it criticized "Wall Street" on this crucial aspect of its legislative program as viciously as it had any Socialist. Third, if the Legion's various stands on the Bonus cost it members at particular times, it retained a core who remained loyal to the organization for other reasons and who did not regard any given Bonus position as the paramount reason for membership. Once the issue was shelved for good in 1936, the Legion's ranks increased steadily until after World War II. Finally, by not consistently embracing the Bonus or immediate payment and by giving first priority to firm but reasonable policies for helping the disabled, the Legion enjoyed a privileged position when it came to creating a system of benefits for World War II veterans. While President Roosevelt, labor leaders, businessmen, educators, and soldiers had suggestions for easing the postwar strains of GIs, the Legion put it all together in the GI Bill, inundated the Capitol steps with petitions on its behalf, and arranged for no less than eighty-one Senators to cosponsor what Senator Ralph Yarborough later called "the most farsighted veterans program in history." Providing free medical care, disability allowances, unemployment insurance, college and vocational tuition, and home and farm mortgages, the GI Bill ensured that the veterans of World War II enjoyed from the start benefits far greater than the Legion had been able to obtain for their AEF counterparts in twenty years. To be sure, the fact that the war had taken fifteen million men away from home for up to six years created an overwhelming obligation. Economists also feared an-

Legion National Commander Warren Atherton with petitions demonstrating public support for the GI Bill, on the steps of the Capitol, with congressmen, 1944. Courtesy of American Legion National Headquarters.

other depression if so many men were dumped at once on the labor market. But at least some credit for the benefits enjoyed by the GIs of World War II must go to the doughboys of World War I, who created and maintained close watch over the Veterans' Administration. Had Legion-inspired benefits not seemed acceptable to the general population, and had the Legion created less effective alliances in the bureaucracy and Congress, the road to compensation for future veterans might well have been more difficult.[63]

The Legion's program and lobbying for veterans' benefits appear in retrospect as its finest and least controversial achievement. Yet even here the Legion can be criticized on two grounds. Especially on the Bonus and the manner of its payment, Legion leaders tried to reach consensus positions determined largely by which strategy would retain the most members. Further, the Legion always kept its eyes fixed on the veteran and his problems and treated him as unique. It never realized that the structure of benefits created in the twenties was in fact America's first reasonable approximation of a welfare state for a sizable number of citizens, a notion that would have appalled conservative Legionnaires. As such, the Legion could not conceive of making common cause with other groups—labor, the aged, blacks, and the unemployed come immediately to mind—who could have benefited from employment and hospitalization programs similar to those veterans claimed should be theirs alone because they earned them through military service.

Nevertheless, the Legion's splendid work in creating the Veterans' Bureau cannot be denied. It offers a prime example of how interest-group politics can employ and shape a basically favorable public opinion to enact specific legislative programs that effectively served a much larger constituency than the interest group itself.

CHAPTER EIGHT

Labor and the American Legion

The American Legion has no interest distinct from other good citizens in the differences between capital and labor. . . . The members of the American Legion are free to follow the dictates of their own consciences within the law of the land whether this leads them to participate in an organized strike, or whether, on the other hand, this may prompt them to volunteer their services as individuals, as was done in the coal strike, to continue the production of the necessities of life temporarily, in order to prevent suffering and alleviate distress. . . . That they should become the tools of either capital or organized labor is unthinkable.

National Adjutant Lemuel Bolles to H. M. Payne, January 13, 1920*

While the purposes of organization of the American Federation of Labor and the American Legion are not the same in all respects, yet fundamentally the aspirations of the two organizations are identical. . . . The real opponents of the American Legion in this great and meritorious issue [the Bonus] have been the Chamber of Commerce and the banking interests of America, and the strongest force of cooperation with the American Legion in pressing the final adoption of its compensation measure has been the uncompromising support of the American Federation of Labor. Thus time has proven the utter preposterousness of the claim that outside interests and particularly the moneyed interest of America controlled the destinies and aspirations of the American Legion.

George Berry, National Vice-Commander of the American Legion and union president ("The American Legion and Organized Labor; The American Legion and its Attitude Toward Organized Labor," c. 1923)*

Liberal and laborite commentators have conceded the strength of the Legion and . . . regard it as a malignant cancer on the body politic. . . . The Legion's founders and officials throughout its history, without exception, have been anti-working class. But . . . they have been forced to disclaim partisanship in the struggle between capital and labor.

Walter Wilson, "Labor Fights the American Legion," American Mercury 34 (January 1935): 1–2

O N SEPTEMBER 23, 1936, President William Green of the American Federation of Labor stood before the assembled American Legion delegates at their National Convention in Cleveland. Legionnaires cheered him repeatedly as he urged the Legion and the AFL to stand united against Communism, involvement in an "inevitable war in Europe," and unemployment. He concluded by linking the two as "thoroughgoing American organization[s]" which should "maintain unbroken the fine relationship we have developed." However, the *Nation* burlesqued the Cleveland lovefest in a cartoon depicting the American Legion as "The New Stepfather," embracing an equally rotund "mother" resembling President Green as a child dubbed "Labor" sulked off on one side.[1]

Green's speech and the left-wing magazine's reaction symbolize the complexity of the American Legion's interaction with the labor movement. Legion leaders repeatedly insisted that "all action by individual posts which would tend to commit the name of the Legion either to Labor or to Capital has been discouraged." Yet this pronouncement is contradicted by both the Legion's cordial relations with America's most prominent labor organization and its unsavory reputation as a strike-breaking weapon of the capitalist class. Most Legionnaires were neither union members nor capitalists, and the Legion's very concept of Americanism eschewed the language of class (indeed, the preamble to its constitution pledged it to "combat the autocracy of the classes and the masses").[2]

Language provides a clue that goes far toward explaining why judgments of the Legion's attitude toward labor varied so greatly. Whatever the personal motivations of the individual Legionnaires, neither National Headquarters nor any Legion post or department officially stated that it was intervening in a labor dispute because it was a labor dispute. Three reasons that appear regularly in Legion correspondence—"law and order," "Communism," and "providing the necessities of life"—removed a given strike from the category of relations between labor and capital and redefined it as an "un-American" threat to community survival. For instance, during the Boston police strike of 1919 the Massachusetts Legion saw no contradiction in "officially assuming a neutral attitude" while drawing up lists of members "who could be relied upon to preserve law and order." In the view of the Massachusetts Legion's historian Claude Fuess, "the city for a few days [was] virtually unprotected against marauders of every description." This "naturally aroused Legionnaires," and veterans joined Harvard students and businessmen in patrolling the streets. (Later the Legion refused to use its influence to reinstate the fired policemen, although they pleaded for it, as this violated Legion "neutrality.") In other strikes, the real or suspected involvement of Communists proved sufficient, or provided an excuse, for Legionnaires to regard the confrontation as an element in a Russian-backed conspiracy to overthrow American democracy. Legion officials in Michigan went to great lengths to demonstrate that Walter Reuther was acting as a Soviet agent when he led the strikes that unionized the automobile industry. They even produced a letter (of questionable authenticity) from his brother claiming him to be "as violent a Red as was ever turned loose on the American public by Russian Communism." Finally, Legionnaires intervened to alleviate acute community distress. In May 1920 the Maplewood, New Jersey, Post was "mighty proud" to have run trains during a railroad strike, thereby furnishing "transportation to those residents of the commuting sections in the vicinity of New York and Newark, whose sole means of geting to business and of securing the necessities of life was the railroads which were tied up by the willful act of a small band of outlaw strikers and revolutionists."[3]

By preserving law and order, fighting conspiracies against the government, and enabling local residents to survive, Legionnaires could act as strikebreakers without defining themselves as such. They thereby sought to refute such attacks as a cartoon in the *Butte* (Montana) *Daily Bulletin* that depicted the American Legion as a wolf in sheep's clothing carrying the label "Capital," biting the throat of a figure representing "Labor," and excoriating "the Exploiters and Plunderers, who wrapped in the folds of the Legion, wolf-like seek to suck the precious blood of the sons of toil." Was the Legion truly impartial or did it mask a blatant prejudice in favor of business with unbiased patriotic rhetoric?[4]

Several arguments and much evidence suggest strongly that the Legion—both posts and National Headquarters—represented and acted as a third, essentially middle-class force that sought to unite capital and labor behind a classless vision of "Americanism." The Legion's conduct in many, though not all, strikes during the two great crisis periods it faced—the Red Scare and the middle and late 1930s—demonstrated unwillingness to act except when requested by the authorities in clear-cut cases of lawlessness or a perceived threat to community survival. Legionnaires at every level examined and questioned the organization's involvement in the labor troubles and stood ready to denounce those who compromised its neutrality. This scrutiny arose because the Legion recruited from the ranks of labor and feared a loss of membership if it offended veterans who were union men and their sympathizers. Finally, Legion cooperation with the AFL went far beyond pro forma exchanges of convention greetings and ironing out local disputes among overzealous members. The two groups shared a common ideology and structure. Even more important, they shared a common enemy—"Wall Street"—and lobbied together for the veterans' Bonus, immigration restriction, and child-labor laws.

Nevertheless, the Legion could function as a procapitalist organization because "middle class Americans'" fears of change, disorder, and challenges to private property coincided with capital's hostility to unionization of mass-production industries. Technically speaking, "lawlessness" was usually required to organize unskilled workers. Sit-down strikes, violations of back-to-work injunctions, coercive picketing, and meetings and demonstrations that communities forbade as disruptive characterized the great labor confrontations of the 1930s and received nationwide publicity. The active participation of Communists, who according to Irving Bernstein by 1941 led 18.9 percent of the 2.5 million workers who had joined the CIO, further convinced Legionnaires the social order was in serious jeopardy.[5] Yet the Legion also struggled against Andrew Mellon and Republican financiers for the Bonus, against the National Economy League for veterans' benefits, and for a "universal draft" of capital as well as labor to forestall profiteering in future wars. If the Legion's behavior can be judged procapital on most occasions, but prolabor on others, its actions sprang from its own traditional ideology of Americanism, which held sacred both law and order and the need to subordinate self and property to communal survival.

The Legion allowed local units to adopt their own policies on labor matters to avoid alienating its diverse membership. Commander Frederic Galbraith informed Samuel Gompers that a policy of other than "strict neutrality" would have been impossible, as "many thousands" of union members belonged to the Legion and it hoped to recruit thousands more. Most other Legionnaires were "working men from the different walks of life" who would not necessarily sympathize with big business. Committed to departmental and local autonomy, National Headquarters intervened only reluctantly when posts compromised the Legion's stated policies, in part because the facts of the case were usually disputed, in part because Legionnaires generally acted "as individuals" when they knew they were violating a national mandate. Galbraith could win Gompers's sympathetic ear when he pleaded that "it is one thing for a great organization to aspire to lofty aims . . . it is another thing . . . to go out and in the daily acts and deliberations of its individual members and small groups" see that these were observed. Gompers had the same problem with obstreperous labor unions. But many labor advocates regarded the separation of "the Legion" and "Legionnaires acting as individuals" as a distinction without a difference. In May 1920 the *New York Evening World* claimed that the Legion had failed to attract significant numbers from the ranks of organized labor because "lawless and thoroughly reprehensible activities of individual members of the Legion were advertised as activities of the Legion." National Headquarters, for its part, tried to reconcile neutrality, federalism, and legality by proclaiming Legionnaires "free to follow the dictates of their own conscience within the law of the land" in labor disputes.[6]

By invoking "the law of the land" during the first years of its existence, however, the Legion put itself at the service of authorities who frequently branded striking workers as revolutionaries. Hence, the Legion could convince itself that it was maintaining neutrality, acting legally, and indeed performing patriotic public service by restoring law and order in a troubled community. Case studies of the Legion's behavior from 1919 through the early 1920s reveal a complex situation. Legionnaires at different times acted as strikebreakers at the request of government officials, maintained law and order in a neutral fashion, acted illegally or in an unauthorized manner against workers, and yet sometimes evinced considerable sympathy for strikers.

For example, the Legion became involved as strikebreakers in the national coal miners' strike of November 1919 at the request of Governor Capper of Kansas. As schools throughout the state closed and inhabitants feared fuel shortages for the upcoming winter, the Kansas supreme court ordered the state to seize and operate the mines. The Thomas Hopkins Post in Wichita, a town already suffering from the cold, volunteered two hundred men, including five who owned steam shovels. For three weeks, Legionnaires worked the pits. National Commander Franklin D'Olier praised the Kansas action as a model, while condemning illegal actions by other posts: "In time of need and emergency, we stand ready as individuals to support, strengthen, and speed up, if necessary, the civil authorities. . . . But always in accordance with competent authority."[7]

The Legion also participated in labor troubles by keeping the peace. In August 1919, five hundred Legionnaires did so for two days in Denver in response to a plea from Governor Shoup that "an emergency existed by reason of rioting, destruction of property and life, all caused by a small, disorderly, and criminal element" in a strike by streetcar operators. Several deaths, many injuries, and thousands of dollars in damage had occurred before the Legion volunteers took charge. Participating Legionnaires kept their pledge to "under no circumstances operate cars, become strikebreakers, or act in any capacity except the maintenance of general order." During the time they patrolled the streets, not one streetcar moved nor was a single shot fired. The following month, four hundred Youngstown, Ohio, Legionnaires received five dollars each per day from the city to protect "life and property." The striking union unanimously commended the Legion's efforts, and Legion leaders "felt proud of the fact that the Youngstown district is reported to be the most orderly of any affected by the strike."[8] But all too many local posts, swept away by the hysteria of the Red Scare, did not bother to seek the approval of government or Legion authorities before taking matters into their own hands.[9]

In other communities throughout the nation, while careful to state "we are not for any radical element, but we are for organized labor," Legion posts strove to attract working men and to achieve good relationships with local unions. In 1922, union leader Sarah Edwards reported to Samuel Gompers that the "St. Louis American Legion boys have been . . . of untold value in smashing the network of bombs and submarines laid and set off against organized labor. They absolutely refused to be strike-breakers in order to get a job." Their counterparts at the Jefferson Post in Louisville condemned an open-shop drive by the Employers' Association as "preaching class antagonism through attacks on union labor," which "reflected on the patriotism of loyal . . . union men." The post found these "radical capitalist agitators" as "un-American" as "radical labor agitators." In 1920, claiming that three-quarters of the state's Legionnaires supported a coke strike, New Mexico's commander refused to allow the governor to employ the Legion to seize the mines.[10]

National Legion officials expressed the belief that the laboring man was loyal and was good Legion material. The 1920 Convention resolved that "the American Legion is not opposed to organized labor when it conducts itself as it normally does in accordance with law and order." The Legion's leading labor spokesman, George Berry, blamed all the trouble on "meddling outsiders"—radicals who misrepresented the Legion to working-class veterans and businessmen who stirred up veterans against labor. John Inzer encapsulated the Legion's philosophy in noting that "the American laborer wants the opportunity to rise. He wants after all to be a boss. . . . Nine times out of ten he is a true American. We want to find these men, and get them organized, and save them" from the "wild dreams" inculcated by Communist agitators. By depicting the righteous Legion and the demonic Bolsheviks as warring for labor's soul, Inzer gave a theological cast to the founders' conviction that most workers shared their ideology and would join up if overzealous posts tempered their excesses.[11]

The Legion worked hard to mend its fences with labor. The action taken by New York's Legion in response to union hostility foreshadowed the sort of accommodation worked out by the national body. On May 1, 1920, news that Legionnaires had served as scabs in the International Longshoremen's strike reached the papers. President John F. Riley of the International Longshoremen's Association, who also headed the New York Council of Central Trades and Labor, the largest local labor body in the world, forbade members of the council from belonging to the Legion at a time when these unions counted several thousand Legionnaires in their ranks. The New York Legion promptly opened negotiations and insisted that no authorized Legion group had participated in the strike. (State Commander Wade Hayes argued that if some Legion men had enrolled as strikebreakers, others were on strike.) By June 17, Hayes had convinced Riley to revoke the ban and "to tell the men that the Legion has proved its neutrality in this affair."[12]

Within a year of its creation, the Legion had gone beyond merely discouraging the antiunion activities of its members and had begun to establish the alliance with the American Federation of Labor that has continued throughout its history. The Legion and the AFL had much in common. The old craft unions had originated as fraternal and social organizations and served the same function for workers as the Legion did for veterans in communities all over America. Composed of established ethnic groups—English, Irish, and Germans—the "aristocrats of labor" who controlled the AFL shared the ethnicity, nationalism, and antiradicalism of the Legionnaires. Both organizations dedicated themselves to mutual helpfulness and offered companionship and support to members who felt vulnerable in the face of twentieth-century capitalism. Both confronted an unsympathetic business community committed to the open shop and stingy in granting veterans' benefits; and both were challenged by equally distasteful "newer Americans" who sought more drastic changes than either the Legion or the AFL desired. The Legion and the AFL were organized in largely autonomous, self-governing units and could thus understand each other's problems with local recalcitrance. Furthermore, both rejected language and action based on class conflict in favor of agitation for specific benefits. With considerable justice, journalist O. L. Warr termed the Legion "the Heroes' Union."[13]

The conflicts that arose between Legion posts and labor locals had almost no long-term effects on relations between the Legion and the AFL. Leaders of both organizations realized that they had far too many common interests to allow a potentially beneficial alliance to be sabotaged by local squabbling. The early years of the Legion witnessed a lengthy and friendly correspondence between Samuel Gompers, who gave his approval to the Legion at its inception in Paris in 1919, and a succession of Legion national commanders. Gompers's complaint in August 1920 that the American Legion in Kansas was "permitting itself to be used as a political catspaw" in opposing farmer-labor organizational efforts received a courteous reply from Commander Galbraith. He first ordered an investigation, which demonstrated that the Legion was not officially involved, and then invited Gompers as "a personal favor" to bring to his attention information "from any source . . . from any part of the country" that the American Legion had either violated the law or taken sides in labor disputes. Gompers took Galbraith at his word. Over the next several years, he informed Legion commanders that AFL members had complained of Legionnaires breaking strikes in West Virginia, denying labor leaders the right to speak in Reading, Pennsylvania, and failing to include representatives of local unions when greeting the Legion's national commander in Wilmington, Delaware. Gompers thus used his access to the Commander to provoke internal Legion investigations of antilabor activity, which in any case diminished as the Red Scare subsided. Gompers considered these investigations, nationwide publicizing of Legion statements recognizing labor's right to organize, and exchanges of convention speakers as strong links in the chain binding the Legion and the AFL.[14]

Antiradicalism also provided a firm basis for Legion-AFL friendship. In November 1920, Gompers reminded Galbraith of his organization's support for the war and reiterated his opposition to pacifism. Four months later, Galbraith congratulated his counterpart for his efforts "to purge his organization of destructive radicals" and his "denunciation of the Soviet government." George L. Berry, an American Legion founder and president of the International Printing Pressmen's and Assistants' Union of North America, the Legion's chief labor publicist and troubleshooter, made antiradicalism the focus of his appeal for Legion-AFL solidarity. Armed with letters of recommendation from Gompers, he traveled around the nation speaking to union meetings and leaders, trying to "break down the [ill] feeling that has been engendered by the Red or Bolshevist element."[15]

In addition to their shared nationalism, the Legion and the AFL found other positive reasons to unite. Gompers and the AFL backed the Bonus for former servicemen, supported the Legion's proposal for Citizens' Military Training Camps—they were "against militarism but for character building"—opposed diplomatic recognition of the Soviet Union, supported restrictive immigration laws, and joined in raising funds for the Legion's five-million-dollar endowment to care for disabled veterans and their children. Given this cooperation, the Legion was willing to look the other way when Gompers disagreed with it. (He supported the presidential candidacy of Robert La Follette—whom Legionnaires detested for his opposition to the war—in 1924, applauded the pardon of Socialist Eugene V. Debs, and opposed the "universal draft" of labor and capital in the event of another war.) All in all, National Adjutant Lemuel Bolles could claim that Gompers "and his crowd have shown much more consideration for the Legion's programs . . . than some of his illustrious opponents."[16]

"Illustrious opponents" were another important common denominator. From September through October 1922, and from

March through June 1923, the *American Legion Weekly* ran more than a hundred pages written by Marquis James condemning business profiteering during World War I. Samuel Gompers coordinated with James's attack the distribution of copies of his *New York Times* article attacking a "Wall Street [that] operates blindly amidst a chaos of forces seeking profits, caring for nothing that does not beget or protect profits." The Harding and Coolidge administrations, which thwarted the approval of the veterans' Bonus for five years, were closely allied with business interests responsible for the "open shop" campaign. This reduced the AFL's membership from over four million to under three million between 1920 and 1924, a five-year span during which the Legion also lost about a quarter of its members.[17]

By the late 1920s, union men had begun to organize their own Legion posts. The Union Labor Post in Los Angeles and the Chicago Labor Union Post both claimed the honor of being the first such group (each began functioning in 1929). However, on the eve of World War II, only five such posts existed, with a total membership of about fifteen hundred. Most state departments frowned, as did Massachusetts, on posts "whose membership is comprised of men in a single trade, profession, craft, or business." The two principal objections were that union posts competed with established community posts for members and that to be fair the Legion would be compelled to grant charters to posts of nonunion workers and those "organized to oppose organized labor." Nevertheless, many skilled laborers (who numbered 13 percent of all Legionnaires in 1938) and some government employees, unskilled workers, and office and clerical personnel (who made up another 24 percent) belonged to unions.[18]

The Legion's cooperation with the AFL reached the point where antiunion Legionnaires in fact wondered whether the Legion was becoming a tool of organized labor. As early as 1921, they had warned that "Sam Gompers [would] hitch the Legion to his kite." In 1923, some members insisted that if the Legion repudiated the Ku Klux Klan it ought not "to divide the allegiance of the people of the United States" by supporting the AFL. Since the AFL had gone on record as opposing antistrike injunctions, which "never interfere with anyone who is not a law breaker," they argued that the Legion had tied itself to an organization led by "criminals" who were "definitely advising the disregard of laws." In phrasing his objections, one critic touched on the most potentially divisive issue between the rank and file of the two organizations—the war

itself. He claimed that "union men seized the opportunity of war
to profiteer. . . . They sheltered themselves behind industrial necessity drawing down big pay and having a glorious time at home
while Legion men stood the brunt and suffered." Given the billions made by industrialists, however, such sentiments were rarely
aired in Legion circles.[19]

The Legion sometimes found itself squeezed between business
and labor on issues more substantive than the publication of
prounion articles. The Legion placed large orders for gravemarkers, buttons, pamphlets, and caps, which could be produced using
either union or nonunion labor. Commanders D'Olier and Galbraith established as official policy in 1920 that the Legion's neutrality in labor matters dictated that it adopt "impartial business
methods." They defined these, in response to Samuel Gompers's
criticism that the Legion had ordered gravemarkers from a nonunion shop, as "asking for bids from all possible manufacturers,"
then selecting those "whose prices and quality were most attrac-
tive" without caring whether they operated open or closed
shops.[20]

By the mid twenties, however, National Headquarters used
only union labor as a matter of policy. In 1925, when Legionnaires
in the Chicago typographical union protested that the Legion had
issued printed material without the union label, the Department
Adjutant in Illinois backed them up by insisting that use of nonunion labor would hurt membership efforts. The National Commander sent assurances to the Indianapolis typographers' union
that "all American Legion printing is done by union labor" and
that henceforth the union label would appear on all posters and
window cards. Nonunion printers who had worked for the Legion in the early twenties protested in vain that "the union demands discrimination in their favor, while the open shop only
asks the right of equal opportunity."[21]

When the Legion issued its pamphlet "The Threat of Communism and the Answer" in 1927, conservative businessmen
praised the contents but strenuously objected to the union label
on the front cover. One protest called the typographical union
oath "un-American" because it stressed fidelity to the union above
"any other organization, social, political or religious, secret or
otherwise." Another observed that "the real damage threatened
by communism is mostly theoretical—the damage inflicted by
organized labor and the closed shop is actual." He concluded, in
disgust, that "if the Legion isn't strong enough to publish anti-

communism literature without the union label, they are weak indeed."[22]

Aside from occasional imbroglios concerning the use of non-union labor, the Legion engaged in few disputes that might be interpreted as antilabor actions between 1921 and the great union drives of the 1930s. When it did so, the labor aspect of the controversy took second place to a more general antiradical element. For instance, the resolution of a Logan County, West Virginia, post in March 1923 pledging to prevent, by force if necessary, a United Mine Workers meeting on the steps of the county courthouse attracted nationwide attention. Legionnaires wondered "what action can we take to get those people down in that state to keep their hands off and out of affairs that don't concern them: namely, labor disputes." Ohio's State Commander scornfully asked: "What does it profit the American Legion if the local post at 'Podunk,' West Virginia, gains a wonderful lot of prestige in 'Podunk' by such resoluting, if it endangers the life of the American Legion in dozens of other communities which know nothing about the situation at 'Podunk' except what they read in press dispatches?"[23]

Nevertheless, in this case National Headquarters told the citizens of "Podunk" "not to have the slightest uneasiness" and applauded them for doing "what is right." For the Logan County post insisted that it was not antilabor, but protesting against the "un-American" Civil Liberties Union, which sponsored a meeting and "invaded" the community with a host of pacifists and radicals, including Roger Baldwin and Arthur Garfield Hays. "We do not believe in bolshevism and anarchy, neither do we believe that slackers should be permitted to invade this state and, under the guise of freedom of speech, propagate pernicious and un-American doctrine," the post argued. The general cooperation between the Legion, especially in West Virginia, and the (at the time conservative) United Mine Workers in the 1920s bears out the exceptional nature of this incident.[24]

Most of the labor controversies in which the Legion became embroiled involved the perennial problem of "the Legion" as opposed to "Legionnaires acting as individuals." In 1929, National Headquarters was in an uproar over an article in the *Chicago Tribune* concerning the violent textile strike in Gastonia, North Carolina. The *Tribune* claimed that the Legion rushed truckloads of strikebreakers to the scene. North Carolina officials had declared that "the American Legion, convinced the textile strike . . .

is of Communist origin, will take a stand to stop it." Even though Communists had in fact organized and directed the strike, National Adjutant James Barton promptly overruled the anonymous source for the statement, claiming rumors of strikebreaking to be "untrue and unauthorized" and that "any such action . . . would violate a well-established policy of our organization." Two days after the original story ran, the *Tribune* printed a Legion rebuttal, which concluded that "if there is any charge of Communistic leadership in a strike, the American Legion is fully confident it will be dealt with properly and promptly, and certainly best, by the union men and women concerned." Nevertheless, the North Carolina Legion expressed its true feelings when it elected A. L. Bulwinckle, who led the vigilantes who crushed the strike, as state commander three years later. But officially, the state Legion stayed out.[25]

Problems arose when overzealous posts and Legionnaires "as individuals" took things into their own hands on other occasions. In 1931, "forty deputies and several American Legion members, armed with tear gas bombs and machine guns" drove back a crowd of striking coal miners in Columbus, Ohio, who hoped to free some strikers who had been arrested. The same year, Legionnaires in New Jersey denied that they had supplied strikebreakers to build the Pulaski Skyway, although a few men guarded the construction site at the behest of the state. To be sure, National Headquarters did not investigate these instances as thoroughly as it might have; nor did it threaten to revoke the charters of posts whose members may have taken an antilabor role. Still, the repeated insistence on official neutrality must have discouraged Legionnaires from involvement in labor disputes on many occasions during the late 1920s and early 1930s, as few accusations against them arose.[26]

By 1933, however, the new political climate produced by the election of Franklin D. Roosevelt encouraged the labor movement to respond more militantly to the Great Depression. With business prestige at an all-time low, and with the election of an administration at least somewhat sympathetic toward labor, union leaders concluded that the time had come to gain acceptance of the rights of workers to organize and bargain collectively. Conditions were so bleak that many rank-and-file workers who felt that they had little to lose risked a policy of confrontation. Consequently, the period stretching from the explosive year 1934 through America's entry into World War II witnessed great industrial turmoil. Union membership increased from under three million to eight million and organized labor emerged as a major political force in American society.[27]

Unlike the AFL, many of whose leaders were hostile to the new unions, the Congress of Industrial Organizations (CIO) offended the Legion's ideology of "Americanism" in at least four ways. Whereas the same "older" American ethnic groups dominated both the craft guilds and the Legion, first- and second-generation Americans from southern and eastern Europe made their first bid for nationwide power during the union drives of the 1930s. The Legion, like other representatives of traditional America, believed these groups ought to embrace the values of the established culture without challenging them. Second, whereas the AFL consisted of loosely organized locals that in many cases worked comfortably with other civic associations, itinerant organizers sent out by centralized directorates flocked to the mass-production industries. They could easily be viewed by local residents as "outside agitators" interfering with communities' efforts to solve their own problems. Third, many important unionization drives in the 1930s were either led by or involved Communists and political radicals who made no secret of their hatred for the values cherished by the Legion; if grass-roots Communism arose out of local distress, the historian Harvey Klehr has shown nonetheless that conservative Americans were not paranoid for arguing that leading American Communists maintained ties with the Soviet Politburo. Finally, even after Section 7(a) of the National Industrial Recovery Act of 1933, and the Wagner Act of 1935, gave labor "the right to organize," both the constitutionality of these laws and the means unions could legally use remained heated issues. The unprecedented lawlessness and number of strikes in the thirties, and the willingness of public officials to deputize Legionnaires in the interest of preserving "law and order," explain the eagerness of veterans to protect by whatever means necessary an America they believed on the verge of collapse. In fact, during the great strikes of the 1930s, local Legion units intervened in labor troubles more aggressively then they had dared to even during the Red Scare, when the organization's fate was still uncertain. This time, National Headquarters backed them up.

The first instances of the Legion's new belligerency appeared in California. In the fall of 1933, it responded to a strike led by the Communist-dominated Cannery and Agricultural Workers Union. The San Jose–based union sought to organize the predominantly Mexican-American farm workers in the Imperial Valley (some five hundred miles to the south), who labored under terrible conditions that historian Irving Bernstein noted "challenge[d] credibility." By January 1, 1934, most of the larger growers had signed an agreement for a nine-hour day at 22½ cents per hour, but when the smaller landholders proved recalcitrant, the union called a strike and increased its demand to 35 cents per hour. During January, police deputized Legionnaires "as a precaution against violence," but in fact they accompanied the police in breaking up union meetings and arresting organizers and participants. Abraham Wirin, an attorney for the ACLU who obtained a court injunction forbidding local authorities to interfere with the meetings, accused the Legion of kidnapping him from his hotel in Brawley and turning him loose in the desert, barefoot, eleven miles from the nearest town. Homer Chaillaux, Commander of the California Legion, publicly called Wirin a "damned liar." Wirin in turned sued Chaillaux for $50,000, but lost his case when he could identify none of the men who abducted him. (A year later, Chaillaux returned the favor by lobbying to have Wirin removed from his new post as chief deputy counsel to the National Labor Relations Board.)[28] But the Commander of the El Centro Post spilled the beans in the weekly publication of the Los Angeles Legion: "The veterans of the Valley, finding that the police agencies were unable to cope with the situation, took matters into their own hands." Beverly Oaten, a Congregational minister who witnessed Wirin's kidnapping, overheard someone ask "How many Posts of the Legion are responsible?" when Wirin was driven to a Legion hall for an intimidation session. If the Legion "officially" remained aloof, unofficially it acted as "an anonymous young man" told a reporter for *Today*: "These outside labor agitators believe in overthrowing the government by violence. We can't wait for legal processes to handle people like that."[29]

As in the Imperial Valley disputes, the California Legion made no secret of its role in breaking the International Longshoremen's Association strike in July 1934 by "forming safety committees ready to assist the constituted authorities when necessary." The San Francisco longshoremen had tied up the harbor for several months in protest against labor conditions "among the worst in the civilized world" that required them to turn out daily at 6 A.M. to be hired. However, respectable citizens and Legionnaires preferred to argue that the "alien Communist" Harry Bridges had provoked a strike that embodied a "revolutionary radicalism" aiming at "the downfall of democracy in America." (If the Supreme Court ruled in 1945 that Bridges was not a Communist, "the Australian immigrant nevertheless worked with them . . . hired them, and . . . adopted their ideas and followed their line," according to the historian Irving Bernstein.) When Bridges called for a general strike to counter the Industrial Association's successful attempt to crash the picket lines and reopen the harbor, the state Legion proclaimed the general strike "not a strike but an usurpation by force by self-constituted groups of the authority duly delegated by the ballots," thereby removing it from the class of labor disputes and placing it in that of social preservation. This statement freed the Legion to "clear [the state] of those who agitate and practice sedition." Chaillaux met with the governor of California and promised him "adequate force" to end the strike. State Adjutant James Fisk reported to Indianapolis that "groups of citizens resentful of Communistic influences assembled and destroyed all red headquarters and hangouts." By July 19, the Legion boasted that "real" union labor was back in control, over three hundred "reds" had been arrested, and "the situation in San Francisco and the Bay area was almost back to normalcy." For his part, National Commander Hayes termed the Legion's action "one of the best things that has recently happened in California" and guaranteed Chaillaux a hands-off policy with respect to labor and radical disputes.[30]

Even so not all Legionnaires endorsed Chaillaux's militant role. Some California posts refused to cooperate, arguing that "nothing in our oath to the American Legion . . . obligates us to be at the call of the Department Commander for strike duties," and called for their Commander's resignation or ouster. An entire post in San Francisco defied Chaillaux by marching in the funeral procession for a striker and war veteran who was killed in a melee. Posts in Portland, Oregon, a city also hit by the longshoremen's walkout, refused to join a Citizens' Emergency League resembling the Industrial Alliance that helped break the strike in San Francisco.[31]

In general, however, the Legion agreed with AFL president William Green, who endorsed Chaillaux's stance as "an expression of determination to oppose those destructive forces which seek to destroy American institutions" rather than as an attack on labor. Foreshadowing one of the Legion's major crusades of the late thirties, the California Department censured U.S. Secretary of

Labor Frances Perkins for not deporting Bridges during the strike. It also promised "one-hundred-percent" support for the AFL in the same breath as it asked the state legislature to "enact a law punishing radical agitation by death or a hundred years in jail." Even more important, the national Legion rewarded Chaillaux for his efforts by appointing him director of the National Americanism Commission. He held this post until his death in 1945 and used it to move the Legion to the forefront of antiradical activities in the United States.[32]

With Chaillaux in Indianapolis, Legionnaires in other states followed his example in what observer Robert R. R. Brooks called "the greatest single industrial conflict in the history of American organized labor": the textile strike that began on Labor Day 1934 and soon spread to 375,000 mill workers from Maine to Alabama. Although this strike had little connection with Communists or other radicals, Legionnaires used their supposed involvement as a pretext for intervention. In Rhode Island, Commander Clarence Quinlan authorized posts to serve as peace-keeping officials on the grounds that strikers were "mobs of hoodlums inspired by Communist agitators." South Carolina Commander W. D. Schwartz called upon the Legion to comply with the governor's request that it "maintain law and order." He justified his action by blaming the strike in the Honea mills on "outsiders," especially a group of Communists from Charlotte, North Carolina.[33]

Not all Legionnaires applauded these actions. When newspapers reported that most of the twenty-five hundred special deputies who killed ten strikers and wounded thirty-three others in South Carolina were Legionnaires, textile union leader Francis Gorman protested that the Legion led "great bands" that had planned a "reign of murder." Union leaders talked Legionnaires out of strikebreaking in Burlington, North Carolina. The Motion Picture Projectors' Post in New York City pleaded with National Headquarters to denounce strikebreaking, as "some of the slain strikers were buddies or comrades of ours." Legionnaire railroad workers in Bonham, Texas, termed the South Carolina Legion's role a "dastardly action" and a "bloodcurdling outrage." But National Headquarters praised Commander Schwartz for the "distinction" he supposedly drew between interference in labor matters and the preservation of law and order.[34]

When the Legion took an antilabor stand it usually justified it as necessary to keep the peace. In September 1934, the Aliquippa, Pennsylvania, Legion placed itself squarely behind the Jones and

Laughlin Steel Company when militant young members of the Amalgamated Association of Iron, Steel, and Tin Workers—whom the NRA's Hugh Johnson (inaccurately) attacked as Communists—attempted to unionize the Beaver Valley area. Aliquippa's police chief, Michael Kane, with a posse of armed men "recruited mostly from a local Legion post," attacked steelworkers in neighboring Ambridge, provoking a battle in which one man was killed and a large number were wounded or gassed. A union organizer reported that the Legionnaires donned their caps and uniforms "while doing company guard duty," which violated the Legion's policy that deputized veterans perform their civic duty as individuals rather than as Legionnaires. Kane followed his triumph by creating the Constitutional Defense League, which he claimed received "instruction, help and advice" from Legion National Headquarters. Given the antiradical community defense schemes covertly organized by Legionnaires throughout the United States in the thirties (discussed in chapter 11), Kane's indiscreet boast is at least plausible.[35]

Law and order coincided with another motive for the Legion's increased readiness to interfere in union troubles in the 1930s. The economic dependence of middle-class Legionnaire merchants on factories and their employees in many communities rendered posts susceptible to threats by businessmen that they might close their plants if unions gave them trouble. In November 1935 a post in New Comerstown, Ohio, that had agreed to rent its hall to organizers for the Machinists Union reneged under heavy pressure from local employers. They insisted that the four factories that dominated the local economy would leave town if the workers joined a union, "which would mean that New Comerstown would practically go off the map." Legionnaires in western Pennsylvania sponsored "Harmony Ads" in newspapers warning steelworkers that if they did not cooperate with management the companies would relocate and put them out of work, a fate in fact suffered by many of the factory towns in the postwar years. In the Hershey strike of 1937, Pennsylvania farmers, including Legionnaires, who supplied the chocolate factory with eight hundred thousand quarts of milk a day, broke a strike that had left them without a market. In the midst of a General Motors strike in Alexandria, Indiana, the town Legion summarized several reasons Legionnaires sided so frequently with capital: "people foreign to our city" had "misinformed" local workers and thrown out of work "more than 11,000 most of whom want to work."[36]

Legionnaires throughout the nation divided sharply on the organization's role in labor disputes. In the truck drivers' strike that paralyzed Minneapolis in May 1934, the state department turned down the chief of police's request to provide fifteen hundred unemployed veterans to drive trucks so that food deliveries might enter the city. The Legion refused to act even though a Trotskyite local of the Teamsters' Union led a violent strike in which other citizens' groups became involved as deputies. In Massachusetts, the state adjutant criticized Legionnaires in Southbridge who "in their zeal to cooperate with the American Federation of Labor" had committed "an error in judgment believing that the strike . . . was carried on and abetted by Communists.[37]

In the great auto- and steel-organizing drives launched by the CIO in 1937, however, the Legion came down squarely on the side of business. Legionnaires in Michigan, Pennsylvania, and Ohio had no trouble volunteering as special deputies to smash strikes in the face of a Communist presence in the CIO, the "invasion" of "their" communities by organizers sent in by John L. Lewis, and the sit-downs and coercive picketing of the United Auto Workers and the Steel Workers' Organizing Committee. However, Legion-management alliances achieved mixed results against tough and resourceful union leaders. Sympathetic state governors and liberal Legion Commander Harry Colmery helped labor by refusing to back local officials who wished to deputize vigilantes.

In the auto industry, Legionnaires proved ineffective in preventing the organization of General Motors in 1937. When the Fisher Body plant in Flint, Michigan, closed down on December 28, 1936, with the workers remaining in the plant for forty-four days, union official Henry Kraus forestalled interference by Legionnaires who intended to denounce the strike and join a "Flint Alliance" that planned to break it. Borrowing a tactic that had prevented Legion involvement in the Goodyear strike in Akron a year earlier, Kraus organized the Union War Veterans, consisting of UAW members. Appealing to solidarity among former servicemen by reminding "the uncommitted that patriotism was not the monopoly of strike opponents," several hundred Union War Veterans guarded strike leaders, while Michigan's Governor Frank Murphy refused to deputize the Flint Alliance and Secretary of Labor Frances Perkins pleaded with GM president Alfred P. Sloan to negotiate. Legion Commander Harry Colmery and Adjutant Frank Samuel did their part, too. They forbade Homer

Chaillaux to accept a speaking invitation from Flint Legionnaires while the strike was on to avoid injecting the Legion into the dispute. (When he finally showed up several months later, Chaillaux denounced the sit-down strike as "virtual anarchy . . . suspension of law, and disregard of courts.") The local radio station refused to allow Chaillaux to speak over the air about the strike while it was in progress, prompting him to complain sarcastically to the American Civil Liberties Union to "believe in your ideals" and defend his right to speak freely. (The ACLU offered to protest to the Federal Communications Commission.) Once the strike had ended, both the Flint post and the state Legion vented their spleen by launching investigations proving (to their satisfaction) that the strikes had been led by "subversive forces . . . seeking to obtain absolute unlawful control of private property," as some union organizers were Communists. They turned their findings over to National Headquarters and testified to the same effect before the Dies committee when it held hearings in Detroit in October 1938.[38]

The Michigan Legion partially recouped its failure at GM by helping to delay the unionization of the Ford Motor Company by several years. Henry Ford had considerable support from Legionnaires in the Dearborn area because he insisted on absolute veterans' preference in hiring; in 1937, 14,000 out of 85,000 workers at the plant were former servicemen. Dearborn Legion and VFW posts repeatedly claimed to be neutral in labor matters, but in June 1937 a *New York Times* investigation showed that the "vigilante army" formed to aid Ford had been organized at secret meetings of the Michigan Legion. Reporter Raymond Daniell found an "identity of sentiment" between business and the "middle class of retail merchants, white-collar workers, [and] farmers" who made up the Legion "against the frankly proletarian worker who has cast his lot with the C.I.O." Ray Smith, Michigan Commander for 1938, said much the same thing, only he praised where Daniell condemned:

> Subversive influences bore from within labor organizations and disrupt communities and bring suffering to innocent people—and when they do Legionnaires are going to do something about it. . . . Can you censure your comrade's activity in actively aiding vigilante groups when he sees irresponsible hoodlums paralyze the capital of a great state? . . . We may talk of neutrality in labor disputes . . . but we cannot indefinitely pussy-foot upon the problem which faces us in the threat of subversive forces gaining power

by manipulating labor movements to put radical leaders in positions where they control the forces of law and order.[39]

The Legion's most publicized action during the CIO's drive in the spring of 1937 to organize the "Little Steel" companies—which included Bethlehem, Republic, and Youngstown Sheet and Tube—also occurred in Michigan. On June 10, about two hundred policemen "reinforced by vigilante deputies, mostly American Legion men, armed with riot clubs, tear gas guns, and gas bombs" routed picketers on a public highway leading to a Republic factory in Monroe and reopened the plant. The Legionnaires then "streamed forth bearing rifles" to guard against the possibility the CIO might send reinforcements, but Homer Martin, president of the United Auto Workers, called off a march threatened by laborers ready to confront the veterans. Local authorities justified the violence by claiming the strikers interfered with the free flow of traffic, but a detailed study by the La Follette Committee investigating strikebreaking found this spurious; the pickets even allowed scabs to enter the plant.[40]

Reports and photographs of the Legion's open participation appeared in newspapers throughout the United States. National Commander Colmery received a barrage of criticism, including at least twenty-six protests from Legion posts. An anonymous citizen asserted that "your organization is getting to be a very hated one." Someone else sent him a photo of two helmeted Legionnaires armed with rifles lying in the grass and asked: "Who are these snakes in the grass, that are waiting to strike down our American men, women, and children with tongues of fire, lead, and death? Are they our heroes of twenty years ago?"[41]

In response to numerous condemnations of its conduct, the Monroe Legion Post issued a defense. It claimed not to object to "the right of labor to organize and to bargain collectively" and denied that it had offered its services "for the protection of private industry." Instead, the post stressed the illegality and arrogance of the CIO's efforts to intimidate a community where it had almost no popular support. (At the outset of the strike, only 125 of 1,352 employees at Republic belonged to the union.) The report, however, ignored such facts as the vicious beating of a black union organizer, Leonides McDonald, the day the strike was broken. The post also insisted that its members only patrolled the downtown area while police handled the strike; the highway patrols were not mentioned.[42]

Although the post left much out, the La Follette committee's investigation of labor unrest backed up its allegation that it had not served as "an instrumentality of the company." Rather, as State Adjutant Donald Glascoff wrote to Commander Colmery, "the situation here in Michigan seems to have outgrown a question of bickering between labor and capital and to be bordering upon a breakdown of law and order." Legionnaires throughout Michigan promoted "law and order leagues." Glascoff expostulated that confronted with simultaneous unprecedented strikes in the auto and steel industry, "it would be an impossible task to convince the 300 members of the Monroe Post that they did the wrong thing, or to convince the Monroe community that its Legion Post did not function as it should."[43]

Nevertheless, National Commander Colmery tried to calm the Michiganders. A moderate who sincerely investigated complaints of Legion excesses brought to his attention by the ACLU and the press, Colmery expressed "deep concern" that the Legion was about to be "put under arms en masse for strike duty." He emphatically insisted that the "Legion is not a strike-breaking organization," and "deplored" instances where it "arrogated to itself police authority." In addition to responding to extensive criticism of the Legion's role in the Michigan riots, Colmery took action after he received protests from all over the nation in April when the Associated Press reported that the local Legion drum and bugle corps had led "a brutal attack" on workers sitting down at the chocolate factory in Hershey, Pennsylvania. The corps then forced women strikers to run a gauntlet to escape as a mob beat them with sticks and clubs. (The local post commander insisted, somewhat disingenuously, he had no control over the drum and bugle corps, which had few Legion members.) Henceforth, Colmery instructed every department commander that if Legionnaires served as deputies in an emergency, they could not wear their uniforms or any Legion insignia. He also took positive action to keep the Legion from becoming involved in labor disputes by forbidding the ever-eager Chaillaux to deliver speeches at the site of strikes in progress.[44]

Not everyone praised Colmery's restraint. Probusiness Legionnaires demanded Michigan's Governor Frank Murphy be thrown out of the Legion because he had refused to call in troops to end the sit-downs. Colmery responded that Murphy was "not accountable to the Legion but to the electorate of that state." Others suggested that the Legion cast off its neutrality and actively fight labor: one realtor complained that "law and order has broken down in Michigan," and warned that if the Legion did not take a more active role authority would "break down throughout the United States as it has done in Spain and France." Michigan Legionnaires "were unable to see why the American Legion . . . cannot do anything about preserving law and order." They backed up their defiance in May 1938 by openly organizing a hundred men to harvest beets in Lewanee County while workers struck. The District of Columbia Legion, over considerable opposition, authorized a "corps of Legion vigilantes" in December 1937. Three months later, Legionnaires in Columbus, Georgia, tried to influence the outcome of a union election by branding the CIO as Communist and intimidating workers who intended to join. Colmery's effort to reassert the Legion's neutrality clearly found little sympathy among members who believed their communities threatened by the CIO's highly publicized organizing drives.[45]

Most notably, posts used the methods repudiated by Colmery to squelch the Steel Workers' Organizing Committee (SWOC) in Youngstown, Warren, Canton, and Massillon, Ohio, and in Johnstown, Pennsylvania. When the SWOC appeared, Youngstown's sheriff hired fifty Legionnaires for policy duty. The Massillon Legion supplied forty after a Republic Steel official planted the false rumor that workers from Canton and Akron were preparing to march on the town to prevent strikebreaking. Mayor Daniel Shields of Johnstown, who claimed the national Legion had secretly authorized his antiunion strongarm tactics in 1935, tried to recruit three hundred Legionnaires for "special police assistance" and deputized an unspecified number. However, Pennsylvania's State Commander, Walter Kress, in town at the time, talked the Johnstown post out of taking official action. Cooperating with industry's "Mohawk Valley" plan to blame labor troubles on "outside agitators" and to unite citizens and loyal employees to break strikes, Legionnaires did their part in postponing the unionization of the smaller steel companies for several years.[46]

Legion activities that offended labor went beyond "peacekeeping" during strikes. The Legion also gathered reams of information on real and assumed radical elements in labor that it made available to private companies and public authorities. To complement Homer Chaillaux's national clearinghouse for reports on subversion, Legionnaires in the states spied on labor leaders and prepared dossiers on their illegal activities and associations with

Communists. California again led the way. Headed by Harper L. Knowles, its Legion Subversive Activities Committee, formed in 1934, gave evidence against Harry Bridges during his deportation hearings five years later. Knowles admitted that his committee used Legionnaires as labor spies and made its findings available to such powerful employer groups as the Industrial Association and the Associated Farmers. Washington's Division of Subversive Activities Investigations, formed the following year, typified how such units worked. It set up branch offices in every district of the state and instructed post commanders to cooperate in collecting and keeping "readily available information on individuals and organizations engaged in subversive or revolutionary movements." Although charged with investigating all radical activities, Washington Legionnaires directed almost all their attention to labor organizations. They filed and passed around numerous reports on the lumber, aircraft, maritime, fishing, canning, agricultural, building services, automobile mechanics, and trucking industries.[47]

Another ostensibly antiradical activity that was in practice antilabor was the Legion's campaign against interference with national-defense production, beginning in 1940. Investigations by the AFL blamed over four-fifths of the walkouts on management's refusal to negotiate in accordance with National Labor Relations Board guidelines. But the Legion generally adopted the opinion, which business inculcated in the public, that "defense objectives are failing of attainment because . . . labor racketeers and profiteers who place personal advantage above the welfare of the nation are crippling industry." Legion posts throughout the country prodded National Headquarters to press for legislative action to halt strikes that they perceived were hindering productivity and thereby jeopardizing the nation's security. As a district commander from Tennessee inquired, "If our government can pass a law putting men in uniforms at $21.00 a month why cannot it also put men in overalls to supply the equipment?"[48]

During the emergency, the Legion urged states to pass "model" defense bills, which offended organized labor. Most obnoxious was the Sabotage Prevention Act, which allowed defense industries to post No Trespass signs and made violations of these warnings a crime; permitted the closing of streets and highways around defense plants; and prescribed harsh penalties for sabotage, defined as intentionally defective work in defense industries. Labor also objected to bills that gave governors the power to mo-

bilize their state police to open struck plants; permitted state
military forces to cross state lines while chasing insurrectionists
and saboteurs; and regulated the ownership, manufacture, sale,
and distribution of explosives. New York, Michigan, and Maryland, among other states, adopted Legion-sponsored codes to this
effect. The attitude of many Legionnaires was expressed in a
California Department resolution of April 1941, arguing that the
"danger of the United States itself being attacked is exceedingly
great" and branding participants in "senseless" strikes and lock-
outs as "treacherous, traitorous, guilty of treason, and unworthy
of the name American."[49]

The Legion took action on the national level as well. Commander Raymond Kelly applauded John L. Lewis's efforts to
purge the CIO of Communist infiltration. At its meetings in May
and November 1941, the National Executive Committee (NEC)
called for "legislation forbidding strikes and lock-outs in national
defense" industries for the duration of the national emergency if
labor failed to restrain itself voluntarily. Other suggestions included the removal of Secretary of Labor Frances Perkins, who
blamed management for most strikes, and the creation of a National Defense Agency, "similar to the War Industries Board of
World War I, to be given full authority and responsibility for
attaining national objectives." Many groups favored such a plan—
President Roosevelt established the War Production Board in January 1942—but the Legion's reasons related to labor unrest. The
NEC also called for utilizing the entire manpower of the nation for
defense, treating any obstruction of military production as a crime
equal to desertion, and regulating wages and prices by government edict. Even before Pearl Harbor, the Legion had asked the
president and Congress to assume control of the national economy
as they had done two decades earlier, but in the present instance
for the primary purpose of ending labor's supposed obstruction
of national defense.[50]

Yet even many Legionnaires realized that labor did not bear all
the blame for defense slowdowns. The NEC equated lockouts—
which of course were rarer—with strikes. Former Commanders
Colmery and Johnson argued that it would be wiser to condemn
obstruction in general rather than to single out labor, as they
knew of businessmen who refused defense contracts to avoid the
requirement that they deal with unions. A minority of Legionnaires went beyond impartiality, spoke up in favor of labor, and
urged that the organization should more actively recruit union

members. Beginning in 1940, George Danfield, chairman of the Cook County Labor Relations Committee and past commander of Chicago's Union Labor Post, badgered National Headquarters with requests for a national Legion Labor Committee to "promote good will and cooperation between the labor movement and the American Legion." Such a committee already functioned in Chicago, where it tried to refute charges that the Legion was antilabor and repudiated interference in labor disputes by "self-seeking" Legionnaires. Danfield and AFL President William Green sent a circular letter to labor unions throughout the nation asking if veterans among them would like to form union posts: they received ninety-one affirmative responses from thirty-one states and Alaska. Remarking that "it is unfortunate that the average men from the ranks of labor have neither the time nor money to work their way to the top of the American Legion," Danfield suggested National Headquarters give "a little recognition" to working men "at the bottom of the ladder plugging along as best we can to put the Legion program over."[51]

Danfield did not make much headway before the United States entered World War II. His requests for a labor representative on the Legion's Defense Committee, which investigated civilian defense in Great Britain, fell on deaf ears. During the war, however, as the Legion's potential membership grew astronomically and large numbers of workers served in the military, the Legion accepted Danfield's suggestion. It created a Labor Relations Committee in 1944; by 1945, the number of union posts had increased from 5 to 120. The union Legionnaires resolved, in Danfield's words, to "keep the Legion free from fascist influence which would destroy labor unions." As during the prewar emergency, they stood up for labor when National Commander Warren Atherton suggested that a good way to handle strikers whose actions threatened production would be "to have some chairs wired up and the current turned on." Despite the Legion's antistrike rhetoric during the war, it extended overtures to the CIO to participate in its Americanism endowment drive and in 1945 began to invite CIO leaders to speak at national conventions. In 1952, 24 percent of the Legion's ranks consisted of laboring men.[52]

Depending on the perspective taken, the Legion's attitude toward labor either shifted four times or it did not change at all. During the Red Scare of 1919–20, the Legionnaires' defense of law and order in a country gripped by the IWW-Bolshevik menace meant a largely antilabor stance. From the 1920s until the early

1930s, the Legion and a conservative labor movement joined forces against even more right-wing presidents and Congresses that favored business interests. Beginning with the great strikes of 1934 and continuing until America joined the Second World War, the Legion again opposed militant unions determined to organize unskilled workers and not afraid of associating with Communists and violating laws designed to prevent mass unionization. Finally, during World War II, after the CIO had completed most of its major campaigns and begun to purge its own radicals, the Legion began to seek the same cordial relations with the newer unions it had developed with the AFL.

Yet one can also say that the Legion's fundamental attitude toward labor never varied. The Legion maintained a law-and-order stand and either embraced or condemned unions based on their adherence to the Legion's definition of Americanism. Efforts by many Legionnaires to remain neutral in labor troubles that did not threaten community safety, and divided opinion within the ranks (even when some of their comrades acted legally as special deputies), demonstrate that the Legion as a whole did not act as a tool of business, although it may have in some localities. A predominantly middle-class American Legion could muster little sympathy for workers driven by unfortunate conditions to join the Communist party or to accept Communist leadership, or for those who failed to adhere strictly to the letter of a law shaped by antiunion legislatures and judges. But cooperation with both the AFL and the CIO once they reached maturity shows the Legion was neither pro- nor antilabor in principle. It put its seal of approval on unions, as on other civic organizations, that worked within the law and supported its commitment to Americanism, even as it showed little restraint in combating unions that failed to respect laws that would have prevented them from organizing. During the first two decades of the Legion's existence, it therefore stood both ideologically and practically opposed to the progressive elements in American labor.

CHAPTER NINE

The Fight Against Subversion Continues:

Communism, Nazism, Immigration, and Education

When I first became a member of the Legion, back in 1919, it never occurred to me, and I dare say it never occurred to you, that you would live to see the day when your number one problem would be to ward off and kill off subversive elements undertaking to eat at the very roots of the government, of the fundamentals for which you in the first place went to war.

W. D. Schwartz at the National Americanism Commission, AL, November 22, 1939, 76

I N THE 1930s, the Legion launched reinvigorated campaigns against Communists, Fascists, immigrants, and leftist educators, who threatened the culturally homogeneous society it equated with "Americanism." The Legion was not simply paranoid: there was indeed a significant Communist and a budding Fascist movement during the Great Depression, and many recent immigrants resisted the Legion's brand of assimilation. But by regarding even refugees from Hitler's tyranny and liberal Legionnaires as subversives, the Legion moved from the middle of the political spectrum in the conservative twenties to the right in an America that had shifted considerably leftward. Seeking at least some consensus, the Legion elected two liberal Midwestern commanders in the mid thirties to counter charges that it had fallen under the thumb of the militantly right-wing California group headed by Americanism Director Homer Chaillaux, who led the Legion's antisubversion programs. But with the rise of Hitler and his subsequent pact with Stalin, Legion fears that a fifth column could undermine American democracy appeared more plausible and led to widespread acceptance of its programs against suspected saboteurs and "un-Americans." The creation of the Legion-sponsored Dies committee in 1938 symbolized the new respectability of the antiradical crusade.

After its relatively low-keyed behavior in the late twenties and early thirties, the Legion's renewed struggle against dissidents may be dated from 1934, when National Commander Frank Belgrano appointed his fellow Californian and former State Commander Homer Chaillaux to head the Legion's Americanism Division. A one-time Los Angeles postmaster whose Legion activity stemmed from his disgust with the radical literature he observed flowing through the mail, Chaillaux came to Indianapolis fresh from his role in breaking the migrant workers'strike in the Imperial Valley and the general strike in San Francisco. For just over a decade, until he suddenly died of a heart attack at forty-eight, Chaillaux, with all "the finesse and subtlety of blasting powder," placed the Legion in the forefront of the nation's crusade against subversion. Chaillaux traveled half a million miles in ten years to deliver speeches "with a voice of thunder." He turned his office into a reinvigorated center for information on "un-Americanism," wrote patriotic tracts, drafted legislation, and led the Legion's important collaborations with the FBI and the House Un-American Activities Committee. Despite some internal questioning of his tactics, most Legion commanders and the rank and file backed him enthusiastically.[1]

When Chaillaux took over the Americanism office, he found, as his predecessor Russell Cook had admitted, "very, very little authentic information regarding either organizations or individuals connected with Communism or subversion." He set out to change that. Within a month of his arrival, Chaillaux sent memorandums to the state departments requesting "authentic reports of all radical activities." Hoping to outlaw the Communist party, Chaillaux wanted to know in which states it was allowed on the ballot and how, in those states, parties qualified to run candidates.[2]

Responses were not long in coming and soon Chaillaux had a sizable file. His own state, California, was already performing the same tasks. Legionnaires there worked hand in glove with the local police, and formed "an organization of men who, upon call, attend the various [radical] meetings scheduled throughout the county and make a written report." San Diego's George Fisher boasted that "this is really military intelligence work and of course, it is secret and confidential, and the men selected are men that know how to stand considerable abuse at a meeting without losing their heads." "One or two" Legionnaires even belonged to the Communist party. The California Legion developed a program, including proposed antiradical legislation, cooperation with such groups as the Elks and the Chamber of Commerce, a publicity campaign and speakers' bureau, watchdogs to prevent the teaching of "Communist propaganda" in the schools, and its own statewide subversive information clearinghouse.[3]

Other states joined California in supporting the new director's initiative. Ohio Adjutant John Saslavsky, who reported a similar program, described Chaillaux's ideas as "very fine . . . exactly what we have to interest our posts in." Chaillaux reimbursed New York's John Snow for the cost of sending in lists of radicals; Tennessee reported Socialist organizers coming from New York; a Michigan Legionnaire who expressed concern about the situation in his state received Chaillaux's assurances that thanks to the state police "I am kept fully well in touch with the continued growth of radicalism in Michigan." Thousands of reports poured in during Chaillaux's tenure.[4]

Chaillaux's general demeanor encouraged local posts, as during the Red Scare, to go beyond the law. On one occasion this took an almost charming form. In April 1935 the Commander of an Atlanta post, "a good-natured, easy-going, very typical little businessman," according to an ACLU informant, persuaded his unit to successfully oppose an appearance by Congresswoman Jeannette Rankin in town on the imagined ground that she was a nudist. "Nudists, Reds, Pacifists, and this Roger Baldwin . . . they all want to overthrow our government by force," he avowed in an interview that would have embarrassed Chaillaux himself. But aside from the labor disputes discussed in chapter 8, the two most spectacular local Legion anti-Communist initiatives of the late 1930s occurred not more than a few miles apart, in Jersey City and Manhattan. They illustrate the Legion's powerful influence even in the nation's eastern urban areas.[5]

The Legion in Boss Frank Hague's fief of Jersey City attracted nationwide attention from December 1937 until February 1939 for its support of the mayor's campaign to keep the city free of CIO "non-resident agitators." These militants "invade[d] Jersey City [to] make us safe for the Reds," Hague's *Jersey Journal* phrased it. The trouble started when forty or fifty "professional radical agitators," according to the *Journal*, appeared from Newark. They began handing out leaflets and holding meetings without obtaining the requisite police permits and "raised the cry of constitutional right of free speech and assembly." "A good Legionnaire" judge sentenced seven ringleaders to serve five days in jail for illegal assembly, while police escorted the rest out of town. Then followed a protracted "invasion" during which Roger Baldwin, the Socialist leader Norman Thomas, and "radical" Congressman Jerry O'Connell of Montana made futile efforts to deliver public speeches in the face of hostile mobs organized by Hague supporters. The crowds pelted Thomas with eggs and roughed up police officers guarding Congressman O'Connell.[6]

The crisis came in May and June 1938. Both Thomas and New Jersey Legion leaders reported to National Commander Daniel Doherty that local posts had organized and participated in the crowds. Newspapers throughout the country condemned the Jersey City veterans' "misguided zeal" and the Legion in general for "always appearing in the forefront of these get-the-hell-out-of-here parties." So did the Legion's labor-union post in Chicago. Taking the advice of National Publicity Officer Edward MacGrail that the Jersey City affair was leading to "dissipation of the friendly regard in which the American Legion was held by the press of the nation," Doherty issued a public statement insisting that no Legionnaire or post "has the right to interfere with, or to impair in any manner," the constitutional guarantees of free speech and expression. He also privately warned New Jersey's State Commander that he would publicly denounce the guilty posts unless they ceased "even semi-official participation" in Hague's rallies. Thomas professed himself satisfied, and even the leftist *Nation* took Doherty's denunciation of Hague's methods as a "healthy sign." Still, Hague's house organ continued to support his refusal to allow "the whoopee-doop congressmen from reed regions, the nit-wit professors from hunky-dunk colleges," and the "front men of the Red Revolution" to "come back here and tell us that we are scum and that we live in a sink hole." As late as February 1939, at a "secret" meeting that somehow became public, Jersey City Legionnaires warned Baldwin, Thomas, "and the rest of your like [that] if you insist on invading our city, the veterans will be compelled to give you a lesson in democracy that you and your kind will never forget as long as you live."[7]

Unlike the Jersey City antics, which provided the Legion with a model to avoid, New York Legionnaires' systematic legal battle against Simon Gerson set a precedent that anti-Communists later used repeatedly to oust "subversives" from government positions. New York's most prominent Legionnaire, Jeremiah Cross, directed the campaign to remove Gerson, an avowed Communist whom Manhattan Borough President Stanley Isaacs had appointed his assistant to reward the Communists for their support of the fusion ticket that had elected Isaacs and Mayor Fiorello La Guardia. Beginning in February 1938, Cross organized rallies and petitioned Isaacs, La Guardia, and Governor Herbert Lehman to remove Gerson. When this failed, he and the Legion lobbied for two years until, in April 1940, the New York state legislature passed a law removing from public office anyone who "advocates, advises or teaches the doctrine that the government of the United States . . . should be overthrown or overturned by force, violence, or any unlawful means." National Headquarters then provided $2,500 for a lawsuit in which the Legion argued that Gerson fit this description simply by virtue of belonging to the Communist party. On September 27, when New York City's counsel refused to take his case, Gerson resigned to avoid "defending the Communist party from the charge that it teaches or advocates the overthrow of government by force." As with the federal Smith Act passed that year, New York's Legion-inspired law and Gerson's resignation established the automatic legal linkage of membership in the Communist party with the advocacy of violent revolution. The Legion thereby paved the way for the wholesale dismissal of real and alleged Communists from government office that followed World War II.[8]

Such legal crusades received enthusiastic encouragement from Indianapolis. To Ohio Legionnaires wondering whether they should "disperse" a group of Communists planning to dupe veterans into joining a march of the unemployed on Washington, Chaillaux warned that "any action of this kind will tend to turn the minds of the public against the veterans." He suggested that the Legion could accomplish "ten times" as much good by obtaining legislation banning Communist organizing. The Legion also participated as a "member organization" in the Chamber of Commerce's similar effort.[9]

Chaillaux vigorously answered critics of such belligerent campaigns. He wrote detailed rebuttals to each of ten American Civil Liberties Union charges that the Legion forcibly denied Communists and radicals their rights to organize, and praised the Legion's "unusual restraint . . . in view of the growth of various subversive movements in this country . . . quite contrary to the methods employed against Legionnaires in Centralia, Washington, who were murdered in cold blood by radicals." Chaillaux also took on Stephen O'Donnell, a reporter from his hometown's *Los Angeles Post Examiner,* who drew parallels between the Legion and Fascist veterans in Italy and Germany. There "a servile leadership" supposedly "went over to the service of extremely wealthy individuals, sold out the rank and file, destroyed every vestige of popular government, and enslaved the nation." Ignoring Legion vigilantism, Chaillaux responded that "ninety percent of our program is our effort to properly present our Americanism ideals to the youth of America," and denied any interest in forming "a fascist outfit, another KKK."[10]

In addition to gathering data on the red menace from others, Chaillaux generated a great deal of his own. In March 1935 he sent out two thousand copies of Congressman Hamilton Fish's radio address "Communism" to Legion Americanism leaders throughout the nation. Fish grouped "left wing socialism" with Communism as "its half brother and sister," and denounced Columbia University, New York University, the City College of New York, and the universities of Chicago, Wisconsin, California, North Carolina, and Pennsylvania as "honeycombed with

Socialists, near Communists and Communists." Chaillaux
warned an Iowa Legionnaire that the figure of 32,000 registered
party members was misleading; some 250,000 Americans voted
for Communists in the 1934 elections, and "several hundred thousands," mostly "transients and foreigners" who could not be
traced, also supported the party. But the Communists' main
strength came from some 3 million "fellow travellers" in "united
front organizations." Chaillaux even attended the 1936 national
convention of the League Against War and Fascism—which had
ten registered Communists on its ninety-member executive committee—to confirm his suspicion of "the close resemblance" of its
program to the Communist party's own.[11]

Some of the Legion's antisubversive fights concerned plays and
films. In October 1935, Chaillaux tried to stop the Dartmouth
College Players from performing Clifford Odets's play *Waiting
for Lefty,* which he described as a piece of "poisonous, un-American propaganda." New Hampshire's American Legion, however,
refused to take any action, thereby restoring the faith of Dartmouth's newspaper editor, Budd Schulberg, in the Legion for its
refusal to countenance "dictatorial methods." In 1938 Chaillaux
went after Irwin Shaw's *Bury the Dead,* an antiwar play he described as "full of blasphemy and immoral sections," including
"scenes of soldiers in houses of ill-fame." He passed on the word
to Legion posts to object to the spread of such "Communist
propaganda." To its credit, the Legion refused in April 1941 to
join Willian Randolph Hearst's crusade against Orson Welles and
his Free Players in the wake of *Citizen Kane,* a film based on
Hearst's unsavory rise to power. When the California Department
attacked Welles for producing such plays as *The Mole on Lincoln's
Cheek,* which might have a "detrimental effect on the effort now
being made to unite this country," the Americanism Commission
preferred to have the nation feel "the Legion has slapped the
California Department in the face" rather than appearing to be
the tool of the Hearst interests.[12]

Such restraint was unusual. Chaillaux painted a variety of
groups and individuals with his red brush. Upon information
provided by Legionnaires in Laredo, Texas, he reported Mexican
Consul Juan Richer to the State Department for sponsoring a
meeting of Mexican-American migrant laborers. Richer and Mexican union organizers supposedly uttered "subversive and un-
American statements," such as comparing Mexican President Lá-
zaro Cárdenas favorably with America's Roosevelt, who allegedly

"had not done one-tenth of what could be done for the laboring class," and whose National Recovery Administration "benefited the rich people." In 1937, Chaillaux condemned the Abraham Lincoln Brigade and financial aid to the Spanish Republicans. The effort to rally Americans around "the united front Socialist-Communist so-called Loyalist Party in Spain," he told Wisconsin Legionnaires, was a "Communist racket" the Legion ought to expose. And in 1939, Chaillaux forwarded to New Orleans businessmen opposed to the National Urban League information that it received money from the leftist Garland Fund which numbered the ACLU's Roger Baldwin among its directors, thereby in his eyes linking it with Communism.[13]

Delivering eighty-nine speeches in twenty-seven states in his first six months in office, including traveling twenty-three hundred miles and making fifty-seven trips at his own expense, Chaillaux warned that "there are more Communists in the United States today than there were in Russia when the government was overthrown." He also stressed that far from being purely an economic system, Communism threatened all the values good Americans cherished:

> Openly denying God; openly an enemy of religion; plans for getting communistic teachers and pupils into schools and colleges to work on the inside against American institutions, including the American home. Children are incited to rebel against home-control; against respect for parents.

Appearing "before state conventions of the Federated Women's Clubs, state conventions of the Women's Christian Temperance Union, Parent-Teachers' Associations, college and university student bodies [and] law and order leagues," Chaillaux drove his point home. The American Communist party ranked him number three on its enemies list.[14]

Chaillaux's greatest triumph came with the publication of *ISMS*, which he announced for distribution to hundreds of prominent Legionnaires on February 27, 1936. The Legion had sent out six thousand copies by May 3; the Michigan Department alone ultimately bought forty thousand; the Mexican veterans' associations printed two hundred thousand copies translated into Spanish to meet their presumed Communist threat. By November, Chaillaux boasted that every library in the nation contained a copy of this "record of revolutionary Communism and its active sympathizers in the United States," which "met the need for

ISMS

A Review of ALIEN ISMS, REVOLUTIONARY COMMUNISM
and their Active Sympathizers in the United States

(SECOND EDITION)

Compiled by the
NATIONAL AMERICANISM COMMISSION *of* THE AMERICAN LEGION
National Headquarters, Indianapolis, Indiana

1937

ISMS—The title page of the controversial volume published in 1936 by the Americanism Commission. Courtesy of American Legion National Headquarters.

reliable proof of the existence of and danger of subversive activities of a revolutionary character."[15]

It is doubtful whether many Legionnaires or other Americans slogged through the 260 pages of *ISMS*. Even a browser, however, would notice the prominent reproductions of Communist posters and captions, intended to show how the reds threatened all the principal American values. *ISMS* reprinted Soviet placards depicting "The New [Red] Star of Bethlehem" shining over a factory, a worker in a dumpster "dumping Jesus Christ overboard," and the hammer and sickle crushing pathetic-looking figures of God, Jehovah, and Allah, which "displayed the attitude of the Communist toward religion." Five illustrations showed the supposed Soviet attitude toward women. One depicted "The Emancipation of Women in Russia"—at what "they call Hard Labor," the caption noted ironically. Beneath pictures of women working in factories, the Legion editorialized: "What a future for girls after college and sorority days—if we tolerate the Communist way," and "would you like to see this for your daughter?" If much of *ISMS* read like a catalogue, those parts that did not vividly showed how Communism would make short work of religion, the family, and traditional attitudes toward women.[16]

Chaillaux also stressed the Communist challenge to baseball, American history, and the police's role in law enforcement. One of the more readable parts of *ISMS* contained a challenge from the *Daily Worker* to sponsor the best of the Young Communist teams against the Legion's Junior Baseball champions to show the Communists "play baseball . . . hold picnics . . . go to summer camp . . . [and] are quite normal beings interested in the same sports and social activities as the masses generally." Besides infiltrating the great American game, the radicals tried to undermine patriotism by depicting George Washington as a slaveowner who "signed the Declaration of Independence" [*sic*], "was one of the biggest drunkards of his day," and "believed in [the] rich having more power than [the] poor." "The Great Emancipator," Abraham Lincoln, only reluctantly freed the slaves "so the northern capitalists could go on exploiting the southern states for their own use," read a Young Pioneer pamphlet the Legion quoted. Two photographs from the San Francisco general strike showed "innocent" policemen being physically and verbally assaulted by workers, "which disproved the Communist Press stories of police brutality" to the Legion's satisfaction.[17]

To its credit, the opening page of *ISMS* warned the public against "descending to the level of Communists" by assuming "police authority" and "taking the law into our own hands," and argued for a "campaign of education" and legislation against subversive utterances. The main message of *ISMS* appeared most prominently in two boxes juxtaposed early in the volume. "WHAT

THE AMERICAN LEGION STANDS FOR" included "God and Country," "Law and Order," "Peace and Goodwill," "Justice, Freedom, and Democracy," and a "Sense of Individual Obligation to Community, State, and Nation." "WHAT COMMUNISM STANDS FOR" consisted of "Hatred of God," "Destruction of Private Property," "Strikes, Riots, Sabotage, Bloodshed, and Civil War," "World Revolution," and "Dictatorship."[18]

Critics objected that while the Americanism Commission gathered information on Communists, it lacked equal vigor in its opposition to Fascism. When a second edition of *ISMS* became necessary in 1937, Chaillaux did add a chapter on Fascism, but it consisted of a mere 16 pages (as opposed to 264 on Communism). Legion conventions repeatedly "reaffirm[ed] our opposition to Communism, Fascism, Nazism," and "any organizations in the United States which are militarily serving Germany, Italy, Russia, Spain, or any other alien power or system." Still, in defense of the Legion, there was little evidence of Fascist activity in the United States before the late 1930s and the rise of Fritz Kuhn's German-American Bund and William Dudley Pelley's Silver Shirts. When the ACLU's Morris Ernst wished the Legion would perceive the danger of Fascism in March 1936, he meant "the Ku Klux Klan, vigilantes, employers, private gunmen, reactionary newspapers, sheriffs, and police." As late as 1937, a liberal Legionnaire feared that the Legion neglected "the rapid spread of Fascist tendencies and the very definite subversive movement of the Nazi groups in this country," which he found "much more frightening and crippling than the so-called Red Menace." Despite Chaillaux's and the National Commanders' public stand against Fascism, complaints continued to arise that the Legion pursued the left with far more vigor than the right.[19]

These charges appear unfair in light of the Legion's record. As the Fascists became more prominent, the Legion faced the same perplexities and responded in the same manner as it did in the case of Communists. Local posts, confronting military camps and uniformed parades in their communities, pressed for anti-Fascist legislation, held counterdemonstrations, and prodded National Headquarters to take a stronger stand. Chaillaux responded with his customary speeches and information gathering. Somewhat ironically, the Nazi controversy arose at the moment when the Legion enjoyed two relatively liberal commanders—Ray Murphy (1935–36) and Harry Colmery (1936–37)—who cared more about civil liberties than most Legionnaires. Although the Legion never generated great amounts of information against the Fascist groups, their menace did appear suddenly and reporting on them had to begin from scratch. Chaillaux explained to the Jewish adjutant of a Missouri post: "We contacted every known agency which investigates Nazi propaganda and asked for facts which would be substantiated and for reliable photographs. We received plenty of promises but very little material." The Legion therefore limited itself to reprinting Congressional hearings on Nazi fronts in the second edition of *ISMS*.[20]

Legionnaires worried especially about the rural youth camps where the Bund spread its doctrine and supposedly trained future storm troopers. Iowa veterans urged Congress to pass a law that "any military or semi-military camp in the United States should be under the direct supervision and control of the War Department." They did so despite Chaillaux's warning that the Bund "forestalled just such a possibility by having only a small percentage of those who attend their camps in uniform," although he offered to support any legislation that might have a chance of standing up in court. New Jersey's Legion, on the other hand, succeeded in pushing through a state law, aimed directly at a Nazi camp in Sussex County, against the "wearing of uniforms of foreign governments by propaganda organizations and the inciting of race, color, or religious hatred." New York, too, acted against Nazi Camp Siegfried at Yaphank, Long Island. Following an investigation demanded by New York Legionnaires, a judge sentenced the camp's organizers to a year in jail "for violating the civil rights law of New York," which required secret societies to file their membership lists.[21]

As with anti-Communist activity, not all Legion posts confined themselves to the letter of the law. Exactly who started the trouble or was involved usually remained unclear, but brawls occurred in February and March 1938 at the time of a major Bund membership drive. Chaillaux warned that "the publicity was not good" when "overzealous individuals," defended by the State Legion Commander, broke the windows of a private home where Fritz Kuhn had attempted to organize a Bund branch in Indianapolis. Buffalo Legionnaires showed even less restraint. A Bund meeting attended by Legionnaires, who verbally challenged the speakers, turned into "a fifteen-minute free-for-all" that required twenty policemen to break up. The County Commander termed the outburst "deplorable," adding that the Legion men originally "came to listen quietly and ask questions" in "the American way."

A post service officer in Youngstown, Ohio, described a similar incident there, and the attendant negative effect on the Legion's image:

> The whole trouble is that we had a meeting here of the Silver Shirt crowd and a few veterans went down and started the trouble and the next day the American Legion headed the newspaper that it was Legionnaires who started the trouble, which of course gives us bum publicity and the American Legion Post took no action on going to any meeting. I told these fellows they could go anywhere as individuals but they could not use the Legion name and put us behind the eight ball all the time. . . . I told them we stood for law and order and this was a good example of it by going out and starting trouble as there were many other ways of getting at these birds and that was by informing people in a nice way what they were doing and their aims and then get laws passed to stop or deport them. . . . I personally believe the Silver Shirt racket like the Klan and others will run its course and die a natural death if the public are wise as to what they are up to.[22]

In Yorkville, the German-American neighborhood on the Upper East Side of Manhattan, the Legion was the victim rather than the aggressor. *Labor News* reported that on April 28, 1938, "storm troopers savagely set upon a group of cap-wearing American Legionnaires who were watching the Bund's celebration of Hitler's forty-ninth birthday and brutally beat them with blackjacks and the heavy buckles from their Sam Brown belts." Ten days earlier, the Bund had warned Legionnaires to stay out of Yorkville upon pain of death. The New York County Legion promptly informed the police, who sent plainsclothesmen wearing Legion buttons into the community to serve as decoys. The resulting arrests enraged the Bund, whose members turned out in such numbers that police at the Hitler rally feared to intervene on behalf of the beleaguered veterans. "The methods now being employed by Nazis against Legionnaires are identical with the methods they used several years ago in Germany," complained Bronx Legionnaire Lou Wolfson. "They started by attacking individuals and small groups who were not in favor with their doctrine of government until they were able to grow to the size where now they are able to control the entire German people." Outraged Stockton, California, Legionnaires extended their sympathies, and suggested their New York comrades retaliate by dealing with the Bund as they themselves had once dealt with the local Communists: "torn down their meeting place . . . burned their records, broke everything they had and when they tried to arrest some of us—the cops just seemed to be unable to find any of those guys." National Headquarters repudiated such strong-arm methods. Commander Murphy took the same line he did against Communists: "We cannot, of course, interfere with free assembly and the right of free speech." Chaillaux set to work gathering information, and on June 24, 1938, sent an eight-page memorandum to every department adjutant and state Americanism chairman listing the locations of Bund offices and camps, the names of leaders, and descriptions of its ideology and activities.[23]

The Legion's greatest opportunity to arouse the public against totalitarianism came with the creation of the House Committee on Un-American Activities in the spring of 1938, commonly known as the Dies committee after its controversial chairman, Martin Dies of Texas. The Legion had staunchly supported the Fish (1930–31) and Dickstein (1934–35) committees, which looked into subversion, and pushed for a permanent committee throughout the 1930s. When the House approved his committee, Dies lost no time inviting Homer Chaillaux "to be one of the first to speak." Thanking him for his help in bringing the committee into existence, Dies gave Chaillaux carte blanche to "present any matters that you see fit without interruption." The Legion, for its part, exulted that the committee would provide the cure for "a diseased condition in our internal affairs, which, if suffered to go unchecked, may cause our national destruction."[24]

Chaillaux appeared twice before the Dies committee in its first two weeks of meetings, on August 9 and 17, 1938. He proceeded to summarize the results of four years' efforts, turning over reams of material on subversives to the Texas congressman. "Sinister forces are expending greater effort than ever before to wreck this nation," he announced, talking mostly about Communists and their "fronts" like the ACLU, the Workers Alliance, and groups supporting the Spanish Republicans. He also "paid his respects to the German American Bund." For the next several years, the Legion strongly endorsed every request Dies made for funds, opened the *Legion Monthly* to committee members, and circulated lists of those congressmen who opposed the committee so that they might be suitably "barraged" with protests from outraged Legionnaires.[25]

The mutual admiration of the committee and the Legion guaranteed that the veterans received criticism for supporting Dies's attacks on church, labor, youth, and hundreds of other groups and individuals. The Legion first ran into trouble in November 1938, when Harper Knowles, head of the California Legion's powerful "Radical Research Committee," began criticizing "practically every Democrat running for office in California" as a Communist sympathizer. Two of them then sued him for $100,000 for slander and libel. Secretary of the Associated Farmers, a group closely linked to the state's Republican machine, Knowles used his Legion connections to mask his capitalist ties. Although the Legion denied that Knowles spoke for it, he remained head of its California espionage network. The same month, the Legion ran afoul of liberal critics, although winning its usual conservative support, for getting behind Dies's attack on Secretary of Labor Frances Perkins when she persistently refused to deport the Longshoremen's leader Harry Bridges. And in December 1940, when the FBI criticized Dies for exposing some of its investigations before it had gathered sufficient evidence to secure convictions, the Legion tried to make peace among its two allies. It argued equitably that "there is need for a committee such as the Dies committee" and "there is need for an FBI with greatly increased personnel" to avert future misunderstandings. In general, Legionnaires agreed with Commander Chadwick's response to Jewish veterans at the City College Post who wanted Dies himself investigated for his (mistakenly) alleged friendliness with Fritz Kuhn: "While the Dies Committee will necessarily thresh out a bunch of chaff, they are getting some wheat and giving us a better audience as to some of the problems with which the Legion has been concerned than we have been able to get for ourselves." The Legion proudly supported Dies to the end and continued to back the permanent Committee on Un-American Activities that succeeded his in January 1945.[26]

Chaillaux' pugnacious antiradicalism provoked an internal Legion struggle in addition to national controversy. Liberals within the organization, especially New York's feisty, left-leaning Willard Straight Post, which risked its charter to oppose him, feared his "red-baiting" was at least as "un-American" as anything he opposed. Commanders Ray Murphy (1935–36) and Harry Colmery (1936–37) also sought to moderate his excesses. By the late thirties, given the annual turnover of the Legion's elected leaders, Chaillaux was once more in the hierarchy's good graces. But for a few years, liberal Legionnaires provided an important counterweight within the organization.

In 1932, the ACLU's Secretary, Lucille Milner, asked Marcus

Duffield, author of the critical *King Legion,* if he knew of "any liberal members or posts" of the Legion besides the Willard Straight Post in Manhattan. He replied he knew of no others. Throughout the 1920s, the Straight Post, which boasted such members as the journalist Walter Lippmann, the publisher W. W. Norton, and Cyrus L. Baldridge, the former editor of the *Stars and Stripes,* pressed the Legion to reevaluate its policies. In the 1923 West Virginia coal strike, it defended the right of the ACLU to send representatives to the state and to encourage the striking miners. That same year the post argued for a more humane peace with Germany, including the forgiveness of loans and the withdrawal of occupying troops. Six years later, it pressed Commander McNutt to investigate the Centralia "Massacre" with an eye toward admitting that the veterans may have provoked the incident. Matters came to a head in 1932, when the Straight Post went too far by repudiating the 1931 National Convention's endorsement of the immediate Bonus payment; it also opposed the Legion's stand on civil-service preference for veterans. In response, the New York Department suspended the post on the pretext that "it has never participated in any of the Legion's activities, and has done no welfare work." From December 1932 until April 1934, the post was technically out of the Legion. Then it won a lawsuit in New York's Supreme Court that reinstated it. Justice Albert Cohn ruled the expulsion "an unwarranted assumption of authority by the national body" and "opposed to the spirit, if not the very letter of the state constitution and the federal constitution."[27]

The Straight Post's most famous controversy, however, occurred with its publication in 1936 of Cyrus Baldridge's twelve-hundred-word pamphlet "Americanism: What Is It?" which stressed "above all else—Freedom of Speech . . . because without Freedom of Speech there can be no search for the Truth." The handsome booklet was intended as a prize for junior-high-school winners of a Legion award. The New York County Committee also approved the tract, printed on high-quality paper and decorated with the Legion emblem and a drawing of the Statue of Liberty. No sooner had it circulated to local Legionnaires than requests for copies came pouring in from all over the nation. The supply was soon exhausted. The pamphlet thereby came to the attention of the Hearst papers, conservative New York Legionnaires, and Homer Chaillaux, who found it "radical." Chaillaux wondered why there was no "reference whatsoever to the many

American Legion programs coming under the heading of Americanism," including youth activities and advocating respect for the flag and constitutional authority: "There is not the remotest mention of the obligation of the young American to good citizenship," he complained, thereby starkly juxtaposing mainstream and liberal conceptions of Americanism.[28]

But Chaillaux and his fellow critics went further. They found in the upraised torch of the Statue of Liberty a "striking similarity to the left-wing Socialist emblem." The booklet was printed on Japanese paper. Supposedly "in typical Stalin fashion," freedom of worship followed freedom of speech and thus appeared secondary. The Legion emblem, in addition to an eagle, and the Statue of Liberty appeared in red. Baldridge's truism that "today the welfare of peoples on the opposite side of the globe is of definite importance to our own welfare" caused Chaillaux to protest this "typical subversive advocacy."

In what Texas Legionnaire and Congressman Maury Maverick described as "one of the most astonishing and asinine controversies in American history," Chaillaux insisted that the New York Department repudiate the booklet and withdraw it from publication. Commander Ray Murphy tried to placate all parties. He wrote a soothing letter to Baldridge, but insisted the pamphlet be withdrawn without discussing its merits because a nonofficial body (the New York County Council) appeared to speak for the Legion without Headquarters' approval. In the course of the affair, it turned out Chaillaux himself had "flown off the handle" by issuing his own unauthorized statement to the press "quite at variance" with Murphy's more moderate view. This provoked Murphy's rebuke that he "exercise a little more diligence in keeping closely in touch with us regarding these public pronouncements."

Thanks to Chaillaux's cries of Stalinism and Socialism, "the road of the liberal became less lonely," as Baldridge wrote in a *Scribners'* article recounting the whole affair. Minus the Legion emblem, thousands of copies of the pamphlet circulated, newspapers reprinted it, and radio stations broadcast excerpts from it. Maverick read it into the *Congressional Record* and sarcastically proposed legislation against red wine, red hair, red herrings, red traffic lights, and red cushions for Supreme Court justices. "If the New York County Legionnaires do not draw criticism from anyone except Mr. Chaillaux and Mr. Hearst, they ought to sleep soundly at night," he added.

Despite the tempest over the Americanism tract, signs of the "liberal movement, unprecedented in Legion history" that Baldridge observed began to appear with the election of Commander Murphy in 1935. Murphy's selection probably indicated a consensus among Legionnaires that Chaillaux and the Legion's California element needed to be balanced. An Iowa Democrat, a lawyer who graduated from the University of Iowa, Murphy was a drinking buddy of the ACLU's Morris Ernst, who wrote to Roger Baldwin, "I can get somewhere with this guy, who really does not want to have groups of Legionnaires go haywire. There will be a gradual sobering influence as far as Murphy has any power." Ernst realized that given the Legion's vast size, "He can no more keep his units in line than you can yours." But Murphy could influence the organization by becoming an apostle for a liberal Legion. While never denying that the "isms" menaced America at home, he spoke eloquently against teachers' loyalty oaths before the National Education Association on the grounds that no special legislation was needed to handle subversives in the classroom. During his tenure, the *Legion Monthly* published the findings of an investigation by the City College of New York Post. City College was not "honey-combed" with Communists, as the Fish committee had charged: not a single faculty member, and only 3 percent of the students ("whose only crime was immaturity"), were Communists. Murphy had no problem with teaching Fascism or Communism as academic subjects, as "the American Legion has never opposed academic freedom, . . . but it believes the subject should be approached with care and with certainty that the information relative thereto is not the product of any school of anti-Americanism propaganda." Murphy added to his pronouncements in favor of freedom of assembly and his sensitive handling of the Willard Straight affair an acceptance of the ACLU's arguments that the Legion had emphasized Communism without equal emphasis on Fascism and Nazism. He ordered Chaillaux to begin to investigate native Fascism. Murphy also instructed the National Office to forego attacking critics and devote "very close attention to our affirmative program" of youth work, "which after all is of such scope and nature as to occupy our full attention." Twenty years after his commandership ended, Murphy was still hopeful: in 1955 he vainly tried to quiet an enraged National Convention that shouted him down and "unanimously" condemned UNICEF as a Communist front.[29]

Murphy's successor, Harry Colmery, shared his temperament.

A Kansas Republican, Oberlin graduate, and former law professor at Carnegie-Mellon, Colmery criticized Legion vigilantism at the height of the sit-down strikes and invited people aware of excesses to call them to his personal attention. He barred Chaillaux from making his inflammatory speeches where labor unrest was occurring. Roger Baldwin praised Colmery's attitude—"we are together on our view of democratic rights"—and proceeded to take him at his word. Unfortunately, the first two incidents the ACLU reported severely damaged its credibility in Colmery's eyes. A union rally in Pocatello, Idaho, the Legion was accused of breaking up had in fact been disrupted by the Ku Klux Klan. In Hudson County, New York, Colmery's investigation revealed that CIO organizers had "the view of fostering conditions where the law enforcement machinery is broken down greatly," and the Legion had cooperated with the local police in restoring order. Colmery's and the ACLU's problem of discerning the facts appeared in another incident. The National Association for the Advancement of Colored People's executive secretary, Walter White, reported "terroristic" tactics by Atlanta Legionnaires who disrupted a meeting and denounced it as Communist. Colmery patiently explained that the chief culprit was not an enrolled Legionnaire. Even if a post had admitted him, Colmery pleaded for understanding on the grounds that "on the whole the organization does a very fine job," and asked White if it would be fair "to have the colored race judged by the excess of a few."[30]

Colmery's rapprochement with the American Civil Liberties Union soon came to an end. The ACLU took advantage of his offer to distribute to Legion posts a pamphlet responding to the Fish committee's charge that the ACLU was a Communist front. However, it prepared a four-page tract that devoted only one paragraph to the Fish committee. The rest attacked "strong and active" Fascist tendencies in a Legion dominated by "the Wall Street and Big Business crowd." Colmery bluntly replied that "when your Mr. [Harry M.] Ward makes the statement in writing that the Legion leaders are taking the boys for a ride, really I am not concerned whether the channels of the Legion are opened up for the distribution of your material." Yet to the end of his term, Colmery insisted that the Legion stick to a moderate course whether its opponents played fairly or not. He summed up the benefits of accuracy and restraint:

> It is true you have so-called Reds in these groups. You have other people too. We have Legionnaires who do things that are bad for

the Legion and we hate like hell to have our organization branded
by what those few do. We have to be damned careful not to brand
other people just because there happens to be that sort of crowd
in there. . . . The best way to get along with these people is to
keep yourselves in a position where you are not vulnerable. . . . I
have been corresponding with Villard and some of these people
who are critical of the Legion. I have been ready to go back and
tell them—"Here are what the facts are and I want you to see how
unfair you have been."[31]

The Legion possessed other liberal voices besides the Willard
Straight Post, Colmery, and Murphy. A postal employees' post
in Los Angeles criticized their former comrade, Homer Chaillaux,
for attacking Communists without seeking to eliminate the "poverty at the bottom of the unrest." The mailmen suggested "that
Legionnaires from now on be more progressive," and not follow
"Hearst headlines like sheep." The critic Alexander Woollcott
belonged to both the Legion and the ACLU; he won Chaillaux's
wrath for his vocal support for the latter. The ACLU also tried to
enlist estranged Legionnaire "Wild Bill" Donovan in its cause of
liberalizing the Legion. In 1936 Pennsylvania Legionnaires heard
their liberal governor and comrade George Earle denounce "men
of great wealth [who] send us on a wild goose chase after so-
called radicals while they continue to plunder the people" and to
treat as Communists "every man, woman, and child who dares
to say a word which does not have the approval of Wall Street."
Some of the more liberal Legionnaires, including Baldridge, General Pelham Glassford, Bennett Champ Clark, Professor Merle
Curti, and Governor Earle signed an introduction to Walter Wilson's ACLU pamphlet *The American Legion vs. Civil Liberty.* There
they attacked a "false concept of Americanism which denies freedom of expression to certain so-called subversive or radical
groups" as "un-American" and "totally unworthy of the men
who fought for democracy."[32]

But such protests were few, and came largely from wealthy,
urban, union, or intellectual Legionnaires who placed a higher
priority on civil liberties than the average veteran. When Daniel
Doherty succeeded Colmery in 1938, the liberal interlude ended.
Doherty denounced Columbia, "the Big Red University," for
granting the doctorate to Legionnaire William Gellerman for the
thesis he published as *The American Legion as Educator.* Washington's Stephen Chadwick, close friend and strong supporter of
Chaillaux, served as national commander in 1938–39. He distinguished himself through extravagant praise of the Dies commit-

tee, and repeated its charges that motion-picture stars, including the young Shirley Temple, had been "dupes" of the Communists. He attacked Frances Perkins for her refusal to support the deportation of Harry Bridges, and garnered negative nationwide publicity for denouncing the governor of California's pardon, after two decades, of Tom Mooney. Although Mooney's defenders had established with almost absolute certainty his innocence of bombing a World War preparedness parade, Chadwick announced to the nation that the pardon was instigated "by persons advocating Communist beliefs. They have made a martyr of him and given him too much importance." Chadwick's response to the ACLU's criticism, when he advised against the renting of meeting halls to radical groups, ended any hope for a rapprochement. "The owner of private property should have the right to rent it only to those people to whom he chooses to rent it."[33]

By the time of Chadwick's regime, the Legion's campaign for a temporary halt to almost all immigration to the United States had reached its zenith. Ideologically, the Legion opposed the sort of "new immigrant" who had been arriving from southern and eastern Europe since the end of the nineteenth century on several grounds. First, the Legion directed considerable anger against these groups because they contained many "alien slackers"—that is, nonnaturalized immigrants, ineligible for the draft, who did not enlist in World War I. Second, the Legion observed that twentieth-century immigrants "were forming themselves into colonies in our larger centers of population," where they adhered to their native tongues, "even read the newspapers printed in their language," and in general "seemed loathe to accept our institutions." Through their refusal to accept the test of self-sacrifice and their segregation in "un-American" enclaves, the newcomers appeared to reject the cultural community that to the Legionnaires represented "America." The Legion, like others who favored greater immigration restriction, ignored the fact that older Americans were perfectly content for the newcomers to live in ghettos and regarded their traditions and cultures with contempt. They also perpetuated the myth that more established ethnic groups had brought "peculiar and appropriate gifts with the friendly purposes of making America greater," forgetting the initial negative reception of the Irish and the Germans in the nineteenth century.[34]

The Legion also charged that immigrants positively menaced the nation by turning to alien "isms" in great numbers. In one of the most astute Legion statements on immigration, Commander John Quinn realized, as many of his comrades did not, that "the chains of industrial slavery" and "exploitation" provided "the fertile bed for sowing radicalism among the embittered immigrants." Most Legionnaires cared little about the economic roots of radicalism. That the immigrants had cause for dissatisfaction was no reason the American community should be sympathetic to attempts to "overthrow by violence the structure we have raised with patient and loving hands." "Communist activities are led within the United States by those who are to a shocking degree aliens," Homer Chaillaux told the House Committee on Immigration in 1940. Unfortunately, he did not follow this indisputably true statement with the more significant fact that only a small proportion of immigrants belonged to the party at all.[35]

In the Legion's eyes, immigrants also undermined the American standard of living. The Legion never lost an opportunity to point out that immigrants took jobs away from citizens and kept wages down as well. Quinn noted in 1924 that "the melting pot has been overstuffed, our absorption power has been overtaxed." Even the 1924 quotas reducing immigration to a trickle proved inadequate for the Legion. "It would seem to be the utmost stupidity," Lemuel Bolles remarked in 1933, "to admit even one hundred more people from abroad" with twelve million Americans out of work. The Legion thus justified its demand that the United States suspend all immigration for ten years "or until such times as our employment problems are back to normal."[36]

Underlying much of the Legion's critique of the new immigrants was the fear that people "of a different interior character," with "no ideals nor any understanding of the spirit of America," were "a menace to American institutions." Legion leaders heaped all the usual canards upon the new immigrants. "They come for gain and offer in exchange ingratitude," Commander Alvin Owsley remarked in terming immigration "the greatest problem facing the United States government" in 1923. Quinn spoke of a "gypsy strain" that "brings foreigners to this country still restless and seeking for something they cannot name." "They take it for granted that this country belongs to anyone and everyone," remarked a Legion press release distinguishing between a public-spirited, intelligent citizenry and an invasion that Quinn compared to "the great immigrations of both Cimbrians and Huns." Legion publications called special attention to the "padrone system," which generated "industrial slavery." The supposed domination of newcomers by sinister bosses and criminals also complemented rather than contradicted the Communist threat of the aliens. As members of older, well-integrated ethnic groups, assured of their own patriotism through wartime service, the Legionnaires regarded the new immigrants' challenge to Americanism as too obvious to require much more support than reiteration of negative stereotypes. In 1923, the Legion set as the theme for its second annual school essay contest "Why America Should Prohibit Immigration for Five Years." The previous year, a Hawaiian Chinese American had won first place for his piece "How Can the American Legion Best Serve the Nation?"[37]

As with its renewed antiradicalism in the 1930s, the Legion's immigration policies received special impetus from California. At California's insistence, the 1919 and 1920 National Conventions called attention to the Japanese problem on the Pacific Slope. It urged the "abrogation of the so-called 'Gentleman's Agreement'" of 1907, which in theory excluded Japanese immigration, but in practice allowed the relatives of Japanese citizens and "the so-called picture brides" to enter the country. Both the national Legion and the California Department set up special committees to lobby for the exclusion of all Japanese immigrants and the barring from citizenship of Japanese Americans and their descendants. These measures became law in 1924. The Legion then led the counterattack when Japanese Foreign Minister Matsui protested such "discriminatory" measures and received support from Secretary of State Charles Evans Hughes and the Federal Council of Churches in a movement to admit at least some Japanese. The Legion termed Matsui's protest a "presumptuous" interference, as "immigration is a purely domestic problem, which it is the privilege and duty of a government to determine, uninfluenced by urge or protest from other nations." The whole question of justice for the Japanese already in the country—many of whom had relatives stranded in Japan—was lost in the smoke of the Legion's preoccupation with Japan's efforts to influence American policy. To Matsui's charges of discrimination, the Legion replied that the 1924 exclusion "applies to all the yellow and brown races, comprising about half the population of the globe . . . of which the Japanese constitute only a small fraction," although the whole furor concerned Japan alone. The Legion reiterated all the usual reasons for stopping immigration in general. While denying any belief in racial inferiority—"Japan has accomplished in sixty years by raising herself from a feudal condition to the modern plane of western political and industrial civilization what it took the white race four or five hundred years to do"—the Legion believed "absorption" of races so "radically different" from the white race in "heredity, tradition, psychology, religion [and] ideals" would be either "impossible" or "disastrous." Even the very success of the Japanese became an argument against them: their admission would be "most dangerous" because of their "advantages in economic competition . . . ambition, aggressiveness, cooperation, [and] pride of race and determination to establish themselves as Japanese wherever they colonize."[38]

The Legion's participation in the West Coast anti-Japanese crusade continued until World War II. Even when the 1924 Exclusion Act passed, the Legion still circulated such pamphlets as "The Japanese Conquest of American Public Opinion" and lobbied against "the Japanese menace." In October 1941, the *Japanese-American Courier* asked the Legion's National Commander Lynn Stambaugh for a message: "how they can contribute to national unity for national defense" as war approached and anti-Japanese sentiment rose. Stambaugh urged them to forget the discrimination they had suffered. This was nothing new, and "the second generation American always has met this challenge by continued devotion to the ideals upon which our republic was founded." "Hard, backbreaking work, and sacrifice," would prove the loyalty of the Japanese, as it had for other groups in past wars. Nevertheless, they could in the long run "be confident that nowhere else in the world would they have a finer possibility of enjoying a satisfying life—under freedom's banner—than here in the United States." Six months later, the sacrifices continued as the government began to relocate Japanese Americans to inland camps.[39]

Although the Immigration Acts of 1921 and 1924 limited newcomers to America to a few thousand carefully scrutinized entrants each year, the Legion continued to support bills halting immigration for five- or ten-year periods, "giving this country time to assimilate the undesirable aliens" already here. The Legion recognized, however, that such legislation had little chance of adoption. It therefore turned to the problem of ridding the nation of illegal and other obnoxious aliens. As Secretary of Labor James Davis, himself an immigrant, told the Legion National Convention in 1923, "the bootlegging of the joy water is not comparable to the bootlegging of aliens." The problem was "no longer an immigration problem; it is what to do with those here, and one

very important angle of that is the deportation question."
Throughout the twenties and thirties, the Legion circulated statistics that between 2 and 3.5 million illegal aliens resided in the United States, "holding jobs that Americans should have and more than 600,000, many of them Communists and other radicals, are on relief."

The California Legion again played a prominent role in dealing with illegal aliens. With the Great Depression, the Mexican migrant workers upon whom the state's agricultural prosperity had rested in the twenties became superfluous as the "Okies" trekked westward. The California Legion therefore urged increasing the border patrol and speeding up deportations to counter an "alarming increase in the numbers and power of unassimilable groups." The Legion even embarked on a minor crusade against the 15,298 aliens employed by the federal government in 1938, although the evidence disclosed that most of them worked in the Panama Canal Zone or in the Philippines, where it was "difficult or impossible to obtain adequate labor from the United States."[40]

While deportation of immigrant laborers troubled only a few regions, the national Legion warmed enthusiastically to the idea of legislation to facilitate the deportation of "alien Communists," among whom Chaillaux numbered author Thomas Mann. Throughout the thirties the Legion battled Secretary of Labor Frances Perkins on this question. She insisted proof that suspect aliens had personally advocated the violent overthrow of the government be presented at formal hearings. The Legion therefore lobbied for bills giving officials no leeway and requiring that they automatically deport Communists on the grounds that membership in the party signified a commitment to violent insurrection.[41]

Beginning in 1938, Commander Stephen Chadwick made a test case of the deportation hearings of Harry Bridges, his friend Chaillaux's old nemesis from the San Francisco strike. Perkins responded that not only was there "no evidence to show that Bridges in his speeches advocates the overthrow of the United States government by force and violence," there was not even proof that he was a Communist. Further, the Supreme Court had ruled party membership was not sufficient grounds for deportation. Chadwick testily replied that ample evidence existed to deport Bridges on both counts. When Perkins remained adamant, he and Chaillaux led the Legion in demanding her impeachment.[42]

The Bridges question touched Legionnaires nationwide as a symbolic issue. Such liberal congressmen as Oregon's Walter

Pierce found themselves "barraged" by telegrams from outraged posts and veterans demanding Bridges's expulsion. (The Senate refused to consider the measure.) Pierce's response to the pressure suggests that on "Americanism" issues, as on veterans' benefits, the "Legion lobby" only served to entrench legislators who took the opposing side:

> Today in Continental Europe thousands of men are being shot, "liquidated," just because they are not liked by the ruling government. That is mob law. That is Hitlerism. Can't you see it, old friend. The Congress [House] just engaged in a legislative lynching. I wouldn't join them. I have no use on earth for Bridges but Lord, I would give my very life, everything I have, to save democratic processes.

When one Legion post went so far as to "condemn the record of Walter M. Pierce" and urge all patriotic citizens to do likewise, he defied them boldly:

> Should this Bridges vote cause my defeat in November, I will return to my home in Eugene, Oregon and wait for the short time that will elapse before the men who are condemning me for this vote will say: "Well, Old Walter was right after all."

"Old Walter" won reelection in 1940. Bridges ultimately won his fight as well and became a naturalized citizen in 1945.[43]

The problem of deporting undesirable aliens was intimately linked to their registration. Except in the cases of such public figures as Bridges, before 1940 the government had no way of knowing which aliens remained in the country or their whereabouts. The Legion had first appeared prominently as an ally of Texas congressman Martin Dies in 1935 to support his "outstanding" bill, as Chaillaux termed it, to register and fingerprint all aliens in the nation. Interestingly, the Legion itself only supported alien registration following a serious internal debate. Liberal Legionnaires complained that "there are aliens who are properly here, and there are others who are improperly here," and that compulsory registration would arouse "fear and suspicion" on the part of "the alien who is here, well-disposed, and complying with all requirements." Furthermore, the "very large additional group of federal officials and large additional expense of federal money" required to keep track of aliens would lead to costs and surveillance anathema to Legionnaires mistrustful of "big government." But such fears troubled only a minority within both the Legion and the nation, as registration of all aliens passed with the Smith Act of May 1940.[44]

Having "done much to initiate and secure" the Smith Act, the Legion defended it from its critics. The Legion cited registration as "An Example of Tolerance," rather than the introduction of a police state, as it only placed aliens on the same level as civilian government employees and young men registering for the draft. And unlike the latter, they had four months, rather than fourteen hours, to register. The Legion used its nearly two thousand citizenship schools to inform aliens of their new obligation, and won the praise of Attorney General Robert Jackson on nationwide radio for being "unusually helpful, understanding, and sympathetic" in the registration program. The director of registration, however, drew the line at providing the Legion with lists of registered aliens to contact as potential recruits for the Legion's assimilation program.[45]

The one group of immigrants the Legion did not think disloyal were repatriated veterans and their relatives. It obtained preference for admission of families of veterans who had proven their Americanism in wartime. Beginning in 1921, thanks to a fight waged by Hamilton Fish, relatives of aliens who fought in the United States armed forces received preference in the 3 percent quota allowed that year. When the 1924 law reduced quotas further, the Legion obtained an amendment in 1925 that allowed alien veterans who lived overseas to return with their families as nonquota immigrants. This law especially permitted two thousand Italian Americans, disgusted by conditions in postwar Italy, to return to the United States. The Legion also used its contacts with the Immigration and Naturalization Service to bring over such "hardship" cases as the mother of two Portland, Oregon, Legionnaires; her sons had threatened to return to England if the aged woman were not admitted. The Legion also supported and obtained easier naturalization laws for immigrant veterans, who until 1937 could become citizens simply by proving five years' residence and having two witnesses attest to their good character. But beginning in 1940, after they were required to register, the Legion refused to back alien veterans' efforts to become citizens on the grounds that they had failed to avail themselves of two decades of almost automatic naturalization.[46]

As the war approached, the Legion also took a hard line on a far more important issue: the admission of refugees from Hitler's tyranny to the United States. The Legion launched a special fight against the Wagner-Rogers Bill, cosponsored by Senator Robert Wagner of New York and Congresswoman Edith Nourse Rogers of Massachusetts, which offered to admit 20,000 refugee children, mostly Jews, from Hitler's Germany in 1939 and 1940. Although never officially voicing any anti-Semitism, the Legion, at the height of its campaign against fifth-column subversives in America, viewed the children's admission as an opening wedge that would permit people to "circulate throughout America propagating their un-American doctrines." At the Americanism Commission meeting of May 1939, California's Archie Closson argued that "there are only two political philosophies in Germany," Nazism and Communism. He maintained that "this bill does not prohibit the entrance into America of 10,000 children from Communist families."[47] Economic reasons also persuaded Legionnaires not to deviate from general opposition to immigration. The Legion maintained that the refugee children would only add to the nation's unemployment and relief problems. "We must first provide for ill-housed and ill-fed American children," John Thomas Taylor argued before the House Immigration Committee. He called attention to the Legion's extensive child-welfare work (which aided 232,000 children in fiscal year 1937) to demonstrate that there were already too many needy children in America. The Legion painted a lurid picture of "distressing" conditions, where "hundreds and thousands of children in the crippled and handicapped class" were part of the 2.5 million American youngsters already on waiting lists for aid. With the states "being bankrupted today taking care of the aged," the Legion predicted a sequence of events whereby refugee children would be followed by their unemployable (and radical) parents—entitled to preferential visas as relatives of residents—thereby taking that much more away from citizens.[48]

Legion opponents of admitting refugees even put their ritual expression of "sympathy . . . to the oppressed children of all lands" and firm commitment to family life to good use. General "sympathy" could stand against "biased" "class legislation" in favor of the mostly Jewish, German children who would be allowed entry. "Although personally I feel the greatest sympathy toward the oppressed children of Germany," Commander Stephen Chadwick informed Assistant Secretary of War Louis Johnson when the latter asked the Legion to make an exception for the victims of Nazi tyranny, "I feel that same great sympathy toward the children of Russia who are rendered orphans by the bloody purges which characterize the Soviet Union, and for the children of China and other lands." To admit any refugees because of extreme hardship would set a precedent whereby "the sentimental phase of the child refugee law proposed [would] lead us toward action weakening the immigration laws." With equally high-minded idealism, some members of the Americanism Commission wondered whether Americans would be acting like the Nazis themselves if they admitted children apart from their families: "It has been the traditional attitude of the American people that we are insistent upon the preservation of home life, and to take these children away from their families would contravene the spirit of Americanism," one member insisted.[49]

The Legion's adamant stand against the Wagner-Rogers Bill aroused more dissension in its ranks than any immigration position it had taken in twenty years. On the Americanism Commission, North Dakota's Joe Rabinovich and New York's Jeremiah Cross led the fight for the children. To arguments that the children would become public charges, Rabinovich shot back that the handful of Jews in his home state alone had raised $30,000 to take care of them: "We are dealing with something which has to do with the heart, and you are dealing with something which has to do with the head," he told his unimpressed colleagues. "We go home and read the papers, our so-called liberal newspapers and liberal magazines of America, pointing another finger at the Legion . . . and saying 'We are a group of men who know only war, a group of men who don't have a heart that beats for the little youngsters.' " For his part, Cross fought for the Wagner-Rogers Bill with the same logic and passion he had used to drive Simon Gerson from public office. To those who opposed bringing in the children, he asked: "How can you reconcile that attitude with active opposition to Communism and Fascism and Nazism?" He maintained that in his home city of New York alone, over 100,000 Jews would be perfectly happy to care for their relatives. "I could lay before you a story so heartrending that even you who have listened to so many of these tales would have tears in your eyes," he stated. Pointing out that the "whole premise" of the Legion's anti-immigration resolutions had been founded on competition with native labor, Cross felt "embarrassed" even to have to argue against the proposition "that now these children who are suffering untold agonies are now to be treated in the same manner as you treated all the other aliens." But with only 8 percent of public opinion favoring the Wagner-Rogers Act, it is perhaps surprising that significant internal debate arose in the Legion at all.[50]

Unlike the American public, the Legion did not suddenly reverse its attitude on the admission of refugee children when the blitzkrieg began in western Europe in 1940, at which time those pleading for admission were the parents of Anglo-Saxon Protestant and French Catholic youngsters. The Legion led a sizable minority (42 percent in June 1940) who favored keeping America's gates closed. Homer Chaillaux again made nationwide headlines when he addressed the Military Order of the Purple Heart and denounced all the "tommyrot" about "the poor little kiddies of Europe." Complaining that America already had over two million juvenile delinquents "for economic and social reasons," he predicted that the United States would be stuck with "refugee children of the Loyalist group in Spain, who were driven from that country because their parents were Communists." New York Legionnaires denounced these "insane vaporings" and suggested "Chaillaux should go and stick his head in the ground somewhere" before "we get a lot more adverse publicity." But Commander Raymond Kelly only questioned his tact, not his position. The Legion also backed North Carolina Senator Robert Reynolds's campaign to thwart the admission of 50,000 Finnish refugees at the same time.[51]

The Legion's firm opposition to providing asylum for alien refugees, even as the horror of World War II became apparent, graphically illustrates the extent to which Legionnaires equated aliens and immigrants with political radicalism and with social and economic unfitness for the American way of life as they defined it. They feared that temporary admission of a few thousand children from war-torn lands would precipitate an avalanche of unassimilable, un-American freeloaders, who would seriously threaten the republic's fiscal solvency and political stability. The tremendous publicity surrounding the refugee question testifies to Legionnaires' belief throughout the twenties and thirties that subversion at home, rather than dictatorships abroad, constituted the primary menace to the republic. It also points to their equation of Americanism with the cultural homogeneity of older ethnic groups.

The Legion regarded schools, and especially liberal teachers and textbooks, as other sources of "un-Americanism" challenging traditional community values. As early as May 1921, Commander Galbraith announced that "We are going to survey every school teacher and every school in the United States, and we will get the teacher reds. If we find them disloyal, we will tell you and you can kick them out." For two decades the Legion harped on this theme. "We do not accord to the so-called word freedom, the right to subvert the adolescent mind," the Wisconsin Legion proclaimed in 1939. It termed the young men who joined the Abraham Lincoln Brigade to fight for the leftist republic in the Spanish Civil War "the army of the misguided" recruited by "murderers and destroyers," "so-called educators whom we as a people, lulled by their new-coined academic freedom, have suffered to teach and preach that we are all wrong in our democratic ideals." While admitting that schools had to teach about the "isms" to show how they threatened the American way, Legion spokesman Jeremiah Cross unintentionally captured the irony of the Legion's position that freedom of speech and "Americanism" were not incompatible when he presented New York State with the Legion's recommendation that teachers swear loyalty oaths. "We don't mind an open discussion of forms of governments, but every safeguard must be taken to prevent advertising any form of government except our own."[52]

The Legion's special attention to the teaching profession in general and universities in particular as purveyors of disloyalty brought forth cries of protest from educators both within and outside the Legion. The Legion's cooperation with the National Education Association was troubled (although not ruined) by mutual distrust: "the school people assumed we were a bunch of drunks and we assumed they had a lot of subversives among their personnel." A member of the University of Southern California Post complained in 1939 that "ninety-nine percent of typical American students get no publicity," but in the mind of the public "they are all Reds because a few are bad on campus." Responding to "Treason in the Textbooks," an article by Homer Chaillaux that appeared in the September 1940 *Legion Monthly,* Wisconsin's Howard Heberle, a leader in a Legion's Schoolmasters' Club movement, which flourished briefly in the late thirties and was intended to educate the Legion and the teachers about each other in the hopes of reconciling them, confessed himself "very disappointed." "No one, not even the Legion," he protested, "can indict an entire profession and the schools."

He might as well call all the Legionnaires drunks, gamblers, and unlawful because they so often violated the Volstead Law, etc.

Some of us are going to have to decide soon whether we can any longer serve as Legionnaires. It seems we schoolmasters are always patriotic Americans whenever the Legion wants something, an oratory contest, Badger Boy cooperation, etc. etc. but we get kicks in the pants nonetheless from the same Legion. Such an article merely incites to countless community squabbles, witch-burning, loss of faith in all public schools, and unAmerican persecutions. The last war taught us nothing and hell will pop soon again. I don't see any bit of difference in our ousting books and teachers and Hitler's doing it—we're Nazified when we do it even if Homer Chaillaux calls it Americanism.[53]

Heberle and the other Legion Schoolmasters never had a chance. Founded in 1936, by Walter B. Townsend of Hollywood, California, the Schoolmasters, with their credo that "both sides of every question be presented without bias, not just one side," were doomed from the start. Townsend's outspoken pronouncements that "I wish we could get rid of the Americanism Commission" and "Homer knows that I hope he gets run over or dies" did nothing to help the splinter group of liberals. The Americanism Commission itself regarded them as a "damned nuisance" that "went over the heads of this office."[54]

College posts, composed of alumni and faculty, combated radicalism in a number of ways. The City College Post of New York made a good effort to calm that troubled campus in the mid thirties. Following a riot in November 1934 widely blamed on campus Communists, "the post didn't do a lot things it might have done," the *Legion Monthly* reported in a feature article. "It didn't issue any denunciation of the student body as a lot of anarchists from whom the devils of radicalism must be chased by red-blooded methods." Instead, it launched a scientific investigation using several tests, which showed only 3 percent of the students were Communists. Amazingly, and inaccurately, they also "found no active Communists on the faculty." To ward off the radical challenge, the post sponsored "extra-curricular activities to keep the student mind occupied," with "special stress laid on athletics, for we find that athletes are also good Americans." It also installed a plaque listing the thousands of CCNY graduates who had served in the war, created several clubs, each advised by a New York Legionnaire (including some of the city's most prominent citizens), and began an employment service to aid graduating seniors at the height of the depression. The post went from 19 to 150 members in a year under the leadership of an alumnus,

Dr. Irving Rattner. Other college posts, however, took less subtle measures "in organizing a campaign of ridicule to offset student strikes." Kings College's Post sent the New York State attorney general a letter protesting "supporting free city colleges which train their students to become Communists," and attempted in vain to subpoena faculty meeting minutes that would supposedly reveal the subversives' intentions.[55]

The Legion used a variety of methods to keep the schools safe for democracy. In Portland, Oregon, and elsewhere, school boards, on which Legionnaires frequently served, allowed the Legion to veto speakers hoping to use school auditoriums. The Legion spent the better part of two decades trying to close Commonwealth College in Mena, Arkansas (a low-tuition school for workers, most closely associated with Kate Richards O'Hare), which, according to the Legion, taught Communism and featured such moral perversions as coed dormitories and nude bathing parties. In 1940, after the Fort Smith and Texarkana posts defeated a motion to "Close Commonwealth," some Arkansas Legionnaires took the law into their own hands and destroyed the buildings. The Legion also sponsored conservative student organizations to counter radical groups at many colleges, and used ROTC units and commanders to report on "Communist or radical pacifist" activities. Legion essay contests enlisted over a quarter of a million high-school students annually, who competed for college scholarships by writing on such themes as "Why Communism is a menace to Americanism" and "Why has the American Legion . . . dedicated itself, first of all, to uphold and defend the Constitution of the United States?"

Legionnaires in many states supported teachers' loyalty oaths, which were required in over half the nation by 1941. Yet although the Miami Convention of 1934 endorsed such oaths, division in the Legion itself was sufficiently strong that National Headquarters refused to make the issue a main priority and left it to the state departments. Commander Ray Murphy, for one, wrote in the Legion's newsletter that he doubted their value, as subversives "could take such an oath with mental reservations without batting an eye or without a qualm of conscience." Privately, he expressed even stronger reservations: a fight for teachers' oaths would make the Legion "ridiculous" and cast aspersions on teachers, "a great body of loyal citizens," who "should not be singled out as a class to take such an oath by compulsion."[56]

The Legion did involve itself in three educational controversies that became national causes célèbres: the firing of two professors at a West Chester, Pennsylvania, teachers' college in 1927; the protest against Marvin Gellerman's *American Legion as Educator* and Teachers' College, Columbia University, which awarded him a doctorate for it; and the campaign against Harold Rugg's social-studies textbooks.

Although National Headquarters took no official stand on the issue, the Legion received wide criticism when, in April 1927, the Board of Trustees of West Chester State Normal College fired Professors Robert Kerlin and John Kinneman, who four years earlier had organized one of the many Liberal Clubs found on college campuses. Following a meeting of the club in which President Coolidge's invasion of Nicaragua was criticized as imperialistic, the Legion post questioned "the right of a tax-supported school to instill in the minds of future teachers a disrespect for the President of the United States." The post then began to investigate the Liberal Club, demonstrating that it "had some connection" with the American Civil Liberties Union, which had supplied it with speakers. This proved to the post's satisfaction that "the Liberal Club was instigated and influenced by Communist influences." At this time, both club advisers, who had a long history of activism in left-wing causes, were fired. The Legion and the trustees denied any connection between the firings and the incident, although the Eastern Pennsylvania Legion, which investigated the West Chester Post, applauded its efforts against "paid propaganda and the exaltation of doctrines which have as their purposes rendering America defenseless" and "accomplishing the destruction of the moral standards of students."[57]

The West Chester Post's denial convinced few people, although the vehement protests from the ACLU and the appearance of several of its leading luminaries in town confirmed the Legion's opinion that the Liberal Club and the professors were indeed closet Communists. One newspaper editoralized that "the prominence of the victims, the widespread publicity given to the cases, the protests of prominent citizens, a petition signed by virtually all the students, the revolt of the Liberal Club, the outspoken opposition of the West Chester newspaper, the *Local News,* and of the Willard Straight Post of the Legion in New York bid fair to make this a case about as famous as the Scopes trial." Even Hamilton Fish took the ousted teachers' side, "deplor[ing] such attacks by the American Legion or any other patriotic organization, which in the name of Americanism deprives American citizens from exercising their constitutional rights." On the other hand, such newspapers as the *Richmond Palladium* and such right-wingers as Harry Jung termed the Legion's campaign "necessary" because "carefree students, free of responsibility even for their own living," would be "attracted by extremes" such as "the revolutionary sentiments advanced by a propagandist." National Headquarters remained silent and the affair blew over, but neither Kerlin nor Kinneman held academic positions again. Other teachers lost their jobs through Legion protests, including professors at Tulane University in New Orleans and high-school instructors in Bangor, Maine. As Kerlin wrote in his unpublished autobiography, "no college president was willing to risk a man whose scalp the Legion had taken. It would scalp him again."[58]

Marvin Gellerman was more fortunate, for Columbia University was no West Chester State Normal College. A former Legionnaire and Washington State high-school teacher on leave from his teaching position at Northwestern University to complete a doctorate at Teachers' College, Gellerman wrote *The American Legion as Educator,* which criticized the Legion as a "Fascist," "unpatriotic," "reactionary" group and as a "tool" of the "privileged classes." Homer Chaillaux was not alone in considering it "as misleading as any one of our bitterest enemies might have written; with certainly more half truths and warped statements than almost any one else could have compiled." Stephen Chadwich protested that "there is not any documentary evidence in the first part of his book to substantiate the conclusions." A post in Mantiwoc, Wisconsin, wondered ironically whether Gellerman considered their "Legion Band, Boy Scouts, Junior Rifles, hockey, archery, Junior Baseball and Junior Basketball" programs "fascist and unpatriotic," and suspected that he was either on the "payroll of the Communist party" or possessed "the shrunken mind of a crackpot."[59]

The national press also spotted the flaws. The *New York Post* described Gellerman's name-calling as "kid's stuff," while the *St. Louis Globe-Democrat* observed "his language is impassioned, his observation emotionalized opinion." Even papers that frequently criticized the Legion found Gellerman out in left field. The *Norfolk Virginian Pilot* agreed with Gellerman that "the educators are extremely tired of self-anointed saviors of Americanism who seek to compel them to take fancy oaths not to poison the minds of their pupils against the Constitution, and equally tired of politicians who seek to put teaching in red, white and blue straitjackets." But the *Pilot* also called it a pity "that a competent book reviewer did not have a crack at his doctorate thesis, before its most purple passages were hauled out of their context." The *New York Times* wrote that Gellerman's work "carried its own rebuttal in the very extravagance of its language and of its allegations." While admitting to have "disagreed emphatically" with the Legion over the Bonus and on civil liberties, the *Times* could not sensibly overlook the Legion's "deep and continued interest in the [disabled] veterans" and "its unflagging efforts to cultivate interest in and reverence for American institutions and traditions," which "have made it a stabilizing force of unquestioned sincerity and patriotism." The *Legion Monthly,* on reprinting this review, said "The American Legion is willing to stand on that." Homer Chaillaux briefly considered suing Gellerman for libel, but did not believe it "would be wise to give Gellerman any more publicity," as "the press of the nation seems to be taking very good care of him."[60]

While Gellerman's inadequate research and outlandish charges quickly disposed of his thesis, Commander Daniel Doherty undid much of the anti-Gellerman backlash by rushing to Columbia University to make an equally absurd attack on "the big red university." Showing a far poorer understanding of academic freedom than his predecessors Ray Murphy and Harry Colmery, Doherty said that if most officials at Teachers' College disagreed with Gellerman's ideas, "why not rid this institution of such baneful influences?" The college's dean, William Russell, defused much of the tension such remarks provoked, including some hissing, by assuring the audience at the speech that Teachers' College was a "conservative place"; of its 151 faculty, ten were "extra liberals," "less radical than the British Labour party," and possibly one was a Communist. Russell went on to placate Doherty by expressing his "utmost contempt" for those who hissed, while concluding with a plea for rational discourse that could be interpreted as opposing either Gellerman or the Commander: "If tonight's plain, courageous talk from the Commander makes us think . . . on the dangers of prejudice, over-statement, innuendo, name-calling, carelessness, bad manners, and bad taste, we shall have had an evening that is worth-while." Doherty and the Legion not only failed to sense any irony, but they invited Russell to address New York State's forthcoming Convention. His speech, "How to Tell a Communist and How to Beat Him," urged Legionnaires to "relieve poverty and distress, stand up for the rights of meeting and assembly and freedom of speech, particularly where you do not agree, and support a liberal education." The Legion again sensed no irony: it warmly applauded and requested thousands of copies of the speech.[61]

Legion reaction to Gellerman marked the culmination of general dissatisfaction with leftism at Teachers' College. Gellerman's thesis supervisor, George Counts, had taught in Moscow, praised Soviet collectivism, and led a small but nationally prominent group at the college in advocating that educators point out the benefits of radical change. In an article supposedly illustrated by William Randolph Hearst, Doherty castigated Counts, using the dichotomy "Educators or Propagandists?" Legion leaders dismissed Gellerman as "a small-town boy who was jockeyed into the position of hooking some of George Counts' chestnuts out of the fire." Gellerman's book lapsed into obscurity, only occasionally to be trotted out for anti-Legion diatribes: in 1944 in the *New Republic,* Arthur Schlesinger Sr. wished that the prospective Legionnaires of World War II could be given pocket editions of Gellerman's book.[62]

The Legion did not leave Teachers' College in peace for long. Beginning in 1939, it joined forces with the National Association of Manufacturers and three other right-wing organizations—the Advertising Federation of America, the New York State Economic Council, and the Friends of the Public Schools of America—to banish from the nation's classrooms the highly popular series of textbooks written by Teachers' College professor Harold Rugg. Rugg's fourteen textbooks, published since the twenties, sold nearly three hundred thousand copies a year and were used by over four thousand schools and fifteen thousand teachers, including the school systems of New York City, Los Angeles, and San Francisco. Although containing many statements appreciative of United States institutions, Rugg also called attention to the insecurity and poverty that stood out in the depression years, stressed the Founding Fathers' elitism and economic interests as well as their idealism, and did not overlook business and political corruption in American history. Such features would have upset the Legion even if Rugg had not linked them with extravagant, uncritical praise for the Soviet Union as "the most daring" and "the most scientific" experiment "that a large nation has ever made." Ignoring the darker side of Stalinism, Rugg hoped that the United States would "transform our exploitive civilization" into "a centrally controlled technology."[63]

The National Association of Manufacturers is usually credited with beginning the drive against Rugg, but an obscure New York Legionnaire from Garden City, Long Island, Augustin Rudd, was trying to enlist Homer Chaillaux in his battle to "expose and fight the Frontier Thinkers in our public schools" as early as January 1939, several months before the other groups picked up the crusade. Not until 1940, however, did Legion Headquarters swing into action. O. K. Armstrong, fresh from his speaking tour on behalf of Charles Lindbergh's isolationist policies, which had angered interventionist Legionnaires, tried to redeem himself with a spectacular article on "Treason in the Textbooks" published in the September 1940 issue of the *American Legion Magazine*. The leading illustration depicted a foreign-looking teacher with a "subversive text book" putting dark glasses on students trying to read a book about "The American Way of Life." Unless Legionnaires worked to remove a list of thirty-eight books and magazines by Rugg, Charles Beard, George Counts, and Carl Becker, among others, from their school systems, Armstrong predicted the "Trojan horsemen" of the classroom would continue to fool students into believing that

> our "capitalist system" is the fault of selfish fellows like Benjamin Franklin and Thomas Jefferson who wanted to save their property, that the poor man wasn't given proper consideration, that in Russia the youth are engaged in creating a beautiful new democratic order, that modern business is for the benefit of profit-makers, that advertising is an economic waste, that morality is a relative value, and that family life will soon be radically changed by state control.[64]

Armstrong's article and the Legion's stand against Rugg provoked a storm of protest. The Silver Burdett Company, publisher of Becker's text, and the publishers of *Scholastic* and five other magazines Armstrong had rashly included on the subversive list forced the embarrassed Legion to apologize publicly. Ginn and Company, Rugg's publisher, showed that Armstrong had not only quoted selectively passages by Rugg critical of the United States, but that he had not even correctly quoted a single one in his entire article. Ginn's manager, H. C. Lucas, wondered why, if the texts were subversive, that after a decade of use "we do not have on file in any of our offices a single statement from any teacher, principal, or superintendent who indicated that these books were subversive or unpatriotic in the slightest degree."[65]

Some of the "thousands of Legionnaire teachers and administrators" who had endorsed and used Rugg's books joined a chorus
of protest against what Rugg termed a "witch hunt." Legionnaire
and teacher John Rudder thought it "a shame that the actual
sentiment of the membership in such matters is not consulted by
a few at the top" who launched the anti-Rugg campaign without
a convention mandate. A California veteran "protest[ed] most
vigorously against the senseless, damaging, inaccurate, unfounded
and unAmerican campaign" against the "school teachers of the
United States." The American Committee for Democracy and
Intellectual Freedom, whose members included such academic
notables as Counts, Ruth Benedict, Paul Douglas, Ralph Barton
Perry, and Edward A. Ross, termed the Legion's action a "red
herring" launched by "purge advocates afraid of democratic public
education" and a "prelude to a large-scale offensive against freedom of speech, press, and thought." The American Civil Liberties
Union pointed out some connections between the New York
State Economic Council and German-American Bund leader Fritz
Kuhn, and joined liberal thinkers in claiming that the Legion and
its allies were being used by "gilt-edged patriots in the NAM."
Even the *American Business Survey* found it "a most amazing
spectacle" that "Dr. Rugg is accused of having observed social
and economic faults, pointed them out, and urged a solution."[66]

Despite the eloquence of Rugg's defenders, the Legion and its
allies struck back and won. Throughout the nation, local posts
and county councils teamed up with Elks, Masons, Parent-
Teacher Associations, Chambers of Commerce, religious leaders,
and others to eliminate the Rugg texts. In 1941, the *Legion Magazine* published a series of articles with correct if selective quotations lambasting Rugg. "Smearing the Minds of Kids," by
former Dartmouth College football star and syndicated columnist
Bill Cunningham, was typical of them. "Imagine the effrontery
of a collectivist like Harold Rugg advocating the elimination of
intercollegiate athletic competition," he argued. "Under totalitarian governments you don't compete, you goosestep." At any
rate, there were no baseball leagues in Russia. The Legion published a four-volume pamphlet series, "Rugg Philosophy Analyzed," which it distributed nationwide as school systems
throughout the land, urged on by the posts, went so far as to
burn Rugg's books publicly. By 1944, sales of Rugg's texts had
dwindled to a pitiful twenty one thousand; in the anti-Communist
atmosphere of the postwar era, they soon went out of print. The

demise of Rugg's textbooks reflected the successful counterattack against progressive education in the forties and fifties, a battle in which the Legion played a major role.[67]

The Legion had much better relations with the conservative National Education Association, made up largely of high-school teachers and administrators, than it did with the "Frontier Thinkers" at Columbia. Overcoming some initial mistrust that they were getting involved with "a lot of parlor Bolsheviks," the National Americanism Commission's members agreed in 1921 to cosponsor National Education Week with the NEA in December. Speeches by Legionnaires and special school curricula covered such themes as "Home, School, and Church," "The Flag, the Emblem of Freedom," and "Universal Use of English." The program also stressed the benefits of physical education and intelligent voting, the need for better training and pay for teachers, and the perils of illiteracy to self and nation. Of course, radicals and liberals objected to the Legion plan. Pennsylvania Socialist leader James Maurer thought the topics and their presentation not only "tend[ed] to stultify the brain, but act as a smokescreen to becloud just grievances." Educator William Kirkpatrick sponsored an alternative week devised by the Rand School and made available to liberal schools, while criticizing the NEA for "singl[ing] out a particular and narrow concept of the country's welfare and sponsoring it." Despite periodic criticism, relations between the NEA and the Legion remained good. The Legion lobbied to "Keep the Schools Open" during the bleak days of the Great Depression, when lack of local revenues threatened to close many districts. It even endorsed the NEA's plan for federal aid to education for this one purpose only, but refused to take a stand on this controversial issue once the emergency had passed. In turn, the NEA allowed Daniel Doherty to present his case against Gellerman at its 1938 convention in New York and maintained a committee to coordinate programs with the Legion.[68]

The Legion did come to grief, however, in its disastrous attempt in 1923 to sponsor a United States history text to solve the National Education Association's perennial problem of how to replace the dull, pro-British, sectionally biased, or overly liberal books from which most schoolchildren allegedly learned the national heritage. Excited by its new alliance with the NEA, the Legion's Americanism Commission made arrangements with Parks, Austin, and Liscomb Publishers in New York and English professor Charles F. Horne of City College to publish *The Story of Our American People* through a newly formed United States History Publishing Company. Its goals were to "inspire the children with patriotism," "express on every page vivid love of our country," "build up character," "emphasize that our ancestors accomplished great deeds at great sacrifice," and "speak in an earnest strain, believing in God," while remaining "non-partisan" among states, sections, and political parties. Such an approach, the Legion asserted with a straight face, would yield "the truth" through "an unbiased presentation of facts." Advised by the DAR, GAR, Confederate Veterans, and Senators Oscar Underwood and Henry Cabot Lodge among other individuals and associations of sterling patriotic credentials, Horne pressed ahead.[69]

Despite many favorable prepublication reviews from educators, government officials, patriotic societies, and religious leaders, who probably did not read the book too carefully, Horne's text was a disaster. With the support of the Legion's National Historian, Eben Putnam, Legionnaire and noted New England historian Claude Fuess castigated it before the National Executive Committee as so "flat and lifeless" that even events like the California Gold Rush and the Battle of Gettysburg passed by in an "uninspiring way." It was also replete with factual errors "which no competent historian would ever have allowed." Horne found "Liberty Girls" who helped the Sons of Liberty, believed the Bill of Rights was inspired by Rousseau rather than by the English Declaration of Right of 1688, and credited the "astronomer" Columbus with "conceiving and measuring a new order of the universe."[70]

Reviewers agreed. The *New Republic* thought the Legion's book "absurd to criticize as history," as it "vindicates the ways of God to the American people, and the ways of the American people to God." The historians Harold U. Faulkner and Claude Van Tyne, respectively, scored it as "a bombastic eulogy" and "sentimental and maudlin" in *Harper's* and the *New York Times*. Mississippi's Legion protested for other reasons: "the petty and prejudiced partisan" text was "grossly sectional," "patronizing and unfair in its attitude toward the South," and did "scant justice" to Robert E. Lee and Jefferson Davis.[71]

The Legion's publisher tried to save the text by arranging for historians to check every fact in the book and eliminate any possible shred of bias (even enlisting Yale's Anglophile Charles M. Andrews to make sure it was not anti-British), but to no avail. The Legion's Executive Committee loyally stood by the text, forty-six to eleven, but intelligently canceled its agreement to profit by 5 percent of the gross sales. Advertisements for the book and its title page continued to bear the Legion's imprimatur, and the National Americanism Commission quietly continued to "give the history every assistance that is possible without [provoking] fault-finding comment." Legion historian Richard Jones tactfully referred to Horne's tome as "a limited success . . . adopted in a number of localities."[72]

The Legion's educational programs testify to its belief that forging a republic of hundred-percent Americans did not just require rooting out subversives and keeping the nation free of foreign influences. Legionnaires took an active role in trying to shape educational goals on both the local and national level to instill a traditional, conservative patriotism in the next generation. But the Legion's concept of education went beyond the schools: it sought to turn the American community itself into a school for Americanism. This is the theme of the next chapter.

CHAPTER TEN

The Legion in the Communities

Some day the country will appreciate the fact that the Legion through its eleven thousand posts is doing more through its program of education, youth activity, community service, and study of subversive groups to preserve Americanism than any other institution in the nation.

Stephen Chadwick to Dalton Spinelli, March 21, 1936, Chadwick Papers, Box 22, Univ. of Washington

If this were all the Legion exists for it would be entirely right and proper. The *Badger* [Wisconsin] *Legionnaire* sets forth an impressive program of genuine constructive effort—safety campaign . . . beautifying the highways—wild game and forest preserve—camp to rebuild the health of ailing members—Boy Scout troops, Junior Baseball teams. It pays out considerable sums each year to destitute comrades in hospitals. It provides home, sustenance, and education for orphans of veterans— community buildings, playgrounds, parks, swimming pools, etc.

Milwaukee Sentinel, *February 16, 1930, quoted in Quetico Superior Council Papers, folder 1928, Minnesota Historical Society, St. Paul*

I N 1931, as he toured Legion meetings throughout the nation, Assistant Americanism Director Charles Wilson recounted how the all-American game of baseball could miraculously banish Communist agitation:

> If I were to make the statement that American Legion Junior Baseball is a medium through which we can combat Communism, one would be tempted to laugh it off. However, this very thing was proven during the past summer in Indianapolis. One hot afternoon, the local Communists were holding a meeting. . . . It so happened that on the other side of the park a kid baseball game was in progress. Soon those who had been listening to the ranting and raving of the Communists relative to tearing down the republican form of government had quit the Communist gathering and gone over to watch the American game of baseball.

Junior Baseball is perhaps the best known of the American Legion's community programs, with school essay contests following a close second. But it represents only one of many educational and local activities undertaken by thousands of Legion posts and the Ladies' Auxiliary throughout the nation. They sponsored Boys' State and Boy Scout camps, built parks, airfields, and playgrounds, aided communities struck by disaster, and engaged in a gamut of constructive projects, including caring for orphans, traffic safety, emergency flood relief, and assisting the American Historical Association in creating the National Archives. The Legion was practicing semiotics a half century before the academics discovered it: acutely aware that patriotism is a way of life inculcated through symbols and ceremonies rather than a set of intellectual principles, the Legion paraded, erected war memorials, and insisted that the flag be saluted, the "Star-Spangled Banner" be sung, and patriotic holidays be honored. Through its sensitivity to ritual and its devotion to establishing a general atmosphere in which what Robert Bellah has termed "American civil religion" could flourish, the Legion kept its vision of Americanism alive in communities that had never seen a red or a Wobbly.[1]

The Legion frequently found itself embroiled with left-wing progressive educators, but, if anything, it went beyond them. If the educators sought a child-centered school that would equip

youth for a democratic citizenship, the Legion took the child out
of the school onto the sandlots and into the Boys' State camps.
The Legion went even further and turned communities throughout the land into schools (with the entire population as pupils)
through patriotic education and celebrations. With over half its
posts sponsoring community programs of some sort as early as
1930, the Legion stole the enemy's tactics. As Homer Chaillaux
noted with respect to more radical rivals of the Legion:

> We are keenly interested in the Scout activity because of the part
> it plays in offsetting the Communist youth-camps and the Com-
> munist-inspired Young Pioneers. You too have probably noticed
> the mental and physical training obtained through scout work leads
> to a greater love of country.[2]

The Legion's local efforts combined public power with the
voluntary effort of concerned citizens. Legion school and civic
programs enabled the veterans to coordinate programs with the
help of such groups as the Kiwanis, Chambers of Commerce,
and churches, winning goodwill for the Legion and lining up
community organizations behind Legion "Americanism." Pre-
empting much of the left's agenda of encouraging communal
solidarity through projects undertaken for the common good, the
Legion provided a popular focus for mixed public and private
endeavors that reinforced capitalist civilization and traditional
American values.

Legionnaires realized their organization's vast potential for
community service almost from the beginning. In February 1920
Theodore Roosevelt Jr. suggested that "the American Legion can
best help the cause of Americanism by taking an active and intelligent interest in community life" and suggested citizenship
schools for immigrants and surveillance of curricula. The same
year, Michigan's Legion pledged to be "a new and powerful force"
in the nation's "volunteer army of social workers." Spurred by
former National Commander Hanford MacNider, Iowa insisted
that Legionnaires in each of some 630 posts in the state "must
each year put over at least one unselfish, conservative, and worth-
while endeavor or have their charter taken away from them."
The motivation for the "Iowa idea" was not totally altruistic:
MacNider believed that if the veterans restricted themselves to
veterans' issues, it would "look like they were just looking for
handouts." "Stub" Allison, athletic coach at the University of
South Dakota, agreed: "What is going to happen to the American

Legion ten years from now?" he asked. "We have got the Grand Army of the Republic and the Spanish War Veterans organizations and the only time we ever hear from them is when? Well, when they want to get a pension or something like that." Arguing that the Legion had stressed the Bonus far too much, Allison insisted that "to the average outsider it [the Legion] was purely selfish."[3]

Legion conventions and leaders acted to dispel this image. In 1921, the Legion began cooperating with the National Education Association in running National Education Week in the schools. Two years later, posts began to sponsor Boy Scout troops. Legion cooperation in a nationwide campaign to eliminate illiteracy and to hold citizenship classes for the wave of immigrants who entered the nation after World War I soon followed. By 1926, with the Legion "free of internal worry," as Commander Howard Savage phrased it, the Philadelphia Convention mandated that each post undertake at least one community-service activity. "Think of the cumulative results of 10,258 betterment projects," Savage said. "Municipal swimming pools, community playgrounds, municipal libraries, public parks. . . . The net result in public improvement will be incalculable. The service given will be truly comparable with that given during war time." In 1926, for the first time, both the Convention and the Commander's annual message to the nation stressed such projects as the Legion's first priority.[4]

By 1931, when the Legion conducted a nationwide poll of post activities, it had come close to reaching its goal. Though the Legion quantified the number of posts performing specific activities rather than whether its units engaged in any service at all, of 10,300 posts 15 percent sponsored Boy Scout troops (by 1941 30 percent), a similar proportion parks and playgrounds, 30 percent auto-safety programs and disaster-relief units, and 50 percent some of the other 150 miscellaneous activities the Legion suggested. Most of the posts not engaging in service activities, the surviving questionnaires indicate, were from poor, rural, or small-town areas that afforded few such possibilities. Some, like the fifteen-member post in Geneseo, Kansas, "merged their activities with the whole community program." Yet others compiled outstanding records. A post in Aguadilla, Puerto Rico, with fifteen members (all of whom regularly attended) built a playground; organized an emergency-relief unit; sponsored vaccinations, health campaigns, and relief work among the poor; helped support the town library; organized baseball, volleyball, and basket-

ball teams; handled thirty-two veterans' claims; and found eight
jobs in 1931. Though most small posts could not match this
record, nearly every post did something. For instance, the Harton,
Kansas, post, membership eighty, average attendance sixteen,
apologized for "not [being] as active as it should be." It still
sponsored a six-team Junior Baseball league, provided Scout leaders, served as deputy police during emergencies, handled veterans'
claims, conducted funeral services, managed a safety program,
and offered boys vocational instruction. Still, the Legion's
strength lay in the "very strong and active posts in communities
of from five to twenty-five thousand" and larger.[5]

   Foreign posts of the Legion tended to be especially active. They
"had a real reason for existence," in the words of Cuba's Walter
Meyers, for they "can make Americanism stand out more forcibly
against its foreign background in carrying on the fellowship, the
sincere desire for comradeship in a good cause." Among other
places, the Legion maintained posts in London, Paris, Rome,
Havana, several Central American and Caribbean countries,
China, India, Korea, Java, Angola, Poland, and Turkey. In part,
the overseas units functioned much as consulates, as France's
Department Commander explained. "They [the veterans would]
get into trouble, lose employment, become despondent and sometimes desperate, and there being no welfare section at the Embassy
or Consulate, we are called upon in every case of misfortune
whether the victims belong to the Legion or not. They were in
the service—that suffices."[6]

   Overseas departments faced special problems and opportunities. Cuba's began slowly, with many original members quitting
when the local organizer issued numerous bad checks drawn on
the Legion's National Headquarters. Italy's was a poor department aided considerably by Benito Mussolini, who provided a
headquarters and financial support. Julia Wheelock, one of the
Legion's two prominent women leaders during the interwar
years—the other was Emma Puschner of the Child Welfare Division—resided in Rome part of the time, where she was "hard
at work trying to get our soldiers back to America." Thousands
of veterans who had emigrated to Italy changed their minds during the crises of the early twenties, but found their way back to
the United States barred by the new immigration laws. "These
soldiers stuck in Italy and deprived of their citizenship were one
time called Yanks and Uncle Sam's Sons. Now they are wops
and aliens," Wheelock protested. Legionnaires in Tientsin,

The American Legion in Paris. Courtesy of Marguerite Anthony.

China—who, as did most of those overseas, worked for United States corporations—had a more "cheerful time," holding sweepstakes that raised hundreds of thousands of dollars. Forty veterans thus built tennis courts, a bowling alley, a library, and an auditorium, as well as contributing to various relief efforts in America and China. All in all, as a Legionnaire from Angola reported, "we get a great deal of satisfaction from the thought that we belong to the Legion. We do not feel out of touch with things."[7]

The Legion also functioned in United States territories. Panama had been exempt from the draft, so its Legionnaires, all employees of the Canal Company, proudly claimed to be the only all-volunteer department. Puerto Rico boasted at least nine Hispanic posts by 1930. In Hawaii, on the other hand, fewer than 10 percent of the Legion's membership was non-Caucasian. One Hawaiian commander dismissed most of the islands' nonwhite majority as not really "membership timber." The department worried a great deal about the Asians' and the native Hawaiians' unwillingness to assimilate: "Vicious doctrines, lying propaganda, and the preaching of a racial unity that has had the effect of binding the Japanese community in a unit" seemed to counteract the department's Americanization efforts, which included an English-language education campaign and numerous patriotic ceremonies.[8]

On the mainland, Junior Baseball proved one of the Legion's more effective contributions to Americanism. The brainchild of K. D. Munro of Milbank, South Dakota, that state's Legion first introduced it in 1924, and in 1926 proposed nationwide Legion sponsorship of leagues and tournaments culminating in a "Junior World Series" at the Philadelphia Convention. "Stub" Allison, Athletic director at the University of South Dakota, persuaded the Americanism Commission to sponsor this program with little trouble. "You will catch them [the boys] when they are just a bunch of clay in your hands," he explained. The Legion could turn the nation's youth from "a bunch of softies" into a "a bunch of hard-fisted fellows who can meet competition at all times." With Babe Ruth reinvigorating a sport damaged by the "Black Sox" scandal of 1920, Allison argued, "how can you teach Americanism with a pencil and paper? . . . When the gong rings again, as it did in 1917, maybe these little cookies will go in there and do their stuff." Sixteen states participated the first year, with the championship going to a team sponsored by an all-woman post of nurses in Washington, D.C. By 1930, with the major leagues contributing $20,000 to partially defray the expenses—they rea-

A Legion parade float honors the founding of Junior Baseball. Courtesy of
American Legion National Headquarters.

soned Junior Baseball both promoted the sport and provided the
first stage of a farm system—and baseball commissioner Kenesaw
Mountain Landis, a big Legion supporter and frequent Convention speaker, throwing out the first ball at the Junior World Series,
all the state departments fielded teams, involving some half million boys.[9]

The Legion sold baseball to the nation and to the boys as a
painless supplement to the patriotic education offered in school.
"It has solved the problem of approach to the red-blooded American boy who has no time for preachments or studious appeals,
to the doctrine of good citizenship" noted a Nebraska Legion
speaker. Fair play, loyalty, teamwork, sportsmanship, democracy,
and success according to merit were some of the values taught by
a sport that mirrored "the game of life." Baseball also provided
a safe outlet for the "excess exuberance of youth" and a surefire
way to influence boys to "turn to the Legion for guidance and
disown the extreme pacifist" and other subversives. If that were
not enough, Junior Baseball provided the bonus of winning enormous prestige for the Legion. "American Legion members,"

Americanism Director Dan Sowers exulted, "are heroes to the boys growing up in our communities, and it is up to them to say what kind of citizens these boys shall grow up to be. The rising generation will eat out of their hands."[10]

The Legion's baseball program worked well, but not flawlessly. Arrangements sometimes became confused and teams in state finals had to sleep on hotel floors or pay their own expenses. Some unscrupulous coaches put ineligible but outstanding over-age or out-of-town players on their rosters. Sowers found those Legionnaires who only cared about winning and who became abusive at ballgames "one of the most disgusting and unsatisfactory things I have seen." And in 1941, when some Junior Baseball alumni had graduated to the majors and the military draft called, the Americanism Commission flinched when some went out of their way to avoid service.[11]

Racial troubles, however, proved to be Junior Baseball's most serious problem. By the 1930s, attendance having been dismal at National Conventions, the Legion discovered it could reliably draw large crowds for the Junior World Series in North and South Carolina, thereby recouping expenses not funded by the majors. Trouble arose in August 1934, when neither the host town of Gastonia, North Carolina, nor the Tampa, Florida, opponents would allow Springfield, Massachusetts, to play Ernest "Bunny" Taliaferro, a black pitcher. The Bay State team received some threats of a "mob menace," but stood behind their star player, refused to play, and consoled themselves with free World Series tickets in New York and a tumultuous welcome back home. The Massachusetts Department angrily carried its case to the Miami National Convention, which backed the South's insistence that "local custom" prevail in racial matters when a city sponsored a Legion activity. The same problem occurred in 1940 when Albemarle, North Carolina, refused to let San Diego, California's, integrated team play. One Americanism Commissioner argued that it would be better to scrap the entire baseball program if "it is going to be in conflict with our protestations about the brotherhood of man." The Commission, however, accepted Homer Chaillaux's argument that since "we get all of our money down there every year, I can't kick them in the pants."[12]

Besides Junior Baseball, the Legion successfully sponsored three thousand Boy Scout troops and, beginning in 1935, the Boys' State program. In the latter, an average of five hundred "representatives" per state who won Legion school awards met in im-

A Legion-sponsored Boys' State meeting, with the boys in their Legion caps.
Courtesy of American Legion National Headquarters.

itation of their state and national governments. Here, too, the
Legion showed an excellent sense of teaching character and patriotism through interesting activities to supplement traditional
classroom methods. It reasoned that "if the American Legion
obtains the confidence of our boys, those same boys will stand
by the principles of the Legion." Events of 1940–41 proved the
Legion correct.[13]
    Legion education did not stop with youth, but extended to the
entire community through patriotic ceremonies. The Legion took
over Lincoln's Birthday, Memorial Day, July 4, and Armistice
Day in many towns. Legion Headquarters suggested all-day programs, including parades, speeches, radio broadcasts, and sports
events, to commemorate these holidays. By the late twenties,
each holiday featured a Legion radio address from the National
Commander stressing the continuity of the Legion's present program with past heroic patriotic endeavors. Speeches in 1933 and
1934, for instance, explained why the disabled deserved better
treatment than that offered by the Economy Act. As the thirties
wore on, the talks emphasized preparedness as the best way to
avoid war. By the late thirties, the Legion was sponsoring radio
plays, such as one in which Abraham Lincoln wrote the nation a
letter from heaven:

The type of funeral Legion posts traditionally provided for comrades. Courtesy of American Legion National Headquarters.

> When I look upon the world these days, I am heartsick with a compassion that far transcends any earthly feelings. I see a world in flames. . . . Yet, through this horror haze, one thing do I see that gives me heart . . . I see America . . . a fearsome giant. I see these things and I thank God for the driving force and support of organizations working for Americanism . . . and organizations of red-blooded Americans. . . . The American Legion is in the forefront.[14]

Despite its careful effort to "link up every element of the community in the observance[s]" of patriotic holidays, the Legion jealously guarded Armistice Day and Memorial Day as its own. It lobbied to make the former a national holiday, finally succeeding in 1938, but could not persuade most businesses to close for the day as the busy Christmas season approached. One minute of silence at eleven A.M., Armistice Day displays in store windows, Legion speakers in schools, and time off with pay for most Legionnaires participating in ceremonies were the best it could obtain. The Legion did successfully keep the Veterans of Foreign Wars from taking part in the annual, nationally broadcast ceremony at the Tomb of the Unknown Soldier in Arlington National Cemetery. The government built the tomb in 1921, following

Dedication of American Legion National Headquarters, Indianapolis, Indiana, 1925. Courtesy of American Legion National Headquarters.

enactment of legislation proposed by Legionnaire Hamilton Fish. The president each year laid a wreath during the Legion observances and frequently addressed the nation. The Legion also courted the dwindling Grand Army of the Republic and Confederate War Veterans to supplant them as the official custodian of Civil War graves. But its efforts to keep Memorial Day one of solemn mourning, free of sporting events and picnics, failed in many cases.[15]

Besides emphasizing holidays that reminded the nation of the veterans' sacrifices, the Legion worked successfully to increase respect for the flag. In the early twenties, Legionnaires complained of widespread "abuse, misuses, and desecration (though unintentional)" of Old Glory, "such as the draping of unmounted flags over greasy, grimy, dirty hoods, sides or tops of autos" and the "flying of flags continually night and day until they are worn out and have lost their identity as the emblem of our country." To establish a uniform flag code, the Legion held a conference attended by representatives of sixty-eight patriotic societies, including the Boy Scouts, American Defense Society, Daughters of the American Revolution, VFW, and GAR. The Legion distributed hundreds of thousands of copies of the code in a booklet entitled "Flag of the United States: The Living Symbol of Our Great Republic—How to Display It." The National Americanism Commission assumed the burden of answering questions as to whether the flag ought to be used as part of costumes or uniforms, decorate napkins or boxes, or be depicted with a patriotic slogan written on it. The Legion discouraged all these uses.[16]

To complement its code, the Legion embarked on a vigorous campaign of flag education. Legionnaires wrote articles in newspapers and gave speeches to civic organizations on flag etiquette. National Headquarters asked posts to be sure every classroom in the nation had a flag and the students knew how to respect it. The Legion sponsored flag quizzes and essays for schoolchildren, which also included substantial doses of the Legion's interpretation of American history. June 14, Flag Day, became yet another occasion for patriotic oratory. A set speech stressing the letters FLAG as symbols of Faith, Loyalty, Amo (Love), and Glory toward the nation was especially popular with elementary-school speakers. Metro-Goldwyn-Mayer collaborated with the Legion on a patriotic film, "The Flag Speaks." The Legion crowned its efforts in 1942 when California Congressman Bud Gearhart, a friend of Homer Chaillaux who had sponsored the Armistice Day holiday legislation four years earlier, succeeded in having the essentials of the Legion flag code enacted into law.[17]

The Legion pioneered and emphasized one more patriotic celebration, the naturalization ceremony for new citizens. Observing the ease with which immigrants had obtained citizenship prior to the world war, and fearful that unassimilated newcomers were more likely to become radicals, the Legion sponsored nearly eighteen hundred citizenship schools during the interwar years. Although intended "to give a proper welcome" to the foreigners and "make friends with them," the schools could also be used to weed out undesirable aliens. Legion posts persuaded judges to quiz applicants for citizenship about their civic responsibilities, and in some localities close collaboration between the Legion and the bench all but gave the Legion control over who would become a citizen.[18]

To cap the process of Americanization, the Legion and local authorities sponsored naturalization ceremonies. The veterans protested against judges who "rushed through [the immigrants] like cattle" with "no dignity, no ceremony, nothing to make a new American proud of his new land." The Legion substituted such festivals as one in 1939 in South Bend, Indiana. Here, 233 immigrants took their oaths of allegiance as the Elks, Legion, VFW, and Boy Scouts paraded before 14,000 spectators in the Notre Dame football stadium. As Judge Dan Pyle explained, expressing his gratitude to the Legion's school:

> In lots of courts a foreigner just had to answer a couple of questions about the Constitution, tell who was President, and he was given the right to vote. Well, that doesn't happen in my court. . . . These folks of mine know more about America than that crowd that could trace itself back to the *Mayflower*.[19]

The Legion did more than preach loyalty to the community and the nation; it practiced it in a variety of public-service programs. Legion assistance at the 1933 Chicago World's Fair, conservation program, campaign for the National Archives, child-welfare services, disaster-relief plan, and the work of the Ladies' Auxiliary stand out as examples of activities that enhanced both its reputation and the quality of national life with little controversy.

The Legion's role in the 1933 Chicago Centennial Exhibition illustrates how the Legion and the nation's second-largest city helped each other during the depths of the Great Depression. Responding to a plea from the Cook County Council of Legion Posts that "men who have had the misfortune to lose their homes and earthly possessions, who are being kept by the Legion Post Welfare Committee" be employed as frequently as possible, the fair hired 39 percent of its workers from the former servicemen's ranks, with 80 percent of these jobs going to Legionnaires. The fair's organizers were not purely altruistic: planning for the event began five years in advance, and the directors hoped to lure the annual Legion Convention, which typically refreshed the local economy to the tune of at least ten million dollars, to Chicago in 1933. "If we cooperate with them . . . we may utilize them to the great advantage of the exposition, both in the matter of attendance and in securing desirable special events," one director commented. Another was not so sanguine. Knowing well the reputation of Legion Conventions for mayhem, E. Ross Bartley wondered, "Can we at the same time accept the sarcophagus of Alexander the Great, and invite people who would consider the nose of Alexander himself a valuable souvenir?"[20]

Nevertheless, the Legion did much good and little harm. Legionnaires hawked tickets to fair events at a 15 percent commission. Thirty-eight Legion bands performed for the entertainment of fairgoers, and the Legion maintained an information booth, rest rooms, and a forty-acre parking facility, as well as providing temporary policemen. The Legion capped its role with a grand Convention parade in Soldier Field. It also sponsored an "American Legion House," which it took as an opportunity "to rekindle the spark of Americanism that should burn in every child's heart." The exhibit emphasized the Legion's constructive role in national life and the AEF's heroic feats during the war. The war-footage film that highlighted the exhibit disgusted the Legionnaire in charge of coordination with the fair as "gruesome. . . . I have no desire whatsoever to live these nightmares over." However, he endorsed it on the grounds "that the dear old American public would go for this picture in a big way."[21]

Conservation was another Legion concern, with the Minnesota Department taking much of the credit. In the mid twenties, power companies proposed to dam rivers and flood much of the 14,500-square-mile Quetico Superior Forest on the Canadian border. The forest was the "only remaining vast wildness area in the central part of North America, blessed with international historic values, rare scenic qualities, and unique recreational facilities." The Minnesota Department lobbied with the Quetico Superior Council, which managed the forest, and the Izaak Walton League to "set [it] aside to be used first for the purposes of reforestation, and secondly to provide for our peoples and our peoples' children a vast area of rare beauty." The Legionnaires defeated the Minnesota Power and Light Company, fending off charges that they were "Communists and Socialists" for being "opposed to the destruction of our natural lakes' land in the interests of power development." "We must fight to Doomsday, if necessary to resist the fat-fingered Midases who would bring our forests and streams under the sway of the dollar sign," *Outdoor Life* quoted one veteran as saying. The Legion's efforts bore fruit with the creation of a national forest in 1927 and the Shipstead-Nolan Act of 1930, which forbade the altering of water levels in Quetico without the consent of Congress. The American-Canadian forest, which still exists, has added millions of acres incrementally over the past six decades.[22]

The Quetico Forest is only one monument to the Legion's efforts. It was also instrumental in securing in 1926 a Congressional appropriation of nearly seven million dollars to build the National Archives. J. Franklin Jameson, noted historian and for two decades the driving force behind both the American Historical Association (AHA) and the movement for the archives, paid tribute to "the American Legion, awakened to the need of a national archive building," which "has exerted itself cordially and effectively in pushing the matter . . . through cooperation with our committee and also independently." The Legion received its primary impetus from Eben Putnam, a prominent genealogist and its first National Historian, who convinced the 1921 National Convention that "the memorials of a nation . . . of incalculable value, which if destroyed can never be restored, are in no other progressive, civilized country so poorly protected, the menaces to their safety so slightly regarded by the nation's legislators, as in our own country." (Government records were scattered in the various department offices and had already suffered from neglect, misfiling, and fire.) Working in tandem with the AHA Committee on Military History, Putnam persuaded the Legion that not only would an archives efficiently house the war and compensation records on which veterans depended, but that as half of all the government documents in United States history had been generated by the war, an archives would serve as an appropriate memorial. Putnam patiently convinced Legionnaires that neither a social gathering place nor another museum was needed, lined up state departments and historians to "barrage" Congress, and helped John Thomas Taylor present his case to skeptical lawmakers bent on fiscal retrenchment. He also worked to persuade fellow Bay Stater Calvin Coolidge to back the project, and Coolidge's support finally resulted in legislation. President Hoover broke ground for the present structure a fortnight before he left office in 1933, a quarter century after Jameson had advanced the idea.[23]

Unlike the archives campaign, Legion interest in child-welfare work never ended. This aspect of the Legion program was an unqualified success thanks to Emma Puschner, ex-director of the St. Louis Board of Children's Guardians, who headed the Legion's Child Welfare Division from 1927 until 1950. After inducing the Legion to abandon its policy of billeting the orphans of war veterans in small rural institutions for one of adoption, and convincing Legionnaires suspicious of social workers not to spend the entire $125,000 in annual child-welfare endowment funds on direct relief, Puschner raised $73 million dollars and launched

National Commander James Drain, a disabled veteran, with orphans cared for by the Legion endowment established during his tenure (1925–26). Courtesy of American Legion National Headquarters.

programs that over the next quarter century aided more than 7 million children. (In 1941, for instance, she recruited 21,000 Legion volunteers, who assisted 629,000 youngsters.) By working to improve juvenile courts and adoption procedures and by inspiring states and localities to devote significant energies to the Child Welfare program (every post had a Child Welfare Officer), Puschner expanded the Legion's role from caring for war orphans to holding a major place among social-service agencies concerned with children in general.[24]

Legion disaster-relief work also made its presence felt throughout the nation. Inspired by the impromptu actions of posts in Indiana during tornadoes in 1923 and an Illinois mine collapse in 1924, National Headquarters worked out a suggested plan. Legion posts would organize rescue, transportation, medical, and supply

Legionnaires building dikes and collecting food for disaster victims (Mississippi, 1927). Courtesy of American Legion National Headquarters.

units, while maintaining close contact with local authorities and the Red Cross for emergency police and fire-fighting duty. The posts could be on the scene of a flood, tornado, earthquake, or fire within minutes, aiding survivors, saving property, and policing the area to prevent looting or curious bystanders from interfering with the rescue work.[25]

Legion posts performed heroically on many occasions. In a 1929 flood in Harriman, Tennessee, when "factories were being swept away," "freight trains were being washed away," and all power was down, the Legion had an emergency refugee center serving food within two hours. For eleven days, Legionnaires policed the city: not one fire broke out and there was no theft. Working among the homeless during the 1927 Mississippi River flood, Mrs. Nannie Julienne, head of the Mississippi Ladies' Auxiliary, discovered "the mortality rate among infants, white and colored, is awfully high, due to the lack of milk which is not being furnished by the Red Cross." Auxiliary members throughout the nation raised $29,000 immediately and spearheaded a drive to collect the milk. When doctors recommended candy to replenish rapidly lost calories, Mrs. Julienne pried ten thousand cartons out of the nation's candy manufacturers. "Tons of clothing" came pouring into Legion centers, so much so that some camps were "littered up with clothes." Such work did wonders for Mississippi's previously ailing Legion: it was "in good condition for the first time." Ten years later, during the 1937 Ohio and Mississippi floods, the Legion distributed five thousand tons of food, three thousand tons of clothing, operated thousands of boats and hundreds of radio units, and flew airplanes for days. The Legion also raised $250,000 in emergency funds, saved lives, established and maintained refugee camps, and provided "money, food, and clothing far more than its share for the half-million who lost everything."[26]

The American Legion Auxiliary, composed of the wives, daughters, sisters, and mothers of Legionnaires or servicemen who died during the war, not only played a major role in disaster-relief work, but in most of the Legion's welfare and educational activities. Although the Auxiliary's membership grew slowly (200,000 in 1925, 400,000 in 1935, and 600,000 in 1945) and never approached the Legion's, it was a more dedicated and single-minded group, concerned primarily with community work and helping the disabled.

The Auxiliary sprang naturally from the part women had

played during the world war. The wife and mother "was a soldier on duty all the time. You did your share of the fighting when you straightened your boy's heart as bravely as you showed him his duty," Legion Adjutant James Barton told an Auxiliary Convention. But women did more than fulfill their traditional female role as helpmates. As the Auxiliary's first historian, Mrs. Joseph Thompson, noted, two million women worked in war industries, the "Women's Land Army of America" took over farms, women knitted fourteen million articles of clothing, and the National Women's Liberty Loan Committee raised $3.5 billion in war bonds. Women served at the front as ambulance drivers and nurses, at home in the Signal Corps, as stenographers, and as recruiters (those in the military could join both the Legion and the Auxiliary). They also provided half the personnel of the YMCA and the Salvation Army. As Mrs. Thompson proudly observed: "That this work in industry was hard or unusual did not prevent the women and girls from undertaking it and seeing it through. In fact, they were willing to serve before their country realized that they could, or that it had to be them." The war provided women as well as men with a noble cause.[27]

Auxiliary units began forming in 1919. Auxiliary leaders like Dr. Helen Hughes Hiescheler—who organized the first Auxiliary department in her home state of Minnesota—and Dr. Kate Barrett of Virginia, founder of the Crittenden Homes for unwed mothers, were women with distinguished records of service in patriotic and philanthropic causes. High office in the Auxiliary, as in the Legion, came through service to the organization itself.[28]

At the 1925 Legion National Convention, Auxiliary President Claire Oliphant won both cheers and chuckles for her remark that "we are unique among women's organizations because we are the only women's organization that takes its entire program of activity from a man's organization." The Auxiliary consisted for the most part of conservative middle- and upper-class women who frequently signed their correspondence *Mrs.* followed by their husband's name. But they took immense pride in their contribution and sometimes drove the Legion to exasperation, if not emulation, by carrying out their tasks with more zeal and competence than the men. In 1928 a Minnesota Legionnaire, recalling the raucous Paris Convention and suggesting that the Legion clean up its act, expressed his gratitude "for the Auxiliary acting as shock troops and protecting the Legion in the Battle of Paris." The Auxiliary lent the Legion its respectability in other ways. When the Americanism Commission needed patriotic speakers in 1925, the men confessed that the women "have to do it. The Legionnaires are not going to take the trouble to do it unless there is somebody to be run out of town or there is a little excitement involved." When the Commission tried to appropriate the Auxiliary's school awards to girls and dispense Legion certificates and medals to both sexes, it was chagrined to discover that the women handed out 90 percent of the prizes. Minnesota Legionnaires observed that Citizenship Clubs for immigrants and child-welfare work "have progressed much better in the Auxiliary than in the Legion."[29]

A more homely story makes the same point. Thirty disabled Minnesota veterans opened a poultry farm and began marketing directly to retailers. They put out a "high class product" at low cost, but went bankrupt because of inept financial managers. A proposal for each Minnesota post to contribute "one thin dime" per member to bail them out fell on deaf ears, but the Auxiliary loaned them $2,500 at once and quickly recovered it. The Veterans' Bureau specialist who had trained the men thanked the Auxiliary for "its prompt recognition of an opportunity to save a going business concern for a group of worthy and disabled servicemen. It has again proved to the world that it is alive to its duties."[30]

The Auxiliary's dedicated troops raised large sums of money through directing the sale of poppies made by disabled veterans in government hospitals. Poppies were sold by both Legionnaires and women, the men especially using such aggressive sales techniques as pinning poppies on people's lapels and glaring at them for money. The Auxiliary successfully persuaded the public not to buy foreign-made or commercial poppies. In the twenties, the Auxiliary was spending at least $500,000 of the poppy profits annually in hospital and welfare work for the benefit of disabled veterans, as well as providing "the inestimable amount of personal attention which is the most valuable thing which can be given." The ladies spent another $120,000 per year on child welfare and donated $25,000 to fund over a fourth of the cost of the Legion's Washington Rehabilitation Office. By 1934 the Auxiliary profited from the sale of eight million poppies annually, by 1944 twenty million. The Legion also depended heavily on the Auxiliary to raise its own $5 million endowment in 1925. As Adjutant Russell Creviston cajoled the women, "we must rely on your charm, for it is a lot harder to turn down our women folks."[31]

The only poppy a good American should buy—made by disabled veterans, sold
through the American Legion or the Auxiliary. Courtesy of American Legion
National Headquarters.

Many Auxiliary posts, departments, and individuals performed
great services and fund-raising feats. In 1924, the South Dakota
Department collected $36,000 for the state's tuberculosis sanitar-
ium; New Jersey's gathered $86,000 for five soldiers' homes. In
New York, $84,000 of Auxiliary money built recreation rooms
and sun parlors "to transform bare cheerless wards into a comfortable home life atmosphere." The Arkansas Auxiliary clothed
a quarter of the men in the state's veterans' hospital. Minnesota's
Poppy Chairman [sic] treated all the men without families who
made poppies in the state to Christmas dinner. The Portland
Auxiliary opened houses for veterans too ill to work or return
home, yet not needing hospital care. Hawaii's visited the lepers
on Molokai.[32]
    Nor did the Auxiliary hesitate to move beyond the community
and women's spheres and join the Legion in lobbying for care for

the disabled and for national defense. In 1920, the Minnesota Auxiliary's Executive Committee protested against men in military hospitals being subjected to "restrictions of personal liberty and confined to particular quarters." "Many of the boys died, not from improper care or treatment, but from lack of the right sympathy and love." In addition to being "mothers to these boys," the Auxiliary lobbied for the Veterans' Hospital system. In 1924, angered that women played so active a role in the nation's peace organizations, the Auxiliary organized a conference of right-wing women's organizations, which became the "Women's Patriotic Conference on National Defense." Meeting annually in Washington, women "who saw the danger of pacifism and disarmament were given a rallying cry and a sounding board."[33]

Auxiliary members never ceased to remind the Legion that women's work had been essential during the war, and that to deprive them of an opportunity for service in peace would contradict the Legions' purpose of "Keeping the Spirit of the Great War Alive." In a rebuke to the 1924 Convention, Mrs. Oliphant remarked that "I am always disappointed when I hear members of the Legion say they are afraid to have an Auxiliary." How could they be

> afraid of their own home folks. Afraid of the women who spent long days in the Red Cross rooms during the war. The women who went without meat and concocted all sorts of substitute dishes in order that you would never want for meat. . . . Who all the while you were away wore heavy hearts and a brave smile that was only wiped away by dread news concerning you. These are the women of the Auxiliary.

One Legionnaire put it more bluntly: "A Legion post without an Auxiliary is like a man without a wife. He simply isn't there." As early as 1923, Kate Barrett's presidential address stressed that the women's outstanding war service continued in peace. "Every hospital, and almost every town and hamlet in the United States has benefited by your loving ministrations. The fatherless, the widow, the discouraged, the needy, all have been ministered unto." If, Barrett added, "we are proud to receive from it [the American Legion] our marching orders," she spoke for an Auxiliary that knew full well that it brought honor and personal fulfillment to its members through the woman's traditional role as helpmate, educator, guardian of children, and comforter of the disabled.[34]

The Auxiliary was a shining star in the Legion's community service efforts, but by no means the only one. Just before World War II began, Homer Chaillaux disagreed strongly with a critic who maintained that "the American Legion has failed to impress the growing generation" with its ideal of Americanism. Reviewing the Boy Scouts, Boys' State, flag education, Junior Baseball, and other programs, Chaillaux maintained that "practically all of the Americanism activities of the American Legion have to do with the youth of America." But they went beyond that. The Legion's patriotic ceremonies and public-service work turned the Legion into an educational institution inseparable from community life, instilling its vision of Americanism on a national scale.[35]

CHAPTER ELEVEN

The Legion, World War II, and an Epilogue

We have the ACLU fighting us all the time, saying that we are a militaristic organization. All right, we are. Are we going to let our children become a lot of pacifists, a lot of crocheting nincompoops?

Americanism Director Garland Powell, May 1, 1926, Minutes of the National Americanism Commission, 91, AL

Had the Legion's advice been heeded we would not today as a nation be tardily, feverishly at the task of our national defense. We would not today be concerned with subversives and fifth columnists among us. We would not today be concerned for the lack of unity born of intolerance and class strife.

Stephen Chadwick to Edward McGrail, January 20, 1941, Chadwick Papers, Box 24 Univ. of Washington

We all know, of course, the American Legion is stronger today than it has ever been in its history because of two things, in my judgment: Because of the attitude and the opinions they had on national defense, and secondly, the program that they have always taken against subversive movements.

Frank McCormick, Minutes of the National Americanism Commission, November 19, 1940, 46, AL

T HE APPROACH of a second world war provided the American Legion, an organization dedicated to preserving the spirit of the first, with great opportunities. The emergency national-defense preparations begun in July 1940 following the fall of France enabled Legion supporters of strong armed forces to see their goals realized. The war also gave the Legion a chance to implement on a large scale its hitherto secret defense plans, designed at the height of the Great Depression to secure communities threatened by radicals, against potential saboteurs and fifth columnists. The Legion expanded its cooperation with the Federal Bureau of Investigation in hunting for traitors and joined with various government agencies in civil-defense work. And while nearly unanimous support for the war gave the Legion few chances to track down subversives, as had the red squads of World War I, its persecution of the Jehovah's Witnesses amply demonstrated the treatment Legionnaires were prepared to mete out to groups and individuals who refused to support America's second great fight of the century.

A strong national defense had always been a key theme stressed by Legion spokesmen. Throughout the interwar years, Legionnaires repeatedly insisted that "adequate preparedness will do more to prevent war than any other thing," as "a reasonably well-armed America need not fear attack, and if we are not attacked, we shall not have war." Conversely, anyone who sought to weaken America's defenses "is an enemy to God and country, and a traitor to the memory of the noble men and women . . . who gave their lives that we may live," as Legion defense expert Major General Amos Fries told Penn State College students on Memorial Day, 1931. The Legion insisted its battle service gave it a special expertise in matters of defense: "Those persons who attack the military training in high schools and colleges as un-American, militaristic, and likely to breed war are cracked idealists who do not know what it is to face a blood-lusting enemy without training," National Commander Savage maintained. Overseas fighting also gave veterans the privilege of asserting that only those who knew war could genuinely point the way to peace. Savage added that "no man or organization desires to maintain the peace any more than the veteran and the Legion. Men who

303

have heard shells burst and machine guns chatter, each burst and each bullet carrying sudden death or horrible mutilation, do not wish again to face death-dealing missiles." Given this outlook, and the considerable overlap of pacifism and leftism, it required no great leap of faith for Legionnaires to suspect, in Fries's words, that "all this pacifism is pure Communism. . . . They have adopted the pacifist argument of 'no more war' just to get armies so small the criminal mob which is always the mainstay of a Communist conspiracy can overpower the people in every hamlet and village and then by the same unparalleled butchery of human beings as has been done in Russia establish the same Communist control."[1]

For most of the twenties and thirties, Legion leaders could muster little support for building up armaments and troops either among the membership or on Capitol Hill. Legion conventions routinely endorsed the National Defense Act of 1920, by which Congress pledged to maintain a regular force of 290,000 men, supplemented by a National Guard of 500,000. However, John Thomas Taylor found it difficult to lobby for appropriations keeping defense strength at even half that level because the posts rarely "barraged" congressmen with the same enthusiasm as they did on the Bonus. The Legion's National Defense Commission had no Washington office and no budget at all. Although Legionnaires mustered more enthusiasm in defending their commissions as reserve officers or with the Citizen's Military Training Camps, throughout the twenties and thirties they could at best lobby for a few more planes and tanks and fight cuts in troop levels that left the United States with the world's eighteenth-largest army in 1939.[2]

When World War II broke out in that year, the Legion was more interested in neutrality than in defense. Two-thirds of all Legionnaires (as well as 62 percent of the nation) believed President Roosevelt was correct in urging Congress to repeal the Neutrality Act, which forbade assistance to belligerents of the recently begun war. But the Legion seemed more concerned with avoiding the divisive issue and placating its isolationist minority. The September 1939 Convention contented itself with a noncommittal resolution "to maintain our neutrality" and pursue a policy that "preserving the sovereignty and dignity of this nation, will prevent involvement in this conflict." Ignoring the vital issue of defense, the Convention elected Michigan's isolationist Raymond Kelly as its National Commander in accordance with a deal worked out with supporters of outgoing Commander Stephen Chadwick the year before. Kelly warned against Roosevelt's "attempt to cloak our neutrality with a biased belligerency which must inevitably lead us straight into war." "Let us determine," he pleaded, "that a widespread rational forbearance resulting from measured and deliberate consideration of the problems of preserving peace will in itself erect a reasonable barrier against the suicide of our civilization by the sword." During his year in office, Kelly stuck to his guns, refusing, as he put it, "to lead the Legion along the path . . . of an unparalleled hysteria" in which "every agency, government and private, seemed to have entered into an informal and fatalistic liaison to whip the fears of the country to fever heat."[3]

By the time the Legion's Convention met in September 1940, the United States had already begun to swap destroyers for British bases in the Western Hemisphere. Fight for Freedom, a group originally formed to support the Loyalists during the Spanish Civil War and closely associated with the Committee to Aid America by Defending the Allies, was determined that the Legion's powerful voice would be raised in behalf of aid. To that end, the organization, led by Herbert Agar and Sanford Griffith, and funded by some $50,000 provided by Metro-Goldwyn-Mayer, Twentieth Century Fox, Skouras, Warner Brothers, and other Hollywood interests, prepared to direct at the Legion the sort of high-pressure lobbying employed by the veterans themselves on so many occasions. Fight for Freedom circled the Convention with a poster truck, distributed 150,000 pieces of pro-Allied literature, and picketed the "America First" Convention headquarters captained by Senator Bennett Champ Clark of Missouri and Congressman Hamilton Fish of New York. Most important, however, it conducted and publicized a poll showing that 80 percent of all Legionnaires favored aiding the Allies.[4]

The poll also provides interesting insights into the attitudes of Legionnaire veterans toward war and foreign policy on the eve of America's entry into World War II. Little sympathy existed in the Legion for the totalitarian powers. Ninety-two percent felt "favorably" or "very favorably" toward Britain, with 7 percent "indifferent." Attitudes toward Germany, the Soviet Union, Japan, and Italy roughly divided into 70 percent hostile or "very hostile," 20 percent indifferent, and around 7 percent favorable. Sixty-three percent of Legionnaires felt the United States would be involved in the war sooner or later, and 90 percent thought the Legion should lead the nation in preparing for national defense. Three-quarters favored sending more destroyers to Britain, 84 percent more bombers, and 66 percent wanted to open American ports to Allied warships. More Legionnaires supported Roosevelt than Willkie in the forthcoming presidential election, although only 47 percent thought a third term was a good idea.

Typical Legion comments on what the president should do were blunt: "Give Britain everything and no pussyfooting around." "Let them have our whole navy to blast hell out of the boches." "Fill the skies with bombers to Britain." The Legion's Convention mandate did not mince words, either:

> We of the American Legion, as lovers of peace and human freedom, devoted to the preservation of Justice, Freedom, and Democracy, condemn aggression and aggressor nations. We condemn all war parties which are leading their own peoples to death and ruin and the world to chaos. To those countries which have been ruthlessly and without just cause invaded, and particularly to our former comrades in arms in the invaded countries, we express our sympathy and the confident hope that soon they will break the chains of the present servitude. To the people of the great British Commonwealth who are so heroically defending their shores and their freedom, and to the gallant Republic of China, we extend our friendship and the assurance of our sympathy. We urge that the government of the United States exercise all lawful means to prevent the shipment of war material to the aggressor nations and that it continue to extend to all peoples who are resisting aggression the fullest cooperation consistent with our obligations, our security, and our peace.[5]

". . . And our peace." In 1940, the Legion followed President Roosevelt's official position that maximum aid to Britain minimized the chance that the United States would have to fight Germany without European allies. The middle ground where the Legion sought to retain membership consensus had thus shifted. Such America Firsters as O. K. Armstrong, who made an impassioned speech urging that the Legion attach a minority resolution to "reaffirm our historic policy of an adequate national defense and support of the Monroe Doctrine [or nonintervention in European affairs] and reaffirm our policy of neutrality and peace," could be dismissed in a voice vote. The Legion's new policy of maximum cooperation with the Allies short of war forged a temporarily acceptable consensus between those who hoped to stay out of war and those who sought to buy time until America was prepared to enter. Virginia's John Wicker made the Convention's most impassioned defense of the Legion's new policy:

> A beast with a foaming mouth . . . has his hands stained and dripping with the blood of innocent children on the high seas but, my friends, his eyes, his aims, his ambitions are right here. This is what he is after, and we ought to do everything we can, as this resolution says, furnishing material aid, consistent with our own national defense, our liberties, and our peace to assist those who are standing over there fighting our battles, holding up the last bulwark of democracy three thousand miles away.[6]

Legionnaires reflected the nation's ambivalence about whether aid to the Allies would lead to war. If nearly two-thirds of those in the Legion polled by Fight for Freedom believed war inevitable, and 40 percent were considering enlisting even though, at age forty-seven, the average Legionnaire was well over draft age, a sizable minority warned that America could only lose by becoming involved in another overseas conflict.

Such Legion isolationists as Massachusetts's Thomas Quinn spoke out against the Convention's resolution in order that "the path to war must be clearly indicated to the people who must do the suffering." Quinn lamented that "the work of the propagandists has been done so well that the people are prepared to accept it and enter into the fray." Conservative Republican Hanford MacNider argued that America was "less endangered by brutalities abroad than by arrogant political plutocrats at home," and sarcastically commented that much as "Chamberlain armed Britain with umbrellas," Roosevelt had squandered money on "flotillas of ornate post offices, court houses, bridges, sewers, apartments, golf courses, [and] dams" that sacrificed defense to "a federal army too fat and too lazy to fight for anything but its public paychecks." And Washington's Stephen Chadwick believed a president "hysterical about" preparedness, who sought "to advance himself and rally the people behind him," had successfully manipulated the Convention. Chadwick reiterated the isolationist case that the people would repudiate the president's policies if they knew his real aim.[7]

Presented with the Legion's new mandate, the new Commander, Ohio's Milo Warner, did more than support aid to Britain. In February 1941, during the air war over England, Warner, in company with former Commander D'Olier and General Frank

Parker, undertook a highly publicized fact-finding tour of the British Isles, with the blessing of the State Department and President Roosevelt, to investigate civilian defense. His report effusively praised the morale and heroism of the British people, commended their home-defense and air-raid warning organizations, and suggested that they serve as a model for the United States. Warner returned urging unconditional "support [for] the President and all our government officials in all our efforts for national defense" and demanded that "all bottlenecks, obstructions, or hindrances . . . delaying the production and delivery to Great Britain . . . of all necessary arms, tools and materials of war be no longer tolerated." He carefully concluded his report by stressing that despite his tremendous admiration for the British, "all this should be done not because of any sentiment for Great Britain, but on the purely patriotic basis of the best possible defense of our own country." The president in turn praised the Legion's "very real contribution to our national defense . . . in undertaking this service" as "truly heartening." Warner continued the Legion's rapprochement with Roosevelt by strongly supporting the new practice of convoying American merchantmen with armed ships. Fight for Freedom commented that "for the first time since World War I, the Legion is giving vigorous leadership."[8]

The Legion's increasingly close cooperation with Roosevelt appeared most strikingly at the September 1941 Milwaukee National Convention, where a speech by the president himself in praise of the Legion's "tremendous importance in stimulating strong backbone and true citizenship" headlined the proceedings. Roosevelt then turned the podium over to Secretary of the Navy Frank Knox, who lauded the Legion as being "directly responsible" for the extension of the Selective Service Law in 1941 and "the salvation of the half-trained American army from dissolution by coming to the support of the administration forces." The measure had passed by one vote in the House after floor leader John McCormack of Massachusetts contacted John Thomas Taylor. Taylor "responded nobly" in motivating "the American Legion [which] immediately went into action" with its customary barrage of letters and telegrams. Selective Service director Lewis Hershey added his approbation of Legion assistance, both in passing the law and in serving on draft boards. An FBI agent reported the general sentiment "that the whole convention was dominated by representatives of the federal government . . . who were trying to high pressure the Legion into supporting the national administration."[9]

"High pressure" was required because the administration faced a tough vote on whether the Legion would endorse its recent decision to aid the Soviet Union in its fight against the Nazis. The Legion had regarded Russia as the hidden hand behind the domestic Communists whose eradication had been a chief Legion priority since the days of the Red Scare. It had never rescinded its earlier convention resolutions that the United States refuse to recognize the Soviet government, even after President Roosevelt extended diplomatic recognition in 1933. The debate over assisting Russia was one of the fiercest ever at a Legion meeting. Two New Yorkers, Herbert Hargrove and Jeremiah Cross, defined the issues for the delegates. Arguing that the Legion should support Soviet aid, Hargrove compared Stalin to a lawyer joined in the same case for whom he had "no regard nor respect": "I'm damned if I'm going to kick him overboard just for spite." Hargrove insisted that "Hitler, as we all know, has the greatest military regime that ever existed in the history of the world. . . . Thank God there are some who have taken him on a while up to this time." Cross responded, "I would rather die fighting Hitler than live supporting Stalin and Communism." Texas Senator Tom Connolly, in his Legion guise, argued the absurdity of the Legion's claiming to support the president in the national emergency and yet opposing him on this issue. Isolationist Chadwick rebutted him: "I don't know why I should be taxed or my children or my children's children taxed to bail Russia out. . . . We do not favor extending our pocketbooks to the man who for years has sought to destroy us."[10]

Several Legionnaires argued cynically, as did Hargrove, that "if Stalin through his forces kills lots of Germans and Germany kills lots of Russians, we will dispose of that problem quite easily." Just as the Legion in part endorsed aid to Britain for the ungenerous reason that it kept America out of a war, proponents of aid to Russia even more blatantly envisioned that if America supplied those who fought Hitler without suffering herself, she would emerge in a stronger position when the fighting stopped. As Wicker of Virginia put it: "Every day we can keep Russia fighting Germany, we are at one time killing off thousands of Nazis and thousands of Russians and I say more power to them." Minnesota's Mike Murray protested against this reasoning. Comparing Hitler and Stalin to a "bedbug and a cockroach," he succinctly remarked: "One of them is going to be licked. The other one we may have to fight afterwards. We seem to be considering ourselves a nation of pansies, and we are willing to help anyone else do our fighting for us."

In the end, the Convention tabled the motion to censure aid to Russia, 874 to 604. In the forefront of the minority was New York's huge 104-person delegation, which, with the sole exception of Hargrove, opposed aid. California, Massachusetts, and Pennsylvania, although strongly for aid to Britain, balked at helping the Soviets. *Time* magazine reported that Bennett Champ Clark and Hamilton Fish, "airtight, waterproof, hermetically sealed isolationists" who led the minority, "Legion heroes for almost a quarter of a century," were "roundly booed" when they spoke out against helping the Soviets and left Milwaukee in a huff. Such isolationist papers as Colonel Robert McCormick's *Chicago Tribune* and the Hearst organs fulminated in vain against New Deal "extremists" and "war mongers."[11]

Fight for Freedom's polls explain the Legion's vote. Fifty-three percent of the Legionnaires distinguished between aiding Russia and supporting Communism. At the Veterans of Foreign Wars convention in Philadelphia the figure was only 29 percent, a sign of the Legion's more educated membership. A full 85 percent of Legion delegates and 79 percent of vfw representatives expressed confidence in President Roosevelt's foreign policy, and 65 percent of the Legion and 60 percent of the vfw believed the United States should enter the war at some point on the Allied side. However, only about a third of all Legionnaires thought the United States should enter immediately, indicating ambivalence remained about committing America to another crusade and about the state of national preparedness. The regional breakdown on this question reflected progressively greater isolationist sentiment as one moved westward, and also the irony that President Roosevelt received the strongest foreign-policy support from the South Atlantic states, which were most hostile to his domestic reforms. As fbi observer Sackett reported, the Midwest and West were "very much against our getting into any war, and do not take the war situation as a serious menace to our American security." Eastern and Southern veterans, on the other hand, "appeared to be very much more excited about the war and felt we ought to get into it right away."[12]

Should the United States enter the war now (September 22–25, 1941):

	Northeast	Central	South Atlantic	Mountain, West
Yes	40%	38%	65%	7%
No	60%	62%	35%	93%

A similar breakdown occurred on the question of whether Hitler planned to attack the United States if he defeated Britain and Russia. However, the percentages were higher, indicating most Legionnaires (except in the West) believed eventual entry into the war inevitable and desirable:

	Northeast	Central	South Atlantic	Mountain, West
Yes	57%	55%	62%	20%
No	43%	45%	38%	80%

Another roll call at Milwaukee in 1941 marked an equally significant landmark in Legion history. Since the Armistice, the Legion's most radical, albeit unsuccessful, proposal had been to implement a "universal draft" in the event of another conflict to "take the profit out of the war." The Legion was convinced the munitions makers and bankers had dragged the nation into a useless war for their own profit. The Legion hoped that if war came again, labor and capital would be drafted and paid wages comparable to those of the men at the front. The proposed law had two advantages in the Legion's eyes. First, it ensured that the United States would never fight again unless its security were truly in danger. "Taking the profit out of war will discourage the activities of militaristic profiteers to foment international discord with a view of amassing wealth," Lemuel Bolles had argued in 1922. Second, as a defense measure, a "universal draft" would either deter potential foes, who would realize that the nation's entire industrial might and manpower would be brought to bear against an enemy, or else permit the nation to prosecute any war "in the most efficient and equitable way possible." The measure obtained President Harding's endorsement, and even passed the House of Representatives in 1935 in the wake of initial enthusiasm for the New Deal and the Nye Committee's revelations of lobbying by industrialists and bankers for American intervention from 1914 to 1917. However, as the New Deal lost its cutting edge in the late thirties, more congressmen and Legionnaires came to agree with North Carolina Senator Josiah Bailey, who was not in favor of the government operating the businesses of the country. In the first place, it would not do this well. In the second place, if it ever started doing this, it would never cease to do it. We would have a socialist collectivism.[13]

The Legion only abandoned its effort "to take the profit out of war" at its 1941 Convention. The universal draft's most distinguished and extreme advocate, New York's former National Commander Edward Spafford, claimed that if Congress drafted manpower and not capital, "I will stand upon the streetcorners and fight the drafting of men. I will fight it until such time as they lock me up for being unpatriotic." Oklahoma's United States Senator Josh Lee was equally ardent:

> The war cost the Americans 29 billion dollars. Five percent of that went to pay the men who fought the war. We find 22,000 million made off the war that cost blood and men and money. They argue against the draft of capital. They argue it would be inconvenient. Go out into our hospitals, ask them about inconvenience.

But such voices as that of New Jersey's Frank Matthews won out. He argued that if the Legion continued to endorse the universal draft "you will be accused, and justly accused, of immediately demanding the abridgement of the Constitution of the United States." Going straight for the Legionnaires' pocketbooks, he predicted the federal government would "take control over everything in the country including your property, your job, your money, your bank account. You would be asking for a Fascist form of government." The 1941 Convention shelved the universal draft by a vote of 1,184 to 184 in favor of a vaguer measure authorizing the president to run the economy.[14]

The Legion also sought to prepare for war by rooting out dissidents and subversives at home. The triumphs of Hitler and Stalin, with some support from European Fascists and Communists, convinced the Legion that America also had to watch out for a "fifth column." Commander Kelly urged the Legion to become a "sixth column" to fight the fifth. Such action took two main forms: collaboration with the Federal Bureau of Investigation and the strengthening of secret Legion emergency-defense plans.[15]

Although systematic FBI recruitment of some 33,000 Legionnaires to serve as official informants only began in December 1940, the Bureau and the Legion had been aiding each other since the Red Scare. In 1921, while visiting friends at the Department

Warren Atherton, chairman of the Legion's National Defense Committee, sharing information with FBI Director J. Edgar Hoover in 1941. Courtesy of American Legion National Headquarters.

of Justice, Legion Judge Advocate Robert Adams was introduced
to "Mr. Hoover . . . the best man in this country on the reds."
Hoover stated "that they were very glad to have our cooperation
and promised to furnish us with anything he thought would be
of value." While specific information on joint Legion–FBI action
is either unavailable or nonexistent, in 1934 the Legion eagerly
responded to the Bureau's suggestion to push for "adequate funds
and power" from Congress "to deal with this scandalous situation" of depression radicalism.[16]

The Bureau began to employ Legionnaires systematically in December 1940 to preempt the overzealous veterans' own investigative efforts. The previous June, responding to Commander Kelly's plea that "we must pull no punches" in rooting out some six hundred "Communazi" subversive groups, the Legion authorized each post to set up an official Internal Defense Committee of three to five members who would carry official identification to facilitate cooperation with government authorities. Although state and national Legion directives stressed that "the committee is not a law enforcement body—and that individual action or threats must in no ways be attempted," the organization clearly resembled the American Protective League and other privately organized red squads of World War I.[17]

Although Attorney General Robert Jackson at first refused the Legion's offer of support in September 1940, J. Edgar Hoover stepped into the breach and persuaded him to recruit the defense committees for the FBI. He welcomed the offer in part to maintain Legion support for the Bureau's funding and activities, in part to keep the Legion from taking matters into its own hands: "Mr. Chaillaux was faced with the problem of trying to keep his people under control." Hoover also hoped (in vain, it turned out) that he could persuade the Legion to repudiate the Dies committee, whose publicized investigations were "injurious to the work carried on by the Bureau."[18]

Hoover's regional offices took less than eight months to identify over thirty thousand Legionnaires who spoke German, Italian, or Russian, were connected with the ethnic communities, or were involved in industrial mobilization, as the Legion had already done most of the work under its own plan. Homer Chaillaux, for one, felt "honored" that the Legion could help, and Hoover returned the compliment by praising an "American Legion which has proven its courage and patriotism." Not all of Hoover's agents shared his enthusiasm, however. In November 1943, in response to Legionnaires' complaints that they were not being employed as investigators and that the agents merely used information the Legion generated by itself, Hoover issued a sharply worded memorandum complaining of "report after report . . . in which absolutely no contact has been made with a member of the Legion." He "expect[ed] to see a marked improvement," and held each agent involved "personally responsible to see that it occurs."[19]

Despite these problems, the Legion-FBI program proved a successful, and for the most part confidential, instance of private-public wartime cooperation. Charged with rounding up draft dodgers, the Bureau found the easiest method was to circulate lists to Legion posts and then let the veterans persuade the boys to register under pain of prosecution. Legionnaires also proved instrumental in exposing suspected spy rings in Detroit, Los Angeles, and Seattle, seizing German agents landed on the East Coast by submarines, and recapturing escaped German POWs. So pleased was Hoover with the results that in February 1945 he made arrangements with the Legion to continue its domestic intelligence activities into the postwar era. The confidential program continued until 1966.[20]

The undercover work for the FBI was not the Legion's only wartime service. Attorney General Frank Murphy reported to President Roosevelt that "the Legion, of course, should not be used for vigilante purposes, but it is a disciplined and patriotic organization, and I believe could be of great value through speeches and otherwise in energizing the people for our common task." The Legion did more than preach: its members, their skills and occupations indexed at FBI offices and Legion posts and State and National Headquarters, assumed a major role in civilian defense, both through the Legion and in cooperation with the authorities. As early as January 1941, Commander Warner and President Roosevelt were discussing how "all of this volunteer service must . . . be fitted into the government's defense program." The Legion assumed primary responsibility for the nation's air-raid warning system, and provided military recruiters, draft-board personnel, and Red Cross volunteers. Over 150,000 Legionnaires—15 percent—reenlisted, including Theodore Roosevelt Jr., who won a posthumous Medal of Honor, and Hanford MacNider, who was captured by the Japanese.[21]

Not all of the Legion's wartime service was either legal or publicized. At the depth of the Great Depression, in 1932, Legion Headquarters had begun planning a secret defense network to deal with expected efforts by Communists or others to overthrow the government. So sensitive was the Legion to adverse publicity that it ordered all written evidence of the "Emergency Disaster Call" be destroyed once the information circulated. Two copies, however, survive by chance in the papers of General Fries (as ABSOLUTELY SECRET!!) and of Missouri State Commander Jesse Barrett (to be "handled in the utmost confidence"). The Legion knew that when rumors of the plans' existence circulated—some overeager veterans in western Pennsylvania's "Constitutional Defense

League" spilled the beans—reporters would be quick to compare the Legion to "storm troopers," as did Amy Shechter in her *Nation* article "Fascism in Pennsylvania."[22]

The first of the "Emergency Disaster Calls" seems to have emanated from southern California's Legion, led by Homer Chaillaux, in April 1932 at a time of labor unrest in the Los Angeles area. General Fries appears to have been a key figure in these plans, for his National Defense Committee distributed the secret information. Working through reliable Legionnaires known to local civic leaders, each city or region's special committee could summon, by telephone chains, as many as two thousand men for special duty within an hour. Upon their arrival at the scene of an emergency, the Legionnaires would be deputized by sheriffs acting in consort with judges, mayors, and other officials. If matters deteriorated to the point of martial law, "outstanding" officers of the Infantry Reserve who belonged to the Legion would commission their comrades as members of the National Guard. As the Legion had already mobilized for flood, earthquake, and other disaster relief in a similar manner, it was easy to maintain publicly that this was the scheme's sole purpose. Similarly, Legionnaires had from the beginning organized firing squads for funerals and other ceremonial functions, "comprising men of high caliber to whom arms may be safely entrusted without creating suspicion," who could thereby serve as the nucleus for emergency military forces.

It is impossible to know in how many states the Legion organized defense plans, or whether they were in fact used on those occasions when local posts became involved in labor and radical unrest during the 1930s. The Montana and South Dakota Departments listed the plans in response to a 1934 request for an activities report from National Historian Thomas Owen. Mississippi elaborated that "to curb subversive organizations a secret organization known as the Mississippi Council for Preparedness and Defense" took note of "all questionable characters, and un-American activities" and reported them to the FBI. In Detroit, "a ranking Legionnaire . . . the Mayor, the Chief of Police, and several F.B.I. agents worked out a plan" that forestalled a Communist-led 1933 May Day parade that was apparently intended to seize the city's power and utility plants. "Without fuss or feathers" Legionnaires parked their cars to seal off the marchers' route and hemmed in the speakers and paraders at Grand Circus Park. The FBI then arrested the ringleaders. The use of Legionnaires in the 1937 strikes in Pennsylvania and Michigan also suggests smoothly functioning emergency plans.[23]

One much-publicized instance in which the Legion almost certainly did *not* put its Emergency Defense Plan to work concerns charges made by General Smedley Butler in December 1934. The former commander of the Marine Corps stated that he had been approached in September 1933 by representatives of the Massachusetts and Rhode Island Departments. They claimed support and funding from the House of Morgan, the American Liberty League, and the du Pont, Rockefeller, and Remington Arms interests, in addition to the Legion. The envoys said they were prepared to recruit the Legion to seize the government of the United States if Butler would lead the coup. But the plot is highly implausible. While Butler may have been approached by Gerald C. MacGuire and Grayson Murphy, neither held any major position in the national Legion. Furthermore, Louis Johnson, Legion commander at the time, was a confidant of President Roosevelt. Given the Legion's diverse membership and the popularity of the new president, Commander Frank Belgrano aptly termed the charges "an insult to every American war veteran." The plan was "treason," and Belgrano promised that "if such an absurd movement ever got started, the first citizens who would spring to suppress it would be the World War veterans." Nevertheless, Butler's charges received wide circulation in newspaper articles published by his friend Paul French, and a special congressional committee duly investigated them. Although nothing was proven, journals as diverse as the Communist *Daily Worker* and *Parade* magazine (an insert in many mainstream Sunday newspapers) have continued to treat them seriously.[24]

When civilian defense planning on a national scale commenced in June 1940, Commander Kelly met with Secretary of War Harry Woodring, General George Marshall, Attorney General Jackson, and Solicitor General Biddle to outline the Legion's "Service of Society" ("SOS for short") plans. "Their duties will be to aid the duly constituted authorities in carrying out all military programs, to survey the community for vulnerable points and arrange for emergency and temporary defense, to preserve the virtue of American womanhood and do all other right things to contribute to the preservation of democracy," Kelly noted. In his article "The Legion Called the Turn," he announced that "many of our Legion posts have prepared disaster relief programs to be effective at the onset of such catastrophes," and offered the government

"Legion support for law and order which is already set up with a fair degree of effectiveness."[25]

Observing the Legion's private law-enforcement machinery, Elizabeth Gurley Flynn exclaimed "it seems like 1919 and 20 over again." There was one major difference. Since the public supported World War II almost unanimously, there was no need for the government to deputize private citizens to maintain law and order or crush opposition. But the Legion's readiness to violate the civil liberties of antiwar groups appeared graphically in its persecution of the Jehovah's Witnesses. The Legion was especially active in running members of this sect out of towns throughout the nation, "none too gently" on at least some occasions as one Illinois post openly bragged. Local posts' rage at a pacifist group, composed largely of poor folk, who "invaded" their communities to proselytize their faith and who made a special point of refusing to salute the flag, earned the Legion hundreds of negative reports in the American Civil Liberties Union files and that organization's "award" in 1940 as the "most active organization interfering with civil rights" in the United States.[26]

National Headquarters made no effort to discourage the widespread attacks and expulsions. The ACLU's request for repudiation of the violence received Commander Stambaugh's curt reply to take complaints to the respective state commanders, as "the national organization intervenes only when asked to do so by department officials." Homer Chaillaux termed the Witnesses a "supposed" religious group, teaching a "doctrine of disloyalty." Observing that "there is nothing in a legal way we can do to curtail the[ir] activities," he suggested communities pass laws prohibiting distribution of materials "which suggest or urge programs of religious intolerance or of religious hatred." These could then be used against the Witnesses, who condemned other churches as "a snare and a racket." The Minersville, Pennsylvania, Legion did its part by supporting the town school board in contesting the *Gobitis* case all the way to the Supreme Court. In a decision reversed in 1943, the Court ruled eight to one that the First Amendment did not give children the right to abstain from flag salutes on religious grounds. Chaillaux also circulated literature that in his opinion "pass[ed] along to all our people the true facts concerning" the Witnesses, and suggested that Legionnaires who administered "verbal lashings" "keep up the good work." By ignoring Legion violence, National Headquarters undoubtedly fueled it.[27]

Attacks on a marginal, unpopular, and defenseless group demonstrated that during the national emergency and then the war, the Legion could promote and implement its programs with far less controversy than in peacetime. "One-hundred-percent Americanism" in the form of united support for strong defense came naturally in wartime. The extended overseas service of millions of Americans ensured that the generous veterans' benefits the Legion had always favored would be a foregone conclusion rather than a hard struggle. And by shifting to an interventionist policy against the Nazis on the eve of war, the Legion positioned itself for a similar stand against Communism in the postwar era. If World War I fortuitously provided the short, successful experience of combat that gave the Legion its initial impetus, the next war enabled it to obtain the consensus on national defense, antisubversion measures, and assistance to veterans that had eluded it during the intervening decades of peace.

With over 12 million prospective recruits returning home from a successful war to a Legion-sponsored GI Bill, it is not surprising that the Legion's membership rose from 1 million in 1941 to 3.5 million in 1946. This number declined over the next decade to about 2.5 million. The Legion has since maintained its strength at about this level, with Korea (1950–53) and Vietnam (the Legion uses the years 1964–73) eligibles filling the places of world war veterans who had died. In fact, the Legion added some 200,000 members during a recruiting drive from 1984 to 1986 specifically aimed at Vietnam-era veterans.[28] Given the tendency of Americans to join voluntary associations as they approach middle age and acquire stability and respectability in their local communities, there is no reason to look for a decline in Legion membership for the rest of the twentieth century. If there are no more wars, the Legion could easily survive by making all veterans eligible. The fact that most Vietnam-era former servicemen did not see combat duty or even serve in Vietnam, and yet may join the Legion, suggests such a course.

The Legion's importance in twentieth-century America cannot be definitively assessed. What would have been different had there been no Legion? The Legion's brand of "one-hundred-percent Americanism" would doubtless have survived in the communities through other voluntary associations. World war veterans would have received some appropriate and reasonable assistance from a grateful nation, although it would have taken longer for the Veterans' Bureau to get under way. The United States adopted large defense budgets and a permanently activist foreign policy because of the events of World War II and the cold war, not because of Legion pressure. And there is almost no radicalism in contemporary America, not because of the Legion's programs, but because—however inexcusable the poverty suffered by a minority—the majority of Americans enjoy a decent standard of living.

May the Legion, therefore, be relegated to a series of footnotes, in company with the Ku Klux Klan, Daughters of the American Revolution, and other reactionary groups, as largely irrelevant to the significant developments in modern American history? It appears in precisely that guise in most general books on the period.[29] However, the Legion has had great (but not easily measured) significance as the conveyor of a mentality held by a large number of Americans—President Nixon claimed they were a "silent majority," although arguably they are neither.

Attitudes supporting antiradicalism, veterans' benefits, national defense, and a patriotic spirit in communities are not just "there." They have a form provided by laws, mentalities, and institutions that interact in a complex and unmeasurable manner. The American Legion has been a major form through which the important strain of the national character stressing community, sacrifice, nationalism, and unity—and opposing individualism, dissent, internationalism, and pluralism—has expressed itself over the past seventy years. It has been a conduit through which the patriotism of Theodore Roosevelt's time still lives in the age of Ronald Reagan.

Further, the Legion can be credited with an important national influence in specific instances. Without the Legion as its principal vehicle, the Red Scare of 1919–20 might not have so effectively stopped American radicalism dead in its tracks. The position is at least arguable. Similarly, by insisting that subversion at home ought to be taken seriously even when little real evidence existed, the Legion kept this idea before the public during the late 1920s and early 1930s. Somehow, and the Legion has helped a great deal here, many Americans still believe in a domestic Communist menace. Legion educational programs, broadly construed—ranging from Junior Baseball to loyalty oaths for teachers to patriotic observances—cannot be dismissed in attempting to explain why so many Americans retain an uncritical loyalty toward the United States and an equally unthinking hatred of the Soviet Union and Communism. Finally, the broad social and economic effects of the GI Bill, and the nature and timing of benefits provided for veterans of all twentieth-century American wars would have been different had the Legion not existed. In one way or another, the Legion has made a difference in the life of every American who served in the armed forces, watched or marched in a patriotic parade, or attended school in a community where Legionnaires monitor teachers and textbooks and maintain local activities.

In its various campaigns, the American Legion broached many of the great issues that have troubled twentieth-century America. The struggle for veterans' benefits raised the question of whether government funding of social-welfare programs ought to take precedence over balanced budgets. The Legion debated with its liberal and radical targets over "what is the United States"— a nation defined by stability or by reform, a homogeneous or a pluralist community? They argued over what sort of loyalty a citizen owes his society—respect for existing institutions, community structures, and public figures, or respect for a spirit that favors the underprivileged, questions authority, and defies the "tyranny of the majority." The Legion insisted as early as the 1920s that only a national defense strong enough to deter any potential aggressor constituted "national security," whereas its critics have argued that this only leads to a suicidal arms race.

The Legion has, for the most part, won: sizable veterans' benefits, the absence of domestic radicalism, and huge defense expenditures are now features of American life taken for granted. The extent of the Legion's role in the triumph of these policies may be questioned: that it had little or no role must be denied.

Notes

Abbreviations

ACLU — American Civil Liberties Union Manuscripts, Seeley W. Mudd Library, Princeton University

AL — American Legion Archives, National Headquarters, Indianapolis

LC — Library of Congress, Manuscript Division, Washington, D.C.

Preface

1. Membership figures in Richard S. Jones, *A History of the American Legion* (New York, 1946), 344; remark of Rev. John Inzer of Alabama, chaplain of the Legion, *Proceedings and Committees: Caucus of the American Legion* (St. Louis, 1919), 114; Eric Fisher Wood, "The American Legion: Keeping the Spirit of the Great War Alive," *Forum* 62 (August 1919):219–22; William Gellerman, *The American Legion as Educator* (New York, 1938), 264–66; Marcus Duffield, *King Legion* (New York, 1931).

2. Keith M. Olson, *The GI Bill, the Veterans, and the Colleges* (Lexington, Ky., 1974), 15–24; Colmery chaired the committee that presented the Legion bill to Congress; Thomas V. Hull, archivist of the American Legion, informed me Colmery drafted it. For benefits distributed under the bill, see "Report of the GI Bill Committee to the National Executive Committee of the American Legion," October 16, 1968, Warren Atherton Papers, Box 2, Univ. of the Pacific. Atherton was National Commander when the GI Bill passed; he chaired the 1968 committee to publicize the bill's benefits so the Legion could attract Vietnam-era veterans. William P. Dillingham, *Federal Aid to Veterans, 1917–1941* (Gainesville, 1952), 223–24; *New York Times*, March 6, 1977, IV, 3, on spending.

3. J. Edgar Hoover, "The Legion and the FBI," in FBI—Americanism—Radicalism—Emergency File, AL; Geoffrey Perrett, *Days of Sadness, Years of Triumph* (New York, 1975), 193, and speech of Secretary of the Navy Frank Knox, *Summary of the Proceedings of the Twenty-Third Annual Convention of the American Legion* (Milwaukee, 1941), 37.

4. Gellerman, *The American Legion as Educator*, is strongest in describing these activities; see also Jones, *A History of the American Legion*.

5. *New York Times*, March 6, 1977, IV, 3.

Chapter One

* Opening quotations from clipping in ACLU papers, vol. 189, 248; Fruit to Roosevelt, October 10, 1920, Box 11, Roosevelt Papers, LC;

Summary of the Proceedings of the Twentieth National Convention of the American Legion (New York, 1938), 13, AL.

1. "Minutes of the National Americanism Commission," November 3, 1936, 40; May 5, 1937, 15–29, 39, 43, AL.

2. Robert G. Simmons, "History of the American Legion," 5, Nebraska Historical Society.

3. "Minutes of the National Americanism Commission," March 12, 1921, 141, AL; exchange of letters, Forrest W. Bailey and Lemuel Bolles, May 23 and 25, 1927, History—Washington—Bolles file, AL.

4. Clipping from *Chattanooga News*, March 15, 1928; speech of Daniel Doherty, July 22, 1938, Americanism—Radicalism—Free Speech file, AL; "Minutes of the National Americanism Commission," March 12, 1921, 6, 31, AL.

5. Clipping on debate between Milo Warner and Roger Baldwin, December 21, 1940, excerpted in Warner biography, History—Ohio—Warner file, AL.

6. John Thomas Taylor, "Traitors—Not Political Prisoners," 5, Americanism—Radicalism—Political Prisoners file, AL; "The Supreme Court's Interpretation of Freedom of Speech," Americanism—Radicalism—Free Speech file, AL.

7. *Summary of Proceedings of the First (Minneapolis, 1919) National Convention*, 50; speech of Frederic Galbraith, July 1, 1920, History—Ohio—Galbraith file, AL.

8. "Speaking of Communist Speakers," *Huddle*, December 1928; for spider-web chart and poem, see Roswell P. Barnes to Morris Ernst, November 22, 1926, ACLU, vol. 303. Fries, who was president of the American Defense Society, is an excellent example of how members of far-right organizations tended to interlock, just as they accused the left of setting up fronts. Fries's papers, at the Univ. of Oregon, demonstrate his role in such links.

9. "Minutes of the National Americanism Commission," May 1, 1935, 14; May 3, 1936, 16; May 12, 1937, 29, AL; Orville Pitt to Stephen Chadwick, September 12, 1936, Box 22, and Daniel Doherty to Chadwick, December 6, 1937, Box 23, Chadwick Papers, Univ. of Washington; Edward A. Hayes, "How Red Is America" [1934], Americanism—Radicalism—Free Speech file, AL.

10. Roy Minn to American Civil Liberties Union, May 15, 1939, ACLU, vol. 2100, 32; statement of National Commander Harry Colmery, October 28, 1936, Americanism—Radicalism—Free Speech file, AL; *Call*, December 3, 1919, clipping in ACLU, vol. 64, 65.

11. See n. 6 above; also "The American Legion and the Communists Discuss Democracy," March 18, 1938, Workers Library Publication, copy at Bancroft Library, Univ. of California, Berkeley; clipping from *Weekly People*, November 22, 1919, ACLU, vol. 64, 54. For other examples of Legion willingness to admit using force against the IWW, see author's interview with Harry L. Foster, October 31, 1980; Edgar N.

Danielson, "The History of the New Jersey Department of the American Legion," 24, Rutgers Univ.; Theodore Roosevelt Jr., *Average Americans* (New York, 1920), 251; J. W. Gardner, "History of the Karl W. Ross Post," *Stockton Legionnaire*, June 30, 1932, 26, Warren Atherton Papers, Univ. of the Pacific; "Minutes of the National Executive Committee Meeting," December 20, 1919, 44, 47, 50, AL.

12. D'Olier's speech of September 1, 1920, History—D'Olier—New Jersey file, AL; Ray Murphy quoted in Edgar N. Danielson, "New Jersey Department History," 905, Rutgers Univ.

13. Harry Colmery, press release of November 5, 1936, in ACLU, vol. 906, 90.

14. For Legion-sponsored antisubversive legislation see, generally, William Gellerman, *The American Legion as Educator* (New York, 1938), 68–134; "Minutes of the National Americanism Commission," May 16, 1928, 131, AL; Stephen Chadwick to Helen Silcox, October 14, 1938; "Speaking of Communist Speakers," *Huddle*, December 1928; exchange of letters, William Mundt and Russell Cook, December 3 and 5, 1930, all in Americanism—Radicalism—Free Speech file, AL.

15. Walter Wilson, *The American Legion and Civil Liberty* (New York, 1936), 24; Maury Maverick to ACLU, January 24, 1933, ACLU, vol. 630, 20. For a sample of accusations that the Legion had "Fascist" tendencies, see clipping from *Boston Herald*, September 25, 1940, ACLU, vol. 2155, 112; Rev. John Mauer, quoted in clipping from *New York Daily Worker*, June 20, 1935, ACLU, vol. 2048, 115; Gellerman, *The American Legion as Educator*, 264–66; Milton S. Mayer, "The American Legion Takes Orders," *American Mercury* (1935): 146–57.

16. Homer Chaillaux to Roger Baldwin, February 27, 1936, ACLU, vol. 906, 18; "Minutes of the National Americanism Commission," May 4, 1938, 11, AL.

17. Good accounts of the Red Scare may be found in William E. Leuchtenburg, *The Perils of Prosperity: 1914–1932* (Chicago, 1958), 66–83; Robert K. Murray, *Red Scare: A Study in National Hysteria* (Minneapolis, 1955).

18. Quoted in Danielson, "The History of the New Jersey Department," 26, Rutgers Univ.

19. For discussions of the twenties stressing this interpretation, which are careful not to make the mistake of equating "older" with "rural," see Paul Carter, *The Twenties in America* (New York, 1968); Stanley Coben, "A Study in Nativism: The American Red Scare of 1919–1920," *Political Science Quarterly* 79 (1964):52–75.

20. Pamphlet of Willard Straight Post cited in Wilson, *The American Legion and Civil Liberty*, 28. A good general history of the ACLU is Charles Markmann, *The Noblest Cry: A History of the American Civil Liberties Union* (New York, 1965), but see also Lucille Milner, *The Education of an American Liberal* (New York, 1954), and Paul L. Murphy, *World War I and the Origins of Civil Liberties in the United States* (New York, 1979).

21. Baldwin/Warner debate cited in n. 5, above.

22. Homer Chaillaux to J. F. Cooke, December 3, 1935, Americanism—Radicalism—Free Speech file, AL.

23. Quotation from Norman Hapgood and Henry Moskowitz, *Up from the City Streets: A Life of Alfred E. Smith* (New York, 1927), as quoted in Paul Carter, *Another Part of the Twenties* (New York, 1977), 184–85.

24. Murphy, *World War I and the Development of Civil Liberties*, 4, 5, 14–17.

25. For Puritan ideology see Perry Miller, ed., *The American Puritans* (New York, 1956), 1, especially 79–83 for John Winthrop's speech "A Modell of Christian Charity," in which the phrase "city upon a hill" appeared. A good discussion of the literature on republicanism is Robert Shalhope's essay "Republicanism and Early American Historiography," *William and Mary Quarterly*, 3d ser. 39 (1982):334–56. Lawrence Friedman, *Inventors of the Promised Land* (New York, 1975), quotation from jacket.

26. These are discussed in the next chapter. When I interviewed ninety-eight-year-old Hamilton Fish, one of three men who wrote the preamble to the Legion's constitution, he stressed repeatedly that the Legion was a "Progressive" organization, moved by the spirit and ideas of Theodore Roosevelt. For aspects of Progressivism particularly pertinent to the Legion, see Robert Wiebe, *The Search for Order* (New York, 1962), and Paul Boyer, *Urban Masses and Moral Order in America* (Cambridge, 1978).

27. Quotation from Levi Pennington to Russell Cook, October 1, 1934, Americanism—Radicalism—Free Speech file, AL. I am indebted to Professor Roberta Kevelson, Director of the Program for Research in the Semiotics of Law, Government, and Economics, Penn State, Berks Campus, for thinking about the issue of "legality" versus "legitimacy." Three works have most influenced my treatment of "legitimate" mobs directed by local elites against "outsiders": Grant Gilmore, *The Ages of American Law* (New Haven, 1971); Pauline Maier, *From Resistance to Revolution: Colonial Radicals and the Development of Opposition to Britain, 1765–1776* (New York, 1972); and Leonard Richards, *"Gentlemen of Property and Standing": Anti-Abolitionist Mobs in Jacksonian America* (New York, 1970).

28. David Potter, *Freedom and Its Limitations in American Life* (Stanford, 1976), 41.

29. Alexis de Tocqueville, *Democracy in America*, tr. Henry Reeve (first edition, Cambridge, 1863), 1, chapter 12, 13. Note also the titles of chapter 29, "That the Americans Combat the Effects of Individualism by Free Institutions," and chapter 33, "How the Americans Combat Individualism by the Principle of Enlightened Self-Interest."

30. Edmund Burke, "Speech on Reform of Representation of the Commons" (1782), in *Collected Works* (Boston, 1865–1867), 3:96; "Re-

flections on the Revolution in France" (1790), ibid., 359, 240; "Letter to M. Dupont, October 1789," in Burke's *Correspondence*, ed. Charles William and Sir Richard Bourke (London, 1844), 3:106. Leo Strauss has noted that Burke's philosophy basically articulated the traditional conceptions held but unarticulated by most of his countrymen: *Natural Right and History* (Chicago, 1953), 306.

31. Robert Dahl, *A Preface to Democratic Theory* (Chicago, 1956); John Hallowell, *The Moral Foundations of Democracy* (Chicago, 1954).

32. Russell Cook to Levi T. Pennington, October 12, 1934, Americanism—Radicalism—Free Speech file, AL; Hallowell, *Moral Foundations of Democracy*, 81.

33. Wilson, *The American Legion and Civil Liberty*, 19–20; speeches of Owsley and McQuigg in history file, AL, under their names and states (Texas and Michigan, respectively). For charges the Legion was Fascist, see n. 15, above.

34. John Diggins, *Mussolini and Fascism: The View from America* (Princeton, 1972); Gellerman, *The American Legion as Educator*, 47.

35. For a discussion of veterans' movements in particular nations during the interwar years, see Stephen Ward, ed., *The War Generation: Veterans of the First World War* (Port Washington, N.Y., 1975).

36. Arno Mayer, *Dynamics of Counter-revolution in Europe, 1870–1956* (New York, 1971). My discussion of characteristics of Fascism relies most on Eugen Weber, *Varieties of Fascism* (New York, 1964); Walter Laqueur, ed., *Fascism: A Reader's Guide* (Berkeley, 1976), especially essays by Weber and Juan Linz (who presents charts on the nature of support for Fascism in Italy and Germany, 59–61); Walter Laqueur and George L. Mosse, eds., *International Fascism: 1920–1945* (New York, 1966), especially the essays by the editors; and Mihaly Vajda, *Fascism as a Mass Movement* (New York, 1976).

Chapter Two

* Opening quotations: William D. Murray, *The History of the Boy Scouts in America* (New York, 1937), 142–43 (lines by Herman Hagedorn); *Summary of the Proceedings of the Twenty-Third Annual Convention of the American Legion* (Milwaukee, 1941), 7.

1. Two interesting, unpublished discussions of the meaning of Americanism are Dorothea Edith Wyatt, "A History of the Concept of Americanism: 1885–1910" (Ph.D. thesis, Stanford Univ., 1936), and James Wallace Webb, "Concepts of Americanism, 1919–1929" (Ph.D. thesis, Louisiana State Univ., 1973).

2. Alexis de Tocqueville, *Democracy in America*, tr. Henry Reeve (New York, 1945), 2:106–7; Arthur M. Schlesinger Sr., "Biography of a Nation of Joiners," *American Historical Review* 50 (1944):1–25. For veterans' movements in general, see Dixon Wecter, *When Johnny Comes Marching Home* (Cambridge, 1941), and Wallace E. Davies, *Patriotism on Parade:*

The Story of Veterans and Hereditary Organizations in America, 1783–1800 (Cambridge, 1965), 74–75.

3. Bruce Stokes, "Self-Help in the Eighties," *Citizen Participation* (Jan.–Feb. 1982), 5; Charles Wright and Herbert Hyman, "Voluntary Association Membership of American Adults: Evidence from National Sample Surveys," *American Sociological Review* 23 (1958):284–94; Richard M. Clutter, "The American Legion in Indiana, 1919–1971" (Ph.D. thesis, Indiana Univ., 1971), 13–14; Richard S. Jones, *A History of the American Legion*, (Indianapolis, 1946), 344.

4. War of 1812 and Mexican-American War veterans are mentioned briefly in Davies, *Patriotism on Parade*, 54–55, 115–16; and 76–78, 211–14, 260–62. The best study of Confederate veterans is William W. White, *The Confederate Veteran* (Tuscaloosa, 1962).

5. *Summary of the Proceedings of the Eleventh Annual Convention of the American Legion* (Louisville, 1929), 4; Minutes of the National Americanism Commission, March 15, 1921, 104, AL; MacNider quotation in Wecter, *When Johnny Comes Marching Home*, 268. See also the comparisons in "Politics and the American Legion," *The World's Work* 37 (July 1919):242–43; *New York Times*, April 10, 1919, 10; and *Outlook* 122 (May 23, 1919):143.

6. Newton D. Baker to Henry T. Allen, September 14, 1928, Box 24, Allen Papers, LC; see also James G. Harbord, speech on "Political Legionnaires," at the Kansas City Convention of the Reserve Officers' Association, September 8, 1926, Hanford MacNider Papers, Hoover Library.

7. Mary R. Dearing, *Veterans in Politics* (Baton Rouge, 1952), and Robert B. Beath, *History of the Grand Army of the Republic* (New York, 1889), are complementary histories of the GAR; Dearing stresses its politics, Beath its social and fraternal activities.

8. Davies, *Patriotism on Parade*, chapter 8; Wecter, *When Johnny Comes Marching Home*, 248–51; Dearing, *Veterans in Politics*, 81–84, 216. Like the American Legion, the Grand Army of the Republic claimed to be nonpolitical; unlike the Legion, it could hardly even justify a narrow definition of "nonpolitical" as "nonpartisan." Beath, *History of the Grand Army of the Republic*, 30.

9. Beath, *History of the Grand Army of the Republic*, quotation on 44.

10. Davies, *Patriotism on Parade*, especially 140–42, 217, 234, 339, 355; Beath, *History of the Grand Army of the Republic*, 70; Dearing, *Veterans in Politics*, 402, 406, 474–76. The GAR published a newspaper (*National Tribune*) beginning in 1876, which, like the American Legion, was headquartered in Indianapolis.

11. B. H. Meyer, "Fraternal Beneficiary Societies in the United States," *American Journal of Sociology* 6 (1901):646–61; Davies, *Patriotism on Parade*, chapter 6.

12. Dearing, *Veterans in Politics*, 342, 400, 441.

13. Davies, *Patriotism on Parade*, 212, 386.

14. Thomas Leonard, *Above the Battle: War-Making in America from Appomattox to Versailles* (New York, 1978), 9, 12.

15. Alfred N. Phillips Jr., "History of the Organization and Evolution of the Army and Navy Association of the Great War, Incorporated, and of the Origins of the Connecticut State Department of the American Legion," History—Connecticut file, AL; "National Americanism Commission Minutes," March 25, 1921, 104, AL.

16. *Proceedings and Committees: Caucus of the American Legion* (St. Louis, 1919), 11; *Summary of the Proceedings of the Sixth Annual Convention of the American Legion* (St. Paul, 1924), 55; *Summary of the Proceedings of the Tenth Annual Convention of the American Legion* (San Antonio, 1928), 58; Russell Creviston, letter of January 31, 1921, History—Washington file, AL; for GAR and Spanish-American War veteran support for the Bonus and opposing cuts in veterans' benefits under the Economy Act of 1933, any good Congressional collection will do. See, for example, Papers of Josiah W. Bailey, Boxes 383, 389, 391, Perkins Library, Duke Univ.

17. Robert Homans to John Emery, August 10, 1921, in History—Massachusetts file, AL; H. T. Dowling to Franklin D'Olier, February 21, 1920, History—Texas file, AL. See also Edgar N. Danielson, "The History of the Department of New Jersey, 1919–1943," 289, Rutgers Univ., and speech of Charles G. Dawes, *Summary of the Proceedings of the Eighth Annual Convention of the American Legion* (Philadelphia, 1926), 83.

18. Davies, *Patriotism on Parade*, quotation on 45; E. Digby Baltzell, *The Protestant Establishment* (New York, 1964), 109–42, has an interesting interpretation of how hereditary societies worked with other institutions formed by the traditional elite to keep themselves apart from undesirable, modernizing developments. President Theodore Roosevelt himself wrote treatises on the content of Americanism: see Wyatt, "A History of the Concept of Americanism," chapter 4, and Rodney G. Minott *Peerless Patriots: Organized Veterans and the Spirit of Americanism* (Washington, D.C., 1962), 54–71.

19. Minott, *Peerless Patriots*, chapter 2; Paul S. Buck, *The Road to Reunion* (Boston, 1937), chapter 10, has good material on reconciliation among Civil War veterans in the latter half of the nineteenth century.

20. C. Howard Hopkins, *History of the Young Men's Christian Associations in North America* (New York, 1951), 4, 15, 32–33; John R. Betts, *America's Sporting Heritage: 1850–1950* (Reading, Mass., 1974), 92.

21. Betts, *America's Sporting Heritage*, 88–117. For an interesting account of how organized recreation in playgrounds was supposed to redirect the energy "wasted" in such frivolous amusements as circuses and amusement parks, see John F. Kasson, *Amusing the Million: Coney Island at the Turn of the Century* (New York, 1978), esp. 102–4.

22. Betts, *America's Sporting Heritage*, 192, 195; *Proceedings and Committees: Caucus of the American Legion* (St. Louis, 1919), 39–41, 169. For

an account of the membership of the Rough Riders and their ideology, see G. Edward White, *The Eastern Establishment and the Western Experience: The World of Frederic Remington, Theodore Roosevelt, and Owen Wister* (New Haven, 1968), chapter 7. The West, like the playing field, built character and promoted equality and mutual dependence. The "dude ranch" movement also is relevant to this trend.

23. Webb, "Concepts of Americanism," 89, 282.

24. Sallie Chesham, *Born to Battle: The Salvation Army in America* (Chicago, 1965), especially 51–52; Herbert A. Wisbey, *Soldiers without Swords: A History of the Salvation Army in the United States* (New York, 1956), especially 121–22, 135.

25. Wisbey, *Soldiers without Swords*, 90, 102, 128; Chesham, *Born to Battle*, 154–67; Hopkins, *History of the YMCA*, 486–500; Theodore Roosevelt Jr. and Evangeline Booth, exchange of letters, June 11 and 26, 1919, Roosevelt Papers, Box 36, LC.

26. William D. Murray, *The History of the Boy Scouts in America* (New York, 1937), 6, 12, 49.

27. Ibid., 9, 46, 59, 93, 101, 106; Edward Nicholson, *Education and the Boy Scout Movement* (New York, 1941), 68.

28. Two accounts of the preparedness movement are John Gary Clifford, *Citizen Soldiers: The Plattsburgh Training Camp Movement* (Lexington, Ky., 1973), and John Patrick Finnegan, *Against the Spectre of a Dragon: The Campaign for American Military Preparedness* (Westport, Conn., 1974).

29. Good narratives of the first American Legion appear in Clifford, *The Citizen Soldiers*, 49–51; Finnegan, *Against the Spectre of the Dragon*, chapter 4 (appropriately entitled "The Private War of General Wood"); and Rodney G. Minott, *Peerless Patriots*, 32–41. Minott is incorrect, however, in asserting the future American Legion grew out of this one; the first Legion disbanded in December 1916, and the second did not form until February 1919, although there is continuity in personnel. See "Theodore Roosevelt the Soldier—Personal Reminiscences by Gordon Johnston" and Frank R. McCoy to Herman Hagedorn, December 7, 1948, both in the Roosevelt Collection, Hagedorn Papers, Houghton Library, Harvard Univ.; *Outlook* 109 (March 10, 1915):548–49.

30. Ralph Barton Perry, *The Plattsburgh Movement* (New York, 1921), supplements Clifford, *The Citizen Soldiers*, very well. For specific information in this paragraph, see Perry, 25, 26, and Clifford, 243. Perry resigned temporarily from Harvard in 1919 in the hope of becoming executive secretary of the present American Legion, but lost the job to Eric Fisher Wood (Clifford, 268).

31. Clifford, *The Citizen Soldiers*, chapter 9.

32. For this American Legion, see Gregory Mason, "Crusaders of Today: An Account of the Personalities, Motives, and Ideals of the Men of the American Legion, Who Voluntarily Fight for the Allies," *Outlook* 113 (June 28, 1916):502–10; *New York Times*, February 14, 1916, 2; April

9, 1916, 1, 24; May 19, 1916, 17; May 28, 1916, 2, 5. Accounts of other Americans overseas include Paul Ayres Rockwell, *American Fighters in the Foreign Legion* (Boston and New York, 1930), and Edward W. Moore, *The Vanguard of American Volunteers* (New York, 1919).

33. H. C. Peterson and Gilbert Fite, *Opponents of War, 1917–1918* (Seattle, 1968); William Preston Jr., *Aliens and Dissenters: Federal Suppression of Radicals, 1903–1933* (New York, 1966); and Harry N. Scheiber, *The Wilson Administration and Civil Liberties, 1917–1921* (Ithaca, 1960).

34. Information from manuscript biographies in American Legion History file by state: Thomas W. Miller (Delaware); Luke Lea (Tennessee); Bennett Champ Clark (Missouri); Louis W. Johnson (West Virginia); Paul V. McNutt (Indiana); Harry W. Colmery and Frank Samuel (Kansas); Ray Murphy and Hanford MacNider (Iowa); and Homer Chaillaux and James Fisk (California) all AL. See Edward Robb Ellis, *Echoes of Distant Thunder: Life in the United States, 1914–1918* (New York, 1975), 347, and David Kennedy, *Over Here: The First World War and American Society* (New York, 1980), 149, for enlistment; John W. Chambers, "Conscripting for Colossus: The Progressive Era and the Origins of the Modern Military Draft in World War I," in Peter Karsten, ed., *The Military in America* (New York, 1980), 287.

35. History—New York—Theodore Roosevelt Jr. file, AL. See also the obituary by Westbrook Pegler, *New York World Telegram*, June 17, 1944, same file.

36. Kennedy, *Over Here*, 214–21; George B. Forgie, *Patricide in the House Divided: A Psychological Interpretation of Lincoln and His Age* (New York, 1979).

37. Glenn Davis, "Theodore Roosevelt and the Progressive Era: A Study in Individual and Group Psychohistory," in Lloyd de Mause, ed., *The New Psychohistory* (New York, 1975), 280–81, 294–96, and works discussed on 303 and 304 for relevant literature; Theodore Roosevelt Jr., *Average Americans* (New York, 1920), 1, 32.

38. Diary of Charles Brent, March 4 and 6, 1919; Charles H. Brent to Bishop Lawrence, March 31, 1919, Brent Papers, Box 16, LC; William H. Taft, et al., eds., *Service with the Fighting Men: An Account of the Work of the American YMCAs in the World War* (New York, 1922), 1:112.

39. Speech of Frank E. Edgerton, 1927, "Eight Years Ago Tonight," in Edgerton Papers, Nebraska State Historical Society; Clark Venable to Stafford King, May 13, 1927, King Papers, Box 23, Minnesota Historical Society.

40. Fred Davis Baldwin, "The American Enlisted Man in World War I" (Ph.D. thesis, Princeton Univ., 1965), especially 95, 103, 121; Mark Sullivan, *Our Times: Over Here*, 335. In *Stars and Stripes*, February 8, 1918, "Army Men Build an Overseas Plattsburgh" is how the army described its training program; Kennedy, *Over Here*, 185.

41. Figures of the United States War Department, *World Almanac* (New York, 1966), 445; Ellis, *Echoes of Distant Thunder*, 477, juxtaposes

the costs and casualties of the United States with worldwide totals: 12 million killed or missing, 20 million wounded, and 21 million civilian casualties, versus 50,000 killed and 230,000 wounded for the United States. Ellis notes that the cost of the war could have provided a comfortable house for every family in France, Belgium, Germany, Russia, Canada, Austria, and the United States, a $5 million library and a $10 million university for each city over 200,000, a fund to train 125,000 teachers and doctors a year indefinitely, and still left a sum equal to the wealth of France and Russia.

42. Sullivan, *Our Times: Over Here*, 343; Kennedy, *Over Here*, 221; Davis, "The American Enlisted Man in World War I," 112, 129, 130.

43. Interviews and scrapbooks of World War I veterans, Oral History Collection, Northeastern Univ.; Wilbur W. Swiger to Earl Smith (1918) in the Earl Smith Box, Clarence Smith Papers, West Virginia Univ.; clipping from "American Legion Section" of *New York Herald*, Paris edition, Paris Convention folder, Box 6, Stafford King Papers, Minnesota Historical Society; *Stars and Stripes* ran these headlines: on May 24, 1918, 1: "Health in AEF Better than in United States"; and on December 20, 1918, "AEF Casualties Lower than Those in Camps at Home." *New Statesman* article quoted in *Literary Digest* 63 (October 15, 1927):21–22.

44. Interview with Alpha Kenna, Chaplain of Kansas Legion, quoted in Richard J. Loosbrock, *The History of the Kansas Department of the American Legion* (Topeka, 1968), 6; "Kate W. Barrett," biographical sketch, and "Scrapbook" clipping, "Dr. Barrett Pleads for All Men in Service," Barrett Papers, LC; *Summary of the Proceedings of the Ninth Annual Convention of the American Legion* (Paris, 1927), 13; speech of Hugh Johnson, September 22, 1937, clippings relating to the New York Convention of 1937, Mississippi American Legion Collection, Mississippi State Archives.

45. Sanford Griffith, "Analysis of the Boston Convention," 22–23, Fight for Freedom Papers, American Legion Folder, Box 1, Mudd Library, Princeton Univ. Also used in next paragraph.

46. Kennedy, *Over Here*, 177–87; *Summary of the Proceedings of the Twenty-First Annual Convention of the American Legion* (Detroit, 1939), 43.

47. Roosevelt, *Average Americans*, 244–45. Roosevelt listed hygiene and development of a spirit of service as other benefits. On the racial and ethnic composition of the army, see Baldwin, "The American Enlisted Man in World War I," 63–74, and Kennedy, *Over Here*, 154–62.

48. Press release, History—North Carolina—Harry Stevens file, AL; clipping from *Hand Grenade*, March 1941, "Old Soldiers," Wisconsin American Legion Papers, Box 3, Wisconsin State Historical Society; William E. Leuchtenburg, "The New Deal and the Analogue of War," in John Braeman et al., eds., *Change and Continuity in Twentieth-Century America* (Columbus, Ohio, 1964), 81–144.

49. Exchange of letters between Col. W. H. Jordan and Theodore

Roosevelt Jr., May 8 and May 15, 1919, Roosevelt Papers, Box 36, LC; Roosevelt, *Average Americans*, 152–57; John J. MacSwain to *Stars and Stripes*, March 17, 1922, MacSwain Papers, Box 1, Perkins Library, Duke Univ.; Jones, *History of the American Legion*, 89.

50. Address of February 6, 1934, History—Washington, D.C.—John Thomas Taylor file, AL; Major William Pryor of Holyoke, Massachusetts, sent Massachusetts Senator David I. Walsh a poem written by a private of the First Division: "We were the first to fight for our country, / The First to feel Hell's hard storm, / All we want now is justice, / SO LET'S BE THE FIRST TO GO HOME." Updated, filed in early 1919, Walsh Papers, Holy Cross College.

Chapter Three

1. John W. Sands to Thomas V. Hull, February 3, 1970, and "Who Blacklisted the World War II Hero Who Might Have Become President of the United States," *Bluebook*, August 1964 clipping, both in History—New York—Theodore Roosevelt Jr., file, AL; Eric Fisher Wood to James H. Doffer, April 8, 1950, Wood Papers, Box 1, Syracuse Univ. (referred to in this chapter as "Wood to Doffer"); Theodore Roosevelt Jr., to Rolland Bradley, August 14, 1920, Roosevelt Papers, Box 11, LC; Speech of John Thomas Taylor, February 6, 1934, History—District of Columbia—Taylor file, AL; "The American Legion: Executive Committee Meeting," May 10, 1919, 54–55, AL.

2. For Comrades in Service, see their file in Box 24 of the Ora D. Foster Papers, Univ. of Iowa, and the Diary of Charles Brent, January through May, 1919, Brent Papers, LC.

3. See, for example, *Stars and Stripes*, January 10, 17, and 24; February 14; March 14; and April 11, 1919; "Memorandum of O. D. Foster," Comrades in Service file, Box 24, Foster Papers, Univ. of Iowa.

4. Rodney G. Minott, *Peerless Patriots: Organized Veterans and the Spirit of Americanism* (Washington, D.C., 1962), chapter 4.

5. "Declaration of Principles and Constitution of the Private Soldiers and Sailors Legion of the United States of America," March 1919, ACLU, vol. 118, 161; Ted Booth to Albert DeSilver, December 30, 1919, ACLU, vol. 109, 219.

6. Roger W. Baldwin to the World War Veterans, June 12, 1923, ACLU, vol. 72, n.p. Employment statistics for the 1920s in David Montgomery, *Workers' Control in America* (Cambridge, 1979), 97.

7. Wood to Doffer; Theodore Roosevelt Jr. to John Greer, March 5, 1920, Box 11, Roosevelt Papers, LC; William Gellerman, *The American Legion as Educator* (New York, 1938), 19; ratio of officers to enlisted men in Veterans' Administration to Josiah W. Bailey, April 1, 1931, Bailey Papers, Box 381, Perkins Library, Duke Univ.

8. For quotation, see typed biographical sketch of Eric Fisher Wood in his papers, Syracuse Univ. The information in the next several para-

graphs is taken from three detailed and considerably overlapping letters of Eric Fisher Wood: to Doffer; to Benjamin H. Griffin, February 9, 1934 (signed by Wood's secretary, Edward Lee Bladen), both in Wood Papers; and to Thomas W. Miller, February 2, 1954 (signed by "Cap" Olson), in History—New York—William Donovan file, AL; see also the speech of John Thomas Taylor, February 6, 1934, History—District of Columbia—Taylor file, AL. These are "inside" accounts of these maneuverings. There are no important discrepancies between Wood and Taylor. For a list of those who attended the morale conference, and its results, see Eric Fisher Wood, "Memorandum for the C. in C. and His Chief of Staff," February 17, 1919, and "Memo to Sub-Committee," March 14, 1919, also in Wood Papers, Syracuse Univ.

9. Frank B. O'Connell, "History of the American Legion in Nebraska," History—Nebraska file, AL. One still finds this opinion in Burl Noggle, *Into the Twenties: The United States from Armistice to Normalcy* (Urbana, Ill., 1974), 120, and in Donald J. Lisio, "The United States: Bread and Butter Politics," in Stephen R. Ward, ed., *The War Generation: Veterans of the First World War* (Port Washington, N.Y., 1975), 43; Wood to Doffer.

10. Wood to Doffer; *Minutes: First Meeting of the Caucus of the American Legion* (March 1919), 3–4, 23–31; *Stars and Stripes*, March 21, 1919; Speech of John Thomas Taylor, February 6, 1934, History—District of Columbia—Taylor file, AL.

11. *Minutes: First Meeting of the Caucus*, 5–6, 15–16; Wood to Doffer.

12. *Minutes: First Meeting of the Caucus*, 9–10.

13. Ibid., 9; *Stars and Stripes*, March 21, 1919; Roy Hoffman to Theodore Roosevelt Jr., March 18, 1919, and Alva J. Niles to Theodore Roosevelt Jr., March 31, 1919, both in History—Oklahoma file, AL; Richard S. Jones, *A History of the American Legion* (Indianapolis, 1946), 28–31.

14. Ogden Mills to Benjamin Kaufman, April 15, 1919, History—Delaware—Thomas W. Miller file, AL; Marquis James, *A History of the American Legion* (New York, 1923), 36–40. For publicity, see *Stars and Stripes*, March 14, 21; April 4, 11; and May 9, 16, 1919. Carbons of Wood's telegrams may be found in the History files of every state at AL; Eric Fisher Wood to "My dear Governor," April 10, 1919, Wood Papers, Syracuse Univ.; Richard M. Loosbrock, *The History of the Kansas Department of the American Legion* (Topeka, 1968), 17.

15. J. S. Miller to John G. Emery, September 23, 1921, History—Illinois file, AL; D. B. McKay to Theodore Roosevelt Jr., May 7, 1919, History—Florida file, AL; Bronson Cutting's list of expenses, Box 13, first item of American Legion file, Cutting Papers, LC; *Proceedings and Committees: Caucus of the American Legion* (St. Louis, 1919), 3–38, for state attendance (hereinafter cited as *Caucus*). "Minutes of [Executive] Committee Meeting," May 6, 1919, AL.

16. *Caucus*, 3–38; Theodore Roosevelt Jr., *Average Americans* (New York, 1920), 244–45; *Outlook* 122 (May 23, 1919):104–5. See also *New York Times*, April 13, 1919, 10, and April 29, 1919, 6.

17. *Caucus*, 3–38, 124–34, 160.

18. John Thomas Taylor, Speech of February 6, 1934, History—District of Columbia—Taylor file, AL; Dorothy R. Harper, "Hawaii—Department History," 11, History—Hawaii file, AL; *Caucus*, passim.

19. *Caucus*, 113–20, describes the issues discussed; J. C. O'Laughlin to Theodore Roosevelt Jr., April 11, 1919, History—Illinois file, AL.

20. Inzer's speech is in *Caucus*, 113–20; for other items see 124–38; 142–51.

21. Ibid., 52, 138–42.

22. Ibid., 118; Bronson Cutting to M. A. Otero Jr., May 16, 1919, Box 13, Cutting Papers, LC.

23. *Caucus*, 154–69. On a tape made in 1979 at the Houston Convention of the Legion (at AL), where Hamilton Fish was named Honorary Life Commander, he relates how he, with Delaware's George Davis and Arizona's Jack Greenway, all of whom "either knew Theodore Roosevelt or were one of his disciples," wrote the preamble, with Davis's draft being the basic text. Later, Eric Fisher Wood, embarrassed by the stridency of the words "one-hundred-percent Americanism," wanted to get Elihu Root to write a new preamble, but Fish commented that "he never served in any war in his life." Fish concluded the interview by stating that the preamble "stood for God and country and the Constitution of the United States and that's a good enough creed for anyone," and constituted a fine definition of Americanism.

24. Wood to Doffer.

25. For "kingmakers," see interview of Thomas W. Miller with Uveija Good, May 5, 1971, History—Texas—Alvin Owsley file, AL; Eric Fisher Wood, "The American Legion: Keep Alive the Spirit of the Great War," *Forum* 62 (August 1919):222.

26. "The American Legion: Executive Committee Meeting," May 10, 1919, 2, 3, 14, AL; Wood to Doffer; see also Eric Fisher Wood's synopsis of the June 9 Committee Meeting, which lists those who attended; Wood Papers, Syracuse Univ.

27. Memorandum outlining "Formation and Present Organization of the American Legion," October 15, 1919, and Eric Fisher Wood to Benjamin H. Griffen, February 9, 1934, Wood Papers, Syracuse Univ.

28. Edward A. Dickson to Theodore Roosevelt Jr., August 23, 1919; Roosevelt to Edward Bok, July 8, 1919; and Mark Wiseman to Roosevelt, May 28, 1929, all in Roosevelt Papers, Box 36, LC. Relating to *Collier's* account of the Caucus, Wiseman wrote that it "caught the spirit of the occasion, and . . . will do a great deal to crystallize the sentiment of the country into a favorable attitude toward the Legion." The Legion itself distributed thousands of copies of this article. "The American Legion: Executive Committee Meeting," June 9, 1919, 15–16, AL. For

more publicity, see *Literary Digest* 63 (November 29 and December 29, 1919):19, 18; "The Birth of the American Legion," *Outlook* 122 (May 21, 1919):104–5; *Caucus*, 3–38; Frank Knox to Roosevelt, June 4, 1919, History—New Hampshire file; *Summary of the Proceedings of the First National Convention of the American Legion* (Minneapolis, 1919), 50.

29. *American Legion Weekly*, July 4, 1919, 11; July 11, 1919, 5.

30. "The American Legion: Executive Committee Meeting," June 9, 1919, 111–12; "Memorandum Outlining Formation and Present Organization of the National Headquarters of the American Legion," October 15, 1919, and "Report of the Chairman of the Publicity Committee," Eric Fisher Wood Papers, Syracuse Univ. A copy of the poster may be found in Marquis James, *A History of the American Legion* (New York, 1923), 69.

31. Oliver H. Shoup to Henry Lindsley, November 7, 1919, History—Colorado file, AL; Richard J. Loosbrock, *The History of the Kansas Department of the American Legion* (Topeka, 1968), 14–20; Eric Fisher Wood to James Cox, May 31, 1919, Wood Papers, Syracuse Univ.; *Caucus*, 15; Edgar N. Danielson, "The History of the Department of New Jersey, 1919–1943," 12, Rutgers Univ.; "A Bit of Unwritten History" (undated), Stafford King Papers, Box 22, Minnesota Historical Society; John J. Pershing to Theodore Roosevelt Jr., June 15, 1919, Pershing Papers, Box 12, LC; Henry D. Lindsley to Pershing, August 24, 1926, Pershing Papers, Box 11, LC.

32. James, *American Legion*, 63; Richard D. Challener, ed., *United States Military Intelligence, 1919–1927* (New York, 1978), 1560; *Congressional Record* 66th Congress, second session, 2875, law loaning army rifles to posts passed February 13, 1920.

33. *Congressional Record*, 66th Congress, second session, 4062–84, 4418, 4823, 4992–94.

34. J. F. J. Herbert to Franklin D'Olier, October 1, 1919, History—Missouri file, AL; "Buck" Private Mendenhall, "A Spasm Relating to the American Legion Headquarters and the Use of Unnecessary Red Tape," one of the earliest items in Bronson Cutting Papers, Box 13, LC.

35. D. M. Davison to J. F. J. Herbert, August 6, 1919; George Seaman, "Report of the Progress of the Organization of the American Legion in Illinois," June 1919; Thomas Gowenlock to Eric Fisher Wood, July 1, 1919; C. L. Dawson, "Survey of the Department of Illinois," April 4, 1921; *American Legion Review* (program for 1924 Illinois State Convention), 33–34; Bion J. Arnold to Hanford MacNider, November 8, 1921, all in History—Illinois file, AL.

36. Report of M. M. Van Valkenburgh on Michigan Legion, 1919–23; Kenneth M. Stevens to Hanford MacNider, June 10, 1922; Augustus H. Gansser to Eben Putnam, September 1921; clipping from *Detroit Journal*, May 13, 1919, all in History—Michigan file, AL.

37. George F. Cutler to John G. Emery, July 30, 1921; Claude M.

Fuess, *A Brief History of the American Legion in Massachusetts* (Boston, 1926), 1–19; History—Massachusetts file, AL.

38. S. C. Crockett to Frank Samuel, September 12, 1925; "Report of Investigation (1921) of the Department of Alabama," History—Alabama file, AL; Lemuel Bolles to Hanford MacNider, March 6, 1922, History— Georgia file; Rex B. Magee to Eben Putnam, July 18, 1925, History— Mississippi file, AL. The Mississippi American Legion Papers, State Archives, Jackson, from this period are largely an account of these woes. C. K. Burgess to Eric F. Wood, May 17, 1919, and A. W. Glenn to Arthur F. Cosby, March 28, 1919, History—North Carolina file, AL.

39. Arthur E. Barbeau and Henri Florette, *The Unknown Soldiers: Black American Troops in World War I* (Philadelphia, 1974); "The American Legion: Executive Committee Meeting," June 9, 1919, 136–38, 148–50, AL; various letters to C. Baxter Jones, Louis H. Bell, and Henry D. Lindsley, August and September, 1919, including a petition by black former captain Austin T. Widen, a lawyer, for a national charter, dated September 25, 1919, all in History—Georgia file, AL; Henry D. Moran to Lindsley, October 25, 1919, History—Kentucky file, AL; John M. Parker to Theodore Roosevelt Jr., April 24 and 25, 1919, History— Louisiana file, AL.

40. For the debate at Legion headquarters, see "The American Legion: National Executive Committee Meeting," June 9, 1919, 136–50, AL; John M. Parker to Theodore Roosevelt Jr., April 15 and 28, 1919, Roosevelt Papers, Box 36, LC; Louis H. Bell to Henry D. Lindsley, July 18, 1919, History—Georgia file, AL; Irvine F. Belser to Lindsley, August 26, August 30, and September 17, 1919, mentioning a petition by Rufus Foster to national headquarters for a separate black organization, History—South Carolina file, AL.

41. Clipping on Kentucky Post, Americanism—Holidays—Flag Day file, AL; Report of Vice-Commander Lawrence A. Oxley of the Negro Division, North Carolina, August 22, 1928, Box 91, Roger Gregg Cherry Papers, North Carolina Department of Archives and History. The David R. Perry Papers, American Legion folder, Perkins Library, Duke Univ., detail the racial arrangements at the 1937 North Carolina State Convention. Black Legionnaires were housed in a separate hotel and held their meetings in a black school rather than the white convention hotels. Blacks and whites, however, joined in the parades and ceremonies. G. W. Hodges to Judge Advocate of the Legion, April 6, 1939, and Wright Patman to Frank Samuel, June 10, 1939, both in Administration and Organization—Organization—District and Posts— "Class" Posts—Black files, AL, which contain more protests and inquiries of the same sort on the eligibility of blacks.

42. B. M. Davison to J. F. J. Herbert, August 6, 1919, History— Illinois file, AL. Roosevelt spoke in thirty states on Legion matters: speaking itinerary, Box 40, Theodore Roosevelt Jr. Papers, LC; Eric

Fisher Wood to Roosevelt, September 19, 1919, Wood Papers, Syracuse Univ.; biography of Harry W. Colmery, History—Kansas—Colmery file, AL; interview of William Pencak with Harry L. Foster, October 30, 1980; John W. Inzer to Roosevelt, March 13, 1919, Roosevelt Papers, Box 36, LC.

43. "Minutes of Meeting, Executive Committee," June 9 and 26, Administration and Organization file, AL; Summary of Minutes of Executive Committee Meeting of July 11, Eric Fisher Wood Papers, Syracuse Univ.; "Treasurer's Report to the Temporary National Executive Committee, American Legion," (New York, 1919), AL; Arthur H. Warner, "The Truth about the American Legion," *Nation* 113 (July 27, 1921):89–90; "Notes Made in Fall of 1919, to Guarantee American Legion Indebtedness" are partially reprinted following the notes to this chapter; Lester P. Barlow to National Headquarters, July 21, 1931; memo, Verna Grimm to Miss Rubrik, July 27, 1931; James Barton to Lester P. Barlow, August 11, 1931; Frank Samuel to William Gellerman, May 13, 1936; all in Administration and Organization—Finance file, AL.

44. "National Treasurer's Report . . . From Inception to October 31, 1919," in Frank Samuel to Dennis H. Haverty, August 9, 1926; A. H. Vernon to Franklin D'Olier, June 8, 1920; Henry D. Lindsley to F. B. Lynch, October 24, 1919, and Lindsley to Lynch, October 27, 1919; note from National Executive Committee Meeting, February 10, 1920; Lemuel Bolles to Mr. Hosk, April 29, 1920; Anna G. Gordon to John G. Emery, October 31, 1921, all in Administration and Organization—Finance—Funds file, AL; "Minutes of the National Convention of the American Legion, 1919," 20, 251, AL (hereafter cited as "Convention"). For private funds, see John W. Inzer to Florida State Attorney General Blanding, May 25, 1919, History—Florida file, AL; and Fuess, *American Legion in Massachusetts*, 10. For war-chest funds, see Robert C. Bancroft et al. v. The City of Springfield and various attached papers, Gilbert Bettmann Papers, Box 15, Univ. of Cincinnati.

45. For fears of politics and a new GAR, see Edward Tyler to Arthur F. Crosby, April 23, 1919, History—Georgia file, AL, and Irvine Belser to Henry D. Lindsley, September 17, 1919, History—South Carolina file, AL; Roger S. Greene to Theodore Roosevelt Jr., September 13, 1919; Charles H. Sherrill to Roosevelt, May 16, 1919; exchange of letters between Leonard Wood and Roosevelt, December 27, 1919, January 8, 1920, and March 6, 1920; exchange of letters between Roosevelt and Bennett Champ Clark, July 30, August 23, and August 26, 1919, all in Roosevelt Papers, Box 36, LC. Eric Fisher Wood quotation in Wood to Benjamin H. Griffen, February 9, 1934, Wood Papers, Syracuse Univ. See biographies in appropriate folders in American Legion History files for Fish, Mills, and Roosevelt (New York); Herbert (Massachusetts); and Clark (Missouri).

46. *Congressional Record*, 66th Congress, first session, 6535 (Tampa

Post) and 7480 (Department of Georgia); Noel Gaines to American Legion Executive Committee, October 5, 1919, and to Henry Lindsley, October 8 and October 11, 1919, History—Tennessee file, AL.

47. "Convention," 12–15, 23, 30–33, 40–46, 334–48.

48. Ibid., 284–95 and 495 is the source for this and the next paragraph.

49. Wood to Doffer; "Convention," 71, 373–97. The problem of the Bonus is discussed more fully later. This Bonus debate is the main source for the next several paragraphs.

50. Wood to Doffer; Theodore Roosevelt Jr. to John Van Sickle, May 11, 1920, Roosevelt Papers, Box 11, LC.

51. "Convention," 386, 470–73.

52. James, *American Legion*, 85–90; "Convention," 54, 416–32.

53. Walter D. Myers, "A Collection of Recollections," 163–71, manuscript in the Indiana Historical Society; "Convention," 112–26.

54. Richard S. Jones, *A History of the American Legion* (Indianapolis, 1946), 344; remark of General Milton Foreman, "Convention," 20; Robert M. Gibson to H. S. Crosby, March 16, 1920, American Legion Papers, Box 16, Wisconsin State Historical Society.

The Continuity of Leadership in the Early American Legion

1. January 1919
   Discuss Legion

   Eric Fisher Wood
   George A. White
   Theodore Roosevelt Jr.
   "Wild Bill" Donovan

2. February 15–17
   Morale Conference

   Roosevelt, chairman
   Wood, secretary
   Franklin D'Olier, Bennett C. Clark, White, present

3. March 15–17
   Paris Caucus

   Wood, secretary
   Clark, chairman
   White, "floor leader"
   D'Olier, present

4. May 8–10
   St. Louis Caucus

   Roosevelt plans, turns down chairmanship
   Wood, secretary
   Henry D. Lindsley, chairman of
     War Risk Insurance Board, elected chairman
   Clark, D'Olier, present

5. May–November
   National Executive
   Committee

   Roosevelt, D'Olier, members
   Lindsley, chairman
   Wood, secretary
   Clark, vice-chairman
   White, runs *American Legion Weekly*

6. November 11–14
Minneapolis Convention

Roosevelt, White, floor leaders
Wood, secretary
D'Olier, major in support services, elected
first National Commander

Occupations of Delegates at St. Louis Caucus
Held by More than One Person

	Officers	Enlisted		Officers	Enlisted
Manufacturer	12	4	Professional Soldier	6	4
Business Executive	44	19	Automobile Salesman	5	3
Banker	25	12	Advertising	7	5
Broker	8	5	Artist/Architect	9	4
Doctor	34	2	Teacher	2	6
Lawyer	152	74	Laborer	0	2
Clergyman	7	1	Tailor	0	4
Engineer	29	14	Painter	1	2
Journalist	40	26	Retired	3	0
Farmer	10	11	Fireman	0	2
Clerk	14	48	Policeman	1	12
Real Estate	12	6	Jeweler	2	1
Salesman	13	33	Accountant	3	3
Merchant	19	23	Contractor	8	3
Public, semipublic	25	15	Carpenter	0	3
Student	18	28	Plumber	0	3
Insurance	8	10	Railroad Worker	3	2
Mechanic	0	7	Shoemaker	1	1
Machinist	1	5	Druggist	2	3
Telegrapher	0	2	Postal Service	5	2
Printer	1	5	Unemployed	0	2

Number of Registered Delegates at St. Louis Caucus

Alabama	15		Nevada	2
Alaska	1		New Hampshire	12
Arizona	7		New Jersey	26
Arkansas	19		New York	92
California	11		North Carolina	0
Colorado	14		North Dakota	9
Connecticut	13		Ohio	60
Delaware	4		Oklahoma	24
District of Columbia	14		Oregon	7
Florida	8		Pennsylvania	80
Georgia	5		Philippines	1
Hawaii	1		Rhode Island	12
Idaho	11		South Carolina	4
Illinois	112		South Dakota	6
Indiana	34		Tennessee	29

Iowa	38	Texas	24
Kansas	37	Utah	11
Kentucky	29	Virginia	12
Louisiana	23	Vermont	7
Maryland	15	Washington	11
Massachusetts	36	West Virginia	15
Michigan	47	Wisconsin	27
Minnesota	39	Wyoming	8
Mississippi	12	American Army Association	6
Missouri	59	American Service League	1
Montana	8	World War Veterans	8
Nebraska	22	Missouri Officers' Association	4

Total 1,132

The $257,000 Loan to the American Legion
66 Lenders, 146 Guarantors (*indicates own guarantor)

Principal Lenders (those under $1,000 not listed)

*Morgan Guaranty Trust Co., New York	$100,000 (30 other guarantors)
*F. M. Alger, Detroit	25,000 (13 other guarantors)
*Chester C. Bolton, Cleveland	25,000 (2 other guarantors)
Robert K. Cassat, Philadelphia	25,000 (9 guarantors)
*William W. Lanahan, Baltimore	10,000
First National Bank, Milwaukee	10,000 (15 guarantors)
Robert A. Elmore, Washington, D.C.	5,000 (10 guarantors)
*E. R. Smith, Little Rock	2,500
*Armour and Co., Chicago	2,500
*E. F. Carry, Chicago	2,500
*R. T. Crane Jr., Chicago	2,500
*Harold F. McCormack, Chicago	2,500
*Edward Morris, Chicago	2,500
*S. Peabody, Chicago	2,500
*A. A. Sprague, Chicago	2,500
*Louis F. Swift, Chicago	2,500
*Garrad B. Winson, Chicago	2,500
*Jerome Harrington, Wichita	2,500
John B. MacDougal, Iowa	2,500 (66 guarantors)
*Kidder and Peabody, Boston	2,000
*Lee Higginson and Co., Boston	2,000

*Lewis Douglas, Jerome, Arizona   1,250
*Hornblower and Weeks, Boston   1,000
*Mosely and Company, Boston   1,000

Legion Expenses and Revenues to October 31, 1919

Revenues

25¢ assessment on members	$186,022.65
Buttons	10,535.62
Advertising and subscriptions, *American Legion Weekly*	29,922.60
Contributions (probably before Legion began to refuse contributions)	1,953.62
Miscellaneous	2,139.20
	$230,573.69

Expenses

American Legion Weekly	$178,882.31
Salaries	36,137.28
Professional Service (accounting, legal, publicist)	16,001.31
Rent and Light	8,967.36
Office Supplies and Publicity	36,298.16
Postage and Express	10,380.96
Telephone and Telegraph	6,650.11
Travel	5,188.86
Purchase of Buttons	53,254.64
Furniture	3,660.41
Washington Office	1,010.25
Pershing Reception, Madison Square Garden	2,965.66
Interest on Notes	3,280.88
Miscellaneous	2,835.00
	$365,513.19

Excess of Expenses over Revenues	$134,939.50

Chapter Four

* Jesse W. Barrett Papers, Box 1, Univ. of Missouri.

1. Ralph T. O'Neil, radio speech, March 23, 1931, History—Kansas—O'Neil file, AL; Henry L. Stevens Jr., "The National Commander Says—There Is More than One Kind of Oil," *American Legion Monthly* (July 1932):17; *Milwaukee Sentinel*, September 16, 1941, Wisconsin

American Legion Papers, Box 3, Wisconsin State Historical Society; Marquis James, *A History of the American Legion* (New York, 1923), 77.

2. W. I. Fruit to Theodore Roosevelt Jr., November 2, 1920, Roosevelt Papers, Box 11, LC; William Gellerman, *The American Legion as Educator* (New York, 1938), 37, 50, 238; Walter Wilson, *The American Legion and Civil Liberty*, American Civil Liberties Union pamphlet (New York, 1936), 19–20, 23–24. A spate of anti-Legion literature appeared in the early 1930s, when the Legion was struggling to retain veterans' benefits in the midst of the Great Depression: see Marcus Duffield, "The American Legion in Politics," *Forum* 85 (May 1931):257–65; "The Legion Prepares for War," *Scribner's* 90 (August 1931):174–81; and *King Legion* (New York, 1931); Walter Davenport, "But the Dead Don't Vote," *Collier's* 89 (June 11, 1932):11–18; and "Taking Allowances," ibid. 90 (August 20, 1932):12–13; Robert C. McManus, "Billions for Veterans," *Current History* 16 (August 1932):558–62; Archibald Roosevelt, "The Enemy Within the Gate," *New Outlook* 161 (October 1932):7–10; and Lawrence Sullivan, "The Veteran Racket," *Atlantic Monthly* 151 (April 1933):393–402.

3. Classic statements of elitist theory include C. Wright Mills, *The Power Elite* (New York, 1956), and G. William Domhoff, *Who Rules America?* (Englewood Cliffs, N.J., 1967); for a pluralist position, see Arnold Rose, *The Power Structure: Political Process in American Society* (London, 1967).

4. Ross Federal Research Corporation Survey of the American Legion, 1938, esp. 1–3, 10–15, AL.

5. Richard S. Jones, *A History of the American Legion* (Indianapolis, 1946), 349; "If These Are the Right Questions, We Have the Right Answers," *American Legion Monthly* pamphlet, 1931, AL; "Analysis of Circulation, November 1937 Issue," *American Legion Monthly*, AL. Post questionnaires for 1923 and 1930, filed by state, in possession of the author.

6. Membership figures in Jones, *The American Legion*, 344–45; Bruce Stokes, "Self-Help in the Eighties," *Citizen Participation* (January–February 1982):5; Charles Wright and Herbert Hyman, "Voluntary Association Membership of American Adults: Evidence from National Sample Surveys," *American Sociological Review* 23 (1958):284–94.

7. "Minutes of the National Executive Committee," February 10, 1920, 37–38, AL.

8. "Minutes of the National Americanism Commission," March 12, 1920, 194, AL; "Minutes of the National Executive Committee," May 18–19, 1920, 389, AL; for Legion antiprofiteer arguments, see *American Legion Weekly*, February 1, 1924, and the exchange between National Commander John Quinn and Andrew Mellon in the *Literary Digest*, February 23, 1924, 10–11.

9. "Proceedings of the Twelfth Annual Convention, 1930" 289, AL; "Executive Committee Meeting of the American Legion," June 9, 1919,

AL; *Greenville* (Mississippi) *Daily Times* clipping, November 27, 1930, History—Kansas—Ralph O'Neil file, AL.

10. Fred Holloway to Jesse W. Barrett, October 20, 1932, and July 6, 1933, Barrett Papers, Box 1, Univ. of Missouri; questionnaires in possession of the author.

11. *Washington Veteran* 2:1 (January 1920), Mark E. Reed Papers, Univ. of Washington; *Summary of the Proceedings of the Nineteenth* (New York, 1937—85), *Sixth* (St. Paul, 1924—76), *Seventh* (Omaha, 1925—79–80), and *Ninth* (Paris, 1927—79) *National Conventions*; Dorothy Culp, "The American Legion—A Study in Pressure Politics" (Ph.D. thesis, Univ. of Chicago, 1939), 27–29; "American Legion News Service," November 17, 1924, and "American Legion File Service," April 24, 1925, Stafford King Papers, Box 19, Minnesota Historical Society; clipping, "Men Outside the Legion," Hanford MacNider Papers, Verne Marshall file, Series 4, Hoover Library.

12. "Minutes of the National Americanism Commission," May 5, 1937, 61–64, AL.

13. Franklin D'Olier to Lemuel Bolles, July 14, 1920, History—New Jersey—D'Olier file, AL; questionnaire in possession of the author; Minutes of Rose City Post, February 1, 1933, Oregon Historical Society; Earl Warren to Mark Requa, November 7, 1931, copy in Herbert Hoover Presidential Papers—American Legion file, Hoover Library.

14. *Reports of Committees to the Thirteenth National Convention* (1931), 81; Hamilton Fish, "In Defense of the Legion," *Forum* 85 (July 1931):29.

15. Earl Warren to Mark Requa, November 7, 1931, Herbert Hoover Presidential Papers—American Legion File, Hoover Library; William Gellerman, *The American Legion as Educator* (New York, 1938), v; Hanford MacNider to L. R. Gignillat, July 23, 1924 (G Series); MacNider to Bert Halligan, July 10, 1924 (Commanders Series); MacNider to Joseph H. Thompson, June 4, 1924 (Box 10), MacNider Papers, Hoover Library; R. A. Cooper to "Commrade," May 3, 1927, copy in Paul McNutt Papers, Indiana Univ.; Jesse W. Barrett to Bruce P. Boyd, February 2, 1933, Barrett Papers, Box 1, Univ. of Missouri; Gilbert Bettmann to Martin David, January 13, 1923, Bettmann Papers, Box 15, Univ. of Cincinnati.

16. Martin M. David, "Manual of Ceremonies," November 1924; James H. Fisk, draft of article for *American Legion Monthly*, June 1933, Administration and Organization—Ceremonies and Rituals file, AL; "Report of Director of Membership" (Minnesota) 1928, and Stafford King to Philip O'Toole, September 25, 1928, King Papers, Box 16, Minnesota Historical Society.

17. Report of Ritual Committee, January 30, 1941; Liszt Lenzen to National Headquarters, November 19, 1935; Wesley H. Morris to Harold K. Phillips, November 10, 1936; Rev. S. M. Egger to Frank Samuel, November 7, 1937; Ray Colson to Samuel, November 5, 1931; Howard Rowton to Samuel, June 27, 1938; all in Administration and Organiza-

tion—Ceremonies and Rituals file, AL; Roswell Barnes to Taylor Miller, March 3, 1928, ACLU, vol. 341, n.p.

18. "Minutes of the National Americanism Commission," November 15, 1931, 53, AL: Stephen Chadwick to W. G. Callow, August 4, 1937, Chadwick Papers, Box 23, Univ. of Washington; Frank Parker to Willard K. Mather, October 29, 1932, Parker Papers, Box 12, Univ. of North Carolina.

19. Omaha post questionnaire (1923) in possession of the author; "Minutes of the Rose City Post," November 29, 1932, Oregon Historical Society; Ernst Angell, "The Legion's Betrayal," *Nation* 136 (November 1936):584–85; for New Mexico, see Bronson Cutting Papers, Box 13, LC; History—New Mexico file, AL; Jones, *The American Legion*, 346.

20. Author's interview with Hamilton Fish, January 24, 1986; Albert Jones to Stafford King, September 11, 1925 (Box 16), King to Henry L. Stevens, March 30, 1928 (Box 23), King Papers, Minnesota Historical Society; Stephen Chadwick to I. A. Lougis, June 25, 1937, Chadwick Papers, Box 22, Univ. of Washington.

21. Jones, *A History of the American Legion*, 335, 336, 342, 371–76.

22. Jones, *American Legion*, 335; Gellerman, *The American Legion as Educator*, 53–64; Ferre C. Watkins to Alvin Owsley, October 21, 1922, Scrapbook 3, Owsley Papers, North Texas State Univ.; "Minutes of the Fifth National Convention" (1923), 134, AL.

23. For use of the term "kingmakers," see, for example, Stephen Chadwick to George Nilsson, June 16, 1937, Box 16, Chadwick Papers, Univ. of Washington; post bulletin from John J. McShane, Roger Gregg Cherry Papers, Box 92, North Carolina Department of Archives and History; Jones, *A History of the American Legion*, 337; oral history memoir of John B. Quinn, 4, 6, Univ. of California, Berkeley. For Henry D. Lindsley's effort to make Pershing national commander, see History—District of Columbia—Pershing file, AL. Also see Royal Johnson to Hanford MacNider, August 27, 1926, MacNider Papers, Johnson Series, Hoover Library. For information on commanders' careers, see their files (under state of residence) in the AL History files. Humphrey Sullivan's letters to Hanford MacNider in MacNider's Papers deal with the maneuvering. For Murphy's efforts, see Wright Patman to Edward Campbell, June 27, 1931, and Ray Murphy to Campbell, August 6, 1931, Campbell Papers, Box 1, Univ. of Iowa; clipping from *Ida Grove Record*, September 26, 1934, Murphy Papers, Scrapbook no. 1, Univ. of Iowa.

24. R. C. Winters to Paul McNutt, August 6, 1927, McNutt Papers, Indiana Univ.; Stephen Chadwick to Julia Wheelock, October 4, 1937, Box 23, and Louis A. Johnson to D. V. Addy, Box 16, Chadwick Papers, Univ. of Washington; list of candidates for commander, 1940, Box 5, Warren Atherton Papers, Univ. of the Pacific; John D. Emery to Frank Parker, July 21, 1930, Box 6, Parker Papers, Univ. of North Carolina.

25. Jesse W. Barrett to George Fiske, November 28, 1934, Barrett Papers, Box 1, Univ. of Missouri; Hamilton Fish, "In Defense of the Legion," *Forum* 85 (July 1931):29; Daniel Steck to Hanford MacNider, September 26, 1925, MacNider Papers, Box 10, Hoover Library.

26. Hanford MacNider to Edward J. Barrett, January 29, 1924 (B Series), and to Bert Halligan, July 30, 1924 (Commanders Series), MacNider Papers, Hoover Library. Clipping from *San Francisco American*, October 11, 1923, Scrapbook 3, and undated letter from Michael Cohen, Alvin Owsley Papers, North Texas State Univ.; *Summary of the Proceedings of the Eighteenth* (Cleveland, 1936—11) *and Nineteenth* (New York, 1937—16) *National Conventions.*

27. Frank Samuel, "Portland, the City of Cities" (1932), History—Kansas—Samuel file, AL; clipping from the *Call*, November 9, 1921, ACLU, vol. 189, 277.

28. Richard Loosbrock, *The History of the Kansas Department of the American Legion* (Topeka, 1968), 50–51, 73; *Nation* 63 (November 23, 1921):594; 71 (October 19, 1927), 420–21; *Christian Century* 48 (October 7, 1931):1,234; Margaret Doty, "The Legion on a Spree," *Forum* 85 (June 1931):333–34; Philadelphia Convention Scrapbook, History—Delaware file, AL; clippings related to the New York Convention (1937), ACLU, vol. 951, 61–66; Carleton B. McCulloch to Meredith Nicholson, October 9, 1940, McCulloch Papers, Indiana Historical Society.

29. Clipping from *Christian Century*, October 6, 1929, ACLU, vol. 362; from New Orleans Convention, October 17, 1922, Scrapbook no. 2, Owsley Papers, North Texas State Univ.; Doty, "The Legion on a Spree," 330.

30. Frank Samuel, "Portland," History—Kansas—Samuel file, AL; *Summary of the Proceedings of the Twelfth* (Boston, 1930—25), and *Twenty-Third* (Milwaukee, 1941—7, 11), *National Conventions*; Raymond Moley Jr., *The American Legion Story* (New York, 1966), 321–22. The secretive nature of the Forty and Eight makes it almost impossible to document its activities.

31. "Preparation for Department Convention" (1925), Stafford King Papers, Box 19, Minnesota Historical Society; "Minutes of the Seventh National Convention" (1925), 535, AL.

32. *Summary of the Proceedings of the Second* (Cleveland, 1920—17), *Eighteenth* (1936—37), *Nineteenth* (New York, 1937—5), and *Twentieth* (Los Angeles, 1938—36) *National Conventions*; clipping from the *Nation*, November 23, 1921, ACLU vol. 189, 281; Emerson B. Nugent, "On to Paris with a Second AEF," copy in Stafford King Papers, Box 16, and Minnesota Executive Committee Meeting Minutes, September 1924, Box 19, Minnesota Historical Society; Loosbrock, *American Legion in Kansas*, 80.

33. Earl L. Bixby, "The Second AEF," Box 15, and Henry D. Lindsley to Stafford King, August 21, 1926, Box 16, King Papers, Minnesota Historical Society; letters to Henry D. Lindsley from Harry Besosa,

September 13, 1926; D. J. Stevens, September 29, 1926; and Robert L. Moorhead, September 20, 1936, John J. Pershing Papers, Box 1, LC.

34. Convention advertisements in Pershing Papers, Box 12, LC, and Stafford King Papers, Box 16, Minnesota Historical Society. Officially, eighteen thousand Legionnaires traveled to the Convention (*Nation*, July 7, 1927, clipping in ACLU, vol. 189, 281); probably twenty-five thousand were present all together, along with families and hangers-on; David Kennedy, *Over Here: The First World War and American Society* (New York, 1980), 363–65. Quotations in this and the next two paragraphs from *Washington News*, September 8, 1926, clipping in Pershing Papers, Box 12, LC: *Literary Digest* 95 (October 1, 1927):5–7, and (October 15, 1927):39–44; Ada Treat, "Is This America?" *Nation* 125 (October 19, 1927):420–22; *L'Illustration*, September 24, 1927, cover; *Summary of the Proceedings of the Ninth National Convention* (Paris, 1927), 6; Stafford King to Henry G. Smith, November 19, 1927, King Papers, Box 23, Minnesota Historical Society.

35. Kennedy, *Over Here*, 365; José Sherwood to James F. Barton, July 7, 1927 (Box 16), and exchange of letters between Sherwood and John Wicker, February 13 and March 19, 1928 (Box 22), Stafford King Papers, Minnesota Historical Society.

36. P. Lincoln Mitchell to Henry D. Lindsley, September 17, 1926, John J. Pershing Papers, Box 11, LC; Loosbrock, *American Legion in Kansas*, 50; Jesse W. Barrett to William Diemer, September 7, 1933, Barrett Papers, Box 1, Univ. of Missouri. Poems follow notes to this chapter.

37. *Christian Century* 48 (October 21, 1931):1315, and (November 13, 1931):1461; *Forum* 86 (August 1931):20. Broun cited in clippings related to the New York Convention (1937), ACLU, vol. 951, 61–66.

38. *Christian Century* 50 (October 18, 1933), 1294; all debates printed verbatim in minutes of appropriate Conventions, AL.

39. "Minutes of the National Americanism Commission," July 8, 1925, 26; May 11, 1926, 8; October 31, 1935, 85; and November 15, 1931, 37, AL. On November 19, 1933 (116), Edward Frazier termed the National Convention "a necessary nuisance" where "resolutions get through . . . that bind the Legion to a policy that does not represent a majority."

40. Gellerman, *The American Legion as Educator*, 26–27; Hamilton Fish, "In Defense of the Legion," *Forum* 85 (July 1931):29.

41. The most convenient listing of committee and commission chairmen and other prominent Legion officials is in Moley, *The American Legion Story*, 403–30. For the Rehabilitation structure, see Jones, *A History of the American Legion*, 208–17; and *The American Legion at Work for the Sick and Disabled: Report of the National Rehabilitation Committee* (New Orleans, 1922), especially 10–13, 22–25, AL.

42. Stephen Chadwick to George Nilsson, December 3, 1927, Chadwick Papers, Box 23, Univ. of Washington; "Minutes of the National

Americanism Commission," August 9, 1925, 326; August 3, 1936, 2–4; on May 1, 1935, 18, Homer Chaillaux admitted to having "chiseled three new types of safety programs," AL; Amos Fries to Edward Hayes, March 14, 1934, Fries Papers, American Legion file, Univ. of Oregon; James W. Duggan to Jesse W. Barrett, October 19, 1937, Barrett Papers, Box 1, Univ. of Missouri; Minnesota Budget, July 21, 1931, Stafford King Papers, Box 19, Minnesota Historical Society.

43. Gellerman, *The American Legion as Educator*, 25. "Minutes of the National Americanism Commission," October 26, 1921, 43–52, and November 1, 1936, 99, AL. "If These Are the Right Questions," *American Legion Monthly* pamphlet (1931), AL.

American Legion Poems—Wisconsin American Legion Papers, Box 2, Wisconsin State Historical Society

The American Legion Comes to Town
Alfred M. Hansen

There is something about a soldier, that thrills a woman's heart,
Something about the Legion, the legislature thinks it's smart,
Both spend time and money to see them on parade,
Bringing with them thousands, to stimulate merchants' trade.

Years ago folks shuddered when the Legion came to town,
When after days of frolic, there was debris all around,
But now they welcome Legion and bid to get the crowd,
With music, drums, and floats, for which the Legion should be proud.

When drums and bugles sounded, they faced death with a will,
Those that escaped alive, have that courageous spirit still,
They proudly march behind flags and banners in color galore,
They promise to meet all comers, that dare intrude our shore.

They swore to protect the flag, and all for which it stands,
But never more to fight for bankers in foreign lands,
They saw horrors of war, they saw their comrades die,
And shudder to think of Flanders, where thousands of them lie.

In Legion banded together, they have fought with pen and voice,
To better the condition, of all the soldier boys,
The drum corps and the buglers have sounded far and wide,
With thoughts of those in need, in towns and countryside.

When they come to town, to frolic for a day,
They are given keys to city, to caper as they may,
And when the stunts are over, and noise has died away,
It may mean a Christmas dinner for some waif on Christmas Day.

A Storekeeper on His Way to the American Legion Convention
Archibald Pennington

A storekeeper was in the company,
He loved a joke as well as you or me,
He was not small nor yet was he slender,
His love of food made him a good spender,
His face was round and red, as was his nose,
With drinking it looked like a full-blown rose.
This worthy man tried to ape the student,
His choice of clothes was not always prudent.
His suit was plaid and his tie was bright red,
His shirt was green with figures overspread.
He loved to tell stories of his great deeds,
Of the time that he was fighting overseas.
He fails to recollect the small detail,
Or when he was peeling spuds into pails,
And he never saw service overseas,
His memory is failing by degrees.
His name was Archibald J. Pennington,
And this is all, this narrative is done.

To My Convention Pals
Francis Roche

The bands were coming down the street,
Their uniforms sparkling indeed,
The two were bending elbows,
A thirst-quencher was in need.

I knew about four in the morning,
These fellows would be traipsing in,
And right around my doorstep,
Would create an awful din.

I went to bed and closed my eyes,
And then—What do you think?
I'll be gol-darned, I'm telling the truth,
I couldn't sleep a wink.

I guess it's put in my system,
To awaken at four A.M.,
During a Legion Convention,
So why should I give a damn?

Now my tale is ended,
And when all is said and done,
The moral of my story is
YAH CAN'T BEAT FUN!

Good-Bye Legionnaires (from Chicago)

(Anonymous)

O! the Legion has departed
And as down the Loop I roam,
I wonder what those roguish lads
Are doing back at home.

Take the guy who stripped the copper
Of his uniform and mount,
I'll bet he's stripping oranges
At the Podunk soda fount.

And the gink who tossed the mattress
Twenty stories—all afire,
Is tossing gems of harmony
In the Sunday morning choir.

And that kissing guy on State Street
Had the time of his young life,
But I'll bet he asks permission
When he wants to kiss his wife.

And the cannoneers on Randolph
With a yen for shot and shell,
Don't even slam the doors at home
For fear of catching hell.

Then the guy who jammed the traffic
Down where Erie crosses Cass,
Is keeping kids in order
At the children's Bible class.

Chapter Five

1. Report of James T. Duane, September 22, 1921, in Clarence Edwards Papers, Box 15, Massachusetts Historical Society.

2. Richard S. Jones, *A History of the American Legion* (Indianapolis, 1946), 363.

3. Clipping, *Call*, June 13, 1920, ACLU, vol. 112, 103; Claude Fuess, *A Brief History of the American Legion in Massachusetts* (Boston, 1926), 13, History—Massachusetts file, AL; "Minutes of the National Executive Committee," February 10, 1920, 44–45, AL; Marquis James, *A History of the American Legion* (New York, 1923), 155–60.

4. Ibid., 230; C. Vann Woodward, *Tom Watson: Agrarian Rebel* (New York, 1938), 471–73.

5. Lemuel Bolles to all state commanders, October 21, 1920, copy in Wisconsin American Legion Papers, Box 3, Wisconsin State Historical Society.

6. The Gibson-Pendill struggle to control the Wisconsin Legion is voluminously documented in Boxes 2 and 3, Wisconsin American Legion Papers, Wisconsin State Historical Society. Specific quotations from

R. M. Gibson to Claudius Pendill, September 15, 1920; clipping from *Wisconsin Rapids Daily Tribune*, October 12, 1920; Bolles circular cited in n. 5, above; and copy of charges against Gibson, all in Box 3.

7. Exchange of letters between Paul S. Andrews and Theodore Roosevelt Jr., October 12 and 17, 1921, Roosevelt Papers, Box 12, LC.

8. "Minutes of the Second National Convention" (1920), 214–37, AL.

9. Anonymous to John Taber, May 11, 1935, Taber Papers, Box 62, Cornell Univ.

10. Marcus Duffield, "The American Legion in Politics," *Forum* 85 (May 1931):261; Stafford King to Paul O. Shell, June 20, 1923, King Papers, Box 20, Minnesota Historical Society.

11. James, *American Legion*, 150; Raymond Scallen to Stafford King, October 1, 1928, Box 17, King Papers, Minnesota Historical Society.

12. Theodore Roosevelt Jr. to George Leach, October 1, 1921, Roosevelt Papers, Box 12, LC; author's interview with Hamilton Fish, January 24, 1986; biographical preface to Hamilton Fish, *Tragic Deception* (New York, 1983); Franklin D'Olier to Thomas M. Owen, January 26, 1934, History—New Jersey—D'Olier file, AL.

13. Clipping from *New York Times*, May 1, 1921, ACLU, vol. 184, 225; Milton J. Foreman to Lemuel Bolles, April 27, 1921, History—Illinois—Foreman file, AL; Robert K. Murray, *The Harding Era* (Minneapolis, 1969), 480–81; Jones, *American Legion*, 54–55; David K. Chalmers, *Hooded Americanism: The History of the Ku Klux Klan* (New York, 1965), 139.

14. "Veterans' File—National Americanism Legislative Committee," Stafford King Papers, Box 18, Minnesota Historical Society; *Summary of the Proceedings of the Twenty-Second Annual Convention* (Milwaukee, 1941), 16.

15. Exchange of letters between Hanford MacNider and Theodore Roosevelt Jr., July 28 through October 16, 1928 (State file—District of Columbia); Thomas W. Miller to MacNider, August 21, 1924 (State file—Delaware); MacNider to Reed Smoot, October 23, 1924 (State file—District of Columbia); Robert Carey to MacNider, August 19, 1924 (State file—Wyoming); all in Box 12, and checks listed from Republican National Committee (Service League file) Box 17, MacNider Papers, Hoover Library; exchanges of letters between Bronson M. Cutting and MacNider, August 30, 1924; and Cutting and Theodore Roosevelt Jr., September 11 and 22, 1924, Cutting Papers, Box 13, LC.

16. Correspondence between Hanford MacNider and Frank Miles, September 23 through October 17, 1924; MacNider to Henry Hess, November 14, 1924; copy of August 1, 1924, editorial in *Iowa Legionnaire*, all in MacNider Papers (General files for 1924), Hoover Library.

17. Hanford MacNider to Torch Press, October 17, 1924; exchange of letters, Henry Hess and MacNider, October 26 and November 14, 1924; exchange of letters, MacNider and John Reardon, September 6 and 11, 1924 (General files for 1924); John Tennel to MacNider, Septem-

ber 22, 1924 (State file—Connecticut), MacNider Papers, Hoover Library.

18. Robert Black to Hugh Martin, October 21, 1926, Black Papers, Letter Book, Cincinnati Historical Society; Hanford MacNider to F. H. Hodges, March 18, 1925 (Adjutants, Post file), and Thomas W. Miller to MacNider, August 21, 1924 (State file—Delaware), MacNider Papers, Hoover Library; William Deegan and others, solicitation for George Berry, John Tuck Papers, #2604, Cornell Univ.

19. Clippings, letters, and scrapbook in Democratic Veterans' Organization file, Henry T. Allen Papers, Box 24, LC. See especially "Stump Speech for Smith"; A. Lacy Price, "Yours for Democracy"; clippings, *New York Times*, September 1 and October 7, 1928; instructions for county chairmen.

20. Alvin Owsley to Patrick Edwards, October 10, 1928; clippings from *New York Times*, September 9, 1928; *New York Herald Tribune*, August 13, 1928; *World Tribune*, August 17, 1928; exchange of letters between Newton C. Baker and Henry Allen, September 14 and 18, 1928, all in Allen Papers, Box 24, LC.

21. See Republican Service League Flyers for Hoover (1932 Campaign Collection) and Landon and Knox (1936 Campaign Collection); press release of September 6, 1928, MacNider Papers, Hoover Library; Henry T. Allen to John O'Laughlin (n.d.), Allen Papers, Box 24, LC. Edward Spafford to Louis A. Johnson, September 30, 1936, copy in Stephen Chadwick Papers, Box 16, Univ. of Washington; clipping from *Chicago News*, August 15, 1940, History—Kansas—Colmery file, AL.

22. Gubernatorial file nos. 8098 and 8191, Lloyd C. Stark Papers, Univ. of Missouri; endorsements of Stark by posts appeared as early as April 1935; Stark to William A. Kitchin, December 29, 1935, and January 27, 1936; Kitchin to Stark, December 26, 1935; January 10 and 25 and February 27, 1936.

23. Charles D. Osborne to Lloyd C. Stark, March 18, 1936, Stark Papers, Univ. of Missouri. Similar maneuverings occurred in other states: in 1939 Leonard Roan reported some "Georgia Gossip" to Assistant Secretary of War Louis Johnson. Besides "the accustomed hilarity of the parades," "some incidents of political significance" occurred at the state convention "although the Legion's bylaws strictly forbid it." Leonard Roan to Louis A. Johnson, September 30, 1939, Johnson Papers, Box 36, Univ. of Virginia.

24. Bruce Brougham to Wright Patman, April 27, 1935, Patman Papers, Lyndon B. Johnson Library, Austin, Texas, quoted in David Lisio, "The United States: Bread and Butter Politics," in Stephen Ward, ed., *The War Generation: Veterans of the First World War* (Port Washington, N.Y., 1975), 55; Albert Somit and Joseph Tannenhaus, "The Veteran in the Electoral Process," *Journal of Politics* 2 (1957):184–201.

25. William Gellerman, *The American Legion as Educator* (New York, 1938); Jones, *American Legion*, 47.

26. Marcus Duffield, "The American Legion in Politics," *Forum* 85 (May 1931):261; information on Taylor in this and following paragraphs from "John Thomas Taylor," *Today*, January 30, 1937; *Time*, January 21, 1935; *North American Review*, January 30, 1950, 86–88, included along with miscellaneous letters and clippings in the History—District of Columbia—Taylor file, AL; *New York Times* clipping January 22, 1927, ACLU, vol. 322; *New York Sun* clipping, January 30, 1932, ACLU, vol. 523, 119. Note on Legion innovation of barrages from *New York Times*, February 7, 1937, VIII, 4.

27. Hanford MacNider to John Quinn, January 26, 1924 (American Legion—Old Papers file); exchange of letters, Bert Halligan and MacNider, January 19, 21, and 22, 1924 (Box 7—Commanders file); MacNider to James Barton, March 26, 1926, and January 20, 1927; Barton to MacNider, January 22, 1927 (Barton file), MacNider Papers, Hoover Library; Herbert Mooney to Paul McNutt, March 11, 1927, McNutt Papers, Indiana Univ.

28. My analysis of lobbying is taken from J. Leiper Freeman, *The Political Process: Executive Bureau–Legislative Committee Relations* (New York, 1965); Karl Schiftgiesser, *The Lobbyists* (Boston, 1951); and Jeffrey M. Berry, *Lobbying for the People* (Princeton, 1977).

29. Hamilton Fish, "In Defense of the Legion," *Forum*, 85 (July 1931):29.

30. *Christian Century* 48 (October 7, 1931):1236; John Thomas Taylor to O. H. Doyle (state commander) April 15, 1930 (Box 5), and Heywood Mahon to John J. MacSwain, May 14, 1928 (Box 4), MacSwain Papers, Duke Univ.; James Boyle to Thomas V. Hull, April 1, 1968, Warren Atherton Papers, Box 2, Univ. of the Pacific.

31. Louis A. Carr to Lemuel Bolles, July 5, 1920, History—West Virginia file, AL; "Legislative file," Stafford King Papers, Box 18, Minnesota Historical Society.

32. "Speech of the Hon. Hamilton Fish in Favor of Outlawing Poison Gas, January 21, 1927"; Stafford King to Fish, February 3, 1927 (Box 16); John Thomas Taylor to King, February 16 and March 31, 1927 (Box 23), King Papers, Minnesota Historical Society.

33. *Summary of the Proccedings of the Fourteenth* (Portland, Ore., 1932), 13, and *Fifteenth* (Chicago, 1933), 11, *National Conventions*; Edward M. Spafford to J. J. O'Connell, October 4, 1932, History—New York—Spafford file, AL; "Minutes of the Fifteenth National Convention (1933)," 163, AL.

34. Address of April 6, 1934, History—District of Columbia—Miller file, AL; Anson Cook's Resolution of April 24, 1934, (Box 16); Homer Chaillaux to Stephen Chadwick, March 23, 1937 (Box 22), Chadwick Papers, Univ. of Washington ; Rufus H. Bethune to Raymond Kelly, May 30, 1940, copy in Louis A. Johnson Papers, Box 37, Univ. of Virginia.

35. Fred A. Boettinger to Lloyd C. Stark, December 6, 1939 (folder

502), and Ralph Smith and others to Stark, March 10, 1937 (folder 491), Stark Papers, Univ. of Missouri; Stafford King to C. D. Hibbard, November 28, 1928, King Papers, Box 15, Minnesota Historical Society; Stephen Chadwick to Charles E. Gates, September 9, 1921, Chadwick Papers, Box 20, Univ. of Washington; W. H. Wallace to Leroy M. Gensman, August 10, 1921, Gensman Papers (folder 110), Univ. of Oklahoma.

36. Arthur E. Nelson to Theodore Christiansen, March 21, 1923, King Papers, Box 21, Minnesota Historical Society; Frank Parker to Ada Mucklestone, October 5, 1931, Parker Papers, Univ. of North Carolina; Hanford MacNider to John Thomas Taylor, January 15, 1925 (State file—District of Columbia); George J. Hatfield to MacNider, December 9, 1924 (State file—California); Frank Miles to MacNider, January 22, 1924 (Iowa Legionnaire file), MacNider Papers, Hoover Library; Leas Greenlee to Paul McNutt, November 22, 1926, and John Smith to McNutt, December 2, 1926, McNutt Papers, Indiana Univ.

37. Exchange of letters between Stafford King and Harold Bain, October 26 and 28, 1928, King Papers, Box 15, Minnesota Historical Society; "Minutes of Theodore Petersen Post," February 17, 1922, Minnesota Historical Society; Stephen Chadwick to Paul M. Potter, November 19, 1940, Chadwick Papers, Univ. of Washington.

38. Boyd Statler to H. K. Phillips, October 8, 1936, and Lawrence Martin to Harry Colmery, October 10, 1936, Administration—Organization—Publicity—Criticism file, AL; C. A. Jackson to Samuel McGarghey, April 14, 1926, and anonymous two-page typescript, McNutt Papers, Indiana Univ. "Minutes of Rose City Post," August 11, 1931, Oregon Historical Society; exchange of letters between Raymond Kelly and M. A. Fields, August 13 and 24, 1940; Frank Samuel to Irwin Couger, July 16, 1940; Samuel to O. K. Armstrong, June 28, 1940; Wilbur M. Alter to Armstrong, September 4, 1940, all in History—Missouri—Armstrong file, AL.

39. Arthur M. Schlesinger Jr., *The Age of Roosevelt: The Politics of Upheaval* (Boston, 1960), 139–41; Bronson Cutting to Henry Ryan, May 6, 1921, and confidential memorandum of M. A. Otero, June 15, 1924, Cutting Papers, Box 13, LC.

40. "Pep" to Bronson Cutting, "On Legion Matters" (1931), Cutting Papers, Box 18, LC.

41. Extract of National Executive Committee Proceedings, copy in Bronson Cutting Papers, Box 18, LC; *Santa Fe New Mexican* clipping, November 22, 1933, Cutting Papers, Box 94, LC.

42. Edward Spafford to Edward Hayes, copy to Bronson Cutting, May 24, 1934, Cutting Papers, Box 18, LC.

43. Schlesinger, *Politics of Upheaval*, 139–41; see clippings from newspapers on Cutting's effort to override presidential veto of the Independent Offices Act, Box 99, Cutting Papers, LC.

44. Richard M. Clutter, "The American Legion in Indiana, 1919–

1971" (Ph.D. thesis, Indiana Univ., 1971), 34; Eugene F. Sidell to Stafford King, December 2, 1923; King to Harry G. Smith, November 19, 1927; exchange of letters, King to Ralph Webb, August 9 and 22, 1930, King Papers (Box 23), Minnesota Historical Society; "Pep" to Bronson Cutting, "On Legion Matters" (1931), Cutting Papers, Box 18, LC; Paul J. McGahon to Russell Creviston, April 28, 1924, and Laura Yost to Edward Spafford, November 4, 1927, Law Enforcement—Prohibition file, AL.

45. Clutter, "The American Legion in Indiana," 34; exchange of letters, Andrew B. Woods to Henry D. Lindsley, August 19 and October 9, 1919, and Woods, "The Legion Should Know," Law Enforcement—Prohibition file, AL; Theodore Roosevelt Jr. to Rev. Elbert Hoag, March 15, 1920, Roosevelt Papers, Box 11, LC.

46. Winifred Adams to Kenneth G. Price, October 30, 1922, Mississippi American Legion Papers, Mississippi State Archives; Scott Lucas to Ralph Collins, June 2, 1928, Law Enforcement—Prohibition file, AL.

47. Cornelius "Con" Hanley to Paul McNutt, September 29, 1929, and H. Nelson Jackson, "What Are We Coming To," clipping from *Burlington Daily News*, August 23, 1930, Law Enforcement—Prohibition file, AL.

48. Editorial on Ketchikan Post, January 21, 1922, and Jim Fisk to Garland Powell, May 12, 1925, Law Enforcement—Prohibition file, AL; Jesse W. Barrett to Charles A. Gray, March 20, 1933; Philip Paris to Barrett, March 31, 1935; Barrett to John W. Burke, April 15, 1933, Barrett Papers, Box 1, Univ. of Missouri; Earl Warren to Mark L. Requa, November 7, 1931, copy in Herbert Hoover Presidential Papers, American Legion file, Hoover Library.

49. Robert A. Adams to Paul J. McGahan, May 2, 1924, and Charles A. Learned Post to National Headquarters, May 28, 1923, Law Enforcement—Prohibition file, AL.

50. Speech of Edward Spafford, December 9, 1927; Spafford to C. C. Hand, August 31, 1928, and to J. F. Moberly, February 10 and March 7, 1930, Law Enforcement—Prohibition file, AL. For reactions to the speech, see Charles Wardery to Stephen Chadwick, October 23, 1931 (Box 5), and Chadwick to Spafford, September 24, 1931 (Box 20), Chadwick Papers, Univ. of Washington, where Spafford receives credit for the Legion's resolution to send Prohibition back to the states; James A. Drain to Spafford, December 10, 1927, copy in Stafford King Papers, Box 23, Minnesota Historical Society.

51. Scott W. Lucas to O. L. Bodenhamer, September 27, 1930, and May 31, 1931, Law Enforcement—Prohibition file, AL; *Summary of the Proceedings of the Twelfth National Convention* (Boston, 1930):50–51.

52. *Chicago Tibune* clipping, September 15, 1930, Law Enforcement—Prohibition file, AL; "Minutes of the Thirteenth National Convention" (1931), 310–33, AL; "What the Legion's Cry for Beer Uncorked," *Literary Digest* 111 (October 31, 1931):24–25.

53. *Literary Digest*, "Legion's Cry for Beer"; *Outlook* 159 (October 7, 1931):169.

54. Exchange of letters, Louis A. Johnson to Clarence T. Price, October 21 and November 7, 1932; Remster A. Bingham to Johnson, January 6, 1933; William McLeod to James F. Barton, March 24, 1933, criticizing Busch's article as "high pressure wet propaganda" motivated by "the same men and the same interests which are behind the National Economy League." All in Law Enforcement—Prohibition file, AL.

55. Clipping, ACLU, vol. 283, n.p.

56. *The Klansman Manual* (n.p., 1925), 7–9; Kenneth T. Jackson, *The Ku Klux Klan in the City, 1915–1930* (New York, 1967), 37, 46, 60, 119, 149, 163, 199, 247; David M. Chalmers, *Hooded Americanism: The History of the Ku Klux Klan* (New York, 1965).

57. Jackson, *Klan in the City*, 237; exchange of letters between F. M. McDermott and James A. Drain, March 5 and 14, 1925, Americanism—Radicalism—Ku Klux Klan file, AL.

58. Chalmers, *Ku Klux Klan*, 139; Daniel Steck–Hanford MacNider Correspondence (Box 10), and MacNider to Harvey Ingham (April 29, 1926) and to John Kelly May 4, 1926, Series 4 Correspondence; Erskine Myer to MacNider, September 29, 1924, State file—Colorado, MacNider Papers, Hoover Library.

59. J. Mitchell Chase to James A. Drain, June 29, 1925; W. T. Mather to John R. Quinn, August 8 and September 17, 1924, Americanism—Radicalism—Ku Klux Klan file, AL; James Collins to Augustus Graupner, November 20, 1923, Graupner Papers, Box 1, Univ. of California, Berkeley; clipping from *Cincinnati Commercial Times*, February 17, 1923, Gilbert Bettmann Papers, Legion Scrapbook no. 2, Univ. of Cincinnati; Floyd Evinger to Paul McNutt, August 16, 1926, McNutt Papers, Legion file, Indiana Univ.; most of the Mississippi Legion Papers in the State Archives, for 1920–23, concern Smith's activities. Clippings from *Cadillac* (Michigan) *News* and *New York Times*, August 15 and 17, 1930, ACLU, vol. 400, n.p.

60. Chalmers, *Ku Klux Klan*, 237, 254; Jackson, *Klan in the City*, 69, 190; Lawrence Doutman to National Headquarters, May 8, 1924, Americanism—Radicalism—Ku Klux Klan file, AL.

61. "Minutes of the National Americanism Commission," October 26, 1921, 76–93, AL, for debate on the Klan, also cited in next paragraph; Chalmers, *Ku Klux Klan*, chapters for Southern states; Jackson, *Klan in the City*, 69.

62. Clippings from *Cincinnati Post*, December 9, 1922, and February 22, 1923; *Middletown Journal*, December 22, 1922, in Gilbert Bettmann Papers, Legion Scrapbook no. 2, Univ. of Cincinnati; "Minutes of the National Executive Committee," May 19, 1923, 310–23, AL.

63. Clippings in Alvin Owsley Scrapbook no. 3, North Texas State Univ., for the 1923 Convention; "Minutes of the Fifth National Convention" (1923), 133–45, AL.

64. Clutter, "Legion in Indiana," 84–91; Loosbrock, *Kansas Legion*, 63; *Summary of the Proceedings of the Fifth National Convention* (San Francisco, 1923), 20; Quinn quoted in clippings, ACLU, vol. 228, 100.

Chapter Six

1. Edgar N. Danielson, "A History of the New Jersey Department of the American Legion," 905, 957 (Rutgers Univ.).

2. Resolution 17 of the Minneapolis Convention, cited in Lemuel Bolles to Joseph Kenecky, December 31, 1919; letters between Samuel McMeekin and National Headquarters, October 27, October 28, October 29, November 22, and November 29, 1919; Franklin D'Olier to Henry Covington, December 3, 1919; clippings from *Dayton* (Ohio) *Herald*, January 9, 1920; German Propaganda file, AL; see also various clippings, ACLU, vol. 64, 39, 95, 102.

3. Lemuel Bolles to Joseph Kenecky, December 31, 1919; clippings from *Cleveland News*, December 21, 1919; *Los Angeles Examiner*, November 24, 1919; *New York Illustrated News*, November 27, 1919; *New York Tribune*, December 7, 1919; *Philadelphia Public Ledger*, December 31, 1919; *Nashville Tennessean*, January 2, 1920, all in German Propaganda file, AL.

4. *Report of National Legislative Committee* (1920), 5, AL; clippings from *New York Times*, April 20, 1919; and various letters on the Von Mach affair, February 1921, German Propaganda file, AL; Marquis James, *A History of the American Legion* (New York, 1923), 173–88.

5. See the Schumann-Heink folder under Memorials, AL; Frederick C. Luebke, *Bonds of Loyalty: German-Americans and World War I* (De Kalb, 1974).

6. Resolutions of Youngstown and Santa Barbara Posts, October 26 and November 21, 1919, Americanism—Radicalism file, AL; Senator Poindexter quoted in *Nation*, November 29, 1919, clipping in ACLU, vol. 150, 243; Patrick Renshaw, *The Wobblies: The Story of Syndicalism in the United States* (Garden City, N.Y., 1967), 2, 215–16; Joseph Conlin, *Big Bill Haywood and the Radical Union Movement* (Syracuse, 1969), 182.

7. John Thomas Taylor, "Traitors—Not Political Prisoners," Americanism—Radicalism—Political Prisoners file, AL; *One Big Union Monthly* 1:10 (1919):9; Conlin, *Big Bill Haywood*, 181; Richard S. Jones, *A History of the American Legion* (New York, 1946), 192.

8. Robert L. Tyler, *Rebels of the Woods: The IWW in the Pacific Northwest* (Eugene, 1967), 8–9, 60. Report of Elmer Smith to ACLU, vol. 294, 640–43.

9. Beryl Green Memoir, 57, Univ. of Oregon; minutes of the Loyal Legion of Loggers and Lumbermen, February 16, 1918, and November 29, 1919, Oregon Historical Society; *New York Times* clipping, November 22, 1919, ACLU, vol. 64, 54; J. W. Gardiner, "History of the Karl Ross Post," June 30, 1932, 26, Warren Atherton Papers, Univ. of the Pacific; author's interview with Harry L. Foster, October 31, 1980.

10. Raymond Moley Jr., *The American Legion Story* (New York, 1966), 97–101; Jones, *A History of the American Legion*, 192–95. Balanced accounts of the Centralia incident may be found in Renshaw, *The Wobblies*, 162–67; Tyler, *Rebels of the Woods*, chapter 6; Robert K. Murray, *Red Scare: A Study in National Hysteria, 1919–1920* (Minneapolis, 1955), 182–89 (quotations on 186).

11. Clipping from *New Solidarity*, November 19, 1919, ACLU, vol. 85, 137; Renshaw, *The Wobblies*, 164. Documents giving the IWW's side of the story may be found in the Rayfield Becker Papers, Oregon Historical Society (microfilm at Univ. of Washington); Citizen's Protective League quotation from Becker to Julia Ruutilla, December 28, 1928; and ACLU, thousands of pages in the volumes for 1919–36, especially vol. 150, 145–339; the Legion Archives also has a great deal of information in its Americanism—Radicalism—IWW file, where copies of the jurors' affidavits are attached to the Centralia Publicity Committee's flyer, "Learn the Truth about the Centralia Case." See also Hubert N. Dukes, "The Centralia Case—Ten Years Afterward," in *The World Tomorrow*, June 1929, 277–79.

12. Quotation from Brett Smith, ACLU, vol. 150, 294.

13. Renshaw, *The Wobblies*, 164.

14. F. R. Jeffrey to Lemuel Bolles, February 27, 1920; Franklin D'-Olier to Jeffrey, March 12, 1920, Americanism—Radicalism—IWW file, AL; "Minutes of Theodore Peterson Post," November 29, 1919, Minnesota Historical Society. Murray, *Red Scare*, 185; *Call*, November and December 22, 1919, ACLU, vol. 64, 53, 70; and *Liberator*, April 1920, ACLU, vol. 150, 232. For Haywood, see various clippings on "Haywood's address in Detroit," Americanism—Radicalism—IWW file, AL.

15. Robert L. Morlan, *Political Prairie Fire: The Non-Partisan League, 1915–1922* (Minneapolis, 1955), especially 179–82; Veblen quoted in William E. Leuchtenburg, *The Perils of Prosperity, 1914–1932* (Chicago, 1958), 128–29.

16. Richard J. Loosbrock, *The History of the Kansas Department of the American Legion* (Topeka, 1968), 46–51; Lucille B. Milner to E. C. MacDougall, June 13, 1920, ACLU, vol. 139, 492–93; various clippings in ACLU, vol. 115, 19–26; Henry M. Lox to Frederic Galbraith, January 3 and 5, 1921; Resolution of Newton, Kansas, Post, January 9, 1921, and various documents in Americanism—Radicalism—Non-Partisan League file, AL.

17. George H. Vlach to Frederic Galbraith, March 15, 1921; Lemuel Bolles to Frank Samuel, January 5 and 7, 1921; Samuel to Bolles, January 7, 1921; copy of Constitution of American Defense League of Kansas; all in Americanism—Radicalism—Non-Partisan League file, AL; Loosbrock, *Kansas Legion*, 46.

18. There are numerous accounts of the American Socialist Party, Eugene V. Debs, and the founding of the Communist Party. See James Weinstein, *Ambiguous Legacy: The Left in American Politics* (New York,

1975) and *The Decline of Socialism in America, 1912–1925* (New York, 1967); David A. Shannon, *The Socialist Party of America* (Chicago, 1967); and Nick Salvatore, *Eugene V. Debs: Citizen and Socialist* (Urbana, Ill., 1982).

19. Clippings in the ACLU files are the best sources for these incidents. See vol. 64, 39–106; vol. 112, 100–119; vol. 115, 18–36; vol. 138, 159; vol. 154, 121–23; vol. 159, 6; and vol. 109, 37–41, 239–99. For Reading (where the author formerly resided), see James Hudson Maurer, *It Can Be Done* (New York, 1938), 236–41 and 263–68, and William Pratt, "The Reading Socialist Experience: A Study in Working Class Politics" (Ph.D. thesis, Emory Univ., 1969), 180–81. (I am indebted to Thomas Gombar, of Alvernia College, for this information.)

20. Albert DeSilver to Edward T. Booth, December 1919, ACLU, vol. 109, 217; "The American Legion Confronted with a List of Its Crimes," in Albert DeSilver to National Commander, July 7, 1921, ACLU, vol. 189, 239, and Americanism—Radicalism—ACLU file, AL. For D'Olier, see chapter 1, n. 12.

21. See ACLU, letters for July 1921 for the posts' responses. For Taft see chapter 1, n. 10; for the Bentley Post, Hugh C. Marten to Lemuel Bolles, September 8, 1920, Americanism—Radicalism—IWW file, AL.

22. *Summary of the Proceedings of the Second National Convention* (Cleveland, 1920), 6; Calvin Coolidge to Morgan Keaton, August 18, 1923, Kate Barrett Papers, Box 1, LC; Aileen Kraditor, *The Radical Persuasion: 1890–1917* (Baton Rouge, 1981); Weinstein, *Ambiguous Legacy* and *The Decline of Socialism*.

23. ACLU quoted in *Christian Leader*, June 11, 1927, 740; John Thomas Taylor to Thomas L. Ross, June 9, 1920, Americanism—Radicalism file, AL. For criminal syndicalism and sedition laws in general, see Paul L. Murphy, *The Meaning of Free Speech, 1918–1933* (Westport, Conn., 1971), chapters 4 and 5.

24. Clipping from *Stars and Stripes*, January 5, 1924, and John Thomas Taylor, "Traitors—Not Political Prisoners," Americanism—Radicalism—Political Prisoners file, AL.

25. Debs quoted in Murray, *Red Scare*, 25.

26. Frederic C. Galbraith to Warren G. Harding, March 14, 1921; Hanford MacNider to Marquis James, November 24, 1921, Americanism—Radicalism—Political Prisoners file, AL.

27. Emmet O'Neal to Frederic Galbraith, April 1, 1921; John Quinn to *New York World*, December 17, 1923, all in Americanism—Radicalism—Political Prisoners file, AL.

28. Clipping from *Washington Post*, April 26, 1923; Taylor, "Traitors—Not Political Prisoners," 2, Americanism—Radicalism—Political Prisoners file, AL; H. C. Peterson and Gilbert Fite, *Opponents of War: 1917–1918* (Seattle, 1957), 265–84 for the Debs controversy.

29. Clippings under "Reading and the American Legion"; "Legion

Men Stop Speaking by Eugene V. Debs"; news release on Colorado, September 1922; letters and telegrams to and from Legionnaires; and *New York World*, December 29 and 30, 1921, Americanism—Radicalism—Political Prisoners file, AL.

30. Frederic C. Galbraith to various prominent Legionnaires, June 9, 1921; Hanford MacNider to William G. Murdock, January 5, 1922, Americanism—Radicalism—Political Prisoners file, AL.

31. Emmett Swisshelm to Legion Headquarters, December 17, 1923; Walter Liggett to John Emery, August 3, 1921, Americanism—Radicalism—Political Prisoners file, AL.

32. Harry Daugherty to Warren G. Harding, December 23, 1921, "In the Matter of the Application for Pardon on Behalf of Eugene V. Debs," 1; see also Department of Justice press release, December 31, 1921, Americanism—Radicalism—Political Prisoners file, AL.

33. American Legion National Americanism Commission, "The Threat of Communism and the Answer" (c. 1928), 8–9; speech of Edward Hayes, "How Red Is America?" May 1935, Americanism—Radicalism file, AL.

34. "Minutes of the National Americanism Commission," May 11, 1926, 87, AL; Hayes, "How Red Is America?" May 1935, Americanism—Radicalism file, AL.

35. Lawrence A. Wittner, *Rebels against War: The American Peace Movement, 1941–1960* (New York, 1969), 1–33, quotation at 1.

36. Wittner, *Rebels against War*, 4. "The Threat of Communism," 15, AL; clipping from *Christian Century*, January 30, 1935, ACLU, vol. 801, 12; clipping from *Chattanooga News*, March 18, 1928, Americanism—Radicalism—Free Speech file, AL; Homer Chaillaux to Oren Sharp, April 12, 1939, Americanism—Radicalism—Pacifism file, AL.

37. Wittner, *Rebels against War*, 4; Memorandum No. 47, July 26, 1921, Americanism—Radicalism file, AL; "Minutes of the National Americanism Commission," May 3, 1932, 98–100, AL; "Speaking of Communist Speakers," *Huddle*, December 1928, vol. 1, no. 10, 1.

38. For early information gathering, see J. F. White to Franklin D'-Olier, November 24, 1919; E. C. Calhoun to D'Olier, March 3, 1920; and T. H. Houston to all Department Commanders, February 10, 1921, all in Americanism—Radicalism file, AL; H. H. Hunter to Bill Roszel, Americanism—Propaganda file, AL; memorandum to Mr. [James] Barton, May 8, 1931, and Ralph M. Easley to John Quinn, May 21, 1924, Americanism—Radicalism file, AL; Frank Cross to E. S. Martin, October 17 and 31, 1925, Americanism—Radicalism—Communism file, AL.

39. Statements of Michigan Department and National Headquarters, June 3, 1932; S. W. Newman Saunders to Russell Cook, June 14, 1932; Frank Cross to Hanford MacNider, November 9, 1925; Russell Cook, April 2, 1931; W. Glenn Elliott to Russell Cook, July 27, 1931; statement

of National Headquarters on "Homeless Youth Homes," June 8, 1933; all in Americanism—Radicalism—Communism file, AL.

40. "Minutes of the National Americanism Commission," May 16, 1928, 131, AL; Frank Samuel to Allison J. Hayes, April 10, 1928, Americanism—Radicalism file, AL.

41. Memorandum to Miss Rubush, March 15, 1933; clipping from *Philadelphia Daily News*, January 28, 1933.

42. Clipping from *Chicago News*, January 23, 1933, ACLU, vol. 629, 4; "Minutes of National Americanism Commission," May 12, 1931, 88, 92, 114; May 3, 1932, 15; AL.

43. Frank Cross to Frank Miles, December 27 and 31, 1926, Americanism—Radicalism—Communism file, AL.

44. David Wallerstein to George Wharton Pepper, March 25, 1924; Daniel Hart to American Civil Liberties Union, January 28, 1924, and ACLU to John Quinn, January 31, 1928; ACLU, vol. 260, 263–85; K. M. Patterson to Garland Powell, May 12, 13, 14, 1924; Powell to Patterson, June 3, 1924, Americanism—Radicalism—Pacifism—Private Peat file, AL.

45. Clippings from *New York Herald Tribune*, February 2, 1927, and *Portland* (Maine) *Press Herald*, January 1927, Americanism—Radicalism—H file, AL; James F. Barton to George T. Woodson, November 3, 1927, and, generally, Cooperation—Law Enforcement—Sacco and Vanzetti file, AL; clipping from *Boston Globe*, August 12, 1927, Massachusetts—History file, AL.

46. Walton B. Hood to National Headquarters, August 23, 1927; Howard P. Savage to Hood, August 23, 1927, Cooperation—Law Enforcement—Sacco and Vanzetti file, AL; Maury Maverick to Roger W. Baldwin and to ACLU, October 10, 1928, ACLU, vol. 350, 4–5.

47. Edward Spafford to various Legion Commanders, December 20, 1927; Spafford to Reid Elkins, January 18, 1928; Sherwood Eddy, "The American Legion and Free Speech," clipping from *Christian Century*, March 1, 1928, 277–78; *Raleigh News and Observer*, February 4, 1928, all in Americanism—Radicalism—Pacifism—Eddy file, AL.

48. J. A. Ellis to Edward Spafford, January 31, 1928; John G. Pipkin to Spafford, March 24, 1928, Americanism—Radicalism—Pacifism—Eddy file, AL.

49. Edward Spafford to John G. Pipkin, June 27, 1928; Albion King to Spafford, March 6, 1928; Spafford to King, March 26, 1928; Homer Chaillaux to E. E. Holdeman, May 9, 1944, Americanism—Radicalism—Pacifism—Eddy file, AL.

50. Copy of American Legion Convention Resolution (1929); clipping from *Boston Herald*, October 4, 1929; "Pastors, Politicians, Pacifists," clipping from *Federal Council Bulletin*, October 1929; Charles MacFarland to Commander of the American Legion, October 3, 1929; Charles C. Cole to O. L. Bodenhamer, November 7 and 11, 1929; Bodenhamer to MacFarland, November 7, 1929; Frederick M. Alger to

Bodenhamer, April 10, April 28, and May 15, 1930, all in Americanism—Radicalism—Pacifism—Investigation of Propaganda file, AL.

Chapter Seven

1. Robert Cruse McManus, "Billions for Veterans," *Current History*
36 (August 1932):557–62; Lawrence Sullivan, "The Veteran Racket,"
Atlantic Monthly 151 (1933):393–402; J. Pendleton Herring, "Scotching
the Veterans' Lobby," *North American Review* 23 (1933):48–54; Marcus
Duffield, "The American Legion in Politics," *Forum* 85 (1931):257–65,
and *King Legion* (New York, 1931); Roger Burlingame, "Embattled
Veterans," *Atlantic Monthly* 152 (1933):385–96, 527–38, 686–96; Bowie
quoted in *Literary Digest*, April 21, 1934, 21; Franklin D. Roosevelt to
Russell Bowie, March 21, 1934, Personal Papers 44, Roosevelt Papers,
Roosevelt Library, Hyde Park, New York; *Boston Sunday Post*, April 15,
1934, clipping in AL—Veterans' Administration—Rehabilitation file
(hereafter AL—VA).

2. William P. Dillingham, *Federal Aid to Veterans, 1917–1941* (Gaines-
ville, 1952), 223–24; see National Economy League literature in AL—
VA, especially clippings from *Chicago Daily Herald*, June 13, 1932, and
Chicago Tribune, June 19, 1932, which are representative of the articles
the NEL managed to have published throughout the nation. For the
Legion's reply, see its January 24, 1934, bulletin, "Veterans' Costs and
Taxation," AL—VA; *Christian Century* 49 (September 14, 1932):1092.

3. Dillingham, *Federal Aid to Veterans*, 223–24.

4. O. L. Bodenhamer, general press release of May 14, 1930, AL—
VA.

5. Davis R. B. Ross, *Preparing for Ulysses: Politics and Veterans During
World War II* (New York, 1969), 12; Robert G. Bodenger, "Soldiers'
Bonuses: A History of Veterans Benefits in the United States, 1776–
1967" (Ph.D. diss., Pennsylvania State Univ., 1971), 135–36; Edward
A. Hayes, "I Want a Square Deal for the War Veterans," clipping from
Real America, March 1934, AL—VA; Eric Fisher Wood to James H.
Doffer, April 8, 1950, Wood Papers, Syracuse Univ.

6. *American Legion Weekly*, February 1, 1924, and exchange between
Treasury Secretary Andrew Mellon and Legion Commander John
Quinn in *Literary Digest*, February 23, 1924; *Summary of the Proceedings
of the Fourth National Convention* (New Orleans, 1922), 18; Marquis
James, "Who Got the Money?" series of articles in *American Legion
Weekly* beginning September 8, 1922, and his "The Profiteer Hunt,"
beginning March 23, 1923; Frank Samuel, speech of September 9, 1934,
in his file, History—Kansas, AL; speech of John Thomas Taylor to the
1933 Chicago Legion Convention, AL—VA and speech of February 2,
1934, in his file, History—District of Columbia, AL.

7. Louis A. Johnson, "Reply to Chamber of Commerce Report,"
AL—VA, and Harold L. Plummer to Stanley Jones, December 1932,
AL—VA; "Special Bulletin No. 1," 1932, AL—VA.

8. John Thomas Taylor to Louis A. Johnson, August 30, 1932, and to Frank Samuel, September 30, 1932; Ray Murphy to W. Reed Blair, December 24, 1935, AL—VA.

9. *Summary of Proceedings of the Fourth* (New Orleans, 1922), 18, and *Sixth* (St. Paul, 1924), 7, *National Conventions.*

10. *Summary of Proceedings of the Third National Convention* (Kansas City, 1921), 28; clipping from *Indianapolis News*, June 9, 1921, Ohio—History—Galbraith file, AL; Frank Samuel to James Deighan, October 17, 1934, AL—VA; *Boston Sunday Post*, April 15, 1934, AL—VA; Louis A. Johnson to Franklin D. Roosevelt, August 3, 1933, Office Files 64, Roosevelt Papers; Roger Daniels, *The Bonus March: An Episode of the Great Depression* (Westport, Conn., 1971), 213.

11. "Report of the GI Bill Committee to the National Convention of the American Legion," October 16, 1968, Box 2, Warren Atherton Papers, Univ. of the Pacific; Ernest Angell, "The Legion's Betrayal," *Nation*, March 24, 1933, 584; Dillingham, *Federal Aid to Veterans*, 223.

12. Bodenger, "Soldiers' Bonuses," 133, 137.

13. *The American Legion at Work for the Sick and Disabled: Report of the National Rehabilitation Committee at the Fourth Annual Convention* (New Orleans, 1922), 212; speech of John Thomas Taylor, February 6, 1934, History—District of Columbia—Taylor file, AL; Report of Organizing Committee, Wisconsin American Legion, July 2, 1919, American Legion Papers, Box 1, Wisconsin State Historical Society; Marquis James, *A History of the American Legion* (New York, 1923), 94–99.

14. James, *American Legion*, 95, 98; Jouett Shouse to Lemuel Bolles, December 27, 1919, AL—VA.

15. James, *American Legion*, 95–101, 161–71.

16. Bodenger, "Soldiers' Bonuses," 140–41; for opposition, see William B. Wilson to Frederic Galbraith, January 24, 1921, and H. S. Cummings to National Commander, American Legion, December 31, 1920, AL—VA.

17. James, *American Legion*, 242–46; Charles Sawyer to A. A. Sprague, July 12, 1924, AL—VA.

18. "Report of [Massachusetts] Department Commander James T. Duane, September 22, 1921, Box 24, Clarence T. Edwards Papers, Massachusetts Historical Society; Edward M. Lewis to Helen Silcox, May 18, 1921, AL—VA; John Q. Young to American Legion Headquarters, February 18, 1921, Alvin Owsley Scrapbook no. 1, North Texas State Univ., and various papers for 1921–23 in History—Texas file, AL; "Proceedings of Second Annual Conference of [Oklahoma] Post Adjutants," 4, Box 15, Courtland M. Feuquay Papers, Univ. of Oklahoma; Report of Sanitarium Investigation Committees, January 7, 1921, Box 94, Roger Gregg Cherry Papers, North Carolina Department of Archives and History; clipping from *St. Louis Star*, July 28, 1922, AL—VA.

19. Mrs. W. E. Hunt to Mrs. O. Lewis [1921] and "for immediate release" report of Mrs. Lowell Hobart, September 1922, AL—VA.

20. Quotations from A. A. Sprague to Charles Sawyer, July 20, 1922; see also Sawyer to Sprague, July 12, 1922, AL—VA.

21. *The American Legion at Work for the Sick and Disabled*; "History of the Legion," in "Reports, 1926–1927," Frank Edgerton Papers, Nebraska Historical Society; "Proceedings of the Fourth (1922) Annual Convention of the American Legion," 219–40, AL; clipping from *Cincinnati Commercial Times*, October 20, 1922, Gilbert Bettmann Papers, Legion Scrapbook no. 1, Univ. of Cincinnati.

22. "Clean-Up Squad Bulletin," August 9, 1921; Charles Forbes to John Emery, October 4, 1921; Abel Davis and A. A. Sprague to Hanford MacNider, November 28, 1921; Emmet O'Neal to MacNider, November 19, 1921; Forbes to Abel Davis, December 9, 1921; Delancey Kountze to MacNider, January 30, 1922; F. B. Flannery to Lemuel Bolles, December 15, 1922; J. B. Ferguson to Bolles, February 5, 1923; all AL—VA; Forbes to M. Bryson, March 7, 1922, Box 91, Roger Gregg Cherry Papers, North Carolina Department of Archives and History; Forbes to Bolles, March 6, 1922; Forbes to Sprague, May 12, 1922, AL—VA; Bodenger, "Soldiers' Bonuses," 143.

23. Robert M. Freed, "What Our Neglected Veterans Want," *Our World*, May 1924, 97; John J. MacSwain to Heywood Mahon, June 7, 1921, December 28, 1921; Mahon to MacSwain, January 18, February 10, February 22, and March 9, 1922, Box 1, MacSwain Papers, Duke Univ.; Charles Forbes to A. A. Sprague, August 14, 1922; Sprague to Forbes, October 4, 1922, AL—VA.

24. Delancey Kountze to Hanford MacNider, January 30, 1924; Edward M. Lewis to Humphrey Sullivan, August 17 and August 19, 1922; Lewis to Fred G. Conick, August 25, 1932, AL—VA; Robert K. Murray, *The Harding Era* (Minneapolis, 1967), 430.

25. Dorothy Culp, "The American Legion: A Study in Pressure Politics" (Ph.D. diss., Univ. of Chicago, 1939), 31–33; Augustus Graupner to John F. O'Ryan, May 18, June 4, and November 7, 1923; Graupner to Walter F. Lineberger, August 22, 1923 (Box 1); Tasker L. Oddie to Graupner, October 12, 1923, and O'Ryan to Graupner, November 12, 1923 (Box 2), Graupner Family Papers, Bancroft Library, Univ. of California, Berkeley. For the investigative committee's report, see United States Congress, Senate, Select Committee on Investigation of Veterans' Bureau, *Hearings*, 67th Congress, 4th session, 1923 (2 volumes).

26. Murray, *The Harding Era*, 461–80.

27. Richard S. Jones, *A History of the American Legion* (Indianapolis, 1946), 136–38; Culp, "American Legion," 41–45; Royal S. Johnson to Hanford MacNider, November 8, 1921, History—South Dakota—Johnson file, AL; National Executive Committee Report, 1924, Box 18,

Stafford King Papers, Minnesota Historical Society; Bodenger, "Soldiers' Bonuses," 177.

28. *Summary of Proceedings of the Tenth* (San Antonio, 1928), 3, *and Ninth* (Paris, 1927), 12, *National Conventions*; Dillingham, *Federal Aid to Veterans*, 184–96; Culp, "American Legion," 33, 86.

29. National Rehabilitation Committee report, April 5, 1929, AL—VA; Jones, *American Legion*, 134–48; Culp, "American Legion," 32–40; "Publicity, September 1938, Rehabilitation," Watson B. Miller to National Rehabilitation Committee, February 27, 1929; "Estimate Budget, 1929," Watson B. Miller to John C. Vivian, April 10, 1930, AL—VA; Herring, "Scotching the Veterans' Lobby," 51.

30. H. L. Plummer to Frank Samuel, November 2, 1938; "Publicity, September 1938, Rehabilitation"; Herbert Barnard, memorandum, May 28, 1938, AL—VA.

31. Dillingham, *Federal Aid to Veterans*, 110–16; 1940 Rehabilitation Program, AL—VA; Culp, "American Legion," 32–38; History—Minnesota—Mayo Brothers file, AL.

32. *Summary of Proceedings of the Eighth National Convention* (Philadelphia, 1926), 15; Dillingham, *Federal Aid to Veterans*, 173–83, 197–206; Richard S. Jones, "My Brother's Keeper," *American Legion Monthly*, May 1928; J. G. Sims to Howard Savage, January 5, 1927; Joseph T. Watson to Savage, January 7, 1921, AL—VA.

33. "National Executive Committee Meeting Minutes," June 1919, 51, AL; Marquis James, *A History of the American Legion* (New York, 1923) 239–43; Richard J. Loosbrock, *The History of the Kansas Department of the American Legion* (Topeka, 1968), 97; *Summary of Proceedings of the Fourteenth National Convention* (Portland, 1932), 51; Richard M. Clutter, "The American Legion in Indiana, 1919–1971" (Ph.D. diss., Indiana Univ., 1971), 145–47; questionnaires in possession of the author; Watson B. Miller to Stephen Chadwick, February 13, 1935, Chadwick Papers, Box 1, Univ. of Washington; Minutes of the Rose City Post, Oregon Historical Society; and Theodore Peterson Post, Minnesota Historical Society, for 1921–22; Ralph T. O'Neil, speech quoted in clipping from *Greenville* (Mississippi) *Daily Times*, November 29, 1930, Kansas—History—O'Neil file, AL; *Business Week*, September 23, 1931, 14–16; January 27, 1932, 16.

34. *America's Duty to Her War Veterans as Interpreted by Governor Smith and Two Republican Administrations* (New York, 1928), Box 24, Henry T. Allen Papers, LC; John O. Quinn Memoir, 49–50, 59–63, UCLA Oral History Collection, copy at Bancroft Library, Univ. of California, Berkeley. See a list of different state programs in "Report of State Legislative Committee, 1924," Stafford King Papers, Box 16, Minnesota Historical Society. J. O. Roberts to Frank Hines, February 5, 1931, Herbert Hoover Presidential Papers, World War Veterans—Bonus Correspondence, Hoover Library; Bodenger, "Soldiers' Bonuses," 260.

35. Bodenger, "Soldiers' Bonuses," 179–82; Jones, *American Legion*,

146–48; John Thomas Taylor to O. L. Bodenhamer, April 23, 1930; Royal C. Johnson to Bodenhamer, June 20, 1930; John Thomas Taylor, Bulletin, July 2, 1930, AL—VA; Donald J. Lisio, *The President and Protest: Hoover, Conspiracy, and the Bonus Riot* (Columbia, Mo., 1974), 15–22; Dillingham, *Federal Aid to Veterans*, 50–54.

36. Chester C. Bolton to O. L. Bodenhamer, April 25, 1930; Bodenhamer to Royal C. Johnson, June 23, 1930; Frank Pinola to Bodenhamer, June 25, 1930, and October 2, 1930; John Thomas Taylor to Bodenhamer, June 17, 1930, and April 23, 1930, AL—VA.

37. "The Fantastic Fact of World War Veterans Pensions Not the Responsibility of the American Legion," *Barron's*, August 22, 1932, 32; "Mr. Hoover Takes Down the Big Stick," *Literary Digest*, July 12, 1930, 5–6; Ernest Angell, "The American Legion versus America," *Nation*, March 15, 1933, 287–88; Sullivan, "The Veteran Racket," 401; Edward M. Lewis to Maclin S. Kemmer, March 19, 1933, AL—VA; see also sources in n. 1, above. United States Congress, Joint Committee on Veterans' Affairs, *Hearings*, 72nd Congress, 2d session, 1932–33 (2 volumes); Burlingame, "Embattled Veterans," 396; Frank Freidel, *Franklin D. Roosevelt: Launching the New Deal* (Boston, 1973), 241.

38. Watson B. Miller to Harry L. Stevens, April 15, 1932; Murphy cited in *New York Times* clipping, March 14, 1933, AL—VA; Burlingame, "Embattled Veterans," 686.

39. Freidel, *Roosevelt*, 242–45; Jones, *American Legion*, 149–52.

40. Johnson quoted in Wright Patman to Louis A. Johnson, September 2, 1933, AL—VA; Burlingame, "Embattled Veterans," 686–88; see Johnson Correspondence with Franklin D. Roosevelt (August 3, September 7, 1933) and Stephen Early (October 16, 1934), also other dates, Office Files 64, Roosevelt Papers; Watson B. Miller, Memorandum to Johnson, March 24, 1933, AL—VA.

41. Dillingham, *Federal Aid to Veterans*, 73–82; Jones, *American Legion*, 149–52.

42. John Thomas Taylor to Louis A. Johnson, April 12, 1933, History—West Virginia—Johnson file, AL; Stephen Early press release, May 10, 1933, AL—VA; Freidel, *Roosevelt*, 448–52; clipping from *New York World Telegram*, June 30, 1933; Wright Patman to Johnson, September 22, 1931, AL—VA.

43. Edward A. Hayes, "I Want a Square Deal for the Veterans," *Real America*, March 1934, AL—VA; Burlingame, "Embattled Veterans," 528–31, 690–91; letters of various Legionnaires and posts to Franklin D. Roosevelt in Office Files 64, Roosevelt Papers, especially from H. George Bruhns, March 21, 1933; James I. Eckford, March 8, 1933, and Morris M. Wolf, March 10, 1933; in the same collection, Louis A. Johnson to Roosevelt, August 3 and September 7, 1933; Jones, *American Legion*, 214; clipping from *Literary Digest*, November 4, 1933, History—Illinois—Edward Hayes file, AL; Child Welfare Conference Report, November 3, 1933, History—Kansas—Frank Samuel file, AL; clipping

from *Tupelo* (Mississippi) *Times*, March 14, 1933, Scrapbook, Mississippi American Legion Papers, Mississippi State Archives; *Summary of Proceedings of the Fifteenth National Convention* (Chicago, 1933), 11–12; Daniels, *The Bonus March*, 228.

44. Lisio, *The President and Protest*, 10–13; Frank T. Hines to Bertrand H. Snell, April 10, 1930, and to Herbert Hoover, November 27 and December 24, 1931, Hoover Presidential Papers—World War Veterans, Hoover Library; *Summary of Proceedings of the Thirteenth National Convention* (Detroit, 1931), 25; American Legion Speakers' Bulletin, October 10, 1932, and Harold K. Phillips, reply to United States Chamber of Commerce, December 31, 1932; Edward A. Hayes, "I Want a Square Deal for the War Veterans," *Real America*, March 1934, AL—VA; John Thomas Taylor to Louis A. Johnson, April 12, 1933, History—West Virginia—Johnson file, AL; Frank Samuel to James Deighan, May 15, 1934, AL—VA.

45. Bert Halligan to Watson B. Miller, November 9 and December 7, 1933, and November 29, 1935, AL—VA.

46. Jones, *American Legion*, 154–56; Dillingham, *Federal Aid to Veterans*, 54; "Proceedings of the National Executive Committee of the American Legion," May 3–4, 1934, 40, AL.

47. Extract of remarks of Hamilton Fish, April 3, 1934; National Rehabilitation Committee, "Report," 1941, AL—VA.

48. J. Frederick Essary, "The Unsolved Problem of Veteran Relief," *Literary Digest* 117 (February 24, 1934):10.

49. For Hearst's support, see his pledge at the New Orleans (1922) Convention, *Summary of Proceedings*, 53. The Bonus struggles are ably recounted in Bodenger, "Soldiers' Bonuses," 198–252; Culp, "American Legion," 94–133; Jones, *American Legion*, 165–90; and much of Daniels, *The Bonus March*, and Lisio, *The President and Protest*.

50. Thomas W. Miller to Henry D. Lindsley, August 29, 1919, Adjusted Compensation file, AL: "Proceedings of the First (1919) National Convention of the American Legion," 7, 373–97, AL; Theodore Roosevelt Jr. to Russell Bowie, November 23, 1922, Box 12, Roosevelt Papers, LC; Lemuel Bolles to Charles W. Scruggs, February 19, 1920, Adjusted Compensation file, AL; Gilbert Bettmann to William Cooper Procter, February 13, 1922, Box 15, Bettmann Papers, Univ. of Cincinnati.

51. Daniel Barrows to Franklin D'Olier, February 20, 1920, Adjusted Compensation file, AL; Ogden Mills to James Hughes, October 16, 1920, Mills Papers, Box 24, LC; E. A. Morin to Wade Hayes, September 25, 1919, History—West Virginia file, AL; Stephen Chadwick to Judge M. I. Gosse, March 19, 1920, Chadwick Papers, Box 20, Univ. of Washington; James, *American Legion*, 128–30; J. M. Johnson to D'Olier, June 16, 1920, and D'Olier to Crompton Harris, April 22, 1920, Adjusted Compensation file, AL; "Proceedings of the Second (1920) National Convention of the American Legion," 35–37, AL.

52. "Minutes of the National Executive Committee," February 10, 1920, 80, AL; Gilbert Bettmann to Franklin D'Olier, May 6, 1920, Box 15, Bettmann Papers, Univ. of Cincinnati; Daniels, *Bonus March*, 31.

53. Address of Henry D. Lindsley to Eastern States Exposition, September 15, 1919, Adjusted Compensation file, AL; Theodore Roosevelt Jr. to R. J. Caldwell, May 11, 1920, and to Frederic Huidekoper, June 3, 1920, Roosevelt Papers, Box 11, LC; John Thomas Taylor, *A History of Adjusted Compensation Legislation* (Indianapolis, 1921); Jones, *American Legion*, 174–76.

54. *American Legion Weekly*, June 6, 1924, special issue on "The Federal Adjusted Compensation Act," especially 17, 26; clipping from *Springfield* (Massachusetts) *Daily News*, January 29, 1921, "State Bonuses," Adjusted Compensation file, AL; Bodenger, "Soldiers' Bonuses," 212.

55. For Rural Settlement, see Box 549, William Borah Papers, LC; Theodore Roosevelt Jr. to Frederic Huidekoper, June 3, 1920, Roosevelt Papers, Box 11, LC.

56. Janet Louise Schmelzer, "The Early Life and Early Career of Wright Patman, 1893–1941" (Ph.D. diss., Texas Christian Univ., 1978), 83–84, 90–92; Culp, "American Legion," 111–16; Lisio, *The President and Protest*, 31–34; Jones, *American Legion*, 181; John Thomas Taylor to Lawrence Richey, August 27, 1930, Herbert Hoover Presidential Papers—American Legion, Hoover Library; "Proceedings of the Twelfth (1930) National Convention," 287–89, 303–6, AL; *Summary of Proceedings of the Twelfth National Convention* (Boston, 1930), 58.

57. Jones, *American Legion*, 183–84; Stephen Chadwick to Edward Spafford, June 9, 1931, Chadwick Papers, Box 20, Univ. of Washington; *Summary of Proceedings of the Thirteenth National Convention* (Detroit, 1931), 50–66; North Carolina—History—Harry Stevens memoir, 8, AL; clipping, *Washington News*, September 29, 1931, Herbert Hoover Presidential Papers—World War Veterans—Bonus—Press Comment, Hoover Library.

58. For the march itself, see Lisio, *The President and Protest*, 72–108, 125–225; Daniels, *The Bonus March*, 65–181; clippings from *East St. Louis* (Illinois) *Daily Journal*, June 22, 1932, *Washington Herald*, June 25, 1932, and Johnstown, Pennsylvania [no paper mentioned], July 30, 1932, George Kleinholz Papers, Univ. of Oregon; Royal C. Johnson to Herbert Hoover, June 10, 1932, Hoover Presidential Papers, World War Veterans—Bonus Correspondence, Hoover Library.

59. *Bonus Expeditionary Force News*, vol. one, no. 1, clipping in George Kleinholz Papers, Univ. of Oregon; Donald J. Lisio, "A Blunder Becomes a Catastrophe: Hoover, the Legion and the Bonus Army," *Wisconsin Magazine of History* (Autumn 1967), 37–50; clippings, *Washington Evening Post*, August 16, 1932, and *Washington Herald*, September 25, 1932, Herbert Hoover Presidential Papers—World War Veterans—Bonus—Press Comment.

60. George Leach, memorandum from Portland, September 11, 1932,

Herbert Hoover Presidential Papers—American Legion, Hoover Library; "Proceedings of the Fourteenth (1932) Annual Convention," 244, 273, AL; *Summary of the Proceedings of the Fourteenth Convention* (Portland, 1932), 11–16, 52–56; S. H. Conner to Frank T. Hines, August 20, 1932, Hoover Presidential Papers—World War Veterans Correspondence, Hoover Library.

61. "Proceedings of the Fifteenth (1933) Annual Convention," 163, 299–308, AL; Daniels, *The Bonus March*, 228.

62. Culp, "American Legion," 125–33; Schmelzer, "Patman," 131–44, quotation, 135; clipping, *New York Times*, September 27, 1935, Adjusted Compensation file, AL; Carleton B. McCulloch to Meredith Nicholson, October 3, 1935, McCulloch Papers, Indiana Historical Society.

63. Yarborough quoted in "Report of the GI Bill Committee to the National Convention of the American Legion," October 16, 1968, Warren Atherton Papers, Univ. of the Pacific; good accounts of the GI Bill may be found in Davis R. B. Ross, *Preparing for Ulysses: Politics and Veterans During World War II* (New York, 1969); Theodore R. Mosch, *The GI Bill: A Breakthrough in Educational and Social Policy in the United States* (Hicksville, 1975); and Keith W. Olson, *The G.I. Bill, the Veterans, and the Colleges* (Lexington, 1974).

Chapter Eight

* First two quotations from Cooperation—Labor file, AL. All quotations in this chapter from this chronologically arranged file are cited under "Labor file, AL."

1. Clippings from *Cleveland Press*, September 23, 1936, and *Nation* 141:456, Ray Murphy Scrapbooks, Univ. of Iowa.

2. George Berry, "The American Legion and Organized Labor" (1921); Paul Beardsley to Franklin D'Olier, April 3, 1920; Labor file, AL.

3. Claude Fuess, *A Brief History of the American Legion in Massachusetts* (Boston, 1926), 13, History—Massachusetts file, AL; Frank Cormier and William J. Eaton, *Reuther* (Englewood Cliffs, 1970), 130–31; Eldorous L. Dayton, *Walter Reuther: The Autocrat of the Bargaining Table* (New York, 1958), 56–57; Victor Traub to National Headquarters, May 4, 1920, Labor file, AL.

4. Clipping from *Butte* (Montana) *Daily Bulletin*, February 26, 1920, ACLU, vol. 112, 111.

5. Irving Bernstein, *A History of the American Worker: The Turbulent Years* (Boston, 1970), 782–83. James R. Green, *The World of the Worker* (New York, 1980), 163, writes that "on a national level, the Communists actually controlled only a few unions, and in others they expanded their influence by allying with various progressives and militants."

6. Frederic Galbraith to Samuel Gompers, November 27, 1920; Le-

muel Bolles to H. M. Payne, November 13, 1920; clipping from *New York Evening World*, May 19, 1920, Labor file, AL.

7. Marquis James, *A History of the American Legion* (New York, 1923), 111–12.

8. Ibid., 116–19; Richard Jones, *A History of the American Legion* (Indianapolis, 1946), 192; Marcus Duffield, *King Legion* (New York, 1931), 169; Martin's Ferry Post to Eric F. Wood, September 23, 1919; Henry Lindsley to Martin's Ferry Post, September 24, 1919, and to Chalmers Wilson, September 30, 1919; clipping from *New York Evening World*, September 29, 1919, Labor file, AL.

9. See chapter 6, nn. 19–20.

10. Sarah Edwards to Samuel Gompers, February 6, 1922 (copy forwarded to Legion headquarters); William H. Barr to Franklin D'Olier, June 5, 1920, Labor file, AL; clipping on New Mexico, ACLU, vol. 156, 17.

11. "Minutes of the Second National Convention" (1920), 97; *Summary of the Proceedings of the Third National Convention* (Kansas City, 1921), 13; "Minutes of the National Executive Committee," June 19, 1919, 153, AL.

12. James, *American Legion*, 113–16; Jones, *American Legion*, 195.

13. Good general discussions of the AFL's characteristics may be found in David Brody, *Workers in Industrial America* (New York, 1980), 21–32, and David Montgomery, *Workers Control in America* (Cambridge, 1979), chapter 1. O. L. Warr, "The Heroes' Union," *American Mercury* 27 (February 1928):175.

14. Exchange of letters, Samuel Gompers and Frederic Galbraith, August 24 and November 2, 1920; Gompers to Hanford MacNider, September 27, 1922; Gompers to Alvin Owsley, July 2, 1923, Labor file, AL; Gompers to MacNider, July 12, 1922, vol. 294, no. 411, Gompers Letter Books in AFL Papers, LC (copy in Boston Public Library).

15. Samuel Gompers to Frederic Galbraith, November 9, 1920; Marquis James to Galbraith, March 1, 1921; Galbraith to Gompers, March 2, 1921, Labor file, AL; Gompers to George Berry: March 11, 1922, vol. 290, no. 709; May 1, 1922, vol. 292, no. 734; May 6, 1922, vol. 293, no. 322; July 11, 1923, vol. 305, no. 322, Gompers Letter Books, LC; George Berry to Lewis E. Burnside, March 8, 1922, Labor file, AL.

16. George Berry to John McQuigg, October 24, 1925; "A.F.L. Declares Against Conscription Bill," *American Flint* (undated clipping, c. 1925), Labor file, AL; *Trades Union News*, October 25, 1924, and clippings from *Seattle Post*, November 20, 1924, Samuel Gompers Scrapbooks, New York Public Library; Lemuel Bolles to T. J. Ross Jr., October 12, 1921, Labor file, AL; clipping from *Federal Press*, December 24, 1920, ACLU, vol. 122, 145.

17. Samuel Gompers to Lemuel Bolles, July 28, 1922, with clipping

from *New York Times*, July 23, 1922, attached; Labor file, AL. Marquis James, "Who Got the Money?" *American Legion Weekly*, September 8 through October 13, 1922; "The Profiteer Hunt," ibid., March 23 through June 8, 1923. For the AFL's membership problems, see "The Labor Council's Report," clipping from *New Haven Union*, November 29, 1924, Gompers Scrapbooks, New York Public Library; for the Legion's, see Jones, *American Legion*, 344.

18. James P. Cotter to Edward Spafford, February 11, 1928; George Berry to Herbert Berger, January 27, 1928; Elmer Sherwood to George Danfield, May 1, 1940; Danfield to Ray Kelly, March 14, 1940, Organization—Post—Class—Labor file, AL.

19. T. J. Ross Jr. to Lemuel Bolles, October 4, 1921; Ross Bowls to John Quinn, November 6, 1923, and to Paul Wiley, November 5, 1923; E. H. Miller to Alvin Owsley, June 4, 1923; A. A. Hastings to National Headquarters, October 22, 1922; W. N. Williams to Alvin Owsley, August 11, 1923; William P. Lindley to John Quinn, June 18, 1924, Labor file, AL.

20. Samuel Gompers to Franklin D'Olier, September 16, 1920; D'Olier to Gompers, September 24, 1920; Frederic Galbraith to Gompers, November 2, 1920, Labor file, AL.

21. Joseph A. Wise to James Drain, April 22, 1925; Guy McCoy to Wise, May 19, 1925; McCoy "To Whom It May Concern," April 6, 1926; Joseph Deutsch to Paul McNutt, November 16, 1928, Labor file, AL.

22. William F. Long to Dan Sowers, July 25, 1927; E. H. Davidson to Sowers, October 12, 1927, Labor file, AL.

23. "Logan Hears 'Free Speech,' " *New York Times*, March 5, 1923, and other clippings for March 5 and 6; George Popkin to Hugh Martin, March 6, 1923; Martin to Lemuel Bolles, March 9, 1923, Labor and Americanism—Radicalism—ACLU—West Virginia file, AL.

24. Lemuel Bolles to Spiller Hicks, March 15 and April 2, 1923; letters between C. C. Chambers and Hicks, February 26, March 7, and March 8, 1923, Americanism—Radicalism—West Virginia file, AL.

25. Clipping from *Chicago Tribune*, April 9, 1929; exchange of letters between James F. Barton and J. M. Caldwell, April 9, and 11, 1929; Barton and Miller C. Foster, April 9 and 19, 1929; and Barton and William Green, April 11, and 15, 1929, Labor file, AL. Irving Bernstein, *The Lean Years: A History of the American Worker, 1920–1933* (Boston, 1960), 20–28. Bulwinckle can be identified by his many letters to North Carolina State Adjutant Roger Gregg Cherry in Cherry's papers for 1932, Box 91, North Carolina State Archives. Bulwinckle was a corporation lawyer for the mill owners.

26. Exchanges of letters between William Vorsanger and Ralph O'Neil, June 12, 1931; O'Neil and John Elden, June 12 and 13, 1931; and O'Neil and Edgar M. Hall, June 17 and 23, 1931; "Strike Breaking

Charge Is Denied," clipping from *Trenton Gazette*, October 6, 1936; exchange of letters between Frank Samuel and Roland Cowan, October 7 and 9, 1936, Labor file, AL.

27. For new trends in unionism, see, generally, David Brody, "The Emergence of Mass Production Unionism," in John Braeman et al., eds., *Change and Continuity in Twentieth-Century America* (Columbus, 1964), 221–62; Bernstein, *Turbulent Years*; Green, *World of the Worker*, 133–73; Harvey Klehr, *The Heyday of American Communism: The Depression Decade* (New York, 1984), for Communist leaders.

28. Bernstein, *Turbulent Years*, 148–49, 160–68; Justin Gray and Victor Bernstein, *The Inside Story of the Legion* (New York, 1954), 135; "Facts Regarding Alleged Legion Participation in Imperial County Riots"; Fred C. Kelly, "Unrest in the Valley," *Today*, May 11, 1935, Labor file, AL; various letters in Americanism—Radicalism—Wirin file, AL, on his appointment to the NLRB.

29. Clippings from Alameda County *Legionnaire*, March 1934, ACLU, vol. 708, 87; "Open Letter to National Commander Hayes . . . ," ACLU, vol. 737, 47; Mark Reisel, "Mexican Unionization in California Agriculture, 1927–1936," *Labor History* 14 (1973):562–79.

30. Clipping from Alameda County *Legionnaire*, March 1934, ACLU, vol. 708, 87; Bernstein, *Turbulent Years*, 252–98 (quotation at 253); Charles P. Larrowe, "The Great Maritime Strike of 1934," *Labor History* 11 (1970):403–51 and 12 (1971):3–37; James Fisk to Boyd Stutler, July 19, 1934, and to Edward Hayes, July 24, 1934; Hayes to Fisk, July 24, 1934; Labor file, AL; Walter Galenson, *The CIO Challenge to the AFL: A History of the American Labor Movement, 1935–1941* (New York, 1961), 429; Gerald C. Macguire (c. July 16, 1934) to Hayes, Labor file, AL.

31. Resolutions—Highland Park Post #206, San Bruno Post #409, and Samuel Gompers Post #386—to Edward Hayes, July 16, 1934, Labor file, AL.

32. Larrowe, "The Great Maritime Strike," Part 2, 34; William Green to Los Angeles Union Labor Post, and to Edward Hayes, July 23, 1934, Labor file, AL.

33. Bernstein, *Turbulent Years*, 298–315, quotation from Brooks at 309; Clarence Quinlan to Edward Hayes, September 14, 1934; clipping from *Charleston* (South Carolina) *News and Courier*, September 7, 1934; W. D. Schwartz to Frank Samuel, September 7, 1934, and to Hayes, September 11, 1934, Labor file, AL.

34. Clipping from *New York Evening Journal*, September 6, 1934; Francis Gorman to Hayes, September 8, 1934; Charles Sherman to Hayes, September 8, 1934; L. C. Richardson to Hayes, September 10, 1934, Labor file, AL; Wilson, "Labor Fights the American Legion," 10.

35. Bernstein, *Turbulent Years*, 197–200; John Tafelski to Edward Hayes, September 18, 1934; Hayes to Otto Messner, September 25, 1934; C. Clinton Stevens to Frank Samuel, September 24, 1934; Samuel

to James Deighan, October 12, 1934, Labor file, AL; Gray and Bernstein, *Inside Story of the American Legion*, 143; Amy Schechter, "Fascism in Pennsylvania," *Nation*, June 19, 1935, filed in ACLU, vol. 801, 26.

36. William Green to Ray Murphy, November 27, 1935; S. A. Wheeler to Milton Campbell, December 17, 1936; Campbell to Murphy, December 18, 1935; Murphy to Campbell, December 20, 1935; clipping from *St. Louis Post Dispatch*, April 8, 1937, Labor file, AL; Bernstein, *Turbulent Years*, 491; William Nelson to Ralph Gregg, January 26, 1937, Labor file, AL.

37. Bernstein, *Turbulent Years*, 229–52; clipping from *Minneapolis Star-Times*, May 22, 1934; M. F. Murray to Boyd Stutler, May 24, 1935; Jeremiah Twomey to Belgrano, March 23, 1935, Labor file, AL.

38. Sidney Fine, *Sit Down: The General Motors Strike of 1936–1937* (Ann Arbor, 1969), 200–203, 280–83, 293, 404; Bernstein, *Turbulent Years*, 501–51; Frank Samuel to Harry Colmery, February 4, 1937, Labor file, AL; clipping from *Flint Journal*, March 23, 1937, ACLU, vol. 982, 35, and in Legion Labor file; for Legion charges the Reuthers were Communists, see n. 2 above; report of Flint Legion Council on subversive activities, April 27, 1938, Americanism—Radicalism file, AL.

39. Clipping from *New York Times*, June 29, 1937; the Communist *Daily Worker* picked up the story the next day, ACLU, vol. 1020, 125, 131; Gordon MacEdward to Raymond Kelly, December 28, 1939; Resolution, Allied Veterans' Council of Dearborn, Michigan, February 17, 1941; A. D. Puttbrese to Frank Samuel, March 4, 1941; Carl Smith (1938), "Subversive Activities of Labor and Their Effect upon the Legion," Labor file, AL.

40. Clippings from various newspapers, June 11–14, 1937, Labor file, AL; United States Senate, Committee on Education and Labor, "The 'Little Steel' Strike and Citizens Committee," Report no. 15, part 4, 132–63; Jerold S. Auerbach, *Labor and Liberty: The La Follette Committee and the New Deal* (New York, 1966), 135.

41. Joe E. Cruse to National Headquarters, June 12, 1937; Calvin Kain to National Adjutant, June 14, 1937; various letters, June 11–July 1, 1937, Labor file, AL; Gray and Bernstein, *Inside Story of the Legion*, 146–47.

42. "Report on the Strike at Monroe," filed July 27, 1937, Labor file, AL.

43. Senate Committee, "The 'Little Steel' Strike," 148–49, 162; Mary H. Vorse, *Labor's New Millions* (New York, 1938), 158; Donald Glascoff to Harry Colmery, June 25, 1937, Labor file, AL.

44. Harry Colmery press release, June 16, 1937; Harry Martin (April 18, 1937), Charles Stoetzer (April 14, 1937), John Harrison (April 13, 1937) to Colmery and numerous letters to Colmery, April 8–19, 1937; Thomas F. Martin to Lynn Adams, police report for activities in Hershey, April 7, 1937; Frank Samuel to Colmery, June 10, 1937; clippings from *St. Louis Post Dispatch*, April 8 and 9, 1937, Labor file, AL.

45. Fred Talbot to Harry Colmery, April 3, 1937; Colmery to Talbot, April 13, 1937; Rex Humphrey to Colmery, March 20, 1937; clippings from *Toledo News-Bee*, May 19, 1938; *Washington Evening Star* and *Washington Post*, September 15, 1937; *Atlanta Journal*, February 8, 1938; *Time*, January 17, 1938, Labor file, AL.

46. Senate Committee, "Little Steel Strike," 231–35, 263; Robert R. Brooks, *As Steel Goes . . . Unionism in a Basic Industry* (New Haven, 1940), 141; Bernstein, *Turbulent Years*, 490–519; Gray and Bernstein, *Inside Story of the Legion*, 143–46; Sam H. Cobb to Harry Colmery, June 17, 1937; *Johnstown Tribune* clipping, June 17, 1937; Walter Kress to Colmery, June 17, 1937, Labor file, AL.

47. Gray and Bernstein, *Inside Story of the Legion*, 139–41; "Subversive Activities Investigations," Department of Washington, October 25, 1935, and reports of Subversive Investigations, Americanism—Radicalism—Communism Reports file, AL.

48. A. G. Dibrell to Milo Warner, November 23 and 25, 1940; W. H. Crawford to Warner, April 17, 1941, Labor file, AL; "Proceedings of National Executive Committee," November 6–7, 1941, 384–85, AL. For a sampling of post antistrike sentiment, see letters to National Headquarters by Indianola Post, March 11, 1941; Kingdom Post, March 26, 1941; Carter Hanner Post, March 27, 1941; Bowling Green Post, March 28, 1941; Camden Post, April 6, 1941; T. P. Johnson Post, April 18, 1941; Lowe-McFarlane Post, April 18, 1941; Bluefield Post, April 11, 1941; California Department, April 19, 1941; Sixth District, Oklahoma, April 8, 1941; and Oneida County Posts, November 17, 1941, in Labor file, AL.

49. *New York Times* clippings, January 6 and 8, 1941; materials relating to Michigan Senate Bill no. 36 in C. R. Crozier to Homer Chaillaux, March 21, 1941; Donald Glascoff, memo to department adjutants, March 17, 1941; National Publicity Division news release, February 3, 1941; clipping from *Boston American*, November 22, 1940; resolution of California department, April 19, 1941, Labor file, AL.

50. Undated letter (1940), Raymond Kelly to John L. Lewis, Labor file, AL; "Proceedings of the National Executive Committee," May 1–2, 1941 (220–23, 418–19, 422–29), and November 6–7, 1941 (213–30, 384–85), AL. Also source for next paragraph.

51. William Green to Officers of State Federations of Labor, February 28, 1940; Letters of George C. Danfield to Elmer Sherwood, March 5, 1940; to Raymond Kelly, March 14, 1940; and to Milo Warner, January 30, 1941, and April 28, 1941; Kelly to Danfield, May 2, 1940, Labor file, AL.

52. Clippings from *Indianapolis Mail*, July 22, 1943, and *New Jersey Labor Herald*, July 1943; Report of George Danfield, June 3, 1944, Organization—Posts—Class—Labor file, AL; Richard S. Jones, *American Legion*, 201–5; Daniel Starch and staff, *Consumer Magazine Report*, prepared for *American Legion Magazine*, November 1952, quoted in Jack M.

McLeod, "A Thematic Analysis of the *American Legion Monthly*, 1919–1951" (M.A. thesis, Univ. of Wisconsin—Madison, 1953), 7.

Chapter Nine

1. Quotations from *Indianapolis Star*, December 12, 1953, and other information from History—California—Chaillaux biography, AL.

2. Russell Cook to Amos Fries, January 17, 1934; Homer Chaillaux to George Fisher, December 20, 1934; National Americanism Memoranda to State Departments, November 30 and December 3, 1934, Americanism—Radicalism file, AL.

3. George Fisher to Homer Chaillaux, December 12, 1934; Thornwell Mullaley to Chaillaux, March 11, 1935; H. L. Knowles to Chaillaux, December 9, 1940, Americanism—Radicalism file, AL.

4. John Saslovsky to Homer Chaillaux, September 14, 1935; John B. Snow to Chaillaux, February 12, 1935; Chaillaux to Snow, March 5, 1935, Americanism—Radicalism file, AL; James D. Cooke to Chaillaux, May 11, 1936; Chaillaux to Conrad Erickson, January 17, 1935; Americanism—Radicalism—Communism file, AL. The various letters to and from Chaillaux may be found in these files.

5. Mary R. Millis to Lucille B. Milner, April 11, 1935, ACLU, vol. 801, 85.

6. Clippings from *Jersey Journal*, May 21, and 28, 1938; William McKinley to Daniel Doherty, January 10, 1938; McKinley to Edward McGrail, January 25, 1938, Americanism—Freedom of Speech file, AL.

7. Norman Thomas to Daniel Doherty, June 6 and 17, 1938; William McKinley to Doherty, June 8, 1938; clippings from *Springfield* (Missouri) *News and Leader*, May 8, 1938, and *Ocala* (Florida) *Morning Banner*, May 29, 1938; Edward McGrail to Doherty, June 6, 1938; statement of Daniel Doherty; Doherty to J. Iredell Wyckoff, May 3 and 14, 1938; clippings from *Jersey Journal*, May 28, 1938; *New York Times*, June 8, 1938, and February 2, 1939; *New York World-Telegram*, February 4, 1939, Americanism—Freedom of Speech file, AL.

8. Clippings from *Chicago Tribune*, March 15, 1938; *New York Times*, February 8, February 9, March 1, 1938; *New York Sun*, April 19, 1940; petition to Governor Herbert Lehman from Jeremiah Cross et al., March 7, 1938; copy of chapter 564, "Laws of New York," April 17, 1940; Legion press release, October 1940, Americanism—Communist Party—New York test case file, AL; "Minutes of National Executive Committee," November 21–22, 1940, 258–71, AL.

9. V. R. Tompkins to Homer Chaillaux, April 22, 1935, and Chaillaux to Tompkins, May 4, 1935; William S. Konold to Chaillaux, December 26, 1934, and Chaillaux to Konold, December 28, 1934; Chamber of Commerce, "Measures to Combat Subversive Activities" sent to "Secretaries of Member Organizations," May 15, 1935, Americanism—Radicalism—Communism file, AL.

10. Homer Chaillaux to Morris Ernst, March 17, 1935, American-

ism—Radicalism—Communism file, AL; clipping from *Los Angeles Post Examiner*, with reply by Chaillaux to Stephen O'Donnell, May 12, 1935, Americanism—Fascism file, AL.

11. Homer Chaillaux to Hamilton Fish, March 26, 1935, with clipping on February 20, 1935, speech on "Communism"; Chaillaux to Eli Parry, January 14, 1936, Americanism—Radicalism—Communism file, AL; National Americanism Commission, AL, *ISMS* (2nd ed., Indianapolis, 1937), 148–52.

12. Homer Chaillaux to Ernst L. Bell, October 9, 1935; Bell to Chaillaux, October 15, 1935; Budd Schulberg to Bell, October 19, 1935; Americanism—Radicalism—Communism—W file, AL; Chaillaux to Conrad L. Rydmark, December 5, 1938; Joe Smith to Chaillaux, December 7, 1938; Betty Davis, et al. to Chaillaux, December 6, 1938, Americanism—Radicalism—B file, AL; "Minutes of the National Americanism Commission," November 4, 1935, 101–4, 126–34, and April 30, 1941, 51–94, AL.

13. Frank C. Heins (through Homer Chaillaux) to Cordell Hull, March 23, 1936, Americanism—Radicalism—Mexican Consul file, AL; Chaillaux to Gilbert Stordock, October 12, 1937, Wisconsin American Legion Papers, Box 49, Wisconsin Historical Society; Chaillaux to Bruce Baird, January 4, 1939, Americanism—Radicalism—National Urban League file, AL.

14. Clipping from *New York World Telegram*, February 27, 1936, ACLU, vol. 906, 18; clipping from the "State," March 21, 1935, Americanism—Radicalism—Communism file, AL; "Minutes of the National Americanism Commission," May 1, 1935, 3, and May 3, 1936, 5; AL.

15. "Minutes of the National Americanism Commission," May 3, 1936, 4, 77, and November 1, 1936, 10; AL. Homer Chaillaux to State Commanders, March 20, 1937, Stephen Chadwick Papers, Box 2, Univ. of Washington.

16. *ISMS*, 247, 251, 253, 231, 133, 235, 236.

17. Ibid., 131–32, 127, 229.

18. Ibid., 7–9, 12–13.

19. See, for example, Morris Ernst to Roger Baldwin, March 20, 1936, ACLU, vol. 907, 51; *ISMS*, 266–83; S. S. Carr to Stephen Chadwick, September 18, 1937 (Box 2) and Chadwick to Clark Frasier, April 22, 1938 (Box 22) Chadwick Papers, Univ. of Washington; Ray Munn to American Legion, May 15, 1939, ACLU, vol. 2100, 22; "Convention Resolutions on Subversive Activities adopted since 1932," Americanism—Radicalism file, AL. For the spread of Fascism, see William E. Leuchtenburg, *Franklin D. Roosevelt and the New Deal, 1932–1940* (New York, 1963), 275–81.

20. Homer Chaillaux to S. Eisenstein, June 16, 1937, Americanism—Radicalism—Nazism file, AL.

21. Homer Chaillaux to Frank Miles, May 12, 1938; Miles to Chaillaux, May 16 and 22, 1938; Legion news release, July 1939; clippings

from *New York Journal-American*, May 12, 1938, and *Chicago Daily Times*, July 13, 1938, Americanism—Radicalism—Nazism file, AL.

22. George Herman to Homer Chaillaux, March 28, 1938; Chaillaux to Herman, March 29, 1938; clippings from *Indianapolis News*, February 14, 1938, and "Ex-Bundsmen to Entertain Legionnaires," filed for May 8, 1938, Americanism—Radicalism—Nazism file, AL.

23. Clipping from *Labor News*, April 29, 1938; Lou Wolfson to Daniel Doherty, April 21, 1938; A. T. Flanagan to Homer Chaillaux, May 7, 1938; Ray Murphy to Chaillaux, March 26, 1936, Americanism—Radicalism—Nazism file, AL.

24. "Convention Resolutions on Subversive Activities Since 1932," Americanism—Radicalism file, AL; Martin Dies to Homer Chaillaux, June 25, 1938; "Finish the Job: Dies Committee Disclosures Important," Americanism—Radicalism—Dies Committee file, AL.

25. F. M. Sullivan to Edward McGrail, August 9, 1938, January 24, 1939, February 9, 1939, and August 17, 1939; Legion news releases, May 22, 1939, September 4, 1940, February 14, 1941, and February 20, 1943; Joe Starnes, "They're on the Run," *American Legion Monthly*, April 1940, 16–17, 44–46, Americanism—Radicalism—Dies Committee file, AL.

26. Clippings from *New York Post*, October 31, 1938, and *New York Times*, November 8, 1938; Paul Y. Anderson, "Behind the Dies Intrigue," November 12, 1938; *Enid* (Oklahoma) *News*, November 26, 1938; "National Legislative Situation" (on Frances Perkins and deportation); news release, December 1940, and "The American Legion is on record for continued support of the Dies Committee and FBI"; Frank Sullivan to Edward Scheiberling, January 9, 1945, Americanism—Radicalism—Dies Committee file, AL.

27. Lucille M. Milner to Marcus Duffield, January 29, 1932; Duffield to Milner, February 17, 1932, ACLU, vol. 533, 90; W. W. Norton to Alvin Owsley, April 6, 1923; *New York World* News Service to Legion News Service, August 2, 1929; Americanism—Radicalism—Free Speech file, AL; "The Ruhr Occupation and Europe's Crisis," February 15, 1923, Administration and Organization—Post Charters—Revocation file, AL; "The Legion Suspends an Independent Post," *Christian Century* 49 (July 27, 1932):925; and "The Legion Declared Opposed to Federal Constitution," ibid. 51 (April 11, 1934):484; clipping from *New York World-Telegram*, June 14, 1932, ACLU, vol. 543, 126; Cyrus L. Baldridge, "Is the American Legion American?" *Scribner's* 100 (September 1936):132–38.

28. Baldridge, "Is the American Legion American?" 132–38; Homer Chaillaux to Maurice Stember, April 2, 1934; clippings from *New York World-Telegram*, March 25, 1936; *New York Tribune*, March 28, 1936; *New York Times*, April 28, 1936; *Indianapolis News*, May 22, 1936; Frank Samuel to Chaillaux, May 23, 1936; Cyrus Baldridge to Ray Murphy, May 23, 1936; Murphy to Baldridge, May 27, 1936; statement by Mur-

phy, May 22, 1936, Americanism—Radicalism—Free Speech file, AL; clippings from *New York Post*, April 30, 1936, and *New York Times*, May 1, May 4, May 22, May 23, 1936, ACLU, vol. 906, 34–40. Same sources used in next two paragraphs.

29. Murphy biography, Iowa—history file, AL; Morris Ernst to Roger Baldwin, November 27, 1935, ACLU, vol. 801, 187; Ernst to Baldwin, March 20, 1936, ACLU, vol. 907, 51; Roger Baldwin to Ray Murphy, May 5, 1936, and Murphy to Baldwin, May 10, 1936, ACLU, vol. 907, 73–77; clipping from *New York American*, November 30, 1935, ACLU, vol. 906, 100; Baldridge, "Is the American Legion American?" 138; "The American Legion Looks at Youth," *American Legion Monthly*, October 1935, 26–30; Ray Murphy to Frank Samuel, May 28, 1936, Americanism—Radicalism file, AL.

30. Notes on Colmery and Roger Baldwin to Harry Colmery, October 22 and November 4, 1936; Colmery to Baldwin, November 5, 1936, ACLU, vol. 907, 149–55; Baldwin to Colmery, October 31, 1936, Americanism—Radicalism—ACLU file, AL; clipping from *Hudson* (New York) *Register*, June 29, 1937; Baldwin to Colmery, July 9, 1937; Colmery to Baldwin, August 23, 1937, ACLU, vol. 951, 48, 52, 62–65; Walter White to Harry Colmery, May 1, 1937; Colmery to White, May 12, 1937, Americanism—Radicalism—Communism—NAACP file, AL.

31. Homer Chaillaux to Roger Baldwin, April 7, 1936; Baldwin to Chaillaux, April 2, 1936, Americanism—Radicalism—ACLU file, AL; Harry Colmery to Roger W. Baldwin, July 11, 1937, ACLU, vol. 982, 31–33; "Minutes of the National Americanism Commission," May 5, 1937, 43–47, 76, AL.

32. Leroy M. Willman to Homer Chaillaux, March 15, 1935, Americanism—Radicalism—Communism file, AL; Alexander Woollcott to Chaillaux, February 19, 1936, ACLU, vol. 906, 39; Roger Baldwin to Bill Donovan, May 10, 1939, ACLU, vol. 2100, 21; foreword to Walter Wilson, *The American Legion vs. Civil Liberty* (New York, 1938), Americanism—Radicalism—Free Speech file, AL.

33. For Doherty and Columbia, see nn. 61 and 62, below; clipping from Seattle *New Dealer*, January 21, 1939 and, generally, Americanism—Radicalism—Mooney file, AL; the Homer Chaillaux–Stephen Chadwick correspondence is in the latter's papers, especially Boxes 2–3, 21–23, Univ. of Washington; clipping from *Des Moines Register*, February 21, 1939; Arthur G. Hayes to Chadwick, February 23, 1939; Chadwick to Hayes, February 27, 1939, ACLU, vol. 2100, 5, 7, 8.

34. V. S. McClatchy to William Green, March 15, 1929; "The Legion and Immigration" (undated; c. 1929); Roland Cochran to Russell Cook, December 18, 1930; Garland W. Powell to Parthenia Gregory, January 24, 1925, Americanism—Immigration file, AL.

35. John R. Quinn, "America and Immigration," clipping from *American Federationist*, April 24, 1924, 295–99; testimony of Homer Chaillaux, May 14, 1940, copies in Americanism—Immigration file, AL.

36. Quinn, "America and Immigration," 296–97; Lemuel Bolles to Louis A. Johnson, January 9, 1933, Americanism—Immigration file, AL.

37. "The American Legion's Stand on Immigration" (c. 1923); Quinn, "America and Immigration," 295–96; "The Legion and Immigration" (c. 1929); Leighton Bloor, "Human Contraband," *American Legion Weekly*, June 19, June 26, and July 3, 1925; Garland W. Powell to Parthenia Gregory, January 24, 1925; Essay Contest press release, May, 1923, Americanism—Immigration file, AL.

38. *Summary of the Proceedings of the First* (Minneapolis, 1919), 38, *and Second* (Cleveland, 1920), 57, *National Conventions*; V. S. McClatchy, "Guarding the Immigration Gates" (San Francisco, 1925); statement, "California Department of the American Legion" (1924), Americanism—Immigration file, AL.

39. James K. Fisk to James D. Phelan, December 3, 1924, and Thomas N. Swale to Phelan, August 27, 1925, under their names, Phelan Papers, Univ. of California, Berkeley; James K. Fisk to Franklin D. Roosevelt, August 30, 1937, copy in Fisk file, Hiram Johnson Papers, Univ. of California, Berkeley; James Sakamoto to Lynn Stambaugh, October 23, 1941, and Stambaugh to Sakamoto, October 31, 1941, Americanism—Immigration file, AL.

40. *Summary of the Proceedings of the Fifth National Convention* (San Francisco, 1923), 11; "Remarks of Mr. Edward J. Shaughnessy," May 3, 1936; California Joint Immigration Committee, "The Problem of Our Reportable Aliens," May 9, 1933; John Thomas Taylor to C. M. Wilson, May 18, 1935; Homer Chaillaux, note on immigration, April 1935; news release on alien employees, January 1938, Americanism—Immigration file, AL.

41. Memorandum of Homer Chaillaux, June 11, 1935; Ray Murphy to Robert P. Reynolds, March 16, 1936; testimony of Homer Chaillaux, May 14, 1940; the Legion began gathering criticism of Perkins as early as 1934, Americanism—Immigration file, AL.

42. The Legion's general role in the case is discussed in Richard S. Jones, *A History of the American Legion* (Indianapolis, 1946), 199–200; the Perkins–Chadwick correspondence may be found as "Appendix A" in Stephen Chadwick to all Congressmen, December 31, 1939, Walter M. Pierce Papers, Box 7, Univ. of Oregon.

43. Walter M. Pierce to J. B. Piercy, July 23, 1940; Redmond, Oregon, Post to Pierce, June 26, 1940; Pierce to Redmond Post, June 20, 1940, Pierce Papers, Box 5, Univ. of Oregon.

44. Memorandums of Homer Chaillaux, June 11 and June 14, 1935; Chaillaux to A Claire Dewey, January 23, 1937, Americanism—Immigration file, AL; "Minutes of the National Americanism Commission," November 15, 1931, 29–35, AL.

45. "An Example of Tolerance," Legion press release, October 24,

1940; Homer Chaillaux to Donald R. Perry, May 15, 1941; Perry to Chaillaux, June 2, 1941; Chaillaux to Wright Tarbell, June 7, 1941; Lemuel B. Schofield to Chaillaux, October 7, 1941; broadcast by Robert Jackson, December 21, 1940, Americanism—Immigration file, AL.

46. Legion press releases on Fish, May 1921 and September 16, 1926 (Alien file); F. A. Montana to James A. Drain, September 14, 1925; K. J. Zink to National Headquarters, November 27, 1924; Garland Powell to Zink, December 2, 1924; W. W. Husband to Powell, December 11, 1924; "Information Concerning Naturalization Laws Now in Effect" (1940), Americanism—Immigration file, AL. Memo, Homer Chaillaux, October 31, 1940, and Chaillaux to J. F. O'Rourke, April 19, 1941, Americanism—Naturalization file, AL.

47. "National Americanism Commission Minutes," May 3, 1939, 53–54; AL.

48. Memorandum to Stephen Chadwick, April 28, 1939; press releases May 1939, June 5, 1940, Americanism—Immigration—Refugee file, AL.

49. Stephen Chadwick to Louis A. Johnson, January 12, 1939; Americanism—Immigration—Refugee file, AL; "National Americanism Commission Minutes," May 3, 1939, 58, AL.

50. "National Americanism Commission Minutes," May 3, 1939, 48–51, 93–94; for posts' protests, see clipping from *New York Times*, December 26, 1938; Frances Scully to Emma Puschner, March 25, 1939; Lowell Limpus to Homer Chaillaux, February 6, 1939; Edward R. Maylan to Americanism Commission, May 6, 1939; Americanism—Immigration—Refugee file, AL; for public opinion, see Lawrence A. Wittner, *Rebels against War: The American Peace Movement, 1941–1960* (New York, 1969), 17.

51. Homer Chaillaux to Don Bolt, September 6, 1940; clippings from *Indianapolis Times*, June 26, 1940, *New York Times*, August 10, 1940, and other papers; Maurice Rosenwald to Frank Samuel, received August 12 and 16, 1940; Raymond J. Kelly to J. P. Hart, August 16, 1940; Robert Reynolds to Chaillaux, March 14, 1940, Americanism—Immigration—Refugee file, AL.

52. Clipping from *New York Times*, May 1, 1921, ACLU, vol. 189, 223; *Madison Star Journal*, March 16, 1939, Wisconsin American Legion Papers, Box 2, Wisconsin State Historical Society; *New York Post*, October 23, 1935, ACLU, vol. 791, 100.

53. "Minutes of the National Americanism Commission," November 19, 1932, 28, and May 3, 1939, 24, AL; H. H. Heberle to Gilbert Stordock, September 11, 1940, Wisconsin American Legion Papers, Box 2, Wisconsin State Historical Society.

54. Walter B. Townsend to Homer Chaillaux, February 24, 1936, and circular letter to "Comrade," 1936, Stephen Chadwick Papers, Box 13, Univ. of Washington; "Minutes of the National Americanism Commission," May 1, 1940, 81, AL.

55. "The Legion Looks at Youth," *American Legion Monthly*, October 1935, 26–30; clippings from *New York Times*, October 1 and 15, 1935; *New York Post*, October 1, 1935, ACLU, vol. 868, 305–8; *New York Times*, March 12, 1938, vol. 2008, 8–9; "Minutes of the National Americanism Commission," May 1, 1935, 10–11, AL; Homer Chaillaux to army officers in ROTC, February 1, 1936, Radicalism—Communism—Colleges file, AL; news release on essay contest, 1924, and Robert Krumholtz, "Puncturing the Windy Bag of Communism," *American Legion Weekly*, May 24, 1925, Radicalism—Communism file, AL.

56. Minutes of Rose City Post, September 27, 1937, Oregon Historical Society; Americanism—Radicalism—Commonwealth College file, AL, especially clipping from *Liberty Magazine*, December 19, 1936; Nathan Oser to ACLU, June 29, 1940, and subsequent documents, ACLU, vol. 2149, 17–104; Russell Cook to Charles C. Hawks, January 10, 1934, and Homer Chaillaux to Department Americanism Chairmen, January 7, 1934, Americanism—Radicalism—Youth Movements file, AL; *National Legionnaire*, March 1936, Ray Murphy to Stephen Chadwick, July 8, 1936, Americanism—Teachers' Oaths file, AL; Marvin Gellerman, *The American Legion as Educator* (New York, 1938), 122–24.

57. Bernhard Schlegel Post investigation, published in *West Chester Daily Local News*, April 18, 1927; Daniel Strickler, "Report of Investigation of the Controversies between the West Chester Post of the American Legion and the Liberal Club of the West Chester State Normal School," June 12, 1927; "Free Speech and the Legion," *Nation* 124 (April 20, 1927), all in Americanism—Radicalism—Communism—West Chester, Pennsylvania file, AL.

58. In addition to sources in n. 57, see Andrew Eric Dinniman, "Academic Freedom at West Chester: The Controversy of 1927" (Ph.D. diss., Pennsylvania State Univ., 1978), especially 97, 221; clipping from *Richmond Palladium*, April 19, 1927, and Harry Jung to Frank Cross, April 21, 1927, Americanism—Radicalism—Communism—West Chester file, AL; Homer Chaillaux to Louis J. Brown, January 19, 1935, and Matt Monaghan to Chaillaux, May 12, 1941, Americanism—Radicalism—Communism file, AL.

59. Homer Chaillaux to Eugene Short, August 4, 1944, Education—Gellerman file, AL; Stephen Chadwick to Chaillaux, June 31, 1938, Chadwick Papers, Box 3, Univ. of Washington; M. Engelbrecht to Editor of *Milwaukee Journal*, July 1, 1938, Wisconsin American Legion Papers, Box 2, Wisconsin State Historical Society.

60. Clippings from *New York Post*, July 1, 1938, *St. Louis Globe-Democrat*, July 1, 1938, *Norfolk Virginian Pilot*, July 1, 1938, *New York Times*, quoted in *American Legion Magazine*, August 1938, 19, all in Education—Gellerman file, AL.

61. Russell's remarks and Doherty's Teachers' College speech, July 21, 1938; clipping, *New York Times*, July 22, 1938; William F. Russell, "How to Tell A Communist and How to Beat Him," speech to New

York State American Legion Convention, August 12, 1938; Cortlandt J. Langley to Edward McGrail, September 30, 1938, and McGrail to Langley, October 4, 1938; Education—Columbia University file, AL.

62. Biographical data on Counts in Education—Columbia University file, AL; Charles M. Frasier to Stephen Chadwick, July 5, 1938, Chadwick Papers, Box 3, Univ. of Washington; Daniel Doherty, "Educators or Propagandists?" *American Legion Magazine*, October 1938; Arthur Schlesinger Sr., "The American Legion," *New Republic*, February 14, 1944, 208–9, Education—Gellerman file, AL.

63. Frances Fitzgerald, *America Revised* (New York, 1979), 37; A. T. Falk to Homer Chaillaux, November 22, December 4, and December 14, 1939, on the Advertising Federation of America; National Association of Manufacturers, "Educational Cooperation Bulletin"; and Amos A. Fries to R. Worth Shumaker, September 8, 1941, all in Americanism—Radicalism—Textbooks file, AL. See also, generally, Irene K. Kuhn, "Battle over Books," *American Legion Magazine*, October 1958, 20–21, 37–40. Quotations from Harold Rugg, *Changing Governments and Changing Cultures* (New York, 1933), 437, and *The Great Technology* (New York, 1933), 185.

64. Augustin A. Rudd to Homer Chaillaux, January 13, 1939, March 18, May 31, 1940; Chaillaux to Rudd, January 23, February 25, 1939; June 22, 1940; Americanism—Radicalism—Textbooks file, AL; Armstrong, "Treason in the Textbooks," *American Legion Magazine*, September 1940, 8–10, 70–72.

65. Homer Chaillaux to Burr L. Chase, October 9, 1940; Walter E. Myers, "The American Legion and Civic Education Service," *Civic Leader*, September 30, 1940; H. C. Lucas to Milo Warner, October 29, 1940; all in Americanism—Radicalism—Textbooks file, AL.

66. *Time*, September 9, 1940; John E. Rudder to R. Worth Shumaker, June 6, 1941; J. W. Getsinger to Milo Warner, November 25, 1940; George G. Axtelle and others to Daniel J. Kelly, May 26, 1940, for American Committee for Democracy and Intellectual Freedom; Roger W. Baldwin, "Gilt-Edged Patriots," *Frontiers of Democracy*, November 15, 1940, 45–47; Alonzo F. Myers, "The Attack on the Rugg Books," ibid., October 15, 1940, reprint; "Let Us Face Realities," *American Business Survey*, January 1940, 19, all in Americanism—Radicalism—Textbooks file, AL.

67. *Time*, September 9, 1940, and Homer Chaillaux to Helen Silcox Trupp, April 25, 1940, Americanism—Radicalism—Textbooks file, AL; Bill Cunningham, "Smearing the Minds of Kids," *American Legion Magazine*, July 1941, 3–19 (fourth of a series beginning in March); "Rugg Philosophy Analyzed," four-pamphlet series published by National Americanism Commission, 1941–42, AL; for Legion posts instrumental in banning Rugg books, see Homer Chaillaux to Charles C. McGonegal, April 9, 1943; Thomas P. Scully to Chaillaux, May 6, 1941; Chaillaux to Gray Sheek, July 10, 1941; clipping from *New York Herald Tribune*,

January 3, 1941; Americanism—Radicalism—Textbooks file, AL; Fitzgerald, *America Revised*, 37.

68. "Minutes of the National Americanism Commission," October 26–29, 1921, 24–26; October 12–15, 1922, 3–10, AL; for Maurer, Kirkpatrick, and other criticism see various clippings in ACLU vols. 251–3, 295–99; Jay Elmer Morgan, "Help Keep the Schools of the Nation Open," *Journal of the National Education Association*, January 1934; Belmont Farley to Russell Cook, January 26, 1934; Resolution no. 760, St. Louis National Convention, 1935, AL; all in National Education Association—Cooperation file, AL; Homer Chaillaux to F. E. Turin, July 11, 1938, Americanism—Radicalism—Gellerman file, AL.

69. For bias and dullness in textbooks, see Fitzgerald, *America Revised*, 168–74; clipping from *Sacramento Bee*, April 1, 1924, Americanism—U.S. History file, AL; "Proceedings of the National Executive Committee," January 12–13, 1925, 166–67, 173, and June 15–16, 1925, 347–49, 402. "Preliminary Statement of Committee on School Textbooks," October 7, 1923; clipping from *American Legion Weekly*, June 27, 1924, Americanism—U.S. History file, AL.

70. "The Story of Our American People," publicity pamphlet, Americanism—U.S. History file, AL: "Proceedings of the National Executive Committee," June 15–16, 1925, 374–88, AL.

71. Clippings, "The Chosen People," *New Republic*, June 23, 1926, 129–30; Harold U. Faulkner, "Perverted American History," *Harper's*, February 1926, 337–64; Claude Van Tyne, "A Questionable History," *New York Times*, July 24, 1925; resolution of Mississippi Department, undated, Americanism—U.S. History file, AL.

72. "Proceedings of the National Executive Committee," June 15–16, 1925, 425–36, AL; Charles F. Horne to James Drain, January 26, 1925; Garland W. Powell to W. F. Austin, July 3, 1936; Frank Cross to Austin, March 23, 1926, and to Robert Byers, April 1, 1926, Americanism—U.S. History file, AL; Richard S. Jones, *A History of the American Legion* (Indianapolis, 1946), 273–74.

Chapter Ten

1. Speech of Charles M. Wilson, 1931, History—Illinois—Wilson file, AL; Robert Bellah, *The Broken Covenant: American Civil Religion in the Twentieth Century* (New York, 1975).

2. Homer Chaillaux to Lucille B. Milner, May 29, 1935, ACLU, vol. 112, 764.

3. Theodore Roosevelt Jr. to William Pearson, February 14, 1920, Box 11, Roosevelt Papers, LC; A. H. Gansser, "Readjustment in Community Building—The American Legion," *Social Welfare Forum: Official Proceedings* (1920), 309–10; Hanford MacNider to James G. Harbord, January 9, 1924 (Box 8), to Frank Milies, January 22, 1924 (Box 9), John L. Griffith, September 9, 1925 (G Series), and Gilbert Bettman, October 22, 1923 (Box 6), MacNider Papers, Hoover Library; "Minutes of the National Americanism Commission," May 11–12, 1926, AL.

4. Minutes of the National Americanism Commission, October 1922, 3, AL; *Summary of the Proceedings of the Fifth National Convention* (San Francisco, 1923), 27; James A. Drain, "The American Legion in the Year to Come," *Outlook* 138 (November 5, 1924):364–65; John R. Quinn, "What the American Legion Is Doing," ibid. 137 (July 9, 1924):397–98; Howard P. Savage, "The American Legion's Program for 1926–1927," ibid. 144:401–2.

5. *Reports of Committees to the Thirteenth* (1931) *National Convention* (Detroit), 81, AL; questionnaires in possession of the author; "Minutes of the National Americanism Commission," November 11–12, 1930, 146, AL; Homer Chaillaux to Albion Roy King, May 6, 1941, Americanism—Radicalism—Textbooks file, AL.

6. Walter E. Myers to Lemuel Bolles, July 15, 1920; Benjamin H. Connor to John Quinn, May 23, 1924, and, generally, other letters in History—Foreign Departments, and France and Italy files, AL.

7. Julia Wheelock to Eben Putnam, March 23, 1921, History—Italy file, AL; C. C. Fitzgerald to Lemuel Bolles, October 25, 1920; "The American Legion in Old Cathay," *American Legion Weekly*, January 4, 1922; Robert H. Warner to Edward Prell, October 29, 1921, all in History—Foreign Departments file, AL.

8. T. M. Drake to Edwin Prell, July 6, 1922, History—Panama file, AL; questionnaires in possession of the author; J. K. Butler to Frederic Galbraith, December 6, 1920, and May 4, 1921, History—Hawaii file, AL.

9. "American Legion Baseball," Fiftieth Anniversary file, and taped interview with K. D. Munro, 1975, AL; "Minutes of the National Americanism Commission," May 11–12, 1926, 8–28, AL; Jones, *American Legion*, 265–66.

10. C. C. Frazier, radio address for 1930, Frazier Papers, Nebraska Historical Society; "Minutes of the National Americanism Commission," January 1928, 64, 75, AL.

11. "Minutes of the National Americanism Commission," January 1928, 46; November 14, 1929, 38; November 1934, 70; May 3, 1934, 79; November 1941, 17–18, AL.

12. Ibid., November 1940, 169–78; *Springfield Union*, August 22, September 1, October 26, 1934, Springfield, Massachusetts, City Library.

13. Jones, *American Legion*, 265–69; "Minutes of the National Americanism Commission," May 11, 1926, 232–36; November 11–12, 1930, 16, AL; C. C. Frazier, speech to the Boy Scouts, January 1928, Nebraska Historical Society.

14. Speeches, skits, and suggested ceremonies for Armistice Day, Memorial Day, July 4, and Lincoln's Birthday are filed by year under each holiday in the Americanism—Holidays file, AL; quotation from "Mr. Lincoln Writes a Letter," 1941, under Lincoln's Birthday, AL.

15. Lemuel Bolles to Frank Cross, January 4, 1926; "Bud" Gearhart to Homer Chaillaux, March 24, March 28, April 2, and September 14, 1938; Frank Samuel to Samuel E. Burns, December 3, 1938; Chaillaux

to Samuel, February 6, 1939; Eugene Van Antwerp to Stephen Chadwick, September 22, 1938; and Chadwick to Antwerp, September 27, 1938; John Thomas Taylor to Samuel, December 19, 1936; E. M. Libonati to Chaillaux, November 13, 1939; J. Leroy to Frank Belgrano, September 28, 1928, all in Americanism—Holidays—Armed Forces Day file, AL; "America's Unknown Soldier" (1921), World War Dead—National Cemeteries—Arlington file, AL; "Plans for Memorial Day," May 30, 1923; Lemuel Bolles, Bulletin, "Observance of Memorial Day," April 7, 1922; Harvey G. Thomas to H. L. Garwood, March 30, 1924; "Indiana Legion Praised for Memorial Day Fight" (1923); Carl Schwarz to Milo Warner, June 18, 1941, and Warner to Schwarz, June 20, 1941, Americanism—Holidays—Memorial Day file, AL.

16. Clipping from "Ohio State Journal"; "Organizations Represented at National Flag Conference," and "The Flag Code," June 14–15, 1923; Charles Wilson to Frank Samuel, September 5, 1941, Americanism—Flag file, AL.

17. "How to Obtain Cooperation of Newspapers for Campaign of Education on the American Flag"; F. G. Condict, "The Stars and Stripes," *Kiwanis Magazine*, November 1927, 592–94; Russell Cook to Robert Smith, November 10, 1930; "Flag Day—June 14," *Huddle*, May 1930; "Chalk Talk on the Flag"; "The Flag Speaks," program advertisement, July 19, 1940; Homer Chaillaux to B. W. Gearhart, October 27, 1941, and flag code, Public Law 623, 77th Congress, 1st session, June 22, 1942, Americanism—Flag file, AL.

18. *Huddle*, 1929, vol. 2, no. 4, clipping in Stafford King Papers, Box 14, Minnesota Historical Society; Homer Chaillaux to Karl Detzer, January 25, 1939, Americanism—Naturalization file, AL.

19. Clipping, Karl Detzer, "Tony Earns His Vote," *American Legion Magazine*, February 1939, 12–13; for South Bend and Judge Pyle; Detzer to Homer Chaillaux, January 17, 1939; various descriptions of schools and ceremonies in Americanism—Naturalization file, AL; see also Gary Gerstle, "The Politics of Patriotism: Americanization and the Formation of the CIO," *Dissent*, winter 1986, 93–101.

20. Leonard Cole to Mr. Tomlin, March 21, 1934; Palmer Edwards to Gold Star Fathers, January 21, 1928; John Sewall to Robert I. Randolph, March 25, 1932; P. M. Kern to Jessie Davies, November 9, 1931; Edward Claye to J. P. Buchanan, December 19, 1929; E. Ross Bartley to Rufus Davies, March 2, 1932, Chicago World's Fair Papers, American Legion file, Univ. of Illinois, Chicago Circle.

21. Edward Claye to J. P. Buchanan, December 19, 1929; program announcement, June 10, 1933; J. A. Donnelly to World's Fair Committee (April 1930); Robert I. Randolph to Edward Kelly, July 25, 1933; Leonard Cole to Russell Cook, December 30, 1933; Cole to G. W. Plumer, April 13, 1934, Chicago World's Fair Papers, American Legion file, Univ. of Illinois, Chicago Circle.

22. South Dakota Legion Resolution, January 18, 1931; Louisville

Convention Resolution, September 30, 1929; "Brief History of the Movement for an International Memorial Forest with Particular Reference to the Part Played by the American Legion," quotation from *Outdoor Life*, September 29, 1927, Quetico Superior Council Papers, folder 1928, Minnesota Historical Society.

23. Victor Gondos Jr., *J. Franklin Jameson and the Birth of the National Archives* (Philadelphia, 1981), 104–8, 128–30, 151–53, 167–68, quotations 168, 111; History—Massachusetts—Eben Putnam file, AL.

24. American Legion, *Child Welfare Guide* (1st ed., Indianapolis, 1931); History—Missouri—Emma Puschner file, AL; Jones, *American Legion*, 255–64.

25. Jones, *American Legion*, 245–53; "The American Legion in Time of Disaster," *American Legion Monthly*, September 1927, and reports of efforts in Disaster Relief File, AL; the plan itself is in Box 1, Stephen Chadwick Papers (1935), Univ. of Washington.

26. Jones, *American Legion*, 247–48, 250–51; Nannie Julienne to Rose Spencer, n.d., and July 18 and 19, 1927, Spencer Papers, Box 3, Minnesota Historical Society; "History of the American Legion Auxiliary," Mississippi American Legion Auxiliary Papers, Mississippi State Archives; Homer Chaillaux to Stephen Chadwick, January 28, 1937, Chadwick Papers, Box 2, Univ. of Washington.

27. Jones, *American Legion*, 328–33; James F. Barton to American Legion Auxiliary, n.d., Iowa—History—Barton file, AL; Mrs. Joseph Thompson, *The American Legion Auxiliary, 1921–1924* (Pittsburgh, 1926), 12, 17.

28. Thompson, *Auxiliary*, 34–36, 55–57; biographical sketch of Helen Hughes Hiescheler in her papers, Minnesota Historical Society; Kate Barrett Scrapbook, Barrett Papers, LC.

29. *Summary of Proceedings of the Seventh National Convention* (Omaha, 1925), 14; "Report of the 1929 Convention" (Minnesota), Box 22, Stafford King Papers, Minnesota Historical Society, St. Paul; Minutes of the National Americanism Commission, August 9, 1925, 249, 253; November 16, 1931, 116; May 3–4, 1932, 16; November 13, 1932, 125 AL.

30. W. T. Molligan to Rose Spencer, March 6, 1926, Spencer Papers, Box 3, Minnesota Historical Society.

31. Report of State Adjutant, Box 3, Rose Spencer Papers, Minnesota Historical Society; Jones, *American Legion*, 331; Thompson, *Auxiliary*, 57.

32. Bess B. Wetherholt, Report of November 18, 1924, Box 19, Stafford King Papers, and Report of State Adjutant (1927), Rose Spencer Papers, Box 3, Minnesota Historical Society; Florence Kallen, *History of the American Legion Auxiliary* (Oregon), 15, Oregon Historical Society.

33. "Minutes of Minnesota Executive Committee, American Legion Auxiliary," September 1920, Helen Hughes Hiescheler Papers, Minnesota Historical Society; Jones, *American Legion*, 331–32.

34. Claire Oliphant to Stafford King, November 18, 1924, Box 19,

and Minnesota Commanders' and Adjutants' Conference Report, March 16, 1928, King Papers, Box 16, Minnesota Historical Society; speech to 1923 Auxiliary Convention, American Legion file, Kate Barrett Papers, LC.

35. Homer Chaillaux to J. W. Hanson, May 21, 1941, Americanism—Flag Salute file, AL.

Chapter Eleven

1. Edward A. Hayes, "Compulsory Military Training in Land Grant Universities," attached to Frank Samuel to Hayes, January 15, 1934, Americanism—Radicalism—Pacifism—Military Training Camps file, AL; Roscoe Baker, *The American Legion and American Foreign Policy* (New York, 1954), 116–17; "Copy of an Address Delivered by Major General Amos A. Fries," Memorial Day file, AL; "Abstract of Armistice Day Speech of Howard P. Savage" (1926), Armistice Day file, AL; Amos Fries to Frank Samuel, January 2, 1934, Fries Papers, Univ. of Oregon.

2. Baker, *Legion and Foreign Policy*, 121; "National Americanism Commission Minutes," May 1930, 126–28, 146–50, AL. Amos Fries to Edward Hayes, March 14, 1934, Fries Papers, Univ. of Oregon.

3. Richard S. Jones, *A History of the American Legion* (Indianapolis, 1946), 73. Statistics on general public opinion used in this chapter from Ralph B. Levering, *The Public and American Foreign Policy, 1918–1978* (New York, 1978), 74–79. Legionnaire opinion in the Fight for Freedom Archive at Mudd Library, Princeton University (hereafter FF); information on Kelly in his biographical file, Michigan—Kelly, AL. Quotation from *Summary of the Proceedings of the Twenty-First National Convention of the American Legion* (Detroit, 1939), 75; Sanford Griffith, "Analysis of Boston Convention, September 23–26, 1940," FF.

4. Griffith, "Boston Convention," FF.

5. *Summary of the Proceedings of the Twenty-Second National Convention* (Boston, 1940), 59.

6. This debate may be read in the "Minutes of the American Legion National Convention, 1940," 329–41, AL.

7. Griffith, "Boston Convention," FF; Thomas Quinn to David Walsh, September 28, 1940, Walsh Papers, Holy Cross College; MacNider quoted in *New York Times*, June 28, 1940 (see his biographical file under History—Iowa, AL); Stephen Chadwick to Raymond Kelly, August 1 and June 3, 1940, Box 24, and to Milo Warner, December 26, 1940, Box 23, Chadwick Papers, Univ. of Washington.

8. Warner's report appears in his communications to J. Edgar Hoover, March 26, 1941, FBI–American Legion Contact Program, file 66-9330, published on microfilm by Scholarly Resources Incorporated (hereafter cited as FBI) and to Franklin D. Roosevelt, March 14, 1941; see also Roosevelt to Milo Warner, February 1, 1941, both in Office Files 64, Roosevelt Papers, at the Roosevelt Presidential Library; Jones, *American Legion*, 107–11; Warner's biographical file under History—Ohio, AL;

"Survey of National Convention, Milwaukee," prepared by Market Analysts, Inc., for Fight for Freedom, 2, FF.

9. *Summary of the Proceedings of the Twenty-Third National Convention* (Milwaukee, 1941), 35–40, 45; John McCormack to Franklin Roosevelt, November 19, 1941, Office Files 64, Roosevelt Papers; Geoffrey Perrett, *Days of Sadness, Years of Triumph* (New York, 1975), 193; B. E. Sackett to J. Edgar Hoover, September 27, 1941, FBI.

10. This debate may be read in the "Minutes of the American Legion National Convention," 1941, 261–314, 388–403, AL.

11. Baker, *Legion and Foreign Policy*, 176–81.

12. "Survey of Milwaukee Convention," FF; B. E. Sackett to J. Edgar Hoover, September 27, 1941, FBI.

13. Bolles quoted in June 1922 news release, "Harding Supports Legion's Universal Draft Program," Profiteers file, AL; "The Legion's Conscription Program," *Literary Digest*, November 5, 1927, 10; Baker, *Legion and Foreign Policy*, 126–30; Josiah W. Bailey to Clare Kearney, April 16, 1938, Bailey Papers, Box 401, Duke Univ.

14. "Minutes of American Legion National Convention," 1938, 319–21, and 1941, 389–99, AL; Edward Spafford to Roy Hoffman, October 7, 1930, in History—New York—Spafford file, AL.

15. Kelly quoted in "Proposed American Legion Defense against Fifth Column Activities" (1940), Americanism—Radicalism—Emergency—FBI file, AL.

16. Robert A. Adams to Russell Creviston, September 9, 1921; Ralph W. Early to Edward A. Hayes, October 21, 1934, Americanism—Radicalism—file, AL; J. Edgar Hoover, "Legionnaires and the FBI" (1946), Americanism—Communism file, AL.

17. Clipping from *New York Herald Tribune*, June 10, 1940; Memorandums, June 4, 5, and 6, respectively, of Indiana, Oregon, and North Carolina Departments; "Proposed American Legion Defense against Fifth Column Activities"; Frank Samuel to Members of National Executive Committee et al., June 27, 1940, all in Americanism-Radicalism—Emergency file, AL.

18. J. Edgar Hoover to Edward Tamm and H. Hugh Clegg, November 18, 1940, FBI.

19. P. E. Foxworth to J. Edgar Hoover, September 3, 1941; Hoover, memos for the attorney general, November 18 and December 2, 1940; Homer Chaillaux to Hoover, June 19, 1942; Hoover to Special Agents in Charge, November 18, 1943, FBI.

20. Hoover, "Legionnaires and the FBI," Americanism—Communism file, AL; David Carlin memorandum, February 1, 1945; G. S. Callen to Alex Rosen, February 6, 1945, FBI; Athan Theoharis, "The FBI and the American Legion Contact Program," *Political Science Quarterly* 100 (1985):271–86.

21. Milo Warner to Franklin D. Roosevelt, January 30, 1941, Office Files 64, and Frank Murphy to Roosevelt, January 5, 1942, Personal

Papers file 1962, Roosevelt Papers; J. Edgar Hoover to Edward Tamm, January 31, 1941, FBI; Raymond Moley, *The American Legion Story* (New York, 1966), 256–63; Jones, *American Legion*, 106–22; for Theodore Roosevelt Jr. and Hanford MacNider, see their files under History— New York and Iowa, AL.

22. See Amos Fries to Clarence Kincaid, March 19, 1932, with a copy to Russell Cook, April 1, 1932, of "American Legion Emergency Disaster Call," American Legion file, Fries Papers, Univ. of Oregon; and Jesse W. Barrett to William Welsh, March 6 and 7, 1933, and to "Small Selected Groups of Legionnaires," March 20, 1933, American Legion file, Barrett Papers, Univ. of Missouri; Amy Shechter, "Fascism in Pennsylvania," *Nation* (140), June 19, 1935, clipping in vol. 801, ACLU. The same sources support the next paragraph.

23. Questionnaires in respective state history files, AL; for Michigan see Alexander Gardiner to James Barton, May 24, 1940, Americanism— Radicalism—Communism file, AL. (Despite the new publicity for the Legion Defense Program, the *Legion Magazine* turned down an article publicizing the previous Michigan effort.) See chapter eight for Pennsylvania and Michigan labor strife.

24. United States Congress, Un-American Activities Committee Investigation of Certain Other Propaganda Activities, House of Representatives, 73d Congress, 2d session (Washington, 1934–35); Belgrano's statement is in his file under History—California, AL; clipping from *Daily Worker*, May 23, 1950, in History—West Virginia—Louis A. Johnson file, AL. (The *Worker* repeats the charge that Johnson, Roosevelt's principal "insider" in the Legion, was trying to overthrow him!); *Parade*, May 16, 1982, 21.

25. Notes on the June 10 meeting in Stephen Chadwick Papers, Box 5, Univ. of Washington; Raymond Kelly, "The Legion Called the Turn," *National Legionnaire*, June 1940, and memorandum to Members of National Executive Committee et al., June 27, 1940, Americanism— Radicalism—Emergency file, AL.

26. Elizabeth Gurley Flynn to Robert Baldwin, September 8, 1939, ACLU, vol. 2127, 178; C. T. Schutt to Bill Mundt, January 13, 1936; Flag Salute file, AL; reports in ACLU, vol. 2215, 4–203; vol. 2216, 287– 92; vol. 2227, 7–14, 63–69, 323–29; vol. 2229, 3–117; vol. 2230, 17–81; vol. 2235, 168–230; quotation from vol. 2155, 112, as reported in *Boston Herald*, September 25, 1940. For a sympathetic discussion of the Jehovah's Witnesses, see H. Rutledge Southworth, "Jehovah's 50,000 Witnesses," *Nation*, August 10, 1940, 110–13.

27. Exchange of letters, Arthur Garfield Hays and Lynn Stambaugh, December 19 and 31, 1941; Homer Chaillaux to Mrs. Q. L. Wright, December 16, 1940, to Mrs. Beatrice L. Hart, July 23, 1941, and to Robert F. Garner, May 20, 1942; C. E. Roudabush to Mary Morrisetti, November 17, 1939; publicity release on *Gobitis* decision, June 5, 1940, all in Flag Salute file, AL.

28. For the Legion's postwar role, see William Pencak, "Veterans' Movements," in Jack P. Greene et al., eds., *Scribners' Encyclopedia of American Political History* (New York, 1984), 1344–47. Legion positions continue to appear in annual convention reports; see also *New York Times*, section IV, March 6, 1977, 3, "Veterans Are at Full Strength in Washington," and May 16, 1986, B, 1–2, "At American Legion Posts, Veterans of Vietnam Fan the Winds of Change." Thomas A. Rumer is currently preparing a scholarly history of the Legion.

29. See, for example, Irving Bernstein, *The Lean Years: A History of the American Worker, 1920–1933* (Boston, 1960), 431, and *The Turbulent Years: A History of the American Worker* (Boston, 1970), 491; Paul Carter, *The Twenties in America* (New York, 1968), 45, and *Another Part of the Twenties* (New York, 1977), 24, 64; William E. Leuchtenburg, *The Perils of Prosperity: 1914–1932* (Chicago, 1958), 92, 205, and *Franklin D. Roosevelt and the New Deal: 1932–1940* (New York, 1963), 56; John D. Hicks, *Republican Ascendancy: 1921–1933* (New York, 1960), 52, 183, 275; David Q. Voigt, *America through Baseball* (Chicago, 1976), 86; Robert Dallek, *Franklin D. Roosevelt and American Foreign Policy: 1932–1945* (New York, 1979), 39, 71; Richard Polenberg, *War and Society: The United States, 1941–1945* (Philadelphia, 1972), 38, 96, 97, 181; and Paul L. Murphy, *The Constitution in Crisis Times: 1918–1969* (New York, 1972), 79, 174, 482.

Scholars who study the Red Scare, veterans' issues, and civil liberties give the Legion more attention. They include Robert K. Murray, *Red Scare: A Study in National Hysteria, 1919–1920* (Minneapolis, 1955), 87–90, 123, 125, 182–89, 264, 265, 270, and *The Harding Era* (Minneapolis, 1969), 88, 164, 266, 311–13, 459, 480; Donald Lisio, *The President and Protest: Hoover, Conspiracy and the Bonus Riot* (Columbia, 1974), especially 7–8, 10–12, 30–36, 43–46, 244–62, 294, and 299; Roger Daniels, *The Bonus March: An Episode of the Great Depression* (Westport, Conn., 1971), especially 23–27, 42–43, 50–52, 203–6, 213–17, 226–28, and 233–41; William P. Dillingham, *Federal Aid to Veterans: 1917–1941* (Gainesville, 1952), forty-one entries on the Legion; Charles Markmann, *The Noblest Cry: A History of the American Civil Liberties Union* (New York, 1965), twelve entries, and a section (278–96) entirely on the Legion; Stanley I. Kutler, *The American Inquisition: Justice and Order in the Cold War* (New York, 1982), seven references; and Victor S. Navasky, *Naming Names* (New York, 1980), fifteen references.

Bibliographical Essay

Manuscripts

The principal manuscript collections used are in the Archives of the American Legion at the National Headquarters in Indianapolis. These are superbly catalogued by topic, such as History (organized by state and leading figures), Administration—Organization, Labor, Veterans' Administration (subsuming Rehabilitation), and Americanism (subheadings include Radicalism, Communism, Nazism, and the Ku Klux Klan). Also at Legion Headquarters are copies of Legion publications, including *Summaries of the Proceedings of the National Conventions*, the *American Legion Weekly* (subsequently the *American Legion Monthly* and the *American Legion Magazine*), and the Americanism Commission's newsletter, the *Huddle* (subsequently the *National Legionnaire*). The Library contains verbatim transcripts of the National Convention, National Americanism Commission, and National Executive Committee proceedings. It also houses a collection of published and unpublished state and post histories and works on American history pertaining to the Legion and twentieth-century military history.

Next to the Legion's own collection, I found most valuable the papers of the American Civil Liberties Union, now catalogued and superbly indexed at the Seeley W. Mudd Library, Princeton University. The American Legion is indexed and appears in several hundred volumes that trace the ACLU's efforts to locate and combat Legion "un-Americanism." The Mudd Library also contains the Fight for Freedom Papers, which show how the Legion was infiltrated by interventionists at its 1940 Convention. This collection also has an important analysis of Legion opinion on the world wars and military service. (Both the Legion and the ACLU extensively filed clippings from newspapers and magazines dealing with the Legion under the appropriate issue.)

Research in Congressional collections in general proved tedious and disappointing, usually yielding only "barrages" of letters and telegrams on issues of major concern to the Legion. Nevertheless, I found occasionally valuable items in the papers of David Walsh (Holy Cross College, Worcester, Massachusetts), John MacSwain, Claude Kitchin, and Josiah Bailey (Perkins Library, Duke University), Walter M. Pierce (University of Oregon), Wesley C.

Jones and Mark E. Reed (University of Washington), Hiram
Johnson (University of California, Berkeley), Courtland M. Feu-
quay and Leroy M. Gensman (University of Oklahoma), and
Ogden Mills and William Borah (Library of Congress).
Far more useful were papers of prominent Legionnaires. The
most important were those of Stephen Chadwick (University of
Washington), Stafford King (Minnesota Historical Society), Jesse
W. Barrett and Lloyd Stark (University of Missouri), Hanford
MacNider (Hoover Presidential Library, West Branch, Iowa),
Paul McNutt (Indiana University), Gilbert Bettmann (University
of Cincinnati), Augustus Graupner (University of California,
Berkeley—which also has a copy of John Quinn's memoir, orig-
inal at University of California, Los Angeles), Warren Atherton
(University of the Pacific, Stockton, California), Amos Fries
(University of Oregon), Frank Parker (University of North Car-
olina, Chapel Hill), Frank Edgerton (Nebraska Historical Soci-
ety), Alvin Owsley (North Texas State University, Denton), Eric
Fisher Wood (Syracuse University), and Theodore Roosevelt Jr.
and Bronson Cutting (Library of Congress). For the Ladies' Aux-
iliary, the Kate Barrett (Library of Congress), Helen Hughes
Hiescheler and Rose Spencer (Minnesota Historical Society), and
Mississippi American Legion Auxiliary Papers (State Archives,
Jackson) were especially helpful.
    Other collections yielding much good information included
Edgar N. Danielson's manuscript "History of the New Jersey
Department of the American Legion" (Rutgers University, New
Brunswick) and a similar work by Robert G. Simmons at the
Nebraska Historical Society. The Wisconsin and Mississippi Le-
gions have filed their department papers at their State Historical
Society and Archives, respectively. I also found the papers of
George Brent (Library of Congress), Ora D. Foster (University
of Iowa), Herman Hagedorn (Houghton Library, Harvard Uni-
versity), Clarence W. Smith (University of West Virginia), and
the Northeastern University World War I Oral History Collection
important for studying the Legion's origins and the veterans'
experience. The papers of Roger Gregg Cherry (North Carolina
Department of Archives and History, Raleigh), David R. Perry
(Duke University), Clarence Edwards (Massachusetts Historical
Society), Henry T. Allen and John J. Pershing (Library of Congress), Samuel Gompers (papers at the Library of Congress; scrapbooks at the New York Public Library), Walter D. Myers and
Carleton McCulloch (Indiana Historical Society), Robert Black

(Cincinnati Historical Society), Edward Campbell and Ray Murphy (University of Iowa), James D. Phelan (University of California, Berkeley), Louis A. Johnson (University of Virginia), Grenville Clark (Dartmouth College), George Kleinholz (University of Oregon), Rayfield Becker (Oregon Historical Society, copy at University of Washington), the Quetico Superior Council (Minnesota Historical Society), and the 1933 World's Fair Corporation (University of Illinois, Chicago Circle) all provided important information. The Oregon and Minnesota Ladies' Auxiliaries have filed numerous unpublished post histories at their respective state historical societies, which also house the minutes of Portland's Rose City and Minneapolis's Theodore Peterson posts. The microfilm copy of declassified documents from the FBI–American Legion contact program, published by Scholarly Resources, Incorporated, and the Presidential Papers of Herbert Hoover and Franklin D. Roosevelt at their libraries in West Branch, Iowa, and Hyde Park, New York, proved valuable; the Harding and Coolidge Papers contain little on the Legion.

Published Works and University Theses on the Legion

There are eight general histories of the Legion, all of which contain much information, but only two of which are sufficiently scholarly and unprejudiced to be wholeheartedly recommended. These are Richard S. Jones, *A History of the American Legion* (Indianapolis, 1946), and Dorothy Culp, "The American Legion: A Study in Pressure Politics" (Ph.D. thesis, University of Chicago, 1939). Although an official history, the former is balanced and is marred primarily by a lack of notes. Culp relies entirely on published sources, but she read them thoroughly. Marquis James, *A History of the American Legion* (New York, 1923), and Raymond Moley Jr., *The American Legion Story* (New York, 1966), are uncritically apologetic. Marcus Duffield, *King Legion* (New York, 1931), William Gellerman, *The American Legion as Educator* (New York, 1938), Justin Gray and Victor Bernstein, *The Inside Story of the Legion* (New York, 1954), and Roscoe Baker, *The American Legion and Foreign Policy* (New York, 1954), are anti-Legion diatribes. Two outstanding state studies are Richard Loosbrock, *The History of the Kansas Department of the American Legion* (Topeka, 1968), and Richard M. Clutter, "The American Legion in Indiana, 1919–1971" (Ph.D. thesis, Indiana University, 1971). See also Jack M. McLeod, "A Thematic Analysis of the *American Legion Monthly*, 1919–1951" (M.A. thesis, University of

Wisconsin–Madison, 1953). Thomas A. Rumer is currently writing a history of the Legion that should complement the present volume.

Newspaper and Magazine Articles

The Legion frequently attracted notice in the *Outlook, Literary Digest, American Mercury, Christian Century, Forum, Harper's, Atlantic Monthly, North American Review, Current History,* and the *Nation.* Many newspapers covered Legion conventions and lobbying: I have generally used clippings from Legion and ACLU archives. The more important articles are cited in chapter 4, notes 28 and 34; chapter 7, note 1; and chapter 10, note 4.

Secondary Works

Works that helped me place the Legion's Americanism in its historical context include Robert Shalhope, "Republicanism and Early American Historiography," *William and Mary Quarterly,* 3d ser., 39 (1982), 334–56; Lawrence Friedman, *Inventors of the Promised Land* (New York, 1975); David Potter, *Freedom and Its Limitations in American Life* (Stanford, 1976); Alexis de Tocqueville, *Democracy in America* (numerous editions; first published 1831); Robert A. Dahl, *A Preface to Democratic Theory* (Chicago, 1956); Ann Firor Scott, *Making the Invisible Woman Visible* (Urbana, Ill., 1984); John Hallowell, *The Moral Foundations of Democracy* (Chicago, 1954); Robert N. Bellah et al., *Habits of the Heart* (Berkeley, 1985); Bellah, *The Broken Covenant: American Civil Religion in the Twentieth Century* (New York, 1975); Grant Gilmore, *The Ages of American Law* (New Haven, 1971); John P. Diggins, *The Lost Soul of American Politics: Self-Interest and the Foundations of Liberalism* (New York, 1985); Pauline Maier, *From Resistance to Revolution: Colonial Radicals and the Development of Opposition to Britain, 1765–1776* (New York, 1972); Leonard Richards, *"Gentlemen of Property and Standing": Anti-Abolitionist Mobs in Jacksonian America* (New York, 1970); Paul Boyer, *Urban Masses and Moral Order in America* (Cambridge, 1978); Robert Wiebe, *The Search for Order* (New York, 1962); Arthur Link, introduction to *The Impact of World War I* (New York, 1969); Dorothea Edith Wyatt, "A History of the Concept of Americanism" (Ph.D. thesis, Stanford University, 1936); James Wallace Webb, "Concepts of Americanism: 1919–1929" (Ph.D. thesis, Louisiana State University, 1973); and Theodore Roosevelt Junior's suggestive *Average Americans* (New York, 1920). See also my "Legality, Legitimacy, and the

American Middle Class," in John Deely, ed., *Semiotics 1984* (Lanham, Md.), 225–36.

Works useful for comparing the American Legion with veterans' movements in other countries and with interwar Fascism include Stephen Ward, ed., *The War Generation: Veterans of the First World War* (Port Washington, N.Y., 1975); Arno Mayer, *Dynamics of Counter-Revolution in Europe, 1870–1956* (New York, 1971); Eugen Weber, *Varieties of Fascism* (New York, 1964); Walter Laqueur, ed. *Fascism: A Reader's Guide* (Berkeley, 1976); Walter Laqueur and George L. Mosse, eds., *International Fascism: 1920–1945* (New York, 1966); John P. Diggins, *Mussolini and Fascism: The View from America* (Princeton, 1972); and Mihaly Vajda, *Fascism as a Mass Movement* (New York, 1976).

General works on United States veterans' movements I found useful included Rodney G. Minott, *Peerless Patriots: Organized Veterans and the Spirit of Americanism* (Washington, D.C., 1962); Dixon Wecter, *When Johnny Comes Marching Home* (Boston, 1944); Wallace E. Davies, *Patriotism on Parade: The Story of Veterans and Hereditary Organizations in America, 1783–1900* (Cambridge, 1955); and Peter Karsten, ed., *Soldiers and Society: The Effects of Military Service and War on American Life* (Westport, Conn., 1975); see also articles in the *New York Times* on March 6, 1977 (section IV, 3) and on May 16, 1986 (B, 1–2), and clipping from the *Springfield* (Mass.) *Union*, June 28, 1981; my treatment "Veterans' Movements" appears in Jack P. Greene et al., eds., *Scribners' Encyclopedia of American Political History* (New York, 1984), 1332–47.

Background information on voluntary associations came from Arthur M. Schlesinger Sr., "Biography of a Nation of Joiners," *American Historical Review* 50 (1944), 1–25; Bruce Stokes, "Self-Help in the Eighties," *Citizen Participation* (Jan.–Feb. 1982), 5; Charles Wright and Herbert Hyman, "Voluntary Association Membership of American Adults: Evidence from National Sample Surveys," *American Sociological Review* 23 (1958), 284–94; B. H. Meyer, "Fraternal Beneficiary Societies in the United States," *American Journal of Sociology* 6 (1901), 646–61; Mary R. Dearing, *Veterans in Politics* (Baton Rouge, 1952), and Robert B. Beath, *History of the Grand Army of the Republic* (New York, 1889), for the GAR; William W. White, *The Confederate Veteran* (Tuscaloosa, 1962); Thomas Leonard, *Above the Battle: War-Making in America from Appomattox to Versailles* (New York, 1978); Paul S. Buck, *The Road to Reunion* (Boston, 1937); C. Howard Hopkins, *History of the Young Men's Christian Associations in North America* (New

York, 1951); John K. Betts, *America's Sporting Heritage, 1850–1950* (Reading, Mass., 1974); Sallie Chesham, *Born to Battle: The Salvation Army in America* (Chicago, 1965); Herbert A. Wisbey, *Soldiers without Swords: A History of the Salvation Army in the United States* (New York, 1956); William D. Murray, *The History of the Boy Scouts of the United States in America* (New York, 1937); and Edward Nicholson, *Education and the Boy Scout Movement* (New York, 1941). For psychohistorical studies of the American elite, see James R. McGovern, "David Graham Phillips and the Virility Impulse of Progressives," *New England Quarterly* 39 (1966); Glenn Davis, "Theodore Roosevelt and the Progressive Era: A Study in Individual and Group Psychohistory," in Lloyd de Mause, ed., *The New Psychohistory* (New York, 1975), and George B. Forgie's suggestive *Patricide in the House Divided: A Psychological Interpretation of Lincoln and His Age* (New York, 1979).

For the World War I context, see John Gary Clifford, *Citizen Soldiers: The Plattsburgh Training Camp Movement* (Lexington, Ky., 1973); John Patrick Finnegan, *Against the Specter of a Dragon: The Campaign for American Military Preparedness* (Westport, Conn., 1974); Ralph Barton Perry, *The Plattsburgh Movement* (New York, 1921); Paul A. Rockwell, *American Fighters in the Foreign Legion* (Boston and New York, 1930); Arthur Barbeau and Henri Florette, *The Unknown Soldiers: Black American Troops in World War I* (Philadelphia, 1974); Edward W. Moore, *The Vanguard of American Volunteers* (New York, 1919); Fred Davis Baldwin, "The American Enlisted Man in World War I" (Ph.D. thesis, Princeton University, 1965); the *Stars and Stripes*; and John W. Chambers, "Conscripting for Colossus: The Progressive Era and the Origins of the Modern Military Draft in World War I," in Peter Karsten, ed., *The Military in America* (New York, 1980). Good works on the home front include David Kennedy, *Over Here: The First World War and American Society* (New York, 1980); Edward Robb Ellis, *Echoes of Distant Thunder: Life in the United States, 1914–1918* (New York, 1975); Mark Sullivan, *Our Times: Over Here* (New York, 1933). For civil-liberties problems, see H. C. Peterson and Gilbert Fite, *Opponents of War, 1917–1918* (Seattle, 1968); William Preston Jr., *Aliens and Dissenters: Federal Suppression of Radicals, 1903–1933* (New York, 1966); Harry N. Scheiber, *The Wilson Administration and Civil Liberties, 1917–1921* (Ithaca, 1960); and Paul L. Murphy, *World War I and the Origins of Civil Liberties in the United States* (New York, 1979).

Useful general works on the interwar period that influenced

my interpretation include William E. Leuchtenburg, *The Perils of Prosperity: 1914–1932* (Chicago, 1958), *Franklin D. Roosevelt and the New Deal: 1932–1940* (New York, 1963), and "The New Deal and the Analogue of War," in John Braeman et al., eds., *Change and Continuity in Twentieth-Century America* (Columbus, 1964), 81–144; Paul Carter, *The Twenties in America* (New York, 1968) and *Another Part of the Twenties* (New York, 1977); Robert K. Murray, *The Harding Era* (Minneapolis, 1969); Arthur M. Schlesinger Jr., *The Age of Roosevelt: The Politics of Upheaval* (Boston, 1960); and Frank Freidel, *Franklin D. Roosevelt: Launching the New Deal* (Boston, 1973).

I found several works on American politics and lobbying especially helpful. These were C. Wright Mills, *The Power Elite* (New York, 1956); G. William Domhoff, *Who Rules America?* (Englewood Cliffs, N.J., 1967); Arnold Rose, *The Power Structure: Political Process in American Society* (London, 1967); J. Leiper Freeman, *The Political Process: Executive Bureau–Legislative Committee Relations* (New York, 1965); Karl Schiftgiesser, *The Lobbyists* (Boston, 1951); and Jeffrey M. Berry, *Lobbying for the People* (Princeton, 1977).

For the Legion's controversies with various "un-American" groups, see Stanley Coben, "A Study in Nativism: The American Red Scare of 1919–1920," *Political Science Quarterly* 79 (1964), 52–75; Robert K. Murray, *Red Scare: A Study in National Hysteria* (Minneapolis, 1956); Charles Markmann, *The Noblest Cry: A History of the American Civil Liberties Union* (New York, 1965); Lucille Milner, *The Education of an American Liberal* (New York, 1954); Burl Noggle, *Into the Twenties: The United States from Armistice to Normalcy* (Urbana, Ill., 1974); Richard B. Challener, ed., *United States Military Intelligence, 1919–1927* (New York, 1978); C. Vann Woodward, *Tom Watson: Agrarian Rebel* (New York, 1938); Kenneth T. Jackson, *The Ku Klux Klan in the City, 1915–1930* (New York, 1967); David M. Chalmers, *Hooded Americanism: The History of the Ku Klux Klan* (New York, 1965); Frederick C. Luebke, *Bonds of Loyalty: German-Americans and World War I* (De Kalb, Ill., 1974); Patrick Renshaw, *The Wobblies: The Story of Syndicalism in the United States* (Garden City, N.Y., 1967); Joseph Conlin, *Big Bill Haywood and the Radical Union Movement* (Syracuse, 1969); Robert L. Tyler, *Rebels of the Woods: The IWW in the Pacific Northwest* (Eugene, 1967); Robert L. Morlan, *Political Prairie Fire: The Non-Partisan League, 1915–1922* (Minneapolis, 1955); James Weinstein, *Ambiguous Legacy: The Left in American Politics* (New

York, 1975) and *The Decline of Socialism in America* (New York, 1967); David A. Shannon, *The Socialist Party of America* (Chicago, 1967); Nick Salvatore, *Eugene V. Debs: Citizen and Socialist* (Urbana, Ill., 1982); Aileen Kraditor, *The Radical Persuasion: 1890–1917* (Baton Rouge, 1981); Paul L. Murphy, *The Meaning of Free Speech, 1918–1933* (Westport, Conn., 1971); Lawrence A. Wittner, *Rebels against War: The American Peace Movement, 1941–1960* (New York, 1969); Irving Bernstein, *A History of the American Workers: The Lean Years* (Boston, 1960) and *The Turbulent Years* (Boston, 1970); James R. Green, *The World of the Worker* (New York, 1980); David Montgomery, *Workers Control in America* (Cambridge, 1979); David Brody, *Workers in Industrial America* (New York, 1980); Harvey Klehr, *The Heyday of American Communism: The Depression Decade* (New York, 1984); David Brody, "The Emergence of Mass Production Unionism," in John Braeman et al., eds., *Change and Continuity in Twentieth-Century America* (Columbus, 1964); Walter Galenson, *The CIO Challenge to the AFL: A History of the American Labor Movement* (New York, 1961); Sidney Fine, *Sit Down: The General Motors Strike of 1936–1937* (Ann Arbor, 1969); Jerold Auerbach, *Labor and Liberty: The La Follette Committee and the New Deal* (New York, 1966); Mary H. Vorse, *Labor's New Millions* (New York, 1938); from *Labor History*: Mark Reisel, "Mexican Unionization in California Agriculture, 1927–1936," 14 (1973), 562–79, and Charles P. Larrowe, "The Great Maritime Strike of 1934," 11 (1970), 403–51, and 12 (1971), 3–37; *ISMS* (two editions, Indianapolis, 1936 and 1937), published by the Legion's National Americanism Commission; Walter Wilson, *The American Legion and Civil Liberty* (New York, 1938); Andrew Eric Dinniman, "Academic Freedom at West Chester: The Controversy of 1927" (Ph.D. thesis, Pennsylvania State University, 1978); and Frances Fitzgerald, *America Revised* (New York, 1979).

For veterans' benefits and the "Bonus," see, generally, William P. Dillingham, *Federal Aid to Veterans, 1917–1941* (Gainesville, Fla., 1952); Roger Daniels, *The Bonus March, An Episode of the Great Depression* (Westport, Conn., 1971); Donald Lisio, *The President and Protest: Hoover, Conspiracy, and the Bonus Riot* (Columbia, Missouri, 1974), and "A Blunder Becomes a Catastrophe: Hoover, the Legion, and the Bonus Army," *Wisconsin Magazine of History* (Autumn 1967), 37–50; Robert Bodenger, "Soldiers' Bonuses: A History of Veterans Benefits in the United States, 1776–1967" (Ph.D. thesis, Pennsylvania State University, 1971); Keith

M. Olson, *The GI Bill, the Veterans, and the Colleges* (Lexington, Ky., 1974); Theodore R. Mosch, *The GI Bill: A Breakthrough in Educational and Social Policy in the United States* (Hicksville, N.Y., 1975); Davis R. B. Ross, *Preparing for Ulysses: Politics and Veterans During World War II* (New York, 1969); John Thomas Taylor, *A History of Adjusted Compensation Legislation* (Indianapolis, 1921); *The American Legion at Work for the Sick and Disabled: Report of the National Rehabilitation Committee at the Fourth Annual Convention* (New Orleans, 1922); Janet Louise Schmelzer, "The Early Life and Early Career of Wright Patman, 1893–1941" (Ph.D. thesis, Texas Christian University, 1978).

For the Legion in the communities I have relied chiefly on manuscript sources, but found Victor Gondos Jr., *J. Franklin Jameson and the Birth of the National Archives* (Philadelphia, 1981), and the histories of the American Legion Auxiliary published every ten years—the first by Mrs. Joseph Thompson in Pittsburgh in 1926—useful. Standard works on foreign policy mention the Legion little or not at all. I used Ralph B. Levering, *The Public and American Foreign Policy, 1918–1978* (New York, 1978), and Athan Theoharis, "The FBI and the American Legion Contact Program," *Political Science Quarterly* 100 (1985), 271–86, for the final chapter.

Index

Abraham Lincoln Brigade, 243, 266
Adams, Robert, 133–34, 313
Addams, Jane, 146, 161, 164
Adjusted compensation. *See* Bonus; Veter-
    ans' benefits
AEF veterans, 49, 52, 62, 80
    See also American Legion
AFL (American Federation of Labor), 114,
    136, 141, 158
    Legion's cooperation with, 209–11,
        214–17, 234
    and Legion union labor posts, 217
Agar, Herbert, 305
Allen, Henry, 114–15, 188
Allison, "Stub," 280–81, 284
All Quiet on the Western Front, 162
Amalgamated Association of Iron, Steel,
    and Tin Workers, 225
American Business Survey, 274
American Civil Liberties Union (ACLU),
    89
    founding beliefs of, 14–15
    Legion's opposition to, 6, 7, 15–16, 20
    Legion's support of, 253–54
    and Sacco-Vanzetti case, 98, 166
    support of labor strikes, 219, 227, 229,
        251
    support of liberal education, 269, 274
    support of radicalism, 155, 157, 246,
        249, 318
American Committee for Democracy and
    Intellectual Freedom, 274
American Defense Society, 36, 290
American Education Association, 103
American Expeditionary Force, 35
American Historical Association (AHA),
    279, 293
Americanism:
    challenged by ACLU, 14–15
    defined by Americanism Commission,
        3–5, 23
    freedom of speech embodied in, 6–8
    influence of Fascism on, 20–22
    patriotism and nature of community,
        16–20, 103, 319–20
    personal freedom embodied in, 5–6
    versus Communism, 8–14, 320
    See also National Americanism Com-
        mission
"Americanism: What Is It?" (Baldridge),
    251–52

American League Against War and Fas-
    cism, 162
American Legion:
    attitudes toward Communism and
        ACLU, 8–17, 160–61
    attitudes toward education, 265–77
    attitudes toward immigrants, 256–65
    attitudes toward labor, 208–34
    Boy Scout and YMCA influence on, 31–
        34
    community action, 279–301
    conventions, 93–103
    creation of, 49, 51–68, 69–72, 73–77
    crusade against radicalism, 145–61
    disputes over Prohibition and Ku Klux
        Klan, 137–43
    fight against subversion of 1930s, 236–
        56
    founding beliefs and motto, 2–8, 17, 34
    GAR influence on, 25–31
    membership and organization, 68–69,
        73–93, 319
    operational funds, 72–73, 85, 103–4
    political partisanship and lobbying,
        106–31
    preparedness for world wars, 34–47,
        302–19
    stance on veterans' benefits and com-
        pensation, 170–207
American Legion as Educator, The (Geller-
    man), 79, 255, 269, 270–71
American Legion Film Service, 86
"American Legion in Politics, The" (Duf-
    field), 106
American Legion Magazine, 273, 274
American Legion Monthly, 81, 104, 136,
    189, 249, 253, 266, 271
American Legion News Service, 86, 163
American Legion vs. Civil Liberty, The
    (Wilson), 255
American Legion Weekly, 64, 72, 73, 173,
    178, 217
American Legion Women's Auxiliary,
    180, 186, 296–301
American Liberty League, 36, 317
American Protective League, 36, 314
American Socialist party, 153, 154–55
American Telephone and Telegraph, 104
Andrews, Charles M., 276
Andrews, Paul Shipman, 109
Angell, Ernest, 176

399